STUDY GUIDE

BUSINESS LAW

PRINCIPLES AND CASES IN THE LEGAL ENVIRONMENT

SIXTH EDITION

DANIEL V. DAVIDSON
RADFORD UNIVERSITY

BRENDA E. KNOWLES
INDIANA UNIVERSITY SOUTH BEND

LYNN M. FORSYTHE
CALIFORNIA STATE UNIVERSITY, FRESNO

PREPARED BY

RONALD L. TAYLOR
METROPOLITAN STATE COLLEGE OF DENVER

WEST
WEST EDUCATIONAL PUBLISHING COMPANY
An International Thomson Publishing Company

Publisher / Team Director: Jack W. Calhoun
Acquisitions Editor: Rob Dewey
Developmental Editor: Kurt Gerdenich
Production Editor: Sharon L. Smith
Sr. Marketing Manager: Scott D. Person
Cover Design: Paul Neff Design
Cover Illustrator: Cathleen Toelke

ISBN: 0-538-86857-0 (Package: Study Guide + CD)

ISBN: 0-538-88871-7 (Study Guide Alone)

1 2 3 4 5 6 7 8 GP 3 2 1 0 9 8 7 6

Printed in the United States of America

I(T)P®
International Thomson Publishing
West Educational Publishing is an ITP Company.
The ITP trademark is used under license.

CONTENTS

CHAPTER 1   Introduction To Law

CHAPTER REVIEW

WHAT IS THE RELATIONSHIP AMONG LAW, ORDER, AND JUSTICE?: The law is a system composed of three elements: law, order, and justice. These three elements balance with one another, subject to limits arising due to practical considerations, such as cost.

- *Law*: Law consists of rules that, when broken, may lead to legal action and penalties, including fines or imprisonment.
- *Order*: Order is the absence of confusion and turmoil, and it usually results when the law is obeyed.
- *Justice*: The process by which the legal system achieves fairness. Sometimes justice is realized by treating everyone the same, called commutative justice, and sometimes it results by treating people individually, called distributive justice.

THE LAW AS AN ARTIFICIAL LANGUAGE SYSTEM: Legal terms must be learned in the context in which they are used. Words used in a legal context may mean something different than when they are used in ordinary conversation.

THE LAW OF BUSINESS: The law of business originated in the English law merchant, which was not part of the formal English court system. Now, the law of business is part of the common law which is comprised of court decisions.

WHY STUDY THE LAW OF BUSINESS?: Having a basic understanding of law helps one to conduct business in a manner that avoids disputes.

WHAT ARE THE NEEDS OF A LEGAL SYSTEM?: There are several elements necessary for a legal system to appropriately balance law, order, justice, and practical concerns. The first element, the need to be reasonable, applies in two ways. First, laws must be enforced based on provable facts. Second, the law must be applied so that people have notice of legal actions that are brought against them.

Another requirement of a legal system is the need for laws to be clear so that people know what is expected so that they may comply with their legal obligations. Also, laws must be available to the public so people are aware of them. In addition, a legal system needs to accommodate the unique facts of each situation, and it must provide practical solutions to legal disputes, rather than mere theoretical possibilities. Finally, a legal system must provide a final solution to disputes.

WHAT ARE THE PURPOSES OF A LEGAL SYSTEM?: One purpose of a legal system is to achieve fairness. A legal system also provides for the creation and enforcement of laws, helps maintain order by resisting excessive change, and allows people to alter their behavior in order to conform to the law. Other purposes of a legal system may include protection of persons and their property, and the preservation of a free and open market which is accomplished in part by allowing people to reach their own agreements.

WHAT ARE THE SOURCES OF LAW IN THE AMERICAN LEGAL SYSTEM?: The American legal system derives its law from several sources, including federal and state constitutions. The federal and state governments also enact statutes, that is, laws passed by the legislature. Treaties with other nations and administrative rules adopted by governmental agencies are additional sources of laws. Finally, laws may arise as a result of court decisions rendered in individual cases. These decisions, called precedents, must generally be followed by lower courts in the same jurisdiction.

HOW IS THE LAW CLASSIFIED?: The legal system is organized into several classifications, some of which have authority over others.
- *Federal versus State Law*: Each state has its own law, as does the federal government.
- *Common versus Statutory Law*: In the American legal system, judges may make laws in those areas that are not governed by statutes. Judge-made law is called common law and is published in opinions issued by judges.
- *Civil versus Criminal Law*: Criminal law consists of those laws that allow the government to punish people who do not follow the law. Civil law involves disputes between private parties rather than the government and a private party.
- *Substantive versus Procedural Law*: Substantive law sets out the standards by which people must conduct themselves. Procedural law sets out the standards by which the substantive laws are enforced.

STUDY HINTS FOR CALL-IMAGE TECHNOLOGY CASE STUDIES

The following study hints may be helpful when resolving the Call-Image Technology (CIT) case studies.

page 6
- When answering whether CIT should provide insurance, consider the concept of justice and whether or not justice is best served by providing insurance for the employees.
- Focus in particular on the two theories of justice, commutative and distributive justice.

page 10
- When responding to Anna and Tom, consider the need of the legal system to be flexible.
- You should also reflect upon the purposes of the legal system, especially providing police power, maintaining peace, and providing protection.

page 20
- To answer Tom and Anna, review the purposes of the American legal system, particularly the need to encourage commercial transactions.
- Consider the nature of statutory law and whether citizens and businesses have access to the legislators who enact this type of law.
- Also, explore the interplay between federal and state law and the priority between these types of law.

MATCHING EXERCISE

Select the term or concept that best matches a definition or statement set forth below. Each term or concept is the best match for only one definition or statement.

Terms and Concepts

a. Administrative regulations
b. Case law
c. Civil law
d. Common law
e. Constitution

f. Criminal law
g. Equity
h. Justice
i. Law merchant
j. Majority rule

k. Moot
l. Procedural law
m. Statutory law
n. Substantive law
o. Treaty

Definitions and Statements

_____ 1. Law that establishes the method for enforcing legal rights or obtaining legal redress.
_____ 2. One goal of the legal system.
_____ 3. Private system of law previously administered outside the regular law courts of England.
_____ 4. Issue that is irrelevant because it can no longer be resolved.
_____ 5. Law that sets forth the rights and duties given or imposed by the legal system.
_____ 6. Legally enforceable rules adopted by governmental agencies.
_____ 7. Unwritten law that is based upon past usage and custom and court decisions.
_____ 8. Legal rules that are applied to resolve controversies when there is no adequate remedy at law.
_____ 9. Law enacted by legislative bodies.
_____ 10. Reported cases decided by federal and state courts.
_____ 11. Fundamental law of a nation.
_____ 12. Private law that allows one person to sue another.
_____ 13. Public law that allows a governmental entity to prosecute a person.
_____ 14. Law that is enacted as an inherent function of a nation's sovereignty rather than by virtue of a right granted by a constitution.
_____ 15. Law that is followed by a majority of states or other jurisdictions.

COMPLETION EXERCISE

Fill in the blanks with the words that most accurately complete each statement.

1. _____ is a fundamental characteristic that distinguishes laws from mere rules.

2. By utilizing _____ _____, one can prevent wrongs before they occur.

3. A government's _____ _____ is used to protect the public's health, safety, and welfare.

4. One purpose of laws is to achieve _____, thereby minimizing chaos.

5. _____ _____ treats all people equally, and _____

_____ takes into account inequalities among people.

TRUE-FALSE EXERCISE

Write **T** if the statement is true, write **F** if the statement is false.

_____ 1. All rules in society are considered laws.

_____ 2. If a person committed a crime against you, then the government, but not you, may criminally prosecute the person who committed the crime.

_____ 3. The concept of "freedom of contract" represents one of the legal system's purposes which is to enforce the intent of individuals and businesses.

_____ 4. The theory of natural law stands for the notion that the law should be based on certain legal and moral values that are indisputably valid.

_____ 5. Laws should be written in such a fashion that they are knowable and definite but so that they can be applied in a flexible manner.

_____ 6. Judicial review is a doctrine that allows the executive branch of government to decide whether laws comply with the U.S. Constitution.

_____ 7. Protection of the individual, the government, and property are three functions of the law.

_____ 8. The U.S. Constitution will, in a conflict with a state constitution, always be favored.

_____ 9. Ordinances are a form of statutory law adopted by Congress.

_____ 10. The doctrine of *stare decisis* generally directs courts to follow precedents previously adopted by higher courts in the same jurisdiction.

APPLICATION OF CONCEPTS

MULTIPLE CHOICE QUESTIONS

_____ 1. Which of the following is an example of case law?
   a. The legislature passes a statute requiring businesses with more than 10 employees to offer a maternity leave program for the employees.
   b. In resolving a legal controversy between two parties, the state supreme court adopts a rule of law that an agreement is not enforceable unless there is both a valid offer and acceptance.
   c. The President of the United States issues an executive order restricting exports to a hostile nation.
   d. The Department of Motor Vehicles changes the fee for renewing a driver's license.

_____ 2. Sherman Television Network aired a show entitled "Do It Yourself." This program instructed the viewing audience on how to manufacture certain illegal drugs and where to buy the necessary ingredients. Sherman Television was notified that it was being charged with violation of a regulation of the Federal Communications Commission, a federal agency. What type of law was Sherman Television charged with violating?
   a. Constitutional law.
   b. Statutory law.
   c. Administrative law.
   d. Common law.

_____ 3. Carol wrongfully breached a sales contract that she had entered into with Arthur, a violation of civil law. Under these facts, which action may be appropriate?
  a. Arthur may sue Carol for damages.
  b. Arthur may sue Carol for an injunction, if damages are an inadequate remedy.
  c. The state district attorney may criminally prosecute Carol.
  d. a and b.

_____ 4. The state treasurer informed the legislature that the state would run a deficit the following year unless taxes were raised. In response, the governor proposed that the legislature adopt the following law: "The tax rates of wealthy residents shall be increased to the extent needed to cover any deficit. It shall be the duty of each resident to determine how much additional taxes, if any, that they must pay." If enacted by the legislature, would this law meet the needs of the state's legal system?
  a. No. The law is indefinite and vague.
  b. No. The law is flexible.
  c. No. The law is not practical.
  d. a and c.

SHORT ANSWER QUESTIONS

Answer the following questions, briefly explaining the reason for your answer.

1. Acme Inc. was sued by a government agency for violating federal nondiscrimination law. At its trial, Acme asserted that the law in question was unconstitutional even though the U.S. Supreme Court had previously found this law to be constitutional. Is the trial court bound by the Supreme Court's decision?

_____

_____

2. The Polks throw all of their garbage and trash into their yard, creating a health risk for the Jacksons who live next door. The Polks have repeatedly refused to clean up their mess, and they intend to continue to dispose of their garbage in this manner. Can the Jacksons sue the Polks under the civil or criminal law? If they sue, what remedy should the Jacksons request?

_____

_____

3. A bill submitted to Congress states: "All persons legally or illegally present in the United States shall be entitled to receive a public education and public welfare." Senator Adams favors this bill because it is a basic moral rule that all people are equal; and Senator Bend favors this bill because it is a way to encourage the social value of equality. What theories of jurisprudence did these senators express?

_____

_____

4. Lexington Manufacturing processed and sold coal to various public utilities. The Environmental Protection Agency, a federal agency, charged Lexington with violation of certain technical environmental regulations. Lexington does not presently have an attorney. Suggest several approaches that Lexington can take to find a qualified lawyer to represent it.

_____

_____

CASE PROBLEMS

Answer the following case problems, explaining your answers.

1. A state statute provides that it is mandatory that anyone who is driving with a blood alcohol level of .015 or higher shall have their driver's license suspended for 6 months and shall be required to obtain counseling for substance abuse. (a) Is this law an example of commutative or distributive justice? (b) What need of the legal system does this law serve? (c) What need of the legal system does this law not serve?

_____

_____

_____

_____

2. Trico Corp. has a patent on a process to artificially create an organism that eats cancerous stomach tumors in humans. Trico believes that a competitor wrongfully infringed upon (violated) its patent in order to develop a competing product that the competitor is now selling. Trico wants to hire an attorney to represent it in a patent infringement lawsuit against the competitor. It is difficult to determine, however, how long this lawsuit may take or how much money Trico may recover from the competitor. (a) Identify and explain the types of fee arrangement that are available to Trico? (b) On balance, what type of fee arrangement is probably the most practical and fair for both Trico and its attorney?

_____

_____

_____

_____

CHAPTER REVIEW

ETHICS AND MORALITY: Ethics is a branch of moral philosophy that is concerned with what is morally "right" or "wrong." Ethics refers to the guiding philosophy of a group, especially societal values regarding what is right or wrong. The laws of a society generally establish an ethical floor, meaning a minimum standard of behavior for each member of society.

Morals, on the other hand, relate to principles of right and wrong as measured by an individual's conscience. Whereas ethics may vary from society to society, the morals of an individual should remain fairly constant over time. A person's perception of what is morally right sometimes differs from what society considers to be right.

ETHICAL THEORIES: There are a number of theories for deciding what is right or wrong, and there is no single "best" theory. Individuals and societies choose to adhere to different theories, sometimes even choosing to follow a combination of theories.

- *Consequential and Nonconsequential Principles*: Broadly speaking, ethical theories fall into one of two broad categories: 1) consequential principles and 2) nonconsequential principles. Theories based on consequential principles evaluate an action by examining the consequences or results that are or may be produced by certain conduct. Theories based on nonconsequential principles focus on the concept of "duty" rather than on what is right or wrong.

- *Consequential Ethics*: Two dominant theories of consequential ethics are egoism and utilitarianism.
  1) **Egoism**: Egoism claims that the rightness of an act is determined solely by the consequences that the act will produce for the person performing the action. Egoism therefore holds that one is obligated to do those acts that will, over time, produce the greatest balance of good over bad for oneself.
  2) **Utilitarianism**: Utilitarianism maintains that the rightness of an act is determined solely by the consequences that the act will produce for one's group (universe). Under utilitarianism, therefore, one should do those acts that will, over time, produce the greatest balance of good over bad for one's group. Act utilitarians believe an act that produces the most good for the group is ethical, even if this requires violating a rule of society. Rule utilitarians, on the other hand, generally advocate strict adherence to all rules of society as the approach for producing the most good for the group.

- *Nonconsequential Ethics*: Two often cited nonconsequential ethical theories are:
  1) **Kant and the Categorical Imperative**: Kant's ethical theory suggested that there are certain universal moral truths that every person must follow in order to be acting both morally and ethically. If a person fails to follow these truths, then the person is acting unethically. Further, Kant suggested that there are perfect truths that must always be followed, and there are imperfect truths that people should follow, although it is not always essential that they do so.
  2) **Rawls and the Veil of Ignorance**: Rawls' theory is based on the premise that the rules to be followed should be developed behind a veil of ignorance, meaning that rules should be created by persons who ignore all of their own characteristics and circumstances. Thus, persons should create rules without considering their own race, religion, economic situation, etc.

A SYNTHESIS FOR ETHICAL DECISION MAKING: When an individual or business is choosing what ethical theory to embrace, factors that should be considered include: 1) the short- and long-term impact; 2) who will be affected; and 3) whether the ethical theory is compatible with the law.

THE GAME THEORY OF BUSINESS:

- *Business as an Amoral Institution*: Originally, businesses were considered to be amoral, meaning they could not act morally or immorally because they were not natural persons.
- *The "Game Theory"*: Under this theory, operating a business is equivalent to playing a game. Thus, the rules that businesses should follow are the same as the rules of a game. This theory is no longer followed, in part because government now establishes the rules (legal regulations) for business.

THE SOCIAL CONTRACT THEORY: Under this theory, businesses owe duties to society because society allows business to exist.

- *The Changing Social Environment*: Over time, business has changed and so has society's view of business. Originally, business was conducted by individual merchants, and the customer had a direct relationship with the business. As business grew, however, this personal link weakened and business gained more power and customers less power. Eventually, government intervened in order to achieve and maintain a balance between the two. For instance the concept of *caveat emptor*, or "let the buyer beware," has largely given way to increasing legal duties that businesses owe to their customers.
- *Problems with Business Ethics*: One problem confronting businesses is the absence of one fixed code of ethics that all businesses must follow. At best, some guidelines are furnished by professional codes of ethics, companies' individual codes of ethics, and legal regulations.
- *The Human Factor*: Traditionally, agents acted with utmost loyalty to the principal. Some critics argue that agents must now act more independently to assure that they are acting in an ethical manner.
- *Legal Aspect*: Since business has sometimes failed to act in a socially responsible manner, the law has stepped in and subjected it to extensive governmental regulation.

MULTINATIONAL ETHICS: Social values differ in other countries, and U.S. firms doing business in foreign countries should try to implement the values of other cultures in their business dealings with them.

A RECOMMENDATION FOR BUSINESS: U.S. firms need to develop their own model for ethical behavior.

STUDY HINTS FOR CALL-IMAGE TECHNOLOGY CASE STUDIES

The following study hints may be helpful when resolving the Call-Image Technology (CIT) case studies.

page 44
- ♦ Review the material dealing with the game theory of business imperative.

page 48
- ♦ Before responding, consider the human factor in the social contract theory.

page 49
- ♦ Explore the differences between consequential and nonconsequential ethical theories to determine what theories are most appropriate for CIT. Then, as a starting point, draft a list of basic consequences or rules that CIT wishes to further. This will help form the framework for a code of ethics.

REVIEW OF KEY TERMS AND CONCEPTS

MATCHING EXERCISE

Select the term or concept that best matches a definition or statement set forth below. Each term or concept is the best match for only one definition or statement.

Terms and Concepts

a. Amoral
b. Categorical imperative
c. *Caveat emptor*
d. Consequential principles

e. Egoism
f. Ethics
g. Game theory
h. Nonconsequential principles

i. Proactive
j. Reactive
k. Social contract theory
l. Utilitarianism

Definitions and Statements

____ 1. Theory suggesting that since society allows business to exist, business owes duties to society.

____ 2. Initiating steps to avoid potential problems before they arise.

____ 3. "Let the buyer beware."

____ 4. Principles of "right" and "wrong" adhered to by a particular person.

____ 5. Theory suggesting that the ultimate goal of business is to win.

____ 6. Initiating steps to deal with existing problems.

____ 7. Theory suggesting that one should act so as to produce the greatest good for oneself.

____ 8. Ethical principles that are determined by rules, not by consequences.

____ 9. Theory suggesting that one should act so as to produce the greatest good for the members of one's group.

____ 10. Ethical principles that are determined by the results of one's actions, not by fixed rules.

____ 11. Quality of not being moral or immoral.

____ 12. Theory suggesting that persons must follow certain universal rules.

COMPLETION EXERCISE

Fill in the blanks with the words that most accurately complete each statement.

1. _____ is society's values regarding what is right or wrong.

2. _____ are comprised of principles of right and wrong as measured by an individual's conscience.

3. Rawls' contract theory of justice is premised on the concept that the rules of society should be crafted

behind a _____ ____ _____ .

4. The game theory of business is based on the belief that businesses are _____.

5. When doing business internationally, businesspeople should bear in mind that the ethics of many

societies may be _____ _____ the prevailing ethics followed in the United States.

TRUE-FALSE EXERCISE

Write **T** if the statement is true, write **F** if the statement is false.

_____ 1. There is no general code of ethics for businesses to follow.

_____ 2. *Caveat emptor* is universally followed in the American legal system.

_____ 3. Governmental regulation came about as a result of businesses' perceived abuses that occurred while the government followed a policy of laissez faire.

_____ 4. Ethical principles often form the basis for fundamental legal principles.

_____ 5. Utilitarians believe that a person should engage in conduct that produces the greatest good for the greatest number of members of a group.

_____ 6. Morals reflect what an individual believes is right or wrong.

_____ 7. According to Kant, each person should act in such a way that his or her action could become a universal law.

_____ 8. There is one universal ethical theory that all persons should follow.

_____ 9. A person's values of right or wrong are not necessarily the same as society's values.

_____ 10. Utilitarians and egoists generally believe that the consequences of an action are not relevant in determining whether the action is right or wrong.

APPLICATION OF CONCEPTS

MULTIPLE CHOICE QUESTIONS

_____ 1. Which of the following is an example of a nonconsequential ethical theory?
  a. If I drive carefully, I will be safe.
  b. If we all drive carefully, we will all be safe.
  c. If we all follow the speed limit, none of us will get hurt.
  d. Following the speed limit is the right thing to do.

_____ 2. Freddy owned a gasoline station. He was approached by other station owners who wanted Freddy to join them in fixing the price for gasoline in their town. Freddy declined because, if all businesses fixed their prices, then this conduct would hurt the financial well being of most townspeople. Freddy is following the ethical theory of:
  a. Egoism.
  b. Act utilitarianism.
  c. Rule utilitarianism.
  d. The categorical imperative.

_____ 3. Fun Toys gave to a local children's charity because doing so is good for its business. Fun Toys is following the ethical theory of:
   a. Egoism.
   b. Act utilitarianism.
   c. Rule utilitarianism.
   d. The categorical imperative.

_____ 4. In most states, adultery is neither a civil wrong nor a crime. However, society views adultery as being morally wrong. If Gina engages in an adulterous relationship, then Gina is acting:
   a. Legally.
   b. Illegally.
   c. Immorally.
   d. a and c.

SHORT ANSWER QUESTIONS

Answer the following questions, briefly explaining the reason for your answer.

1. A&A Used Cars sold a car to Fred after its salesman told Fred that the car "ran like a top." In fact, the car ran poorly. If Fred sues A&A, what legal doctrine might A&A raise as a defense?

_____

_____

2. Mighty Machines Corp. determined that it would cost more to recall and repair its Ajax jack hammer that has a hidden defect, than it would cost to pay damages to persons who were injured due to the defect. Therefore, Mighty Machines decided against a recall of the jack hammer. What ethical theory supports this analysis?

_____

_____

3. Pal's Publishing was committed to taking care of its employees. Therefore, it decided to make all of its employees undergo mandatory drug testing at least once a year. It undertook this action because drug use is illegal and a crime. What ethical theory supports this analysis?

_____

_____

4. Wally's Shoe Warehouse has had trouble collecting accounts receivables from certain customers. Wally told his general manager to "do whatever is necessary to get paid." The general manager responded by hiring a collection agency that has a reputation for making threats and using physical force if necessary to convince customers to pay their debts. Evaluate the morality of the general manager's conduct.

CASE PROBLEMS

Answer the following case problems, explaining your answers.

1. Gordon, president of Ace Cigarettes, believed that all people have the right to freedom of choice and action. Thus, he directed his marketing department to actively pursue sales to younger individuals, including minors. Society, on the other hand, has determined that it is both morally and legally wrong to sell cigarettes to minors. (a) Evaluate whether Gordon acted morally. (b) Evaluate whether Gordon acted ethically. (c) Evaluate whether Gordon acted legally.

---

2. For many years, U.S. companies manufactured, sold, and used asbestos. Hypothetically, assume that these companies engaged in this conduct even after they became aware of the potential health hazards posed by their conduct. Eventually, the government forbid the sale and use of asbestos in many situations, and thousands of people sued these companies for massive damages. Only then did some of these firms stop using asbestos. (a) Is the conduct of these firms representative of proactive or reactive conduct? (b) What could these firms have done differently to avoid this situation? (c) Did these firms act ethically or not in this case?

CHAPTER 3 International Law

CHAPTER REVIEW

INTRODUCTION: When "going global," U.S. businesses can choose from several options. Agents can help businesses find foreign buyers, or distributors may resell businesses' goods to foreign customers. Alternatively, U.S. firms may use franchising whereby the firms, as franchisors, grant a license to a franchisee to conduct business under the name of the U.S. firms. Another option is a joint venture whereby a U.S. firm and a foreign firm form an association to carry out an enterprise. Finally, U.S. firms can create a new company (subsidiary) to engage in business in one or more foreign countries.

EXTRATERRITORIALITY: U.S. LAWS, INTERNATIONAL APPLICATIONS: In some cases, U.S. laws apply to business conduct that is in other countries.
- *Antitrust*: Under one test, the "direct and substantial effect" test, U.S. courts apply U.S. antitrust laws to business conducted outside of the United States if there is a significant effect on U.S. commerce. Nonetheless, most courts choose to balance U.S. interests with those of foreign countries in order to decide whether American law should apply.
- *The Foreign Corrupt Practices Act (FCPA)*: The FCPA forbids U.S. companies from giving money or anything of value to high-level foreign government officials in order to influence their conduct. However, payments made to low-level officials to expedite routine services are allowed.
- *Employment*: U.S. nondiscrimination laws protect Americans working for U.S. companies abroad.

THE EUROPEAN UNION (EU): The EU is an organization of Western European countries, and it has four objectives: 1) eliminate duties among EU nations and set uniform tariffs for nations that trade with the EU; 2) allow citizens of EU nations to move to other member nations; 3) allow firms from EU nations to offer services anywhere in the EU; and 4) establish a common currency (EUU).

The EU has competition laws that are similar to U.S. antitrust law. Businesses can apply for an exemption from EU competition law by requesting issuance of a negative clearance from. Conduct anywhere in the world is subject to EU competition law if it affects the EU market.

The EU has the following four main governing bodies:
- *The Council of Ministers*: Acts as the legislative branch of the EU. It issues directives (instructions) asking member nations to adopt laws that are consistent with EU policy. It also issues regulations which are legally binding on member nations and override the laws of each member nation.
- *The European Commission*: As the enforcement branch of the EU, the Commission can impose fines on firms for violating EU law, and it can issue negative clearances relating to EU competition law.
- *The European Parliament*: Parliament is primarily an advisory body.
- *The Court of Justice of the European Communities*: Is the final arbiter of all disputes within the EU.

THE NORTH AMERICAN FREE TRADE AGREEMENT (NAFTA): This agreement, between the U.S., Mexico, and Canada, seeks to eliminate all tariffs on goods traded between member nation by 1998. NAFTA also promotes greater movement of workers and investments between member nations.

THE GENERAL AGREEMENT ON TARIFFS AND TRADE (GATT): GATT was an international convention that reduced tariffs and quotas between member nations and promoted fair trade. GATT approved the WTO.

WORLD TRADE ORGANIZATION (WTO): The WTO is comprised of 117 nations, including the United States. The WTO can adopt rules relating to international transactions involving goods, services, and intellectual property, and its rules are binding on all member nations.

EXPORTS AND IMPORTS: All U.S. exports must be licensed. U.S. goods imported into a foreign country must pass customs, which usually requires payment of a tariff or duty.

LETTERS OF CREDIT: These documents help minimize some of the risk of international transactions. A letter of credit is a promise by a bank to pay the contract price, even if the goods turn out to be defective.

INFORMATION AND TECHNOLOGY: Although there are no global laws protecting intellectual property, there is increasing international protection of copyrights, patents, and copyrights.

NATIONALIZATION: Nationalization occurs when a foreign government converts a private business into a government-owned business. Nationalization is legal under international law only if the state had a proper public purpose and paid just compensation. This practice is common in developing countries.

ACT OF STATE DOCTRINE AND SOVEREIGN IMMUNITY: The act of state doctrine prohibits courts from judging the acts of a foreign government performed within its borders. Sovereign immunity prohibits individuals or countries from suing a foreign government based on its political activities. However, it is permissible to sue a foreign government based on its commercial activities.

DISPUTES: All international contracts should provide for a way to settle disputes, and arbitration is the most common way to resolve international disputes.

STUDY HINTS FOR CALL-IMAGE TECHNOLOGY CASE STUDIES

The following study hints may be helpful when resolving the Call-Image Technology (CIT) case studies.

page 62
- ♦ In support of Lindsay's position, consider how new technological and communication advances have contributed to a great increase in international trade and competition.
- ♦ In support of Dan's position, consider potential problems with going "global," such as international unrest, cultural differences, differences in foreign laws, and nationalization.

page 67
- ♦ When preparing your paper, explore the differences between the U.S. relationship with NAFTA member nations and EU member nations.
- ♦ Also, consider the issue of tariffs and duties when deciding where CIT should do business.

page 74
- ♦ Consider the pros and cons of the various ways that CIT can do business internationally.
- ♦ Review Articles 85 and 86 of the Treaty of Rome, and U.S. licensing requirements.

MATCHING EXERCISE

Select the term or concept that best matches a definition or statement set forth below. Each term or concept is the best match for only one definition or statement.

Terms and Concepts

a. Act of state doctrine
b. Antitrust laws
c. Arbitration
d. CISG
e. EU

f. Franchising
g. GATT
h. Letter of credit
i. NAFTA
j. Nationalization

k. Negative clearance
l. Remand
m. Sovereign immunity
n. Uniform Commercial Code
o. World Trade Organization

Definitions and Statements

_____ 1. Foreign government's act of converting a private business into a public enterprise.

_____ 2. International doctrine that prohibits courts in one country from reviewing the legality of acts of a foreign government that are undertaken within the foreign country's borders.

_____ 3. New international organization that can adopt binding rules for international transactions involving goods, services, and intellectual property.

_____ 4. International convention that establishes uniform rules for the international sale of goods.

_____ 5. Creates a free-trade zone among its member nations in Europe.

_____ 6. U.S. laws that help protect competition.

_____ 7. Nonjudicial resolution of a case by a third person.

_____ 8. State statutory law that governs many types of commercial transactions in the United States.

_____ 9. Trade agreement between the United States, Mexico, and Canada.

_____ 10. Doctrine that holds that a nation is immune from liability for its actions.

_____ 11. Permission by a company that allows another to do business under the company's name.

_____ 12. Act of sending a case back to another court from which it came.

_____ 13. International convention that promoted nondiscriminatory trade among its members and established the World Trade Organization.

_____ 14. Bank's promise to pay a stated sum of money, such as the contract price for goods, upon presentment of required documents.

_____ 15. Exemption from EU competition laws that is granted by the EU Commission.

COMPLETION EXERCISE

Fill in the blanks with the words that most accurately complete each statement.

1. Under the _____ _____ _____ _____, a U.S. company cannot give "anything of value" to foreign officials with the intent to corrupt.

2. The _____ _____ _____ _____ is an international court in which nations may sue one another.

3. In the EU, the _____ _____ proposes legislation and enforces EU law.

4. In the EU, the _____ _____ _____ issues directives and regulations.

5. Identify three methods that a U.S. company can use in order to conduct international business.

   a. _____.

   b. _____.

   c. _____.

TRUE-FALSE EXERCISE

Write **T** if the statement is true, write **F** if the statement is false.

_____ 1. U.S. law recognizes that sovereign immunity protects foreign nations from being sued for both their governmental and commercial activities.

_____ 2. U.S. antitrust law does not generally apply to conduct occurring outside of the United States if the conduct does not affect commerce within the United States.

_____ 3. Foreign countries are generally prohibited from imposing tariffs that may interfere with the sale of U.S. goods.

_____ 4. U.S. firms doing business in Europe are generally subject to the competition laws of the EU.

_____ 5. A private person can go to the International Court of Justice to resolve a grievance with a foreign company.

_____ 6. A popular method for conducting international business is franchising.

_____ 7. The FCPA prohibits a U.S. firm from paying low-level foreign officials to do their job.

_____ 8. In the EU, the European Parliament is an influential law-making body.

_____ 9. In general, an international contract can state which country's law will govern the parties' rights.

_____ 10. Nationalization describes how much a foreign citizen identifies with his or her own nation.

APPLICATION OF CONCEPTS

MULTIPLE CHOICE QUESTIONS

_____ 1. Kirsten wishes to expedite a sale of household goods to a customer in a foreign country. Which of the following actions may Kirsten take without violating the Foreign Corrupt Practices Act?
   a. Kirsten may bribe a high government official in order to gain the official's approval.
   b. Kirsten may make valuable gifts to high government officials to gain their approval.
   c. Kirsten may pay low-level government officials to expedite routine paperwork.
   d. Kirsten may not make any kind of payment to any government official.

_____ 2. Jensen Corp., a U.S. firm, wants to form a joint venture with a foreign company to engage in the coffee business in a third world country. However, Jensen fears that its business could at some point be nationalized by this country. What actions may be available to Jensen in order to reduce the financial risks associated with nationalization?
   a. Purchase insurance to protect it against losses resulting from nationalization.
   b. Require a short payback period for its investment in the joint venture.
   c. There is nothing that Jensen Corp. can do to minimize the risk of loss from nationalization.
   d. a and b.

_____ 3. AllTech is a U.S. firm that has a plant in a foreign country staffed with U.S. employees. Jane, a U.S. citizen, works in AllTech's foreign plant. Jane was discriminated against by AllTech because she is a woman. This discrimination would violate U.S. law (Title VII of the Civil Rights Act), but not the law of the foreign country where Jane works. In this case, Jane can:
   a. Sue AllTech in the foreign nation's court for discrimination.
   b. Sue AllTech in U.S. court for violation of U.S. law.
   c. Do nothing because U.S. law does not apply in foreign nations.
   d. a and b.

_____ 4. Vigneti Company, a foreign firm, sued GeoMap, a U.S. firm, in a foreign court. Following a full and fair trial before an impartial court during which GeoMap was allowed to present a defense, the foreign court issued a $50,000 judgment in favor of Vigneti Company. If Vigneti Company seeks to enforce this judgment against GeoMap in the United States, a U.S. court will likely:
   a. Recognize and uphold the foreign judgment because foreign judgments are legally binding in the United States.
   b. Recognize and uphold the foreign judgment based on the principal of comity.
   c. Hold a new trial because U.S. firms cannot be sued in a foreign court.
   d. Hold a new trial because foreign judgments are unenforceable in the United States.

SHORT ANSWER QUESTIONS

Answer the following questions, briefly explaining the reason for your answer.

1. Gill wants to do business with firms located in countries belonging to the EU. Gill plans to grant exclusive sales territories to each foreign firm, and he also plans to establish mandatory, uniform resale prices for his products. What foreign law should Gill be concerned with? What can Gill do, if necessary, to assure that his actions will not violate this foreign law?

_____

_____

2. Pedals-2-Go wants to sell its bicycles to a foreign firm, but it is worried that the foreign firm may not pay. Suggest several ways that Pedals-2-Go can assure that it will receive payment?

_____

_____

3. ArmorTech, a U.S. firm, produces a secret computer chip for the U.S. military. A foreign government has approached ArmorTech with an offer to purchase some of the chips. What must ArmorTech do in order to sell its computer chips to the foreign government? What problem may ArmorTech encounter?

_____

_____

4. Jacob has decided that his business should "go global" and sell its goods in North and South America. He is concerned, however, that there may be international laws that could affect his international dealings. Identify and briefly discuss two treaties or organizations that may be relevant to Jacob's plans.

_____

_____

CASE PROBLEMS

Answer the following case problems, explaining your answers.

1. Bill wants to do business with companies from the African country of Ruritania. Ruritania is a former British colony, and its businesspeople are generally quiet, reserved, individuals who prefer to proceed cautiously. Ruritanians emphasize honor, politeness, and personal relationships when negotiating. Bill is a forceful negotiator, who speaks quickly, roughly, and to the point. He also has a habit of gesturing, interrupting others, and yelling in order to get his point across. What matters should Bill think about when preparing to negotiate with his Ruritanian counterparts?

_____

_____

_____

_____

2. Coal companies from the nation of Abuk have gained an increasing share of the international coal market by fixing prices with one another and entering into uniform pricing agreements with their customers. These actions are legal under Abuk law, but would violate U.S. antitrust law. The Abuk coal companies have not yet sold coal in the United States, but they intend to do so in the near future. (a) Can U.S. coal producers presently sue the Abuk coal companies for violation of U.S. antitrust law? (b) Will the U.S. firms have the right to enforce U.S. antitrust law against the Abuk coal companies if they begin to sell their coal in the United States?

_____

_____

_____

_____

CHAPTER 4   The American Legal System and Court Jurisdiction

CHAPTER REVIEW

THE FEDERAL CONSTITUTION:

- *Allocation of Power*: The federal Constitution allocates legislative, executive, and judicial power among the branches of the federal government. Federal courts may hear only actual cases and controversies; they cannot issue advisory opinions, consider moot points, hear cases where the plaintiff lacks standing, or decide political questions.
- *Limitation of Power*: The federal Constitution limits governmental power by granting certain rights to individuals. These rights include:
  1) **Writ of *habeas corpus***: Order directing that a detained person be brought before a court and that the detaining party, such as a state, obey any order issued by the court relating to the detained person.
  2) **Bill of Attainder**: Congress cannot pass a bill of attainder, meaning Congress cannot convict a person of a felony or worse.
  3) ***Ex Post Facto* laws**: Congress cannot pass any ex post facto laws, meaning that Congress cannot pass a law that retroactively declare that a past act is a crime.
- *Amendments to the Constitution*: The first ten amendments to the Constitution, called the Bill of Rights, protect important individual rights such as the right to face one's accuser in a criminal case.

THE COURTS AND JURISDICTION: Jurisdiction is the power of a court to hear and decide a case.

- *Subject Matter Jurisdiction*: Subject matter jurisdiction determines the types of disputes that a court may review.
- *Jurisdiction Over the Persons or Property*: To decide a case, a court must have authority (jurisdiction) over the persons or property involved. Also, the defendant must receive either actual notice or constructive notice of a lawsuit. Types of jurisdiction include:
  1) ***In personam* jurisdiction**: *In personam* jurisdiction means a court has authority to decide the rights of a specific person or corporation in a civil case. This jurisdiction is present when defendants consent to jurisdiction or they are served with process while present within the state in which they are being sued. Long-arm statutes may be used to give a court *in personam* jurisdiction over persons who live in another state.
  2) ***In rem* jurisdiction**: *In rem* jurisdiction occurs when property that is the subject of a lawsuit is located in the state where the court is located, and this jurisdiction allows a court to decide all persons' rights in the property.
  3) ***Quasi in rem* jurisdiction**: *Quasi in rem* jurisdiction allows a court to decide the rights of only certain persons in specific property.
- *Concurrent versus Exclusive Jurisdiction*: When only one court has jurisdiction over a case, it has exclusive jurisdiction. If more than one court has authority, the courts have concurrent jurisdiction.
- *Venue*: Venue refers to the geographical area or district where a lawsuit may be filed.

- *Choice of Laws*: If parties from more than one state are involved in a lawsuit, choice of law rules determine which state's substantive law is used to resolve the dispute. However, the procedural law where the court is located is generally used in this situation.
- *Federal Courts*: Federal courts may hear: 1) cases involving a federal question, meaning the dispute primarily involves some sort of federal law, or 2) cases involving diversity of citizenship, meaning the plaintiffs and defendants reside in different states, if the lawsuit involves more than $75,000.
- *Specialized Courts*: Some federal courts, such as the tax court, hear only one type of case. There are 13 federal circuits, each with its own circuit court of appeals. Appeals from U.S. district courts are heard by the circuit courts of appeals. The U.S. Supreme Court hears appeals from the circuit courts of appeal.
- *State Courts*: Trial courts may have either general jurisdiction or limited jurisdiction. Appellate courts may review decisions of lower courts to determine if errors of law occurred.

ALTERNATIVES TO LITIGATION: To avoid the cost and uncertainty of litigation, many people and businesses submit their legal disputes to arbitration or mediation instead of filing a lawsuit.

HOW TO FIND THE LAW: Federal court decisions are reported in a series of publications. Separate publications print the opinions rendered by: 1) U.S. district court cases (*Federal Supplement*); 2) circuit court of appeals (*Federal Reporter*); 3) U. S. Supreme Court cases (*United States Reports*, *Lawyers Edition, Second*, and *Supreme Court Reporter*); and 4) cases from specialized courts.

Regional publications report state appellate court decisions.

STUDY HINTS FOR CALL-IMAGE TECHNOLOGY CASE STUDIES

The following study hints may be helpful when resolving the Call-Image Technology (CIT) case studies.

page 95

- ♦ Review the power of the federal and state governments to regulate business in order to evaluate whether the states can regulate the Kochanowskis' product.
- ♦ As a practical matter, consider ways that the Kochanowskis can assure that their product complies with both existing and proposed regulations.

page 97

- ♦ Determine what courts may have subject matter jurisdiction over this type of case.
- ♦ Consider carefully the material dealing with allocation of power among the branches of government, particularly the limits on the power of the courts to hear and decide cases.

REVIEW OF KEY TERMS AND CONCEPTS

MATCHING EXERCISE

Select the term or concept that best matches a definition or statement set forth below. Each term or concept is the best match for only one definition or statement.

Terms and Concepts

a. Advisory opinion
b. Appellant
c. Attachment
d. *Certiorari*
e. Defendant

f. *Ex post facto* law
g. Garnishment
h. *Habeas corpus*
i. *Mandamus*
j. Nonjusticiable issue

k. Plaintiff
l. Political question
m. Reverse
n. Standing
o. Subject matter jurisdiction

Definitions and Statements

_____ 1. Authority of a court to hear and decide a certain type of case.
_____ 2. Overturning of a lower court decision.
_____ 3. Court order directing that a person be brought before a court or judge.
_____ 4. Question that intrudes upon the power of the legislative or executive branch.
_____ 5. Person who files a civil lawsuit.
_____ 6. Seizure of property owned by a defendant.
_____ 7. Process to take possession of defendant's money which is held by another person.
_____ 8. Writ issued by a higher court, agreeing to review a case.
_____ 9. Person against whom a lawsuit is filed.
_____ 10. Writ issued by a superior court, directing that a governmental officer do or not do something.
_____ 11. Opinion rendered by a court relating to a question submitted by the legislature or executive that is not involved in an actual case.
_____ 12. Question cannot be properly decided by a court.
_____ 13. Person appealing a court decision.
_____ 14. Right to sue.
_____ 15. Law that retroactively makes a past act a crime.

COMPLETION EXERCISE

Fill in the blanks with the words that most accurately complete each statement.

1. The federal courts can hear only cases that involve an actual _____ and

    _____.

2. The doctrine of _____ requires that only a person who has been injured can sue.

3. The power of a court to hear and decide a case is called _____.

4. A court's authority over a person is referred to as ____ _____ jurisdiction.

5. A _____- _____ statute allows a court to exercise jurisdiction over a person or corporation who is domiciled in another state.

TRUE-FALSE EXERCISE

Write **T** if the statement is true, write **F** if the statement is false.

____ 1. Federal courts can properly decide cases that involve only a political question.
____ 2. By filing a lawsuit, plaintiffs generally grant a court *in personam* jurisdiction over themselves.
____ 3. A court with *quasi in rem* jurisdiction can determine the rights of all persons in a particular item of property.
____ 4. A foreign corporation generally grants *in personam* jurisdiction to the courts of a state in which the corporation is doing business.
____ 5. Questions involving interpretation of a federal statute are not appropriate for a federal court.
____ 6. Cases involving diversity of citizenship can be heard by a federal court, regardless of the amount of money that is in controversy.
____ 7. The U.S. Supreme Court must hear all cases that are appealed to it from a lower court.
____ 8. A state juvenile court is an example of a court of general jurisdiction.
____ 9. In the federal government, the executive branch has the primary power to make laws.
____ 10. The power of judicial review allows the courts to review the validity of actions taken by the legislative or executive branch of government.

```
APPLICATION OF CONCEPTS
```

MULTIPLE CHOICE QUESTIONS

____ 1. In which case is the defendant given *constructive* notice of the lawsuit?
   a. Karim sued Tonya and the summons and complaint was sent to Tonya by registered mail.
   b. Jack sued Ron and, when Ron could not be located, the summons and complaint were published in the local newspaper.
   c. Pat sued Rene and a licensed process server delivered the summons and complaint to Rene.
   d. a and b.

____ 2. Jessica sued her employer, Enco Corp., for violation of federal nondiscrimination law. The U.S. district court ruled in favor of Enco and the circuit court of appeals upheld the trial court judgment. Jessica wants to appeal her case to the U.S. Supreme Court. Under these facts:
   a. Jan has no right to request the U.S. Supreme Court to hear her appeal.
   b. Jan has no right to request the U.S. Supreme Court to hear her appeal unless the circuit court of appeals admits that it made a mistake.
   c. Jan may request the U.S. Supreme Court to hear her appeal, but the Court is not required to do so.
   d. Jan may request the U.S. Supreme Court to hear her appeal, and the Court is required to do so.

_____ 3. Luke sued Rosa for breach of a contract, and Luke has requested that the court award him $5,000 in damages. What type of jurisdiction must the court have to grant this relief?
   a. *Quasi in rem* jurisdiction.
   b. *In rem* jurisdiction.
   c. *In personam* jurisdiction.
   d. No jurisdiction is required.

_____ 4. Peg works for a lawyer while attending college. Peg's employer asks her to locate several decisions rendered by various federal courts. Under these facts:
   a. Peg can locate U.S. district court cases in a regional reporter.
   b. Peg can locate circuit court of appeal cases in the *Federal Supplement*.
   c. Peg can locate U.S. Supreme Court decisions in the *United States Reports*.
   d. Peg can locate U.S. Supreme Court decisions in the *Federal Reporter*.

SHORT ANSWER QUESTIONS

Answer the following questions, briefly explaining the reason for your answer.

1. The state legislature recently passed a statute authorizing a tuition increase at the state's public university. Lisa graduated from this university 10 years previously and she is opposed to this increase in tuition because she thinks it will make a college education unavailable to poorer people. Although this tuition increase does not affect her, she wants to sue the state, challenging the validity of this statute. Does Lisa have standing to challenge this statute?

_____

_____

2. Jim is a political activist who believes that elected officials should have to disclose their personal financial statements. The state legislature considered, but rejected, a bill that would require this type of disclosure. Jim has now filed a lawsuit in order to obtain a court order requiring elected state officials to disclose their personal financial information. Will a court grant Jim's request?

_____

_____

3. Roger and Teresa owned competing grocery stores. Roger told a group of Teresa's customers that she had previously been convicted of selling spoiled meat. Teresa claimed this statement was false, and she sued Roger for $50,000 for defamation (i.e., the wrongful injury to the reputation of another). Roger asserted two defenses: (a) He did not commit this wrong because what he said was true; and (b) the court lacked jurisdiction over him because he had never been served with process. Are Roger's defenses based on substantive or procedural law?

_____

_____

4. The state legislature is concerned with health risks associated with domesticated lizards and other reptiles. Thus, the legislature passed a statute that makes it a crime for anyone to sell live lizards or other reptiles. The statute applies to any sales made within the past two years and any future sales. Is this statute valid to the extent that it applies to past sales? Is this statute valid to the extent that it applies to future sales?

_____

_____

CASE PROBLEMS

Answer the following case problems, explaining your answers.

1. Tortilla Wonders Corp. (TWC) and Ramon jointly own a chain of restaurants called "Chips Ahoy." TWC was incorporated under Arizona law and its principal offices are located in New Mexico. Ramon is a California resident. TWC and Ramon own and operate restaurants in 10 states, including Nebraska. Ginger, a customer, was injured in a Chips Ahoy restaurant located in Omaha Nebraska. Ginger wants to file suit against both TWC and Ramon in Nebraska state court. (a) Do TWC and Ramon have sufficient minimum contacts with Nebraska to enable its courts to hear and decide this lawsuit? (b) Can the Nebraska state court obtain *in personam* jurisdiction over TWC and Ramon?

_____

_____

_____

_____

2. Janet, a resident of Florida, plans to sue Carson, a resident of New York, for $100,000. Janet intends to sue for breach of contract, a claim that is based on Florida state law. Janet plans to file her lawsuit in U.S. district court. Would the U.S. district court have jurisdiction to hear and decide this case?

_____

_____

_____

_____

CHAPTER 5   Torts

CHAPTER REVIEW

OBJECTIVES OF TORT LAW: Tort law provides a remedy for individuals and businesses who have been intentionally or unintentionally damaged by the wrongful acts or omissions (meaning, failures to act) of others. The remedy usually awarded under tort law is monetary damages.

THEORIES OF TORT LIABILITY: A tort is a civil wrong which involves: 1) conduct that causes a harm or injury to a party, 2) thereby entitling the party to recover damages, and 3) the right to damages does not depend on the breach of a contract. There are three basic theories of tort liability: 1) intentional torts, 2) negligence, and 3) strict liability.

INTENTIONAL TORTS: Intentional torts are wrongs that impose liability on persons who either wanted a wrongful act to occur or knew that it would occur. Intentional torts include:
- *Assault*: An assault is conduct that causes someone else to fear an immediate battery.
- *Battery*: A battery is the wrongful physical contact of another.
- *Defamation*: Defamation is conduct that wrongfully harms another person's reputation. Slander is spoken defamation, and libel is defamation made in a writing, photo, or similar manner.
- *Disparagement*: Disparagement arises when one makes a false statement about a company, its reputation, or its products or services.
- *False Imprisonment*: False imprisonment is the unlawful detention of a person against his or her will without just cause.
- *Mental Distress*: Liability arises if a person intentionally causes another to suffer serious indignity (severe emotional harm) by engaging in outrageous conduct.
- *Invasion of Privacy*: Invasion of privacy is conduct that wrongfully invades another's privacy. This tort is committed when a person without permission: 1) uses someone else's name, likeness, or life story for its own commercial benefit, 2) invades someone else's physical privacy, or 3) discloses to the public private facts about someone else and the public has no legitimate interest in this information.
- *Trespass*: Trespass occurs when a person ventures onto another's land without permission.
- *Conversion*: A person is liable for conversion when he intentionally exercises exclusive control over another's personal property without permission.
- *Misappropriation of Trade Secrets*: This tort occurs when someone unlawfully acquires and uses trade secrets (confidential information) of another business.
- *Fraud*: Fraud occurs when one party intentionally deceives a second party regarding a factual matter in order to benefit from the second party's reliance on the false information.
- *Civil RICO Violations*: Civil liability may be imposed under certain statutes if a person or business commits two or more racketeering acts within a 10-year period.
- *Defenses to Intentional Torts*: Consent, privilege, necessity, and truth (with regard to defamation) are potential defenses that defendants may use to avoid liability under tort law.

NEGLIGENCE: Liability for negligence may be imposed when people act in an unreasonably careless manner and, as a result, harm someone else. Negligence exists when the following four are established:
- *Duty*: Everyone has a duty to act as a reasonable and prudent person would act under the same circumstances. Stated another way, everyone has a duty to act in a reasonable manner to prevent

foreseeable harm to others. In some cases, a statute defines the standard by which a person's duty is measured. In most states, the breach of this statutory standard is called "negligence per se."

- **Breach of Duty**: Breach of duty means to violate a legal obligation. One may breach a duty by acting carelessly or by failing to act (an omission) when action is required.
- **Causation**: A person's act or omission must be both 1) the actual cause and 2) the proximate cause of the plaintiff's harm. Actual cause means that, as a factual matter, the breach substantially produced the harm. Proximate cause is a policy question, but generally means the breach is so closely related to the plaintiff's injuries that the law will hold the defendant responsible.
- **Harm**: There generally is no liability for negligence unless harm is caused.
- **Defenses to Negligence**: Defenses to negligence include: 1) assumption of risk (plaintiff knowingly and voluntarily undertook risk); 2) contributory negligence (plaintiff's negligence bars recovery); 3) comparative negligence (plaintiff's negligence reduces recovery).

STRICT LIABILITY: Strict liability imposes liability on persons who engage in ultrahazardous activities and, as a result of these activities, harm others. Liability is imposed even if the person acts as carefully as possible and does not intend to harm anyone.

PRODUCT LIABILITY: Manufacturers may be held liable for harm caused by their defective products. Common theories for imposing liability include: 1) fraud; 2) breach of express or implied warranties; 3) negligence; and 4) strict liability.

TORT LIABILITY OF BUSINESS ENTITIES: Employers can be held liable for the torts of their employees that are committed while the employees are carrying out the business of the employers.

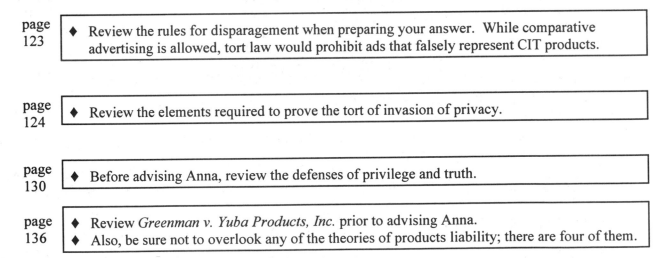

STUDY HINTS FOR CALL-IMAGE TECHNOLOGY CASE STUDIES

The following study hints may be helpful when resolving the Call-Image Technology (CIT) case studies.

| page 123 | ♦ Review the rules for disparagement when preparing your answer. While comparative advertising is allowed, tort law would prohibit ads that falsely represent CIT products. |

| page 124 | ♦ Review the elements required to prove the tort of invasion of privacy. |

| page 130 | ♦ Before advising Anna, review the defenses of privilege and truth. |

| page 136 | ♦ Review *Greenman v. Yuba Products, Inc.* prior to advising Anna.
♦ Also, be sure not to overlook any of the theories of products liability; there are four of them. |

MATCHING EXERCISE

Select the term or concept that best matches a definition or statement set forth below. Each term or concept is the best match for only one definition or statement.

Terms and Concepts

a. Assault
b. Bar
c. Conversion
d. False imprisonment

e. Foreseeable
f. Implied consent
g. Libel
h. Negligence per se

i. Privilege
j. Replevin
k. Slander
l. Trespass

Definitions and Statements

_____ 1. Permission that is inferred from one's words, actions, or other conduct.
_____ 2. Oral defamation.
_____ 3. Barrier; something that prevents one from suing on a claim.
_____ 4. Wrongfully causing another to fear an immediate, unlawful touching.
_____ 5. Presumption that a defendant was negligent.
_____ 6. Capable of being anticipated.
_____ 7. Wrongful detention of another.
_____ 8. Wrongful going upon or other interference with another person's land.
_____ 9. Written defamation.
_____ 10. Wrongful taking or other interference with another's personal property.
_____ 11. Action brought to recover possession of one's goods.
_____ 12. Legal right to do something.

COMPLETION EXERCISE

Fill in the blanks with the words that most accurately complete each statement.

1. A tort involves a _____ wrong whereas a crime involves a _____ wrong.

2. _____ torts are wrongs in which the defendant has acted in a willful manner and either wanted the act to occur which resulted in harm or knew that the act would probably result in harm.

3. Fraud requires proof that the defendant misrepresented a _____ _____.

4. A merchant who wrongfully detains a customer without having a sufficient legal basis for the detention may be liable for the tort of _____ _____.

5. Identify the four elements that must be established in order to establish liability for negligence:

a. _____.

b. _____.

c. _____.

d. _____.

TRUE-FALSE EXERCISE

Write **T** if the statement is true, write **F** if the statement is false.

_____ 1. A tort is a crime against the public which is punishable by fines and imprisonment.

_____ 2. Remedies in a tort action are most often money damages.

_____ 3. Under the doctrine of *res ipsa loquitur*, an inference of negligence arises if the instrument that caused the plaintiff's injury was under the exclusive control of the defendant and the injury suffered by the plaintiff ordinarily occurs only as a result of someone else's negligence.

_____ 4. A person cannot be liable for defamation if the person speaks only the truth about someone else.

_____ 5. Libel and slander involve the same basic violation - wrongful injury to the reputation of another.

_____ 6. A person commits the tort of trespass by going upon another's land without permission, and proof of actual damage to the land is not required.

_____ 7. A person who gives a resume to a prospective employer stating that he is a Harvard University graduate, when in fact he is not, is committing a fraudulent act.

_____ 8. There is no trespass if someone goes upon another's land due to a necessity.

_____ 9. The defense of contributory negligence is a complete bar to a lawsuit for negligence.

_____ 10. An employer cannot be held liable for an employee's tort - only the employee is liable.

APPLICATION OF CONCEPTS

MULTIPLE CHOICE QUESTIONS

_____ 1. Joe was angry with a clerk and, standing a foot away from the clerk, Joe drew his arm back with a clenched fist and stated, "I am going to punch your lights out." What tort did Joe commit?
   a. Libel.
   b. False imprisonment.
   c. Battery.
   d. Assault.

_____ 2. One afternoon, Carrie slipped on grapes that had fallen on the floor in the produce department of Acme Groceries, injuring herself. Acme inspected the floor once in the morning and once at closing for spilled produce, even though it knew that produce was dropped on the floor more often. Is Acme liable for negligence?
   a. No, Acme owed no duty to Carrie.
   b. No, Acme did not breach its duty to Carrie.
   c. No, Acme's conduct was not the cause of Carrie's injuries.
   d. Yes, Acme was negligent and is liable to Carrie.

_____ 3. John and Ken went to a baseball game at their college. They sat high up in the stands behind first base even though they knew that foul balls often landed in this area. In the third inning, a foul ball struck John in the head, causing him serious injuries. John sued the college for negligence. In all likelihood, is the college liable to John?
   a. Yes, the college was negligent in allowing spectators to watch the baseball game.
   b. Yes, the college is liable under strict liability because baseball is an ultrahazardous activity.
   c. No, John assumed the risk that foul balls would sometimes land in the stands.
   d. No, colleges owe no duty to protect students from unreasonable risks of harm.

_____ 4. Which of the following is fraud?
   a. Nigel offered to sell his car to Jawan, explaining that the clutch was worn out.
   b. When negotiating to sell his car to Maureen, Jack stated that the car was "a beauty - worth every penny" of the asking price. Actually, the car was a worn-out junk heap.
   c. Sally offered to sell her car to Mark. She stated to Mark that all of the car lights worked, not knowing that one rear tail light had just burned out.
   d. Guillermo sold Kim a car that he claimed had two years left on the warranty even though he knew that the warranty had run out six months before.

SHORT ANSWER QUESTIONS

Answer the following questions, briefly explaining the reason for your answer.

1. Bob spread a false rumor at a party that Margo had a sexually transmitted disease. Identify the type of tort Bob has committed and list the elements that Margo must prove in order to recover.

_____

_____

2. Fran, a security guard for Northern Department Store, believed that she saw Ben shoplift a watch from a display cabinet. As Ben attempted to leave the store, Fran blocked Ben's exit and detained him for a few minutes to ask some questions in order to determine whether he was in fact guilty of the suspected theft. When Fran determined that Ben was innocent, he was released. Are Fran and Northern Department Store liable to Ben for the tort of false imprisonment?

_____

_____

3. Jessie and a group of other teenagers entered Dan's Candy Store. Dan decided that there were too many teenagers in his store, so he grabbed a purse that was slung over Jessie's shoulder and pulled her towards the door, telling her to leave. Jessie suffered a displaced shoulder as a result of this encounter. Is Dan liable for the tort of battery?

_____

_____

4. Patsy was fired as a waitress at the Blue Bull Cafe. To get back at the cafe owner, Patsy stood in front of the cafe and falsely told prospective customers that the cafe served spoiled food. As a result, a number of potential customers decided to eat elsewhere. Has Patsy committed a tort?

_____

_____

CASE PROBLEMS

Answer the following case problems, explaining your answers.

1. Will was hired to prepare a registration statement (disclosure document) for an offering of stock in "You're Connected," an Internet company. Will misstated important information in the statement regarding the risks that were associated with this company in return for a $50,000 bonus paid by "You're Connected" management. Management did not want Will to fully disclose the risks so that investors would not be scared away. Lilly bought stock in the company based on the information in the statement and, as a result, she suffered large financial losses. Analyze what tort claim, if any, Lilly may have against Will and "You're Connected."

_____

_____

_____

_____

2. For many years, Waste Disposal Corp. (WDC) intentionally dumped toxic wastes in porous soil near Megalopolis, a growing metropolitan area. WDC did not investigate the potential dangers associated with its dumping. Over time, the toxic wastes migrated towards Megalopolis. Five years later, a new residential subdivision was built in the Megalopolis suburbs, but many of the homes had to be abandoned because the toxic wastes previously dumped by WDC rendered them uninhabitable. (a) What tort duty, if any, did WDC have in connection with its dumping activities? (b) Analyze whether WDC has any tort liability in this case?

_____

_____

_____

_____

CHAPTER REVIEW

INTRODUCTION: The six basic steps in a civil lawsuit are 1) pleadings, 2) service, 3) discovery, 4) pretrial motions, 5) trial, and 6) enforcing the judgment.

CLIENT'S INTERVIEW WITH A LAWYER: During an initial interview with a potential client, an attorney will obtain the facts of the case and determine whether there is a conflict of interest in representing the potential client. Attorneys may charge a flat rate based on the nature of the work, an hourly fee, or a contingency fee, meaning the attorney receives a percentage of any damages awarded or settlement paid to the client. Attorneys are licensed by the state, not the country. Any attorney licensed in a state may appear before any court in that state.

INVESTIGATION OF THE FACTS: An attorney will investigate the facts of a case by obtaining any readily available documents and interviewing witnesses. The attorney will then develop a theory of the case to be used as a basis for settlement negotiations.

NEGOTIATION OF SETTLEMENT: Lawsuits should be filed only after attempts to settle have failed. A lawsuit must be filed within the statute of limitations, or deadline, for filing.

FILING THE SUIT: Filing of the suit requires the filing of a complaint with the clerk of the civil court and service of the complaint, and in some states a summons, on the defendant. A defendant must be served with notice that a lawsuit has been filed before the lawsuit is considered to have commenced. The defendant must file an answer to the complaint or a default judgment will be entered against the defendant.

PRETRIAL PROCEEDINGS: After the complaint and answer are filed, the discovery process begins. Discovery allows each party to learn facts about the case that will help both sides determine the issues that are disputed in the lawsuit. Many more facts can be discovered than can be admitted as evidence in a trial. Methods of discovery include:

- **Depositions**: Depositions are the sworn testimony of witnesses that is taken outside of court. Depositions can be used to preserve testimony of witnesses who cannot appear at trial. They may also be used to show inconsistencies in trial testimony, called impeaching a witness.
- **Interrogatories**: Interrogatories are written questions that are served by one party on the other. The interrogatories are not as spontaneous as depositions but serve essentially the same purposes.
- **Production of Documents and Things**: A subpoena duces tecum requires witnesses to turn over specified documents and records that might be relevant to the case.
- **Physical or Mental Examination**: If the physical or mental condition of a party is an issue, the court may, upon request, order the party to submit to an examination by a physician or psychiatrist.
- **Request for Admission**: Parties may submit written questions asking the other side to admit to certain facts.
- **The Result of Discovery**: Evidence found out during discovery can help parties know how to proceed with a lawsuit. Evidence found out during discovery may not be admissible as evidence at a trial.
- **Pretrial Conferences**: Pretrial conferences are often required by the court to try to settle the case without an expensive and prolonged trial. The judge may take an active part in this phase of the case.

- *Demurrer, Motion to Dismiss, and Motion for Summary Judgment*: A demurrer challenges the legal sufficiency of a party's pleading. A motion to dismiss requests the court to dismiss a complaint because, even if the allegations in complaint are true, the plaintiff has failed to state a valid claim. Summary judgment may be awarded if there are no genuine, material, factual issues and one party is entitled to win as a matter of law.

THE TRIAL: Unless both parties agree that the case should be heard by the judge, the selection of the jury is first. Prospective jurors are asked questions (voir dire) to determine whether they are fit to serve on the jury. Prospective jurors who are potentially biased are eliminated for cause. Prospective jurors may also be eliminated for no reason by either party's using of a peremptory challenge.

After the jury is selected, each side gives an opening statement, outlining what they propose to prove. Beginning with the plaintiff, each side then calls witnesses and submits documentary evidence; direct and cross-examination is used to get to examine witnesses. Expert witnesses may be called to offer an opinion regarding a disputed issue.

Closing statements summarize the "truth" that each side believes it has proved. The judge then informs the jury of the applicable law (jury instructions) and asks them to resolve the case by applying the facts to the law. The jury renders a verdict, general or special. The judge then enters a judgment based on the jury's verdict. The judge can enter a judgment that disagrees with the jury's verdict (judgment n.o.v.) only if the judge finds that there is no substantial evidence to support the jury's verdict.

POST-TRIAL: The losing party may appeal if it believes that an important issue of law was incorrectly decided.

A COMMENT ON FINALITY: The doctrine of *res judicata* prohibits parties from suing a second time on a claim that has been decided by a final judgment.

STUDY HINTS FOR CALL-IMAGE TECHNOLOGY CASE STUDIES

The following study hints may be helpful when resolving the Call-Image Technology (CIT) case studies.

| page 142 | ◆ In advising the Kochanowskis about hiring a lawyer, recognize that civil litigation and practicing commercial law involve different legal skills and knowledge. |
| | ◆ Anna and Tom should look at ways to show that their company is proactive in taking measures to prevent or reduce accidents. |

| page 145 | ◆ Refer Anna and Dan to Exhibits 6.1 and 6.2. |
| | ◆ Also, emphasize to Anna and Dan that it is best not to hold anything back from their attorney. |

| page 161 | ◆ Look at the reasons for dismissing a juror for cause, including the issue of juror bias. |
| | ◆ If cause cannot be established for dismissing the juror, then Mr. Jones may want to consider using a peremptory cchallengeto disqualify the potential juror. |

MATCHING EXERCISE

Select the term or concept that best matches a definition or statement set forth below. Each term or concept is the best match for only one definition or statement.

Terms and Concepts

a. Answer
b. Complaint
c. Contingent fee
d. Deposition
e. General verdict

f. Group bias
g. Impeach
h. Interrogatories
i. Peremptory challenge
j. Petit jurors

k. Request for admission
l. *Res judicata*
m. Subpoena duces tecum
n. Summons
o. Voir dire

Definitions and Statements

_____ 1. Attorney's fee that is a percentage of any amount the attorney recovers on behalf of the client.
_____ 2. Plaintiff's initial pleading that states the plaintiff's claim against the defendant.
_____ 3. Writ served upon a defendant, giving the defendant notice that he or she has been sued.
_____ 4. Sworn testimony taken outside of court.
_____ 5. Written request for a party to admit or deny facts that are relevant to the lawsuit.
_____ 6. To call into question the truthfulness of a witness.
_____ 7. Panel of citizens who decide issues of fact in civil and criminal trials.
_____ 8. Defendant's response to the plaintiff's complaint.
_____ 9. Doctrine holding that a final judgment bars the parties from filing a new lawsuit on a claim that has already been litigated.
_____ 10. Decision of a jury.
_____ 11. Court order directing a witness to produce specified evidence.
_____ 12. Examination of potential jurors to determine whether they are fit to serve on a jury.
_____ 13. Presumption that jurors cannot be fair because they belong to a particular race or other group.
_____ 14. Right of a party to exclude a potential juror without having to justify the rejection of that person.
_____ 15. Written questions that are served on the opposing party in a civil lawsuit to be answered under oath within a required time.

COMPLETION EXERCISE

Fill in the blanks with the words that most accurately complete each statement.

1. _____ is the process by which parties obtain evidence from one another.

2. Once the jury has issued its verdict, the court then generally issues a _____ based on the verdict.

3. _____ - _____ occurs when a witness is questioned at trial by the lawyer who did not call the witness to the stand.

4. The losing party at a trial will often _____ a question of law to a higher court.

5. Identify five basic discovery devices:

    a. _____.

    b. _____.

    c. _____.

    d. _____.

    e. _____.

TRUE-FALSE EXERCISE

Write **T** if the statement is true, write **F** if the statement is false.

_____ 1. A potential juror cannot be disqualified except for cause.

_____ 2. A demurrer is a motion for a new trial that is made by a party who loses at trial.

_____ 3. The plaintiff initiates a civil lawsuit by filing a complaint and having it served on the defendant.

_____ 4. Voir dire is the process for examining witnesses to determine if they are fit to serve on a jury.

_____ 5. People can keep filing new lawsuits on the same claim until they get a judgment they like.

_____ 6. A party in a civil lawsuit cannot be required to undergo a physical or mental examination.

_____ 7. Failure to respond to a request for admission will result in the matter being deemed admitted without need for further proof.

_____ 8. The purpose of a jury is to decide questions of fact and render a verdict.

_____ 9. In appropriate situations, expert witnesses may be called to testify as to their opinions.

_____ 10. A pretrial conference is a proceeding in which the judge decides the case without having a trial.

APPLICATION OF CONCEPTS

MULTIPLE CHOICE QUESTIONS

_____ 1. Lawrence plans to sue Diane, his former partner, in order to recover partnership property that was wrongfully taken by Diane. Under these facts:
    a. Lawrence will commence the lawsuit by filing a judgment with the court.
    b. Lawrence will commence the lawsuit by filing a complaint with the court.
    c. Diane will respond by filing a request for deposition with the court.
    d. b and c.

_____ 2. Wendy sued her former tenant, Frank, for damaging the leased premises. Frank denies damaging the property. Wendy wants Frank to be personally questioned during the discovery process in order to obtain a spontaneous statement admitting that he damaged the premises. Which discovery technique would best serve Wendy's purpose?
    a. A subpoena duces tecum.
    b. Interrogatories.
    c. Demurrer.
    d. Deposition.

_____ 3. Jim sued Carol for breach of contract, and the case will be tried before a jury. Which of the following potential jurors is most likely to be dismissed for cause by the judge?
    a. A person who years ago was sued for breach of contract.
    b. All female prospective jurors.
    c. A business associate of Carol.
    d. All of the above.

_____ 4. Ellen sued SuCorp for breach of contract. Based on substantial evidence, the jury returned a general verdict in favor of Ellen for $10,000, and the judge entered judgment in favor of Ellen for this amount. If SuCorp appeals this judgment to an appellate court, the appellate court:
    a. May reverse the judgment if the lower court committed serious errors of law.
    b. Will not review the proceedings of the lower court.
    c. Will have the witnesses testify again.
    d. Will conduct a new trial.

SHORT ANSWER QUESTIONS

Answer the following questions, briefly explaining the reason for your answer.

1. Hin was involved in an automobile accident, and he suffered personal injuries and his vehicle was damaged. Hin is preparing for his first meeting with his attorney. What should Hin do to prepare for this meeting? What, if anything, should Hin bring to this meeting?

_____

_____

2. Chad needed a living will, which his attorney agreed to prepare for $120. Chad also was injured by a product and wanted to sue the manufacturer of the product for $10,000. Chad's attorney agreed to represent him in this suit and take 40 percent of the amount recovered as her fee. What type of fee arrangements have Chad and his attorney made? How much in fees will the attorney receive?

_____

_____

3. Joe's Diner bought all of its vegetables from Acme Farms. Joe's claims that one shipment of Acme vegetables was tainted, and Acme denies the allegations. Acme has now sued Joe's for breach of contract, and a jury trial is scheduled. In this case, what specific matters will the jury determine?

_____

_____

4. Sammy sued Franklin Corp. for injuries he suffered while using a tool manufactured by Franklin Corp. The trial court issued a judgment in favor of Franklin. At this point, is there a final judgment? If Sammy appeals the judgment and the appellate court upholds the judgment, can Sammy file a new lawsuit against Franklin for the same injuries?

_____

_____

CASE PROBLEMS

Answer the following case problems, explaining your answers.

1. Randy was injured in a car accident. Randy claimed the other driver, Karen, negligently ran a red light causing the accident, but Karen insists that Randy ran the red light. Randy sued Karen, the parties have filed all pleadings, and Randy has now filed a motion for summary judgment. (a) Describe the purpose for a motion for summary judgment. (b) Under the facts stated, will the court grant summary judgment in favor of Randy? (c) If Karen admitted that she ran the red light, but defended that she is not liable because she didn't mean to collide with Randy, would the court grant summary judgment in favor of Randy?

_____

_____

_____

_____

2. Suiter Corp. sued Pizza Man Corp. for breach of contract and Suiter was awarded a $100,000 judgment by the trial court. Pizza Man Corp. appealed the judgment to the appellate court. Describe the legal effect of the following actions that the appellate court might take: (a) The appellate court affirms the judgment. (b) The appellate court reverses the judgment, finding that serious errors of law were made and Pizza Man Corp. was entitled to win. (c) The appellate court reverses the judgment finding that important evidence was excluded by the trial court, and the appellate court remands the case.

_____

_____

_____

_____

CHAPTER 7   Alternate Dispute Resolution

```
CHAPTER REVIEW
```

THE NEED FOR ALTERNATIVES: Alternate dispute resolution (ADR) refers to a number of procedures that allow parties to settle legal disputes without going to court. ADR is generally a voluntary approach for settling disputes, although courts and legislatures are increasingly making it mandatory in some situations. Advantages of ADR include: 1) it lessens burden on the judicial system; 2) it is quicker and less expensive than litigation; and 3) it may help businesses avoid becoming adversaries, thereby allowing them to maintain a business relationship.

NEGOTIATION: Negotiation involves the discussion and resolution of a controversy by the parties who have a disagreement.

MEDIATION: Mediation is an out-of-court procedure whereby parties submit a dispute to a neutral third party who tries to help the parties find a solution. One mediation approach is caucusing, whereby the mediator meets with the parties separately. Another approach, shuttle mediation, involves the mediator's placing the parties in different rooms and then speaking privately with each party in an attempt to clarify the issues and explore possible options. The mediator then runs messages back and forth between the parties in an attempt to reach a mutually acceptable settlement.

The mediator does not make a decision that is not legally binding. Also, the matters discussed in mediation are generally confidential. It is best that the parties agree that any discussions during mediation should not be used at trial.

- *Standards of conduct*: The American Bar Association has drafted model standards of conduct for mediators.
- *Compensation*: There are no set rules on whether mediators should be compensated or the amount of compensation they should be paid.

ARBITRATION: Arbitration is an out-of-court procedure whereby parties submit a dispute to a one or more neutral third parties called an arbitrator. In a voluntary arbitration, the parties mutually select the arbitrator or agree upon the process for selecting the arbitrator.

Arbitration is most often a voluntary process to which the parties have freely consented. In most situations, voluntary arbitration is provided for in contracts which identify the types of disputes that must be arbitrated. An agreement to arbitrate is legally enforceable (unless the agreement is unenforceable due to fraud or other defenses). If parties have a valid arbitration agreement, they must arbitrate the dispute, and they have given up their right to have this dispute decided by a trial court.

The arbitrator's decision is called an award. In most voluntary arbitrations, the award is legally binding on the parties. However, parties may agree to an "advisory arbitration," in which case the award is not binding.

Broadly speaking, parties cannot appeal an award. If one party fails to perform in accordance with the award, the other party may file a petition with a court seeking its enforcement.

- *Controls on arbitration*: States have developed their own rules on arbitration, and some have laws that do not permit arbitration for certain types of disputes. Despite these laws, parties must still arbitrate a dispute if they have contractually agreed to do so. This is because a federal law provides that arbitration agreements must be enforced and state laws cannot make them unenforceable.
- *Statutory coverage*: Most states have adopted the Uniform Arbitration Act for the purpose of regulating arbitration. At the federal level, the Federal Arbitration Act provides limited regulation. At the international level, more than 80 countries follow the UN Convention on Recognition and Enforcement of Arbitral Awards.
- *Organizations*: There are many organizations that offer arbitration services including the American Arbitration Association (AAA). The AAA also offers other services such as mediation, minitrial, and fact-finding. In fact-finding, an arbitrator investigates a dispute and issues findings of fact and a nonbinding report.

MINITRIAL: Another procedure that may be used to settle disputes is a minitrial. This procedure is frequently used to decide a dispute between two companies.

A minitrial is an informal, out-of-court procedure that is conducted by a neutral advisor. A shortened form of the case is presented, with senior executives from both companies watching. After the presentation is completed, the executives try to resolve a dispute and reach a settlement.

RENT-A-JUDGE TRIAL: This procedure entails two parties to a dispute hiring a judge or retired judge to hear their case and render a judgment. It is quicker and less expensive than a normal trial. Typically, the decision in these proceedings can be appealed to public appellate courts.

SMALL CLAIMS COURT: Small claims courts are public courts and, therefore, their proceedings are actually trials. Nonetheless, these courts, which typically have limited subject matter jurisdiction, are a relatively quick, inexpensive method for resolving small legal disputes.

STUDY HINTS FOR CALL-IMAGE TECHNOLOGY CASE STUDIES

The following study hints may be helpful when resolving the Call-Image Technology (CIT) case studies.

page 173	◆ First, you should advise John to review his insurance policy. In all likelihood, the policy allows his insurer to use its own discretion in deciding how to handle the dispute, so long as it acts in good faith. ◆ You may want to suggest to John that he encourage his insurer to try various ADR approaches in order to achieve a fair result.

page 176	◆ You should review the material dealing with mediation, especially those portions dealing with the selection, qualifications, and compensation of mediators.

MATCHING EXERCISE

Select the term or concept that best matches a definition or statement set forth below. Each term or concept is the best match for only one definition or statement.

Terms and Concepts

a. ADR
b. American Arbitration Association
c. Arbitration

d. Award
e. Caucusing
f. Mediation

g. Mediator
h. Negotiation
i. Shuttle mediation

Definitions and Statements

_____ 1. Out-of-court proceeding whereby a third person renders a legally-binding decision regarding a dispute between two parties.

_____ 2. Type of mediation whereby the mediator meets separately with the parties in hopes of finding a common ground for settlement of their dispute.

_____ 3. Person who conducts a mediation.

_____ 4. Organization that provides experts to serve as arbitrators.

_____ 5. Out-of-court proceeding whereby a third person tries to help parties reach a settlement of a dispute. The third person does not render a legally-binding decision.

_____ 6. Assortment of out-of-court procedures that help parties to settle legal disputes without going to court.

_____ 7. Decision of an arbitrator.

_____ 8. Type of mediation whereby the mediator separates the parties and goes back and forth between the parties, carrying messages and settlement proposals.

_____ 9. Procedure whereby parties themselves try to reach a settlement of a dispute.

COMPLETION EXERCISE

Fill in the blanks with the words that most accurately complete each statement.

1. The _____ is the person who conducts a mediation.

2. The _____ _____ _____ is a uniform act that most states have adopted to regulate arbitration.

3. Some mediators believe that their role is only to help _____ the settlement of disputes while other others believe that their role is to _____ the parties' proposals.

4. _____ _____ is a type of arbitration in which the arbitrator's decision is not legally binding on the parties.

5. List three advantages of ADR.

    a. _____.

    b. _____.

    c. _____.

TRUE-FALSE EXERCISE

Write **T** if the statement is true, write **F** if the statement is false.

_____ 1. Businesses are increasingly opposed to arbitration and other forms of ADR as a means for resolving legal disputes.

_____ 2. Small claims court is not a real court; rather it is a group of citizens who decide the legal rights of others.

_____ 3. Increasingly, courts are requiring people to attempt ADR before allowing them to seek a judicial determination of their rights.

_____ 4. Agreements to arbitrate a dispute are illegal and void.

_____ 5. ADR is appropriate for resolving all disputes.

_____ 6. States generally have the power to declare that arbitration agreements are null and void.

_____ 7. An agreement to arbitrate cannot be enforced if the agreement was procured by fraud or other wrongdoing.

_____ 8. Arbitration is a common method that is used for resolving disputes in international business.

_____ 9. An arbitration may be heard by one arbitrator or a panel of arbitrators.

_____ 10. A mediator should be a disinterested party.

APPLICATION OF CONCEPTS

MULTIPLE CHOICE QUESTIONS

_____ 1. Jason and JoJo submitted a dispute to binding arbitration. The arbitrator issued a decision in Jason's favor and awarded him $5,000 to be paid within 60 days. JoJo has refused to pay the $5,000 or any portion of it. Under these facts:
    a. Jason can do nothing to enforce the award.
    b. Jason can have JoJo imprisoned for failing to comply with the award.
    c. Jason can file an action in court to obtain judicial confirmation of the award, thereby enabling him to legally enforce the award.
    d. b and c.

_____ 2. Todd has a dispute with Carla and he wants to use some type of ADR or equivalent procceding that will produce a legally binding decision. Which of the following would meet Todd's needs?
   a. Arbitration.
   b. Mediation.
   c. Minitrial.
   d. a and c.

_____ 3. Advantage Corp. and Disadvantage Corp. had a trade name dispute. Advantage claimed that Disadvantage's name was deceptively similar to its name and confused consumers regarding their companies and their respective products. Advantage and Disadvantage agreed to retain an arbitrator to conduct a fact-finding regarding this dispute. Under these facts:
   a. The findings of fact determined by the arbitrator will be legally binding on the parties.
   b. The report issued by the arbitrator will be legally binding on the parties.
   c. The findings of fact determined by the arbitrator and the arbitrator's report will NOT be legally binding on the parties.
   d. a and b.

_____ 4. Richard sued Quint in Small Claims Court for $500. Select the answer(s) that are probably correct regarding this lawsuit.
   a. The parties may represent themselves.
   b. The parties should not worry about being prepared when they go to trial.
   c. The court's judgment is not legally binding.
   d. All of the above.

SHORT ANSWER QUESTIONS

Answer the following questions, briefly explaining the reason for your answer.

1. Neuron Corp. agreed to arbitrate a trade secret dispute with Biomed, another nuclear physics company. The dispute involved a technical point of law and science. Explain who will select the arbitrator. Discuss who might be an appropriate person to arbitrate this type of dispute.

_____

_____

2. Two businesses owned adjoining property. When a flood destroyed a common roadway they shared, each insisted the other repair it. Unable to reach a solution, they submitted their dispute to mediation. Discuss two approaches the mediator may use to help the parties resolve their dispute.

_____

_____

3. Rigatoni Corp. had a dispute with a client regarding the client's unpaid bill. Both parties wanted to maintain their business relationship, but the client disputed the amount owed to Rigatoni. The parties are considering using a minitrial in order to help settle their dispute. Discuss what would occur in a minitrial of this dispute. Is the outcome of the minitrial legally binding on the parties?

_____

_____

4. Gina claims that her landlord has wrongfully failed to return $250 of her security deposit. The landlord refuses to negotiate this matter with Gina and refuses to agree to any type of ADR. Under these facts, what can Gina do in order to enforce her legal rights in a relatively quick, inexpensive manner?

_____

_____

CASE PROBLEMS

Answer the following case problems, explaining your answers.

1. West Fabricating installed a powerful grinder to use in its manufacturing operation. West operated its plant around the clock. Paul, who lives next door, is considering filing a lawsuit against West because noise from the grinder disturbs his family at night. (a) Discuss the advantages that mediation may offer to West and Paul in this case. (b) Analyze how the parties might settle this dispute without going to court.

_____

_____

_____

_____

2. Carson Trucking bought a forklift from Dependable Equipment Sales. The forklift's engine went out one week later. Carson demanded its money back, but Dependable refused. The sales contract for the forklift states, "All disputes arising out of this agreement shall be submitted to binding arbitration."
(a) Must the parties arbitrate this dispute? (b) If the dispute is arbitrated, is the arbitrator's award legally binding? (c) If the arbitrator makes factual and legal errors in deciding this dispute, can Carson or Dependable appeal such errors to an appellate court?

_____

_____

_____

_____

CHAPTER 8

Crimes and Business

CHAPTER REVIEW

WHY STUDY CRIMINAL LAW?: Businesses are constantly confronted with the effects of crime.

OBJECTIVES OF CRIMINAL LAW: Objectives of criminal law include:
- *Protection of Persons and Property*: Protection of the public from harm, which is accomplished under the criminal law by fines and imprisonment.
- *Deterrence of Criminal Behavior*: Criminal behavior is presumably deterred by punishment. Under the U.S. Constitution, however, punishment cannot be excessive.
- *Punishment of Criminal Activity*: Criminals are punished by fines and/or deprivation of their freedom.
- *Rehabilitation of the Criminal*: Criminals generally receive education and training in an attempt to reform them.

BASES OF CRIMINAL RESPONSIBILITIES: In general, all crimes have two elements: a criminal act and a criminal mental state.
- *The Act*: Conduct is criminal only if it is prohibited by law and the actor voluntarily engages in such conduct. Criminal liability cannot be based solely on thoughts or involuntary acts. In some cases, the failure to perform a legally required act can be the basis of a crime.
- *Mental State*: Depending on the crime, a person can be held criminally liable only if they acted with:
  1) purpose, meaning, with a conscious objective to commit the act;
  2) knowledge, meaning, with awareness of what the person is doing;
  3) recklessness, meaning, with disregard for a substantial and unjustifiable risk of harm to others;
  4) negligence, meaning, the person should have known of a substantial, unreasonable risk of harm to others; or
  5) no particular mental state, meaning, the law imposes strict liability and requires no mental state.

SERIOUSNESS OF THE OFFENSE: There are three categories of crime:
- *Infractions or Violations*: Petty offenses that are generally punishable only by fines.
- *Misdemeanors*: Minor offenses punishable by fines or short jail sentences.
- *Felonies*: Major offenses punishable by long prison terms.
- *Treason*: Waging war against the state or giving aid and comfort to the enemy.

SELECTED CRIMES: The following crimes may occur in connection with business activities:
- *Murder*: Deliberate killing of another human being.
- *Manslaughter*: Involuntary killing of a human being.
- *Arson*: Intentional burning of property.
- *Burglary*: Breaking and entering into a structure with the intent to commit a felony.
- *Embezzlement*: Taking of money or property by an employee.
- *Forgery*: Making or altering negotiable instruments, such as checks, or credit card invoices.

- *Credit Card and Check Legislation*: Bad check laws typically provide that a person commits a crime when: 1) the person issues a check that is not paid; 2) knowing there are insufficient funds to pay the check, and 3) (in some states) with the intent to defraud another
- *Criminal Fraud*: Theft by deception.
- *Larceny*: Wrongfully taking and carrying away another's personal property.
- *Robbery*: Larceny that is committed with violence or the threat of violence.
- *Computer crime*: In many states the following acts may be a crime: 1) unauthorized use of computers or computer-related equipment; 2) destruction of a computer or its records; 3) alteration of legitimate records; and 4) accessing computer records to transfer funds, stocks, or other property.
- *Corporate Liability for Crimes*: Historically, corporations were not charged with crimes because courts held that corporations could not form the intent required to be guilty of a crime. Today, corporations may be held criminally liable for crimes that are committed by their employees when they are acting within the scope of their employment. This is especially true if a crime is *mala prohibita*.
- *RICO (crimes)*: Crimes designed to prevent a pattern of racketeering activity.

SELECTED DEFENSES: Four classic defenses to criminal liability are:
- *Duress*: An accused is coerced into criminal conduct by the threat or use of force.
- *Insanity*: An accused did not know an act was wrong or could not stop himself or herself due to a mental disease or defect.
- *Intoxication*: Voluntary intoxication may be a defense only to crimes that require an accused to form a specific intent to commit the crime.
- *Justification*: When the act is necessary to prevent harm to the accused.

THE LAW OF CRIMINAL PROCEDURE: Criminal law is the area of law that assures an accused due process in connection with criminal prosecutions. Among other things, an accused must generally be afforded the following minimal protections: 1) notice of the criminal charges; 2) an opportunity to face his or her accusers and to present a defense, and 3) due process, including a requirement that there be probable cause to arrest and/or search an accused.

STUDY HINTS FOR CALL-IMAGE TECHNOLOGY CASE STUDIES

The following study hints may be helpful when resolving the Call-Image Technology (CIT) case studies.

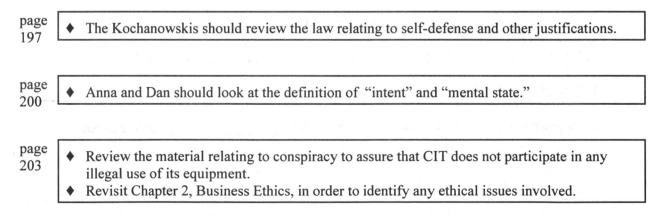

page
197

♦ The Kochanowskis should review the law relating to self-defense and other justifications.

page
200

♦ Anna and Dan should look at the definition of "intent" and "mental state."

page
203

♦ Review the material relating to conspiracy to assure that CIT does not participate in any illegal use of its equipment.
♦ Revisit Chapter 2, Business Ethics, in order to identify any ethical issues involved.

MATCHING EXERCISE

Select the term or concept that best matches a definition or statement set forth below. Each term or concept is the best match for only one definition or statement.

Terms and Concepts

a. Arraignment
b. Bail
c. Beyond a reasonable doubt
d. Currency transaction report
e. Defraud

f. Deterrent
g. Due process
h. Equal protection
i. Grand jury
j. Indictment

k. *Mala prohibita*
l. *Nolo contendere*
m. Retainer
n. Sentence
o. U.S.C.

Definitions and Statements

_____   1. Concept that all persons are treated the same by the law.
_____   2. Report that banking authorities must file whenever a customer deposits $10,000 cash or more.
_____   3. Abbreviation for United States Code, the federal statutory code.
_____   4. Punishment of a criminal, as pronounced by the court.
_____   5. Attorney's fee paid in advance for legal services.
_____   6. Act that is considered wrong only because it is prohibited by law.
_____   7. Proper exercise of judicial authority.
_____   8. Something that prevents or discourages criminal conduct.
_____   9. Written accusation of criminal conduct issued to a court by a grand jury.
_____ 10. Degree of proof required to find a person guilty of a crime.
_____ 11. Accused's appearance in court for the purpose of entering a plea.
_____ 12. Money paid to obtain the temporary release of a person charged with a crime.
_____ 13. Jury that determines whether a crime has been committed and whether to indict an accused.
_____ 14. Plea that has the effect of a guilty plea, without actually admitting one's guilt.
_____ 15. Depriving another of his property by deceit.

COMPLETION EXERCISE

Fill in the blanks with the words that most accurately complete each statement.

1. One of the objectives of criminal law is to protect _____ and _____.

2. In general, a crime cannot occur unless there is an _____ and a required

   _____ _____.

3. _____ is an acronym for federal and state laws that are intended to prevent and punish patterns of racketeering and criminal activities by organized crime.

4. In general, a person cannot be arrested unless there is _____ _____ to believe that the accused committed a crime.

5. Identify four classic defenses to criminal liability:

   a. _____.

   b. _____.

   c. _____.

   d. _____.

TRUE-FALSE EXERCISE

Write **T** if the statement is true, write **F** if the statement is false.

_____ 1. One assumption of criminal law is that punishment for crimes will deter criminal behavior.

_____ 2. In general, proof of both a criminal act and a criminal mental state are necessary in order to convict a person of a crime.

_____ 3. Misdemeanors are the most serious category of crimes.

_____ 4. Embezzlement includes the taking of money or property by an employee who has been entrusted with such money or property by his employer.

_____ 5. Larceny is the wrongful taking of another's personal property with the intent to permanently deprive the owner of the property.

_____ 6. Corporations cannot be held answerable for crimes committed by their officers.

_____ 7. Insanity is no longer a valid defense to criminal acts.

_____ 8. The purpose of the preliminary hearing is to decide the guilt or innocence of an accused.

_____ 9. Once an accused is charged with a crime, the next immediate step is for the accused to be tried.

_____ 10. The burden of proof for the prosecutor in a criminal case is to prove the accused's guilt beyond a reasonable doubt.

APPLICATION OF CONCEPTS

MULTIPLE CHOICE QUESTIONS

_____ 1. Roger, an employee, systematically took tools from his employer whenever he was left to lock up his employer's store. Roger was arrested one night while taking more tools. What crime has Roger committed?
   a. Larceny.
   b. Burglary.
   c. Embezzlement.
   d. Criminal fraud.

_____ 2. In which case does Janice commit the crime of forgery?
   a. Without permission, Janice took a blank check belonging to Kim. Janice then filled the check out, signed Kim's name, and cashed the check.
   b. Without permission, Janice took a credit card belonging to Sarah. Janice bought goods, charged the bill to Sarah's card, and Janice signed Sarah's name to the charge card slip.
   c. Without permission, Janice printed and passed fake $20 bills.
   d. a and b.

_____ 3.   In which case did Kelly probably commit a crime?
      a.   Kelly cashed a check for $50. Unknown to Kelly, she had insufficient funds in her account and the check was not paid. When informed that her bank refused payment, Kelly immediately paid the check.
      b.   Kelly cashed a check for $1,000. She knew that she had inadequate funds to cover the check, but she planned to move soon and she figured the bank could write off her overdraft as a tax loss.
      c.   Kelly took her roommate's credit card without permission and charged $200 merchandise.
      d.   b and c.

_____ 4.   Select the correct answer.
      a.   Bob parked his bike outside a classroom while he attended class. Unknown to Bob, Lex stole the bike while Bob was in class. Lex has committed the crime of larceny.
      b.   While drunk, Hal stole some beer. Hal knew what he was doing, but he wouldn't have done it if he was sober. Hal can assert the defense of intoxication to avoid criminal liability.
      c.   Ted shoplifted a coat from J&J Department Store. Ted stole the coat because he was cold. Ted can assert the defense of justification to avoid criminal liability.
      d.   All of the above.

SHORT ANSWER QUESTIONS

Answer the following questions, briefly explaining the reason for your answer.

1. Norma was fired as manager of the Java House, a small coffee shop. To get back at the owner of the coffee shop, Norma deliberately set fire to the premises. What crime has Norma committed? What elements must be established to prove Norma's guilt?

_____

_____

2. Sami forced open the door of a fur warehouse and entered it with the intent to take $10,000 worth of furs. What crime has Sami committed? What elements must be established to prove Sami's guilt?

_____

_____

3. Cal owns a cafe, and he unintentionally left raw fish at room temperature for several hours. Cal proceeded to serve the fish to customers who became quite ill as a result. Cal was charged with violating a strict liability health regulation that made it a misdemeanor to leave raw fish unrefrigerated for this long. What elements must be established to prove this crime? Can Cal be convicted of this crime?

_____

_____

4. Samuel offered to sell a plot of land to Roland. In order to induce Roland to buy, Samuel stated that there was an underground spring on the property with an attached irrigation system. Samuel knew that his statement was false. Since Roland was planning to grow corn on the land, the existence of adequate water and irrigation was important. Relying on Samuel's statement, Roland purchased the land for three times its actual value. What crime did Samuel commit? What must be established to prove Samuel's guilt?

_____

_____

CASE PROBLEMS

Answer the following case problems, explaining your answers.

1. Acme Electrical employees were repairing power lines when an Acme "cherry picker" came into contact with a power line, electrocuting a worker. Prior to this accident, the employees had complained to Acme supervisors that operation of this equipment so near to the power lines was unsafe and exposed the workers to a significant risk of injury or death. The supervisors responded: "We can always replace one of you if necessary, but we can't replace the client for whom we are doing this work." (a) What crimes, if any, have the Acme supervisors committed? (b) Can Acme be held criminally liable for its supervisors' conduct?

_____

_____

_____

_____

2. Over a period of four years, Allen knowingly and willfully engaged in numerous transactions that entailed the fraudulent sale of worthless swampland to elderly persons who lived in various parts of the United States. Mrs. Hinton unsuspectingly bought some of this worthless land from Allen, and she paid him $10,000 for the property. (a) What crimes did Allen commit? (b) What criminal penalties may be imposed against Allen? (c) What remedies does Mrs. Hinton have against Allen?

_____

_____

_____

_____

CHAPTER 9
Introduction to Contract Law and Contract Theory

CHAPTER REVIEW

THE IMPORTANCE OF CONTRACT LAW: Contracts occur in all aspects of daily life. Examples of common contracts include buying a car, leasing an apartment, purchasing insurance, making credit purchases, and writing a check.

- *Commercial Law Contracts*: Contract law was once part of real property law. Separate rules developed to deal with commercial transactions, and mercantile courts developed apart from courts of law. The Law Merchant was replaced by the Uniform Sales Act and the Uniform Negotiable Instruments Act. Eventually these were replaced by the Uniform Commercial Code (UCC). Among other things, the UCC deals with sale of goods, commercial paper, and secured transactions. Other uniform acts have been adopted to deal with partnerships and credit transactions.
- *Common Law Contracts*: Common law rules regarding contracts develop from court decisions. The common law supplements the UCC when the UCC is silent on certain matters.
- *Definition of a Contract*: A contract is a legally enforceable promise made by two or more parties who are legally competent. Social promises or obligations are not legally enforceable.
- *Elements of a Contract*: A valid contract requires:
  1) an agreement that is comprised of a valid offer and acceptance;
  2) consideration;
  3) legal capacity of the parties;
  4) genuine assent by the parties;
  5) legal subject matter; and
  6) certain formalities, such as a writing for certain types of contracts.

FROM STATUS TO FREEDOM OF CONTRACT AND BACK AGAIN: In feudal society contracts were relatively unimportant because individual rights were determined by status. As society grew increasingly dependent upon commercial activities, the freedom to contract became more important along with rights to enforce contracts. Today, there is once again growing interest in limiting contractual freedom in order to protect persons whose status places them at a disadvantage when making a contract.

CLASSIFICATIONS OF CONTRACTS: A contract may fall into several of the following categories:

- *Formal versus Informal Contracts*: Formal contracts require the formality of being sealed with a wax insignia. Today, most contracts are informal (without a seal). Informal contracts may be oral or written, or they may by implied from the parties' conduct.
- *Unilateral versus Bilateral Contracts*: A unilateral contract is an agreement pursuant to which the offeror promises to do something in exchange for the actual act or forbearance of the offeree. An offer for a unilateral contract can be accepted only by the offeree's actual performance of the act or forbearance requested by the offeror. A bilateral contract is an agreement in which the offeror and the offeree both promise to do, or not to do, something.

- *Valid, Voidable, Void, and Unenforceable Contracts*: A valid contract is legally binding and enforceable, and it is not subject to any defenses. A voidable contract may be affirmed or rejected at the option of one or more of the parties. A void agreement cannot be enforced and it is not legally a contract. An unenforceable contract, although apparently valid, will not be enforced by a court because it violates certain requirements for the creation of a valid contract.
- *Express versus Implied Contracts*: An express contract specifically sets out the parties' agreement and it may be either oral or written. An implied contract, on the other hand, is inferred, in whole or in part, from the parties' conduct. A contract is when, based on the facts, it is clear that the parties intended to enter into a contract even though they do not expressly create a contract.
- *Executory versus Executed Contracts*: An executory contract is one that has not been fully performed by both parties. An executed contract has been fully completed.
- *Quasi Contracts versus Contracts Implied in Fact*: A quasi contract is implied in law by a court in order to avoid one party being unjustly enriched at another's expense. Although no actual contract exists, in order to achieve justice a court imposes a quasi contractual obligation to pay. On the other hand, a contract implied in fact is an actual contract and it is implied by a court because this is what the parties clearly intended.

STUDY HINTS FOR CALL-IMAGE TECHNOLOGY CASE STUDIES

The following study hints may be helpful when resolving the Call-Image Technology (CIT) case studies.

page 226

- ◆ When a contract requires one party to both provide a service and sell goods, the parties' predominant purpose for making the contract determines which type of contract law will govern most contractual issues. However, you should also review the discussion relating to how the common law may supplement UCC rules.
- ◆ You should discuss with Tom and Anna the relative importance that services play in their sales contracts.

page 241

- ◆ Tom should consider whether Dan and his friend intended to form a binding contract.
- ◆ Review the section on quasi contract, paying particular attention to the discussion of volunteered services.

REVIEW OF KEY TERMS AND CONCEPTS

MATCHING EXERCISE

Select the term or concept that best matches a definition or statement set forth below. Each term or concept is the best match for only one definition or statement.

Terms and Concepts

a. Commercial paper

b. Counterclaim

c. Free enterprise

d. Goods

e. Mercantile

f. Public policy

g. Restitutionary

h. Secured transaction

i. Security interest

Definitions and Statements

____ 1. Dealing with business, commerce, or trade.

____ 2. Equitable basis for restoring injured parties to their original position.

____ 3. Defendant's legal cause of action (claim) against the plaintiff.

____ 4. Items of identifiable and movable personal property.

____ 5. Interest that is held by a creditor in property of a debtor to assure payment of a debt or performance of an obligation.

____ 6. Negotiable instruments, such as checks, that are governed by UCC Article 3.

____ 7. Credit sale or loan transaction in which a creditor retains a security interest in the debtor's property to assure payment.

____ 8. Fundamental value of society.

____ 9. Carrying on free, legitimate businesses for profit.

COMPLETION EXERCISE

Fill in the blanks with the words that most accurately complete each statement.

1. A contract is a _____ _____ agreement between two or more parties.

2. In order to form a valid contract, an agreement must be supported by _____.

3. Parties must have the _____ _____ to form a valid contract.

4. There must be _____ _____ of the parties to the agreement; that is, they should not be influenced by fraud or duress.

5. The subject matter of a contract must be _____ and must not violate a statute or public policy.

TRUE-FALSE EXERCISE

Write **T** if the statement is true, write **F** if the statement is false.

_____ 1. Historically, freedom of contract has been an important part of the American free enterprise economy.

_____ 2. The UCC has completely replaced the common law of contracts.

_____ 3. In feudal society, contractual rights were of little importance.

_____ 4. Labor laws enacted by statute may restrict the freedom to contract.

_____ 5. Formal contracts are commonly used in modern life.

_____ 6. The agreement in a unilateral contract is formed by reciprocal promises made by the contracting parties.

_____ 7. The absence of certain required formalities may render a contract unenforceable.

_____ 8. A contractual offer that may be accepted by the offeree's promise to do a requested act is an offer for a bilateral contract.

_____ 9. A quasi contract is a judicial remedy, not an actual contract.

_____ 10. A voidable contract may be affirmed by the parties.

APPLICATION OF CONCEPTS

MULTIPLE CHOICE QUESTIONS

_____ 1. A contract implied in fact is created in which of the following situations?
  a. John voluntarily fixed his sister's car.
  b. Kami and Tom entered into a complete, written contract to sell Kami's condominium to Tom.
  c. Luci and Mary orally agreed that Luci would make a suit for Mary for $100.
  d. Mark requested that Clay's Roofing repair his roof and Clay's did so. The parties did not expressly agree upon all of the terms of the transaction, but Clay's expected to be paid for its work and Mark knew this.

_____ 2. Eddie agreed to sell stolen bicycles to Foster for $500 and Foster agreed to buy them. Which statement accurately describes their agreement?
  a. The agreement is a voidable contract which the parties may later affirm.
  b. The agreement is void and unenforceable.
  c. The agreement is enforceable if it is stated in writing.
  d. The agreement is a valid contract.

_____ 3. In which of the following situations would a court recognize a quasi contractual obligation to pay?
   a. Unknown to Grace, Todd's lawn service mistakenly mowed her lawn while she was at the store.
   b. Linda voluntarily cared for Sally's children for a week.
   c. Franklin and Lamar orally agreed that Franklin would paint Lamar's boat for $300.
   d. None of the above.

_____ 4. Roger promised to sell his car to Reggie and Reggie promised to pay Roger $3,000 for the car. The parties have not yet performed their respective promises. This contract may be classified as:
   a. An executed, bilateral contract.
   b. An executory, bilateral contract.
   c. An executed, unilateral contract.
   d. An executory, unilateral contract.

SHORT ANSWER QUESTIONS

Answer the following questions, briefly explaining the reason for your answer.

1. For years, Dave's Deli has supplied box lunches to Kelly's Construction Company. Each week, Dave called Kelly's ordering the required number of lunches. The lunches were then delivered in accordance with Dave's instructions and, at the end of month, Kelly's sent a check to Dave for the lunches delivered. This month, Kelly's refuses to pay Dave for the lunches delivered, arguing that the parties did not enter into a contract for the delivered lunches. Does a contract exist between the parties?

_____

_____

2. Martha accepted an invitation from Jeff to attend a charity ball. She purchased an expensive dress and spent the entire afternoon at the hairdresser. As she was preparing for her date, Jeff called to say that he had decided not to attend. Martha is furious and is considering legal action. Does Martha have a claim for breach of contract against Jeff?

_____

_____

3. Jason bought a car from Leo's Auto Sales. The sales contract described the car's engine as recently rebuilt. Soon afterwards, Jason took the car to his own mechanic and it was discovered that the engine had not been rebuilt. Is this contract valid, voidable, void, or unenforceable? What are Jason's options concerning this contract?

_____

_____

4. Merlin bought a new power saw from Brady's Hardware. Brady's offered to sell him the saw on credit if he signed a contract agreeing not to sue them for any accident which might result if the saw proved defective. Will a court uphold this contract?

_____

_____

CASE PROBLEMS

Answer the following case problems, explaining your answers.

1. Serena recently moved to town and she entered into the following transactions: (a) she granted Last Bank a security interest in her home to assure that she repaid the bank a loan; (b) she purchased a new TV; and (c) she hired Barb to paint her home. What types of transaction did Serena enter into? What law governs these transactions?

_____

_____

_____

_____

2. Ken took his car to Acme to get an estimate for painting one fender. Ken overheard an Acme employee tell others that he was preparing to completely paint Ken's car, but Ken did nothing to correct the employee's misunderstanding. Acme proceeded to paint Ken's car. Ken refuses to pay, arguing that he has no contractual obligation to pay. (a) Discuss whether the parties entered into a contract. (b) Does Ken have any legal obligation to pay for Acme's services?

_____

_____

_____

_____

CHAPTER 10

Contractual Agreement: Mutual Assent

```
┌─────────────────────────────┐
│  ┌───────────────────────┐  │
│  │    CHAPTER REVIEW     │  │
│  └───────────────────────┘  │
└─────────────────────────────┘
```

THE FIRST STEP IN CONTRACT FORMATION: The agreement is the basic element of a contract. An agreement is comprised of a valid offer by the offeror and a valid acceptance by the offeree.

MUTUAL ASSENT: An agreement cannot arise unless both parties agree to exactly the same terms. Without this mutual assent (agreement), a contract cannot be formed.

THE OBJECTIVE THEORY OF CONTRACTS: Formation of a contract requires that both parties intend to agree to a transaction. The law evaluates the parties' intent by an objective standard, that is, by what a reasonable person observing the parties' words and actions would believe was intended. Conversely, the parties' secret or subjective intentions do not generally control questions relating to intent.

OFFER: An offer is an expression to enter into a legally binding agreement upon the terms stated.
- ***Clear Intention to Contract and Definiteness of the Offer***: An offer must be a clear and definite expression in order to give rise to a contract. However, the common law and the UCC differ regarding how definite an offer or agreement must be in order to form a contract.

    At common law, an offer must specifically state all important terms of the proposed contract. The UCC, however, applies a more relaxed standard and finds that a sales contract is sufficiently definite if: 1) the parties intend to contract and 2) there is a way to determine the essential terms of the agreement.
- ***Advertisements and Auctions***: In general, advertisements are not offers; they are instead viewed as invitations to do business. Similarly, unless an auction is stated to be "without reserve," the placement of goods for auction is not an offer; a person's bid is the offer.
- ***Communication of the Offer to the Offeree***: An offer must be communicated to the offeree. An offer cannot be accepted by a person to whom it was not made.
- ***Duration of the Offer***: An offer may terminate due to: 1) lapse; 2) revocation; 3) rejection; or 4) acceptance.

    An offer lapses (expires):
    1) at the time stated in the offer;
    2) if no time is stated, upon expiration of a reasonable time; or
    3) upon the death or insanity of either party, supervening illegality, or destruction of the offer's subject matter.

    The right to revoke an offer prior to acceptance may be limited by:
    1) an option (contract to keep an offer open for a stated period of time);
    2) UCC § 2-205 (an offer to buy or sell goods that is made by a merchant in a signed writing which promises that the offer will remain open); or
    3) the doctrine of promissory estoppel (a person makes a promise and should expect that another person will act in reliance on the promise, the other person rely on the promise, and injustice can be avoided only by enforcing the promise.

ACCEPTANCE: An acceptance is the offeree's agreement to all of the terms of the offer.

- *Mirror-Image Rule*: The common law mirror-image rule provides that an acceptance is valid only if the acceptance and the offer are identical. The acceptance can neither delete or change any term of the offer nor add any term not stated in the offer. Any deviation is a counteroffer which effectively terminates the original offer and creates a new offer by the offeree.
  UCC § 2-207 establishes a different rule regarding contracts for the sale of goods.

- *Manner and Time of Acceptance*: An offeree must accept in exactly the way stated in the offer. If the offer is silent, then an offeree may accept using any reasonable method of communication. Under the mailbox rule or implied agency rule that is followed in most states, a properly sent acceptance is effective when it is sent, even if it is never received by the offeror. If an acceptance is sent using an unauthorized method of communication, then the mailbox rule does not apply and the acceptance is effective only upon receipt by the offeror. Other communications, such as revocations or rejections, are effective only upon receipt.

- *Silence*: As a general rule, an offeree's failure to respond to an offer, that is an offeree's silence, is not a valid acceptance.

- *Bilateral versus Unilateral Contracts*: An offer for a bilateral contract may be accepted either by: 1) making a promise to the offeror to perform as requested or 2) by inferring a promise from surrounding circumstances or the offeror's conduct, such as the offeree's performance of the requested act. An offer for a unilateral contract can be accepted only by the offeree's actual performance of the requested act.

STUDY HINTS FOR CALL-IMAGE TECHNOLOGY CASE STUDIES

The following study hints may be helpful when resolving the Call-Image Technology (CIT) case studies.

page 253	♦ When distinguishing sales talk from contractual statements, Tom should bear in mind the objective theory of contracts and the requirement that an offer be clear and definite. ♦ Regarding the definiteness requirement for sales contracts, review UCC § 2-204.

page 256	♦ Tom should review UCC § 2-205.

page 262	♦ Tom should first review the UCC § 2-206 relating to the manner and time of acceptance. ♦ Tom should then review the mailbox rule.

CHAPTER 10 - CONTRACTUAL AGREEMENT: MUTUAL ASSENT

MATCHING EXERCISE

Select the term or concept that best matches a definition or statement set forth below. Each term or concept is the best match for only one definition or statement.

Terms and Concepts

a. Bona fide
b. Constructive acceptance
c. Declaratory judgment
d. Lapse
e. Objective standard

f. Option contract
g. Output contract
h. Promissory estoppel
i. Rejection
j. Requirements contract

k. Revocation
l. Specific performance
m. Subjective standard
n. Supervening illegality
o. Vacate

Definitions and Statements

_____ 1. Offeror's termination of an offer.
_____ 2. Contract that requires the buyer to purchase all of the seller's production of a good.
_____ 3. Expiration of an offer due to the passage of time.
_____ 4. Contract in which the offeror promises to keep an offer open for a definite time.
_____ 5. Acceptance that is implied or inferred from the actions or words of an offeree.
_____ 6. Offeree's termination of an offer.
_____ 7. To nullify or make void, such as setting aside a judgment.
_____ 8. Court decision that determines the parties' rights in a particular transaction.
_____ 9. Standard that is used to evaluate a person's intent based on the party's words and conduct.
_____ 10. Doctrine that prohibits an offeror from revoking a promise if the offeree has reasonably relied upon the offer and justice requires enforcement of the promise.
_____ 11. Standard that is used to evaluate a person's intent based on the party's feelings and actual intent.
_____ 12. Unexpected event that makes it illegal to perform an act.
_____ 13. Equitable remedy by which a court orders the parties to perform the contract.
_____ 14. Honest and in good faith.
_____ 15. Contract that requires the seller to provide as much of a product as the buyer needs.

COMPLETION EXERCISE

Fill in the blanks with the words that most accurately complete each statement.

1. A contractual agreement cannot arise without the _____ _____ of the parties to the same terms.

2. Advertisements are usually considered to be _____ _____ _____.

3. A contractual agreement is comprised of a valid _____ and a valid _____.

4. A _____ is a statement by an offeree whereby the offeree rejects the original offer but indicates a willingness to enter into a contract upon newly stated terms.

5. Identify the four basic methods for terminating an offer.

    a. _____.

    b. _____.

    c. _____.

    d. _____.

TRUE-FALSE EXERCISE

Write **T** if the statement is true, write **F** if the statement is false.

_____ 1. Under the mailbox rule, an acceptance that is sent in the proper manner is not effective until it is received by the offeror.

_____ 2. If an offer states the exclusive method by which it can be accepted, any other method of acceptance will generally render the acceptance invalid.

_____ 3. Silence by an offeree in response to an offer may be a valid acceptance if the parties' prior dealings with one another establish that they intended the offeree's silence to be an acceptance.

_____ 4. A unilateral contract comes into existence the moment the offeree promises to perform the requested act.

_____ 5. A merchant is a party who regularly deals in (e.g., buys and sells) goods that are the subject matter of an offer or contract.

_____ 6. Under the UCC, merchants who make signed, written promises to buy or sell goods and promise not to revoke these offers give up their right to revoke their offers for the time stated.

_____ 7. An offeree can accept an offer after it has been terminated.

_____ 8. An offer must be communicated to the offeree in order to form a contract.

_____ 9. At an ordinary auction (i.e., one that is not conducted "without reserve"), bids made by persons wanting to buy an item are only offers that the auctioneer may accept or reject.

_____ 10. An option is not formed unless the offeree gives consideration (legal value) for the offeree's promise not to revoke the offer.

APPLICATION OF CONCEPTS

MULTIPLE CHOICE QUESTIONS

_____ 1. In which case was Don legally entitled to revoke his offer?
    a. Don offered to sell his carpet business to Wilma. Don promised not to revoke the offer for 24 hours in consideration for $500 paid by Wilma. One hour later and before Wilma had accepted, Don revoked his offer and offered to return the $500 to Wilma.
    b. Don offered to build a home for the Burkes for $100,000. While they were considering this offer, Don revoked his offer.

c. In a signed writing, Don (a merchant) offered to sell Pat a TV and Don promised not to revoke the offer for two days. The next day, Don revoked before Pat could accept.
d. a and c.

_____ 2. In which situation did the offer NOT terminate prior to its acceptance?
a. Ty offered to sell a patent to Hal. Ty died, and Hal sent an acceptance two days later.
b. ChemCo offered to sell chemicals to Wes. Congress then passed a new law making the sale of these chemicals illegal. Wes sent his acceptance after the new law was enacted.
c. Ray offered to sell a parcel of land to Ely. The offer stated that it would lapse on May 1. On May 2, Ely sent an acceptance of the offer.
d. Sissy offered to sell a stereo to Carl, and Carl accepted. Sissy then changed her mind and told Carl, "I revoke my offer."

_____ 3. Sal offered to do certain accounting work for $5,000 for a new client, Louise. The offer stated that Louise's failure to expressly reject the offer within 24 hours would be an acceptance of the offer. Which of the following expressions or actions would be a valid acceptance?
a. In writing Louise stated: "I accept your offer if your price is lowered to $4,000."
b. Louise did not expressly reject or accept the offer.
c. In writing Louise stated: "I accept your offer. Also, I would appreciate it if you did not smoke when you are working at my office."
d. All of the above.

_____ 4. On May 1, Lilly mailed Patton an offer to buy his home. Patton received the offer on May 5. On May 6, Patton deposited a properly addressed, stamped acceptance in the mail. Lilly received the acceptance on May 10. On May 8, Lilly changed her mind, and she personally delivered a written revocation of the offer to Patton. In most states:
a. A contract was formed on May 5.
b. A contract was formed on May 6.
c. A contract was formed on May 10.
d. A contract was not formed.

SHORT ANSWER QUESTIONS

Answer the following questions, briefly explaining the reason for your answer.

1. Kelly drove off to the side of the road and yelled to her companion, Lorenz, "I'd take $10 for this car and be happy to get it!" Lorenz replied, "Here's $10, I'll take it." Did the parties form a contract?

_____

_____

2. Johnson Appliance Store placed an ad that read, "We will sell a new 24" Zenith® television set for $10 to the first person in line when our doors open on Monday, June 21." Jake appeared two nights before, camped out, and was first in line when the store opened. However, the store refused to sell the TV to Jake for the advertised price. Was Johnson's ad an offer in this case?

_____

_____

3. Tricia offered to sell Jason her hang-glider for $3,000. Jason replied that he accepted, if Tricia would accept $2,500 instead. Tricia responded that she agreed to take $2,500. Was a contract formed?

_____

_____

4. Jerry's Van City offered to sell a new van to Susie's Caterers for $10,000. Susie's returned a signed, written "acceptance" of Jerry's offer, but the acceptance stated that Susie would take delivery of the van in 14 days, not 10 days as stated in the offer. Was Susie's acceptance valid?

_____

_____

CASE PROBLEMS

Answer the following case problems, explaining your answers.

1. Sally advertised a parcel of land for sale. Bryan delivered a signed, written purchase offer to Sally. The offer appeared to be sincere, and it stated all of the proposed contract terms. Unknown to Sally, Bryan did not intend to buy the land unless he first obtained financing. Sally accepted Bryan's offer. (a) Was Sally's advertisement an offer? (b) Did Bryan indicate a clear intention to contract? (c) Was a contract for the sale of the land created?

_____

_____

_____

_____

2. Fred offered to sell his gasoline station to Bess. Fred mailed the offer to Bess via first-class U.S. mail. The offer was silent regarding the required manner of acceptance or when it would lapse. (a) Can Bess accept the offer by remaining silent, or must she communicate an acceptance to Fred? (b) When will Fred's offer lapse? (c) How can Bess communicate an acceptance of the offer? (d) If Bess sends an acceptance via first-class U.S. mail, when will her acceptance be effective?

_____

_____

_____

_____

CHAPTER 11   Consideration: The Basis of the Bargain and Contractual Capacity: The Ability to Agree

CHAPTER REVIEW

INTRODUCTION: A valid contract requires both consideration and the legal capacity to contract.

THE BARGAIN AS A CONTRACT THEORY: Consideration shows that parties intend to be legally bound.

DEFINITION OF CONSIDERATION: Consideration is what a party gives up in exchange for the promise.
- *Consideration as an Act or Forbearance to Act*: In a unilateral contract, the considerations are the offeror's promise and the offeree's actual performance of an act or forbearance (not doing) of an act.
- *Consideration as a Promise to Act or Forbear*: In a bilateral contract, the considerations are the promises made by the offeror and the offeree.
- *Adequacy of Consideration*: As a general rule, the law does not examine the adequacy of the considerations that contracting parties give. In other words, the requirement that each party must give consideration is met even if the considerations exchanged are not of equal value.

CONSIDERATION IN SPECIAL CONTEXTS: Special situations involving issues of consideration include:
- *Contracts for the Sale of Goods*: Under the UCC "firm offer" rule, if a merchant states, in a signed writing, that an offer will not be revoked, then the offer must be held open for the stated time (up to three months) even if the promise was not supported by consideration.
- *Suretyship Contracts*: A "surety" agrees to pay another's debt if the debtor fails to pay. The surety's promise to pay must be supported by separate consideration from the creditor unless the surety's promise to pay is made in exchange for the creditor's promise to extend credit to the debtor.
- *Liquidated Debts*: Part payment of a liquidated (definite, undisputed) debt is not consideration for a discharge from the entire debt. In this situation, the debtor remains liable for the unpaid balance.
- *Unliquidated Debts*: Part payment of an unliquidated (uncertain or disputed) debt that is paid and accepted by the creditor is supported by consideration and does discharge (terminate) the entire debt.
- *Composition Agreements*: A composition agreement is an agreement by a debtor to pay, and the debtor's creditors to accept, partial payment of their claims as payment in full. This agreement is valid.

ABSENCE OF CONSIDERATION: The below promises are NOT enforceable due to a lack of consideration:
- *Illusory Promises*: Promisors are free to decide whether or not to do a promised act.
- *Preexisting Duty*: A promise to do an act that the promisor is already legally obligated to perform.
- *Moral Consideration*: A person's promise to pay for a benefit already received is not legally enforceable even if the promisor feels a moral obligation to pay.
- *Past Consideration*: A benefit already given is not consideration for a later promise to pay.

EXCEPTIONS TO THE BARGAINING THEORY OF CONSIDERATION: Consideration is not required below:
- *Promissory Estoppel*: A promise is enforceable if: 1) a promisor should expect a promisee rely on a promise; 2) the promisee does rely; and 3) injustice can only be avoided by enforcing the promise.

- *Charitable Subscriptions*: A promise to make a donation to a charity is enforceable.
- *Promises Made After the Expiration of the Statute of Limitations*: A promise to pay a debt after the statute of limitations has run (i.e., a creditor has waited too long to sue on the debt) is enforceable.
- *Promises to Pay Debts Covered by Bankruptcy Discharges*: A promise to pay a debt that may be discharged (terminated) in bankruptcy is enforceable if certain requirements are met.

LEGAL CAPACITY: Legal (contractual) capacity is the legal ability to enter into a contract. Both contracting parties must have contractual capacity in order to form a valid contract.

MINORS: In most states, a minor is a person (infant) under the age of 18. In some states, persons under the age of 18 are not treated as minors if they are married or emancipated (free from parental control).
- *Disaffirmance/Rescission*: Minors have the right to disaffirm (avoid) most contracts that they make prior to becoming an adult. To disaffirm, a minor must: 1) be a minor at the time of contracting; 2) give the other party notice of the minor's intent to disaffirm either prior to, or within a reasonable time after, becoming an adult; and 3) return all contract benefits received, at least to the extent that the minor still has such benefits. In most states, a minor may disaffirm even if the benefits received have declined in value, and the minor is not liable for paying for the decline in value.
- *Misrepresentation of Age*: Sometimes, minors lie about their age. Despite this deception, most states permit disaffirmance by the minor. But, courts in some of these states hold the minors liable for any actual losses suffered by the other party as a result of the minors' deception.
- *Ratification*: Ratification is a party's approval or confirmation of a contract. A minor cannot disaffirm a contract if the minor expressly or by implication ratifies the contract.
- *Necessaries, Special Statutes, Torts and Crimes*: A necessary is a good, service, and other thing that is required to maintain a minor's life or that is a basic necessity of life when the minor's personal circumstances are considered. Although minors may disaffirm contracts for a necessary, they must pay the reasonable value for any benefit received under the contract. Special statutes may prohibit minors from disaffirming certain contracts. In general, minors cannot disaffirm liability for crimes or torts.

INSANE PERSONS, INTOXICATED PERSONS, ALIENS, CONVICTS ,AND MARRIED WOMEN: Insane persons may avoid a contract if they were actually insane when they made the contract. Legal aliens and married women have the capacity to contract, but the contractual capacity of convicts is limited in some states.

STUDY HINTS FOR CALL-IMAGE TECHNOLOGY CASE STUDIES

The following study hints may be helpful when resolving the Call-Image Technology (CIT) case studies.

page 275
- ♦ You should consider the concepts discussed in the "Suretyship Contracts" section.
- ♦ As a practical matter, you should also consider who the bank would accept as a surety.

page 277
- ♦ Determine whether other creditors are agreeing to similar revised payment terms and whether a composition agreement (or similar arrangement) may be appropriate.
- ♦ Think about what benefits, if any, CIT should request in exchange for the extended credit terms.
- ♦ Also, consider whether payment of the debt is secured by adequate collateral.

REVIEW OF KEY TERMS AND CONCEPTS

MATCHING EXERCISE

Select the term or concept that best matches a definition or statement set forth below. Each term or concept is the best match for only one definition or statement.

Terms and Concepts

a. Bankruptcy
b. Bona fide purchaser
c. Circumscribe
d. Default
e. Emancipation

f. Firm offer
g. Guarantor
h. Illusory promise
i. Promisee
j. Promisor

k. Promissory estoppel
l. Rescission
m. Stipend
n. Summary judgment
o. Waiver

Definitions and Statements

_____ 1. Doctrine that may require performance of a promise if another has detrimentally relied upon it.
_____ 2. Voluntary surrender of a legal right.
_____ 3. Promise that allows the promisor to decide whether or not to do the promised act.
_____ 4. Person who makes a promise.
_____ 5. Person to whom a promise is made.
_____ 6. Judgment that may be granted prior to trial if there are no genuine issues of fact.
_____ 7. Person who purchases in good faith, for value, and without notice of any illegalities.
_____ 8. State of being free from parental care and exercising legal independence.
_____ 9. To avoid, cancel, or terminate something.
_____ 10. Person who promises to pay a debt if the principal debtor fails to do so.
_____ 11. Sum of money paid for services or to defray costs.
_____ 12. Irrevocable offer to buy or sell goods that is made by a merchant.
_____ 13. Limit the range of an activity.
_____ 14. Area of law designed to give an honest debtor a "fresh start."
_____ 15. Wrongful failure to perform a legal obligation.

COMPLETION EXERCISE

Fill in the blanks with the words that most accurately complete each statement.

1. A _____ _____ is an agreement by a debtor to pay, and the debtor's creditors to accept, partial payment of their claims as payment in full.

2. _____ _____ is the legal ability to be bound by a contract.

3. A contract that is grossly unfair is _____, and courts may examine the adequacy of consideration in such contracts.

4. A _____ _____ is an act that a person is already obligated to perform.

5. A _____ _____ is a merchant's offer to buy or sell goods that cannot be revoked for a stated period of time and consideration is not required to make this offer irrevocable.

TRUE-FALSE EXERCISE

Write **T** if the statement is true, write **F** if the statement is false.

_____ 1. In most states, a minor who misrepresents his or her age can still disaffirm a contract.

_____ 2. An agreement is not legally binding unless each party to the agreement gives consideration.

_____ 3. A promise not to trespass on someone's land (a tort) is consideration if the promisor does in fact refrain from trespassing.

_____ 4. A minor cannot avoid a contract if the minor cannot return all of the benefits that the minor received from the other person.

_____ 5. Legal aliens in the United States do not have the capacity to make contracts.

_____ 6. Anyone who is intoxicated at the time that he or she makes a contract may avoid the contract.

_____ 7. A promise to do something only if the promisor decides that he or she wants to do it is an illusory promise and is not consideration.

_____ 8. Under promissory estoppel, a court will enforce any promise that is relied on by another person.

_____ 9. A creditor cannot sue for the unpaid balance of a debt if the creditor received an agreed-upon partial payment pursuant to a composition of creditors.

_____ 10. If a person agrees to pay more for something than it is worth, then the agreement is not a contract and it is not legally binding due to a failure of consideration.

```
APPLICATION OF CONCEPTS
```

MULTIPLE CHOICE QUESTIONS

_____ 1. ABC Corp. hired Derrick for a fixed, three-year contract. One year after entering into the contract, ABC realized that Derrick's contract did not include an agreement not to compete. ABC drafted a separate agreement not to compete and Derrick signed it as requested by ABC. Under these facts, the agreement not to compete is:
   a. Enforceable because ABC signed the agreement.
   b. Enforceable because ABC gave Derrick consideration in exchange for signing the agreement.
   c. Unenforceable because ABC did not give Derrick consideration in exchange for signing the agreement.
   d. a and b.

_____ 2. Nina wanted to buy a VCR on credit from Seller. In exchange for Seller's agreement to sell the VCR to Nina, Sue agreed to guarantee Nina's obligation for the purchase price. Under these facts:
   a. A suretyship contract is created.
   b. Sue has no obligation to pay if Nina defaults because the Seller did not give Sue any consideration in exchange for her promise to pay.
   c. Sue is obligated to pay if Nina defaults because the Seller gave Sue consideration in exchange for her promise to pay.
   d. a and c.

_____ 3. Cindy purchased a TV when she was 16 years old. Two months ago, Cindy turned 18, the age of majority in her state. Cindy now wants to disaffirm the TV contract. Under these facts:
   a. Cindy can disaffirm the contract, but she must pay for depreciation to the TV.
   b. Cindy can disaffirm the contract, and the seller must repay all money paid by Cindy.
   c. Cindy can disaffirm the contract only if she shows that she acted in good faith.
   d. Cindy cannot avoid the contract because she failed to disaffirm before she turned 18.

_____ 4. Maggie sold 50 acres of land to William for $2,000 below its market value. Two months later, Maggie was committed to a mental institution, and Maggie's son, Jeff, was appointed her guardian. Jeff wants to rescind the land sales contract made by Maggie based on her lack of contractual capacity. In order to rescind, Jeff must prove:
   a. Maggie was actually insane at the time she entered into the contract.
   b. The contract was unfair.
   c. The other party knew that Maggie was insane.
   d. All of the above.

SHORT ANSWER QUESTIONS

Answer the following questions, briefly explaining the reason for your answer.

1. When Stacy was 16 years old, she bought a pedigree dog on credit for $300. While Stacy was a minor, she made numerous payments, paying the entire contract price. Stacy is now 17 and the dog has developed a serious illness. Regrettably, Stacy has decided she can no longer care for the dog and she wants to disaffirm the purchase contract for the pet. Can Stacy disaffirm the contract?

_____

_____

2. Aunt Millie wanted her nephew, Jim, to become a lawyer. She offered to pay Jim $10,000 if he graduated from law school. In response to this offer, Jim enrolled in and ultimately graduated from law school. After graduation Jim requested payment from Aunt Millie. However, she refuses to pay, arguing that the parties' agreement is not enforceable because Jim suffered no detriment by becoming a lawyer and she realized no benefit. Is the agreement between Aunt Millie and Jim enforceable?

_____

_____

3. Ina and Homeowner entered into a bilateral contract whereby Ina agreed to completely paint and prep Homeowner's home for $2,000. Due to higher than expected labor costs, Ina requested that Homeowner pay Ina an extra $500. Ina and Homeowner subsequently agreed that Homeowner would pay Ina an extra $500 in consideration for Ina's promise to completely paint and prep the house as originally agreed. Is the agreement regarding payment of the additional $500 enforceable?

_____

_____

4. Linda needed to print her Master's thesis, which was due the next day. Unfortunately, her printer did not work, and the computer center at her college was closed. At 3:00 a.m., she woke Fred, the only person with a printer that was compatible with her computer, and asked Fred if she could print her thesis. Annoyed at being awakened, Fred said she would need to pay five times the per-page rate charged by the computer center to print her document. Desperate, Linda agreed. Was this adequate consideration?

_____

_____

CASE PROBLEMS

Answer the following case problems, explaining your answers.

1. RDM, Inc. took the following actions: (a) RDM agreed to pay Sandy $500 for extra work she voluntarily performed last year; and (b) RDM agreed to pay Ralph, a subcontractor, a $1,000 bonus in exchange for two promises: (1) his promise to complete an existing project by the date already required by a contract with RDM; and (2) his promise to perform some new work. Evaluate the enforceability of these agreements.

_____

_____

_____

_____

2. Luis lived in Georgia. CompuTech, a Wyoming firm, called Luis and told him that they would be interested in hiring him if he moved to Wyoming. Luis and CompuTech never entered into a formal employment agreement. During their last conversation, CompuTech mentioned to Luis that although they were cutting back their staff, they were still interested in him. In response, Luis quit a well-paying job in Georgia, sold his house, and moved his family to Wyoming. When he arrived, CompuTech refused to hire him. (a) Was it reasonable for Luis to rely on CompuTech's promise? (b) Is CompuTech's promise enforceable under promissory estoppel? (c) What would you have advised Luis to have done differently?

_____

_____

_____

_____

CHAPTER 12

Legality of Subject Matter and Reality of Consent

```
┌──────────────────────────────────────────┐
│            CHAPTER REVIEW                  │
└──────────────────────────────────────────┘
```

THE REQUIREMENTS OF LEGALITY OF SUBJECT MATTER AND REALITY OF CONSENT: A valid contract requires that the subject matter of an agreement and its objectives be legal and not violate public policy. A genuine assent by both parties is an additional requirement for a valid contract.

MALA IN SE **AND** *MALA PROHIBITA*: In most states, a contract that violates a statute is void whether the prohibited act is evil in itself (*mala in se*), which includes all crimes and torts, or simply prohibited by a statute (*mala prohibita*). Some courts, however, do not invalidate a contract if it only violates a statute that does not further a strong public policy.

AGREEMENTS VIOLATIVE OF STATUTES: Important types of conduct prohibited by statute include:
- *Price Fixing Agreements*: Agreements between competitors to fix prices are illegal and void.
- *Performances of Services Without a License*: An agreement is unenforceable if it requires violation of a regulatory-license statute, but it is enforceable if it only violates a revenue-license statute.
- *Sunday Laws*: These laws forbid the formation or performance of contracts on Sunday.
- *Wagering Statutes*: Wagering is paying consideration in the hope of winning a prize by chance.
- *Usury Statutes*: These statutes set a limit on interest rates. Interest that is charged in excess of the lawful limit cannot be collected in most states.

AGREEMENTS VIOLATIVE OF PUBLIC POLICY: A court may hold that a contract is void if it violates an important public interest, meaning a fundamental value or interest of society.
- *Covenants not to Compete*: A covenant not to compete is an individual's promise not to compete against another party. In general, a covenant not to compete is legal if: 1) it is made as part of or in connection with a contract for the sale of a business or an employment contract; and 2) it restricts competition for only a reasonable time and for only a reasonable geographic area.
- *Exculpatory Clauses*: An exculpatory clause is a contract term that eliminates a party's liability for certain wrongs that he or she may commit. The legality of these clauses are evaluated on a case-by-case basis.

EXCEPTIONS: UPHOLDING ILLEGAL AGREEMENTS: In some situations, a court may enforce an illegal agreement if the person suing has already performed his or her contractual obligations. This may occur in the following situations:
- *Parties not* **in Pari Delicto**: If one party is less guilty than the other, i.e., the party is not *in pari delicto*) then that party may recover under the contract if doing so will further the public interest.
- *Repentance*: If a party tries to undo or rescind an illegal agreement, then the law may allow that party to recover what has already been given under the agreement.
- *Partial Illegality*: If a contract involves both legal and illegal undertakings and these portions of the contract can be fairly separated, then a court may enforce the legal part and void the illegal part.

THE REQUIREMENT OF REALITY (OR GENUINENESS) OF CONSENT: A contract that looks valid may not be.

FRAUD: Fraud is an intentional misrepresentation of a material fact that is made with the intent to induce a person to enter into an unfair contract.

- *Elements of Fraud*: The elements of fraud are: 1) misrepresentation (misstatement) of a fact (does not generally include statements of value, future predictions, or mere opinions); 2) the fact is material (important); 3) the misrepresentation is made with scienter (the person knew or should have known the fact was false); 4) it was made with the intent to deceive; 5) the innocent party reasonably relied; and 6) the innocent party suffered injury or detriment as a result.

- *Silence*: In most states, a party must voluntarily disclose to the other party latent (hidden) defects relating to the subject of the contract. Fiduciaries also have a duty to disclose all material information.

MISREPRESENTATION: Misrepresentation (often called innocent misrepresentation) is a defense that includes the same elements as fraud except for the requirements of scienter and intent to deceive. While a plaintiff may recover punitive damages for fraud, such damages are not available for misrepresentation.

MISTAKE: Mistake is when the parties are wrong about a past or present material fact.

- *Unilateral Mistake*: If only one party is mistaken, the contract will generally be upheld.
- *Bilateral Mistake*: If both parties are mistaken about an essential element of the contract, then either party may elect to rescind the contract.
- *Reformation*: If a court can remedy a mistake, such as correcting a typographical error, then the court will in effect rewrite the contract to reflect the parties' actual intent and then enforce the contract.

DURESS: Duress is coercion that is so extreme that it prevents a party from freely assenting to a contract. Duress may be personal (e.g., threats against a person) or economic (e.g., threat to breach a contract).

UNDUE INFLUENCE: Undue influence is the use of a relationship of trust to unfairly obtain a contractual advantage. Undue influence often involves elderly persons who are the victims of wrongful persuasion.

UNCONSCIONABILITY: A contract may be set aside if one of the parties' used their superior bargaining power to achieve a contract that it commercially shocking or unreasonably oppressive.

STUDY HINTS FOR CALL-IMAGE TECHNOLOGY CASE STUDIES

The following study hints may be helpful when resolving the Call-Image Technology (CIT) case studies.

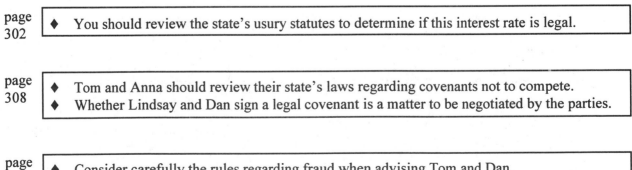

page
302
♦ You should review the state's usury statutes to determine if this interest rate is legal.

page
308
♦ Tom and Anna should review their state's laws regarding covenants not to compete.
♦ Whether Lindsay and Dan sign a legal covenant is a matter to be negotiated by the parties.

page
314
♦ Consider carefully the rules regarding fraud when advising Tom and Dan.

REVIEW OF KEY TERMS AND CONCEPTS

MATCHING EXERCISE

Select the term or concept that best matches a definition or statement set forth below. Each term or concept is the best match for only one definition or statement.

Terms and Concepts

a. Acceleration clause
b. Ambiguity
c. Chattel
d. Conditional sales contract
e. Contract of adhesion

f. Exculpatory clause
g. Fiduciary
h. Monopoly
i. Oligopoly
j. Prepayment clause

k. Reformation
l. Scienter
m. Time-price differential sales contract
n. Tortious
o. Warranty

Definitions and Statements

_____ 1. Economic condition when one firm controls an entire market.
_____ 2. Economic condition when a small number of firms dominate a market.
_____ 3. Relating to private wrongs or injuries.
_____ 4. Contract with different prices, one price for immediate payment and another price for a later payment.
_____ 5. Contractual clause that limits the potential liability of a party.
_____ 6. Contractual clause that allows a creditor to advance the date that a debtor must pay.
_____ 7. Contract that is not open to negotiation, i.e., a take-it-or-leave-it contract.
_____ 8. Contractual remedy whereby a court corrects an error in how a contract is stated in order to make the contract conform to the parties' original intent.
_____ 9. Type of personal property.
_____ 10. Contractual clause that allows a debtor to pay a debt before it is due.
_____ 11. Uncertainty about the meaning of a contractual term.
_____ 12. Sales contract in which the transfer of title is subject to a condition.
_____ 13. Person who holds a position of trust or confidence, and is expected to act in good faith.
_____ 14. Knowledge that a misrepresentation is false.
_____ 15. Contractual guarantee relating to the nature or quality of goods.

COMPLETION EXERCISE

Fill in the blanks with the words that most accurately complete each statement.

1. A contract to steal the property of another is an example of a bargain that is _____ _____ _____ and, therefore, such a bargain is always illegal and void.

2. A _____ - _____ _____ is an agreement between competitors to charge certain prices for their goods or services.

3. _____ is the lending of money for an interest rate that exceeds the legal rate of interest.

4. A _____ mistake occurs when only one party is mistaken about a fact.

5. A _____ mistake occurs when both parties are mistaken regarding the fact.

TRUE-FALSE EXERCISE

Write **T** if the statement is true, write **F** if the statement is false.

_____ 1. An agreement may violate public policy even if the agreement does not require a party to commit a crime, tort, or require a party to violate a statute.

_____ 2. Duress that renders a contract voidable may be personal or economic.

_____ 3. A contract may be rescinded for fraud even if the fraud does not cause any injury or detriment to the defrauded party.

_____ 4. If a single contract requires performance of two services, one legal and one illegal, then the entire contract is always illegal and void.

_____ 5. The legality of exculpatory clauses are evaluated on a case-by-case basis.

_____ 6. The fact that a party agreed to pay more for an item than it is worth does not, standing alone, establish the defense of economic duress.

_____ 7. The traditional common law rule that a contracting party does not have a duty to voluntarily disclose facts to the other party is still uniformly followed by present-day courts.

_____ 8. The defense of misrepresentation does not require proof of scienter or an intent to deceive.

_____ 9. If a salesperson says "This is a great car" and the car turns out to be a lemon, then the salesperson has committed fraud.

_____ 10. In an illegal agreement, courts may allow a less guilty party to recover.

APPLICATION OF CONCEPTS

MULTIPLE CHOICE QUESTIONS

_____ 1. Which contract is voidable due to mistake?
   a. Earl contracted to sell a cabin to Phil. Unknown to either party, the cabin had burned down the previous week.
   b. Subcontractor submitted a bid to Contractor for $15,000. Contractor accepted the bid, not knowing that Subcontractor had made a mistake and the bid should have been $16,000.
   c. Andie purchased stock of ABC, Inc. from Paul. Both Andie and Paul expected the stock to increase in value, but it did not.
   d. a and c.

_____ 2. Pete and Gail agreed to pay Jason, an employee of Rayon Corp., to steal valuable trade secrets belonging to Rayon. Pete gave Gail his share of the money, and Gail was to give the money to Jason. After Gail had paid Jason the money and received the stolen trade secrets, Pete reconsidered and told Gail that he did not want to participate in this undertaking. Under these facts:
   a. Pete cannot recover his money from Jason because the agreement is illegal and void.
   b. Pete cannot recover his money from Jason because he had a contractual obligation to pay the money to Jason.
   c. Pete can recover his money from Jason because the agreement is illegal, but not void.
   d. Pete can recover his money from Jason because he effectively repented.

_____ 3. Which contract is voidable due to fraud?
   a. During negotiations, Joe falsely stated to Susan that a car offered for sale was a 1965 Mustang when it was actually a 1967 Mustang. Susan bought the car, but she did not rely on Joe's false statement because she knew the car was a 1967 model.
   b. Kelly contracted to sell an antique desk to Pedro. Kelly told Pedro that she believed the desk was worth $3,000. The desk was actually worth $2,500.
   c. Al contracted to sell a vending machine to Maria. Al intentionally lied about the machine's prior earnings, showing Maria false income statements that inflated the machine's earnings for the past three years.
   d. All of the above.

_____ 4. Nell was hired as president of a soft drink distributor located in Fizz City. When hired, Nell agreed not to compete in the soft drink industry after she quit. Under these facts, Nell's agreement not to compete would be:
   a. Valid if it prohibited Nell from competing in Fizz City for one year after she quit.
   b. Valid if it prohibited Nell from competing anywhere in the state in which Fizz City was located for ten years after she quit.
   c. Not valid, because all agreements not to compete are unenforceable.
   d. a and b.

SHORT ANSWER QUESTIONS

Answer the following questions, briefly explaining the reason for your answer.

1. Slick Larry has a reputation as a pushy car salesperson. Angela went to Larry and, after talking to him for two hours about a particular car, Angela bought the car just so Larry would "leave her alone." Angela has now decided that she doesn't want the car. Can Angela rescind the sales contract because of duress?

_____

_____

2. A state statute requires self-storage facilities to pay an annual fee and to obtain a license to operate. The statute does not protect the public, but is only intended to raise revenue for the government. U-Stor failed to obtain this license. Sally, who stored goods at a U-Stor facility for the past year, now refuses to pay the bill. Sally argues that her storage contract is unenforceable because U-Stor violated the statute in question. Is the contract between U-Stor and Sally void?

_____

_____

3. Ben is a financial planner and his client, Dee, completely relies on him to manage her financial affairs. Ben used his position of trust to convince Dee to buy stock in Star Corp., a speculative company that Ben owns an interest in. Ben knew that this investment was risky, but he wanted to earn the commission and obtain new capital for Star. If Dee loses money on her investment, can she rescind the purchase contract?

_____

_____

4. Bob and Earl are both sophisticated merchants who deal in antique automobiles. Bob contracted to purchase an antique car from Earl for $30,000. The day after the purchase, Earl took the car to an auto show, but the highest offer for the car was only $20,000. Is this contract unconscionable?

_____

_____

CASE PROBLEMS

Answer the following case problems, explaining your answers.

1. Luis agreed to employ Jim as an architect to design an addition to his house. Individuals are legally required to be licensed by the state to be architects, but Jim did not have this license. To assure the competency of architects and to protect the public from unqualified work, this license requires extensive education and successful completion of an exhaustive examination. (a) Is the required license a protective (regulatory) license or a revenue-raising license? (b) Is the agreement between Luis and Jim valid or void? (c) If Jim performs the work but Luis fails to pay him, can Jim collect his fee?

_____

_____

_____

_____

2. Laredo Ranch sold a parcel of land to Dynamic Developers. Prior to the sale, the parties retained Lawrence to do a survey and determine how many acres were in the parcel. Lawrence informed the parties that the parcel contained 100 acres. Unknown to the parties, the parcel actually contained only 75 acres. Laredo and Dynamic computed the contract price based on 100 acres. (a) Can Dynamic rescind this contract based on mistake? (b) What elements must Dynamic prove to establish this defense?

_____

_____

_____

_____

CHAPTER 13

Proper Form and Interpretation of Contracts

CHAPTER REVIEW

THE IMPORTANCE OF FORM: Because of the potential for fraud, the law places certain requirements on the form of contracts and certain limitations on their interpretation.

STATUTE OF FRAUDS: Every state has adopted the Statute of Frauds which requires certain contracts to be evidenced by a signed writing in order to be enforced in court.

- *Types of Contracts Covered*: The Statute of Frauds requires the following categories of contracts to be evidenced by a sufficient writing in order to be enforceable:
  1) Contracts to Answer for the Debt of Another If the Person So Defaults: Includes contracts of guarantee or suretyship.
  2) Contracts for Interests in Land: Includes land sale contracts, mortgages, easements, and (most) real estate leases, sales contracts for standing timber or buildings attached to the land.
  3) Contracts Not to Be Performed Within One Year of the Date of Their Making: Measure the one-year period starting from the date the contract is made, not from the date the work is to actually begin.
  4) Contracts of Executors and Administrators of Estates
  5) Contracts Made in Consideration of Marriage
  6) Contracts for the Sale of Goods for $500 or More, and Contracts for the Lease of Goods Where the Total Lease Price Is $1,000 or More: Despite this rule, an oral sales contract for $500 or more is enforceable *to the extent* that: (a) the party who refuses to perform admits in judicial proceedings that the contract was made; (b) the goods are delivered by the seller and accepted by the buyer; or (c) the buyer pays the contract price and payment is accepted by the seller.
- *Writing*: The writing required to satisfy the Statute of Frauds need not be a complete contract, but under the common law it must identify: 1) the parties to the agreement; 2) the subject matter of the agreement; and 3) all material terms and conditions.
- *Signature*: The writing need not be signed by both parties, only by the party who opposes enforcement of the contract. A signature is anything intended to be a signature, including stamped signatures and letterheads.

PAROL EVIDENCE RULE: The parol evidence rule is a rule of substantive law that prohibits a party from using evidence of prior statements or writings to add to or change the terms of a final and complete written contract.

EXCEPTIONS TO THE PAROL EVIDENCE RULE: Exceptions to the parol evidence rule include the following

- *Partially Integrated Contracts*: If a contract is partially integrated (i.e., it is the final statement of only part of the contract), evidence of prior statements or writings may be used to establish terms that are not stated in the writing.
- *Mistake, Fraud, and Other "Reality-of-Consent" Situations*: Evidence that shows mistake, fraud, duress, and lack of consideration is permitted.

- *Ambiguities and Conditions Precedent*: Parol evidence may be used to explain the meaning of ambiguous terms. Evidence is also admissible to show that a contract was not to become binding until a certain event occurred (i.e., obligations were subject to a condition precedent).

- *Uniform Commercial Code*: UCC §§ 2-202 and 2-208 allow evidence a course of performance, course of dealing, or usage of trade in order to explain contract terms even if the contract is not ambiguous. Also, the UCC allows evidence of additional consistent terms unless a court finds that the parties to a contract intended the writing to be the final and exclusive statement of the agreement.

JUDICIAL INTERPRETATION: Courts use the objective or reasonable person approach when interpreting contracts. In other words, the courts interpret a contract from the perspective that a reasonable person would have in the same situation.

- *Standards*: Typically, courts use the "general usage" standard to decide the meaning of terms, that is, the courts ascribe the meaning that a reasonable person would give them. Sometimes, a court may use the standard of "limited usage," that is ascribing the meaning given to a word in a particular locale.

- *Total Integration*: Courts assume that a writing supersedes any terms discussed during negotiations.

- *Partial Integration*: If a writing is incomplete, courts will allow the parties to add terms as long as the additional terms do not contradict the written terms.

- *Rules of Integration*: If a writing looks formal and complete, courts will more likely find that the writing is totally integrated. If a writing is not integrated, some courts use the reasonable expectations standard to fill in missing terms. Some courts use the limited usage standard, which looks to local custom and trade usage, to fill in missing terms.

- *Rules of Interpretation*: The four most important rules of interpretation state that courts should: 1) attempt to give affect to the indicated intentions of the parties; 2) look at the contract as a whole to find the parties' intent; 3) give ordinary words their ordinary meaning and technical words their technical meaning unless the situation suggests otherwise; and 4) look at all of the circumstances of a transaction when interpreting it (subject, however, to the limits imposed by the parol evidence rule).

- *Conduct and Usage of Trade*: Courts will look at past dealings between the parties to help interpret an agreement. The UCC also allows evidence of usage of trade to aid in interpreting a contract.

STUDY HINTS FOR CALL-IMAGE TECHNOLOGY CASE STUDIES

The following study hints may be helpful when resolving the Call-Image Technology (CIT) case studies.

page 335
- ♦ Tom should review UCC § 2-201 regarding written confirmations between merchants.

page 340
- ♦ Tom should again consider UCC § 2-201, focusing this time on the exception relating to specially manufactured goods.

page 341
- ♦ You should review the parol evidence rule and UCC § 2-202.
- ♦ Also consider the different rules of interpretation that apply when one is determining the meaning of partially integrated and totally integrated contracts.

MATCHING EXERCISE

Select the term or concept that best matches a definition or statement set forth below. Each term or concept is the best match for only one definition or statement.

Terms and Concepts

a. Administrator	f. Merchant	k. Partially-integrated contract
b. Affirmative defense	g. Mortgage	l. Perjury
c. Condition precedent	h. Novation	m. Statute of Frauds
d. Easement	i. Parol evidence	n. Surety
e. Interpretation	j. Parol evidence rule	o. Usage of trade

Definitions and Statements

_____ 1. Defense to a cause of action that the defendant must assert.
_____ 2. Law that requires certain contracts to be evidenced by a writing to be enforceable.
_____ 3. Contract that is the final statement of only a portion of the parties' agreement.
_____ 4. Person who manages a decedent's estate.
_____ 5. Law that prohibits prior evidence from being used to alter a final, complete written contract.
_____ 6. False statement made under oath during judicial proceedings.
_____ 7. Substitution of a new contract in place of a preexisting one.
_____ 8. Evidence of oral statements.
_____ 9. Limited right to use the land of another.
_____ 10. Person who promises to pay if the principal debtor fails to do so.
_____ 11. Process for discerning the meaning of a contract and unclear contractual language.
_____ 12. Event or action that must occur before a party has a legal obligation to act.
_____ 13. Regularly observed practice in an industry or profession.
_____ 14. Conditional transfer of real property to secure payment of a debt.
_____ 15. Person who regularly deals in certain kinds of goods.

COMPLETION EXERCISE

Fill in the blanks with the words that most accurately complete each statement.

1. A _____ _____ contract is one that represents the parties' entire, final agreement.

2. An _____ _____ contract is one that represents only a portion of the parties' final agreement.

3. Parol evidence is admissible to show that certain contractual defenses may exist, such as _____ _____ and _____ .

4. The _____ _____ standard gives words the meaning that would be given by a reasonable person who was acquainted with the circumstances surrounding the transaction in question.

5. Identify six types of contracts that must be in writing.

   a. _____.

   b. _____.

   c. _____.

   d. _____.

   e. _____.

   f. _____.

TRUE-FALSE EXERCISE

Write **T** if the statement is true, write **F** if the statement is false.

_____ 1. All oral contracts are unenforceable.

_____ 2. A contract term should be interpreted without considering the other terms of the contract.

_____ 3. An executor's promise to personally pay the debts of an estate must be evidenced by a writing to be legally enforceable even if the executor intended to be personally liable.

_____ 4. Mechanic agreed to install "ABS" brakes on Fred's car. In this case, Mechanic must install brakes that would comply with the technical meaning for "ABS" brakes. Installing brakes that would comply with the ordinary meaning for normal car brakes would not be sufficient.

_____ 5. The Statute of Frauds requires that writings be signed by all contracting parties.

_____ 6. The parol evidence rule requires all contracts to be evidenced by a writing to be enforceable.

_____ 7. Evidence of prior oral statements may be used to prove terms that are not stated or implied in an incomplete contract.

_____ 8. The Statute of Frauds (at common law) requires a writing to state all material contract terms.

_____ 9. Only formal writings signed by all parties can satisfy the Statute of Frauds.

_____ 10. When interpreting a contractual term, a court can generally use any meaning that the court chooses in order to produce a contract that is fair and balanced.

APPLICATION OF CONCEPTS

MULTIPLE CHOICE QUESTIONS

_____ 1. On March 1, Julia orally contracted to work for Moose's Diner from April 1 through March 30 of the following year. Under these facts:
   a. The contract violates the Statute of Frauds because it cannot be performed within one year from the date the contract was made.
   b. The contract violates the Statute of Frauds because all service contracts must be written.
   c. The contract does not violate the Statute of Frauds because it can be performed within one year from when the work begins.
   d. The contract does not violate the Statute of Frauds because it may be terminated at any time due to a party's breach.

CHAPTER 13 - PROPER FORM AND INTERPRETATION OF CONTRACTS

_____ 2. Which of the following oral contracts is unenforceable?
a. Bubba orally contracts with Madison to lease Madison's apartment for three years.
b. Lewis orally contracts to grant High Finance, Inc. a mortgage on Lewis' home.
c. Linda orally contracts to sell a parcel of land to Andy.
d. All of the above.

_____ 3. Paul orally contracts to sell land to Angela. Angela takes possession of the land, and Angela makes valuable improvements, the value of which is hard to determine. This contract is:
a. Enforceable because the Statute of Frauds does not apply to land sale contracts.
b. Enforceable due to Angela's part performance.
c. Voidable and cannot be enforced because the contract violates the Statute of Frauds.
d. Void and cannot be enforced because the contract violates the Statute of Frauds.

_____ 4. Which oral contract violates the Statute of Frauds?
a. Frank and Joe make an oral contract whereby Frank promises to make Joe the general manager of a company in exchange for Joe's promise to marry Frank's daughter.
b. Tim orally contracts to buy a TV for $400.
c. Ursula orally contracts to buy a car for $10,000.
d. a and c.

SHORT ANSWER QUESTIONS

Answer the following questions, briefly explaining the reason for your answer.

1. Bob orally told his good friend and employee, Steve, "You have a job at my company for the rest of your life." Steve is 26 years old. The next month, Bob fired Steve and hired someone more qualified. Does this contract violate the Statute of Frauds?

_____

_____

2. Al's Butcher Shop has a long-term contract with Snortin' Pig Ranch to buy its "pork chops" from Snortin'. For the past year, Snortin' has always sent and Al has accepted center-cut pork chops. In the latest shipment under this contract, Snortin' sent loin-cut pork chops, an inferior type of pork chop. If Al sues Snortin' for breach of contract, what evidence can Al use to interpret the meaning of "pork chops"?

_____

_____

3. The Top Secret Research Center (TSRC) contracted to hire Ivan as a scientist. The contract stated that TSRC did not have a duty to hire Ivan unless he first passed a security check. Ivan failed the security check and was not hired by TSRC. Can Ivan sue TSRC for breach of contract?

_____

_____

4. Anna and Bob, both merchants, orally agreed that Anna would sell Bob's Vegetable Store 600 pounds of carrots per week. Anna sent Bob the following letter: "This confirms my sale to you of 600 lbs. of grade A carrots at $1.00/lb., delivery every Monday /s/ Anna." Ten days went by and Bob did not reply. Discuss whether this contract is enforceable or not?

_____

_____

CASE PROBLEMS

Answer the following case problems, explaining your answers.

1. Jim advertised a parcel of land for sale, and Edna orally made a generous cash purchase offer, which Jim orally accepted. Eager to seal the deal, Jim grabbed a piece of paper that had his letterhead on it and wrote down his name, Edna's name, a description of the land, and the cash purchase price. Edna took this paper with her as she left. After Edna left, Jim received a better offer, and he told Edna that he would not sell the land to her. (a) Does the contract between Jim and Edna come within the Statute of Frauds? (b) If so, does the piece of paper satisfy the requirements of the Statute of Frauds? (c) Does Edna have an enforceable contract against Jim?

a. Yes - Contract for land falls under the statute of fraud

b. It was in writing therefore satisfy the requirement

c. Yes

_____

2. Sally offered to sell Ralph her computer. When Ralph saw the computer, it had a color monitor. Sally and Ralph entered into a written contract that stated "Sally sells to Ralph her computer system for $1,000," with no other description of the computer. The contract also contained a merger clause and was signed by both parties. When the computer arrived, it did not come with the monitor. Sally says that she did not intend the "computer system" to include the monitor, whereas Ralph intended otherwise. (a) Identify the nature of this contract in terms of its completeness. (b) If a lawsuit arises regarding this transaction, could Ralph use parol evidence to prove the meaning of the term "computer system"? (c) What rules of interpretation may a court use to interpret this term?

_____

_____

_____

_____

CHAPTER 14

The Rights of Third Persons

CHAPTER REVIEW

ADDITION OF THIRD PARTIES TO THE RELATIONSHIP: As a general rule, a contract only affects the rights of the two (or more) parties who enter into the contract. One exception to this rule permits a third-party beneficiary to enforce a contract that others have made for his or her benefit.

THIRD-PARTY BENEFICIARY CONTRACTS: In a third-party beneficiary contract, the contracting parties typically agree to perform an act for a third person, known as a beneficiary. The beneficiary may be an incidental or intended beneficiary. How the third party is classified determines what rights, if any, that he or she has to enforce the third-party beneficiary contract.
- *An Incidental Beneficiary*: An incidental beneficiary is one who may receive a benefit merely by accident or chance, not because one or both of the parties intended to directly benefit the beneficiary. An incidental beneficiary has no right to enforce a contract.
- *An Intended Beneficiary*: An intended beneficiary is a third party whom one or both of the contracting parties *clearly* intended to benefit. An intended beneficiary has the same (but no greater) right to enforce the contract as does the original contracting party who intended to benefit the beneficiary.
- *A Donee Beneficiary*: A donee beneficiary is an intended beneficiary whose benefit is intended as a gift from one of the contracting parties. In some states, the donee's rights are vested (cannot be terminated) once the contract is made; in other states the donee's rights vest only if the donee has accepted the contract, either expressly or by reliance.
- *A Creditor Beneficiary*: A creditor beneficiary is an intended beneficiary whose benefit is intended as payment of a debt that is owed by one of the contracting parties to the beneficiary.
- *Analysis of Third-Party Beneficiary Contracts*: When deciding whether a third party is an intended beneficiary of a contract between others, ask yourself three questions: 1) Did the contract benefit the third party from the beginning or was the benefit bestowed upon the third party later? 2) Was the benefit clearly intended by one or both contracting parties or was it merely accidental? 3) Was the benefit a gift from one of the contracting parties or did it satisfy an obligation owed to the third party?

DEFINING ASSIGNMENTS AND DELEGATIONS: If a third party is granted rights or duties under a contract after the contract was created, then the third party is not a beneficiary of the contract. Instead, there may have been either an assignment of rights to the third party or a delegation of duties to the third party.

ASSIGNMENTS: An assignment is the transfer of a contractual right to another. The person transferring the right is the assignor, and the party receiving the right is the assignee.
- *Formalities Required for Assignments*: An assignor must indicate a present intent to vest a right in another person. The assignment must be in writing if the contract in question was required to be in writing. Consideration is not required to make a valid assignment.
- *Notice of the Assignment*: Notice of assignment is not required. If the person obligated to perform the assigned right (the promisor) is given notice of the assignment but nonetheless delivers performance to the assignor, then the promisor remains obligated perform for the benefit of the assignee. If one right is assigned more than once to different assignees, courts may use one of three theories to determine the

assignees' priority to the assigned right: 1) first person to whom an assignment was made; 2) first assignee to give notice to the promisor; and 3) the "Massachusetts Rule."

- *Nonassignable Rights*: Courts generally favor and will enforce assignments. However, an assignment is not permitted if the assignment will significantly: 1) change the promisor's duty; 2) impair or reduce the value of a return performance; or 3) increase the burden or risk of performance.
- *Contract Clauses Restricting Assignments*: Courts interpret these clauses narrowly and many courts allow assignments despite these clauses. However, strong contractual language prohibiting assignments, such as "all assignments shall be null and void," are typically enforced, thereby barring any assignment of rights.
- *Warranties Implied by the Assignor*: An assignor warrants to the assignee that: 1) an assigned right is valid and actually exists; 2) the right is not subject to any defenses or limitations that are not stated or apparent; and 3) the assignor will not interfere with the assignee's rights.
- *Rights Created by the Assignment*: An assignee receives the same rights that the assignor possessed.
- *Waiver of Defenses Clauses*: In a waiver of defense clause, the promisor agrees not to assert any defenses against an assignee that the promisor may have had against the assignor. The validity of these clauses depends on the nature of the transaction and the parties, and what law governs the transaction.

DELEGATIONS: In a delegation, the promisor (delegator) appoints a new party (delegatee) to perform one or more of the delegator's contractual obligations. A delegation is not valid unless the delegatee assumes the delegated obligations.

In general, the delegator remains liable for the proper performance of the delegated obligation. Whether the delegatee can be held liable generally depends on whether the delegatee contractually agreed to perform the obligation (delegatee may be liable) or agreed to perform the obligation as a favor or gift for the delegator (delegatee is not liable).

UNIFORM COMMERCIAL CODE PROVISIONS: UCC § 2-210 covers assignments and delegations for contracts involving sales of goods.

STUDY HINTS FOR CALL-IMAGE TECHNOLOGY CASE STUDIES

The following study hints may be helpful when resolving the Call-Image Technology (CIT) case studies.

page 358
- ♦ First, ask yourself the three questions used for analyzing third-party beneficiary contracts.
- ♦ You should then determine whether CIT is a beneficiary of the BG-Joe's Trucking contract and what rights, if any, it may have to enforce the contract against Joe's Trucking.
- ♦ Also, review material in other parts of the textbook regarding a common carrier's (shipper's) obligations for the care of goods during shipment.

page 363
- ♦ When deciding how to advise CIT, you should consider all of the issues surrounding assignments, paying particular attention to the rights that CIT, as assignee, would receive.

page 368
- ♦ You should review the discussion of delegations, especially the portions relating to the delegator's continuing liability and the duties of delegatees, if any.

MATCHING EXERCISE

Select the term or concept that best matches a definition or statement set forth below. Each term or concept is the best match for only one definition or statement.

Terms and Concepts

a. Assignee
b. Assignment
c. Assignor
d. Creditor beneficiary

e. Delegation
f. Donee beneficiary
g. Extinguish
h. Incidental beneficiary

i. Insured
j. Mortgage insurance
k. Post-loss duty
l. Vested interest

Definitions and Statements

_k_ 1. Obligation of an insurance company after a loss.
_c_ 2. Party who transfers a contractual right to another.
_l_ 3. Legal right that is fixed and cannot be arbitrarily taken away by another.
_i_ 4. Party who is covered under a policy of insurance.
_e_ 5. Transfer of a contractual obligation to a third party.
_d_ 6. Beneficiary who is intended to receive a contract benefit as satisfaction of an obligation owed by one of the contracting parties.
_h_ 7. Beneficiary who may by chance receive a benefit under a contract between others.
_g_ 8. To destroy or terminate something.
_f_ 9. Beneficiary who is intended to receive a contract benefit as a gift from one of the contracting parties.
_b_ 10. Transfer of a contractual right to another.
_j_ 11. Insurance that will pay a mortgage if the mortgagor dies.
_a_ 12. Party to whom a contractual right is transferred.

COMPLETION EXERCISE

Fill in the blanks with the words that most accurately complete each statement.

1. The presence or absence of an ___intent___ to directly benefit a third party under a contract is a primary factor in deciding whether the third party is an intended or incidental beneficiary under the contract.

2. Under the ___First___ - ___in___ - ___Time___ approach, the first assignee to whom an assignment is made receives all assigned rights.

3. A ___Waiver___ ___of___ ___defense___ clause attempts to shield an assignee from defenses that the promisor may assert in order to avoid performance of an obligation.

4. When assigning rights, an assignor creates three implied _Warantees_.

5. Identify three situations when an assignment may be prohibited:

   a. _____.

   b. _____.

   c. _____.

TRUE-FALSE EXERCISE

Write **T** if the statement is true, write **F** if the statement is false.

_F_ 1. Courts disfavor both assignments and delegations.

_F_ 2. An assignment of rights under a contract automatically terminates the assignor's duty to perform any duties under the contract.

_F_ 3. An incidental beneficiary may sue a contracting party in order to compel performance of the contract.

_T_ 4. An assignment must be in writing if the original contract was required to be in writing.

_F_ 5. An assignment is invalid unless the assignor notifies the promisor of the assignment.

____ 6. In general, a delegator remains liable for the proper performance of a delegated task.

_T_ 7. A third party beneficiary can enforce a contract only in accordance with the terms of the contract.

____ 8. If a party is legally entitled to assign a contract right, then the party may assign this right without first obtaining the consent of the other contracting party.

____ 9. A party cannot assign a right to be insured because the assignment may significantly increase the risk or burden to the insurer.

____ 10. An assignment is not valid unless consideration was paid by the assignee to the assignor.

APPLICATION OF CONCEPTS

MULTIPLE CHOICE QUESTIONS

____ 1. Ace Imports sold a car to Trent on credit for $30,000. Ace assigned to C&C Credit all of Ace's right to payment under its contract with Trent. Trent was not informed about the assignment and he never consented to it. Trent later paid the entire $30,000 to Ace. Under these facts:
   a. Trent is obligated to pay nothing to C&C Credit because he was never informed about the assignment and he in good faith paid Ace.
   b. Trent is obligated to pay nothing to C&C Credit because he never consented to the assignment.
   c. Trent is obligated to pay $30,000 to C&C Credit.
   d. a and b.

_____ 2. In which case is a third party entitled to enforce the contract in question?
   a. Jake lent Moe $2,000 to pay bills. The loan contract states that the parties do not intend for any of Moe's creditors to be third-party beneficiaries. Third party is one of Moe's creditors.
   b. Lewis contracted with West Life Insurance to pay Lewis' wife $20,000 on Lewis' death.
   c. Head Ache is a rock group that contracted to perform at City Coliseum. Ned's Hot Dog Stand, located near the coliseum, will benefit from sales to persons going to this concert.
   d. b and c.

_____ 3. Leo agreed to paint a portrait of Mona. Leo has a very talented student, Angelo, who wants to paint his first portrait. Will a court allow Leo to delegate the work to Angelo?
   a. No, because this is a personal service contract.
   b. No, because delegations are illegal.
   c. Yes, if Angelo is talented.
   d. Yes, because courts favor delegations.

_____ 4. Brett owed Fred $1,000. Fred orally told Brett and Alicia: "I transfer to Alicia my right to collect $1,000; Brett, pay Alicia the $1,000." Alicia did not give Brett anything in return. Assume no special statutes apply to this assignment. Under these facts, the assignment is:
   a. Invalid because Fred did not use the word assign.
   b. Invalid because the assignment is not in writing.
   c. Invalid because Alicia did not give consideration for the assignment.
   d. Valid.

SHORT ANSWER QUESTIONS

Answer the following questions, briefly explaining the reason for your answer.

1. Steve told a customer who owed him money to make all payments to Last Bank, a bank to whom Steve was indebted. Last Bank knew about this arrangement and verbally accepted it. If Steve changes his mind about this arrangement, does he have the legal right to unilaterally decide that payments should once again be paid to himself and not to Last Bank?

No, Last Bank knew about and accepted the assignment and therefore the right at vested.

2. Brent Auto Trades (BAT) sold Laurie a personal car on credit. The contract contained a standard waiver of defense clause, whereby Laurie agreed not to assert any defenses against an assignee of the contract. BAT assigned its rights under the contract to Third Bank. As it turns out, the car is defective and Laurie does not want to pay. Was the assignment to Third Bank valid? Can Laurie assert her defense of breach of contract against Last Bank in order to avoid paying for the car?

Yes the assignment was valid. under the Federal Trade Commission, as a consumer, she can assert he defense of breach against Third Bank.

3. Mike is a pilot for Air Freight, Inc. Air Freight assigned Mike's service contract to Thailand Air Freight. This assignment requires Mike and his family to move to Thailand. It also requires Mike to fly in unfamiliar regions, under somewhat risky flying conditions. Is this assignment valid?

_____

_____

4. Jasper contracted to build a storage shed for Juan. The contract price is $3,000. Jasper owes Rosa $3,000, and the contract states that Juan is to pay the $3,000 directly to Rosa in order to satisfy this debt. Jasper built the shed, but failed to install shelving worth $300. How much, if any, must Juan pay to Rosa?

_____

_____

CASE PROBLEMS

Answer the following case problems, explaining your answers.

1. The City of Hope contracted with Virgil's Construction to build a parking garage on 23rd Street, a rundown area. Businesses on 23rd Street, including Harry's Cafe, may benefit from the construction of this garage. The city council approved the project in order to revitalize and stimulate economic growth in this part of town. (a) Is Harry's a beneficiary under this contract and, if so, what type of beneficiary is it? (b) If Virgil's Construction fails to properly build the garage, can Harry's sue to enforce the contract against Virgil's?

a) Yes - incidental beneficiary

b) No he has no legal right to any benifit was was not named in the contract

_____

2. JobFinders helps recent college graduates find jobs. JobFinders contracted with Trina to help her locate a job. As part of its obligation, JobFinders was to design a resume and provide her with 50 copies of it. JobFinders subcontracted out the typing of all resumes, including Trina's resume. The subcontractor made numerous errors in typing Trina's resume. (a) The typing subcontract is what type of third-party transaction? (b) Was JobFinders legally entitled to subcontract the typing of Trina's resume without first obtaining her permission? (c) Is JobFinders liable to Trina for the improperly typed resumes?

a. a Delegation

b. Yes because they are standardize duties anyone can perform

c. Yes, as delegators - they remain reliable.

CHAPTER 15

Contractual Discharge and Remedies

TERMINATION OF THE CONTRACT: A contract may be discharged (terminated) in four ways: 1) discharge by performance; 2) discharge by agreement of the parties; 3) discharge by operation of law; or 4) discharge by nonperformance.

DISCHARGE BY PERFORMANCE: A duty may be discharged by complete or substantial performance.
- *Complete Performance*: A contract is discharged by the exact performance (or tender, meaning offer, of performance) of their contractual duties.
- *Substantial Performance*: Substantial performance means that a party has in good faith fully performed a duty with the exception of minor, unintentional errors. In most cases, parties may discharge their contractual obligations by substantial performance so long as the errors were not material and were unintentional.

DISCHARGE BY AGREEMENT OF THE PARTIES: Parties may agree to discharge contractual obligations.
- *Release*: A release discharges a legal claim that one party has against another. A release generally requires: 1) a writing; 2) consideration; and 3) an immediate relinquishment of the claim.
- *Rescission*: A contract of rescission is a mutual termination of another contract.
- *Accord and Satisfaction*: An accord is an agreement to accept a substituted performance as fulfillment of an existing duty. A satisfaction is performance of the accord. The original duty is not discharged until the satisfaction is completed.
- *Novation*: In a novation, a new party is substituted for one of the original parties.

DISCHARGE BY OPERATION OF LAW: Bankruptcy law and statutes of limitations are examples of laws that may discharge contractual obligations.

DISCHARGE BY NONPERFORMANCE: Discharge by nonperformance may occur in the following situations:
- *Impossibility*: The doctrine of impossibility excuses a party from a contractual duty if, after the contract is made, performance of the duty is made impossible because of an unforeseeable event. The event must be such that performance is objectively impossible, meaning no one can perform the contract. The fact that a particular contracting party cannot personally person is not sufficient.
- *Commercial Frustration*: Commercial frustration discharges a party if an unforeseen event destroys the value of and purpose for a contract. However, the occurrence of foreseeable events and the fact that a contract is simply made less profitable than expected do not excuse performance.
- *Actual Breach*: The complete (actual) breach of a contract by one party generally discharges the other party's obligation to perform.
- *Anticipatory Breach*: An anticipatory breach of contract is: 1) a definite, unqualified refusal to perform contractual duties 2) that is made prior to the time that performance is required.
- *Conditions*: A condition is an event that may create or discharge a contractual duty to perform. Conditions may be express or they may be implied from the nature of the contract or implied by law. Conditions are classified as conditions precedent, concurrent conditions, or conditions subsequent.

TYPES OF REMEDIES: The two types of contractual remedies are legal (damages) and equitable. The purpose of contractual remedies is to make a contracting party whole if the other party breaches.

DAMAGES: In a breach of contract, the injured parties are entitled to recover damages to compensate them for their foreseeable financial losses.

- *Compensatory Damages*: Compensatory damages place the injured party in the same economic position as if the contract had been performed.
- *Consequential Damages*: Losses that are suffered because of the parties' particular needs or circumstances are called consequential (special) damages. Consequential damages may be recovered only if they were reasonably foreseeable by the breaching party.
- *Duty to Mitigate*: An injured party has a duty to mitigate (minimize) its losses.
- *Punitive Damages*: Punitive damages cannot be recovered for a typical breach of contract.
- *Liquidated Damages*: A contract may validly state the amount of liquidated damages to be paid if a party breaches if: 1) the amount is reasonable and 2) it is difficult to foresee the amount of damages.
- *Nominal Damages*: Nominal damages are a token amount given for a minor breach.

EQUITABLE REMEDIES: Equitable remedies may be awarded when money damages are inadequate. Equitable remedies include:

- *Rescission and Restitution*: Rescission means termination of a contract. Restitution means the return of goods, money, property received under a contract (or their value if they cannot be returned).
- *Specific Performance*: Specific performance is a court order that requires contracting parties to perform their contract.
- *Quasi Contract/Reformation/Injunction*

LIMITATIONS ON REMEDIES: A contract may limit damages. Under UCC § 2-719, a contract may not provide for an exclusive remedy if such a remedy is inadequate. Also under UCC § 2-719, a contract may not limit remedies for consequential damages for personal injuries caused by defective consumer goods.

WAIVER OF BREACH: A contracting party may agree to accept less than complete performance by waiving a breach of contract that is committed by the other party.

STUDY HINTS FOR CALL-IMAGE TECHNOLOGY CASE STUDIES

The following study hints may be helpful when resolving the Call-Image Technology (CIT) case studies.

page 376
♦ You should review the material dealing with complete and substantial performance, and make sure that the contract specifically requires exact, complete performance.

page 381
♦ Recall, that a party cannot assert these defenses if the events in question are foreseeable. Therefore, careful wording of the contract may help minimize this potential problem.

page 393
♦ Consider the purpose and requirements for a valid liquidated damages clause. Pay attention to the material discussing whether parties can use liquidated damages to penalize a party.

MATCHING EXERCISE

Select the term or concept that best matches a definition or statement set forth below. Each term or concept is the best match for only one definition or statement.

Terms and Concepts

a. Condition
b. Discretionary
c. Election of remedies
d. Forfeiture
e. Indemnify

f. Insolvency
g. Novation
h. Prima facie
i. Remedy at law
j. *Respondeat superior*

k. Restitution
l. Specific performance
m. Treble damages
n. Unconscionable
o. Waiver

Definitions and Statements

_g_ 1. Substitution of a third party for one of the original parties to a contract.
_k_ 2. Return property or money previously received from another.
_e_ 3. Reimburse a person for expenses or liability already paid or incurred.
_n_ 4. Blatantly unfair.
_h_ 5. Something presumed to be true "on its face" unless disproved by contrary evidence.
_i_ 6. Money damages.
_o_ 7. Voluntary surrender of a legal right.
_l_ 8. Equitable remedy that compels parties to perform a contract.
_b_ 9. Freedom to make or not to make a decision.
_a_ 10. Event or act that may create or destroy the obligation to perform a duty.
_m_ 11. Damages multiplied three times; a remedy usually given by statute.
_d_ 12. Loss of a right or privilege that is imposed as a penalty for certain conduct.
_f_ 13. Inability to pay one's debts as they become due.
_c_ 14. Doctrine that requires a plaintiff to choose between two inconsistent remedies in order to prevent the plaintiff from recovering twice.
_j_ 15. Doctrine that holds employers liable for torts committed by employees while acting within the scope of their employment.

COMPLETION EXERCISE

Fill in the blanks with the words that most accurately complete each statement.

1. _Discharge_ is the termination of a contract or contractual duty.

2. When one contracting party breaches a contract, the other party generally has a _duty to mitigate_ its losses if it can reasonably do so.

3. _Consequential_ (special) damages are indirect damages that may result from a breach of contract due to the particular circumstances of the parties.

4. _Punitive_ damages are awarded in order to punish a wrongdoer and to deter future wrongdoing.

5. _Specific Performance_ compels a party to perform a contract and may be an appropriate remedy if the subject matter of the contract is unique and irreplaceable.

TRUE-FALSE EXERCISE

Write **T** if the statement is true, write **F** if the statement is false.

_T_   1. A party cannot recover consequential damages unless that type of loss was foreseeable.

_F_   2. Quasi contract is a remedy that is imposed by a court to prevent unjust enrichment.

_T_   3. If performance is contingent on the occurrence of a condition and that condition does not occur, the duty to perform is discharged.

_F_   4. Liquidated damage clauses are void and unenforceable.

_T_   5. Subject to certain exceptions, contracting parties are generally free to impose limits on the remedies that may be sought if there is a breach of contract.

_F_   6. A suggestion by one party that he or she might be unable to perform a future contractual obligation constitutes an anticipatory repudiation.

_T_   7. Specific performance is typically available for enforcing land sale contracts.

_T_   8. A court will discharge a contract under the doctrine of impossibility only if the event in question was unforeseeable.

_T_   9. A contract may be discharged if both parties agree to cancel or rescind the contract.

_F_   10. Courts commonly award punitive damages in breach of contract cases.

APPLICATION OF CONCEPTS

MULTIPLE CHOICE QUESTIONS

_____ 1. William, a CPA, contracted to provide accounting services for Tyler. William promised to perform the work to Tyler's personal satisfaction. William rendered the required services. A reasonable person in Tyler's position would be satisfied with the services, but Tyler is not. Under these facts:
   a. Tyler's contractual duties are discharged because he is dissatisfied with William's services.
   b. Tyler's contractual duties are discharged because personal satisfaction contracts are illegal and void.
   c. Tyler's contractual duties are not discharged because a reasonable person would be satisfied with William's services.
   d. a and b.

_____ 2. Which contract would be discharged under the doctrine of impossibility?
   a. Ventricle Corp. contracted to sell a heart medicine to Aorta. The contract was legal when made. Prior to performance, the FDA unforeseeably declared sale of the medicine illegal.
   b. Acme contracted to sell a standard Yomo stereo to Bob. Prior to performance, Acme's inventory of stereos was destroyed by a fire. Acme can obtain a replacement Yomo stereo elsewhere, but doing so will diminish Acme's profits on the contract.
   c. Larry contracted to buy a house. Prior to either party performing, Larry died.
   d. All of the above.

_____ 3. Juan contracted to sell coffee beans to the Wide-Eye Cafe each week. Delivery was required to be made every Friday. One week, Juan failed to deliver the beans until the following Monday, a breach of contract. The Wide-Eye Cafe waived Juan's breach. Under these facts:
   a. Wide-Eye Cafe cannot cancel the contract due to Juan's breach.
   b. Wide-Eye Cafe can cancel the contract due to Juan's breach.
   c. Wide-Eye Cafe has given up its right to insist that future deliveries be made on Friday in accordance with the contract.
   d. a and c.

_____ 4. Pat contracted to buy a boat from Steve for $6,500. A dispute arose regarding the amount of the debt because the boat failed to satisfy certain warranties. Later, Pat and Steve entered into a second agreement whereby Pat agreed to pay, and Steve agreed to accept, $4,000 as payment in full for the disputed debt. Under these facts:
   a. The second agreement is an accord.
   b. Pat's $6,500 obligation was discharged when the parties entered into the second agreement.
   c. Pat's $6,500 obligation will not be discharged until the second agreement is performed.
   d. a and c.

SHORT ANSWER QUESTIONS

Answer the following questions, briefly explaining the reason for your answer.

1. Theo contracted to build storage shelving for Casey. The shelving is not unique, and any carpenter can perform the work. As Theo was working on the shelving, he severely cut his hand and he cannot complete the work. Is the contract discharged under the doctrine of impossibility?

No. Event is not unforeseeable, other people can perform. Fayed the fact that he cannot personable perfor is not sufficient

2. Josh's Delivery Service contracted to buy a truck from Big Rig to use in its delivery business. Big Rig failed to deliver the truck on the required date, and it has informed Josh that delivery will be 5 days late. Discuss Josh's duty, if any, to mitigate his damages.

Josh has a duty to mitigate loss. He should try to obtain another truck and sue for any extra it cost incurred, due to the late delivery of the truck.

3. Leonardo, a sculptor, contracted with Albert, an eccentric millionaire, to cast a bronze sculpture of Albert. Albert told Leonardo how much the sculpture meant to him. The sculpture was a masterpiece; it received world acclaim. However, Albert is not pleased with the sculpture. Must Albert accept the sculpture and pay for it?

No. It is a personal contract which involve Albert's personal taste therefore he has the right to personally determine whether he is satisfied

4. Craftsman Co. contracted with Todd to build him a pool for $20,000. Craftsman had barely begun, when it quit the job. As a result of Craftsman's default, Todd lost $500 in permit fees. Todd hired another company to complete the work. Todd had to pay this company $23,000 to complete the work. What type of breach has Craftsman committed? For how much can Todd sue Craftsman Co.?

Actual Breach - He can sue for compensatory damages in the amt. of $3500

CASE PROBLEMS

Answer the following case problems, explaining your answers.

1. Mark contracted to purchase a business that drills for natural gas. After the parties entered into this contract, the price for natural gas declined significantly, making it unprofitable to operate the business. It is well known in the natural gas industry that prices can rise and fall sharply and unpredictably, although prices had never before fallen this low. (a) When can a contract be discharged under the doctrine of impossibility? (b) When can a contract be discharged under the doctrine of commercial frustration? (c) Can Mark discharge the purchase contract under either of these doctrines?

a) If an unforeseeable event makes it impossible for anyone to perform.
b) When an unforeseeable frustrate the essential purpose of the contract.
c. No. Mark should have foreseen the possibility of price fluctuation. Furthermore court do not make up for bad deals

2. Wainwright Construction contracted to build a house for the Johnsons for $100,000. Wainwright completed the house in accordance with the parties' contract, except it inadvertently painted the garage a different shade of white than the remainder of the house. It will cost the Johnsons $500 to hire someone else to repaint the garage the correct color. (a) Discuss the nature of Wainwright's contractual performance. (b) Can Wainwright enforce the contract or is the Johnsons' duty to pay discharged? (c) How much, if any, must the Johnsons pay?

a) He has substantially performed that can discharge the contract. The breach is immaterial and the and was not wilfully done. b) he can enforce the contract for the full amt.
c) The contract price less $500 for damages

CHAPTER 16   Formation of the Sales Contract: Contracts for Leasing Goods

---

CHAPTER REVIEW

INTRODUCTION: The Uniform Commercial Code (UCC) has been adopted in whole or in all part in all states. It has been adopted in order to modernize the law relating to a variety of commercial transactions, including sales, leasing of goods, banking, negotiable instruments (such as checks and negotiable promissory notes), secured transactions, and documents of title.

THE SCOPE OF ARTICLE 2: UCC Article 2 governs sale of goods.

A sale is a transaction in which 1) a seller passes title (ownership) to a buyer 2) for a price. The price may be any type of consideration, including the payment of money or exchange of goods or services. Goods are movable personal property, but do not include most forms of intangible property, such as money, investment securities (stocks and bonds), promissory notes, accounts receivable, and trademarks.

Article 2 governs sales between merchants (e.g., persons who deal in the type of goods being sold) and nonmerchants, and it governs sales of new and used goods. All parties are required to act in good faith and to cooperate with each other. Merchants must also act in a commercially reasonable manner.

FORMING THE CONTRACT: Sales contracts are basically formed in the same manner as other contracts except: 1) less formalities are required for sales contracts and 2) some special rules apply, especially if merchants are involved. For example, an acceptance may vary from the exact terms of the offer and yet still form a contract. Also, the courts may uphold a contract even if not all terms have been set forth as long as 1) the parties intended to contract and 2) there is a way to determine the essential terms. A seller may accept a purchase offer that requests prompt shipment by 1) promptly shipping the goods, 2) promptly shipping nonconforming goods, or 3) notifying the buyer that goods will be shipped.

- **Standard Form Contracts:** UCC § 2-207 states that an acceptance may form a contract even if its terms are not exactly the same as the offer. In this case, these general rules apply in most situations: 1) an acceptance cannot add or change terms if nonmerchants are involved; and 2) if both parties are merchants, then the acceptance can add minor, standard (not important) terms if the buyer has not or does not object and the offer is not expressly stated to be limited to its terms.
- **Firm Offers:** A firm offer is 1) an offer to buy or sell goods 2) made by a merchant 3) in a signed writing 4) which promises that the offer will not be revoked. A firm offer cannot be revoked for the time stated (not to exceed 3 months) and, if no time is stated, it cannot be revoked for a reasonable time. A firm offer is binding even if the offeree does not give consideration to keep the offer open.
- **Statute of Frauds:** A contract for the sale of goods for $500 or more must be evidenced by a writing to be enforceable. The writing must: 1) be signed by the party who is using the Statute of Frauds as a defense; 2) indicate that a contract has been made; and 3) state the quantity of goods involved. If both parties are merchants and one merchant sends the other merchant a sufficient writing confirming the contract, then the confirmation is binding on the merchant receiving it if the merchant does not object to it in writing within 10 days from its receipt.

    UCC § 2-201(3) provides that a writing is not required if the goods must be specially made and cannot be resold to another buyer and the seller has substantially started making the goods. Also, a sales contract is enforceable *to the extent*: 1) the defendant admits in legal proceedings that a contract existed, the goods have been delivered and accepted, or 3) the price has been paid and accepted.

When interpreting a sales contract, terms are determined in the following order of preference: 1) express terms, 2) course of performance (repeated performances under the present contract), 3) course of dealing (repeated performances under past contracts between the same parties), and 4) usage of trade (trade customs).

The parol evidence rule prohibits *contradicting* the terms a *final, complete* written sales contract by using evidence of prior oral statements or writings.

SPECIAL RULES UNDER ARTICLE 2: A contract is unconscionable if it is grossly unfair to one party. A court that finds a contract unconscionable may refuse to enforce the contract, refuse to enforce any unconscionable clauses, or limit the application of any unconscionable clause to avoid any unfair result.

- *Open Terms*: If the parties do not state a term in a sales contract, then the court may supply the missing term by referring to certain "gap-filling" provisions of the UCC that supply most missing terms. See UCC §§ 2-305 to 2-309.
- *Options*: Article 2 leaves some decisions, such as product mix and shipping arrangements, to the option of the buyer or seller.
- *Cooperation*: Failure to cooperate or interference with a party's performance can be treated as a breach of contract or excuse for delayed performance.

CONTRACTS FOR LEASING GOODS: UCC Article 2A governs contracts for the lease of goods. Many of the provisions of Article 2A are the same or similar to those stated in Article 2 relating to the sale of goods. Leases are generally classified as consumer leases or finance leases. A lease of goods for $1,000 or more must be evidenced by a writing to be enforceable.

STUDY HINTS FOR CALL-IMAGE TECHNOLOGY CASE STUDIES

The following study hints may be helpful when resolving the Call-Image Technology case studies.

page 408	◆ Review the scope of both Articles 2 and 2A when deciding how to advise the parties. ◆ Also, do not overlook the fact that two or more areas of law may be crucial to CIT's business.

page 417	◆ Before advising Amy and Tom, consider UCC § 2-207, and the textbook materials dealing with the battle of the forms. ◆ Also, consider the advantages of CIT using a standard form contract that includes all appropriate protections, such as a clause limiting the contract to terms stated in the CIT form.

page 424	◆ Review the material on cooperation of parties. While this should not be a problem, remember that sometimes the best business decision is *not* to fully assert one's legal rights. ◆ Consider whether the vendors have made a firm offer or are simply negotiating.

REVIEW OF KEY TERMS AND CONCEPTS

MATCHING EXERCISE

Select the term or concept that best matches a definition or statement set forth below. Each term or concept is the best match for only one definition or statement.

Terms and Concepts

a. Accommodation
b. Chose in action
c. Confirmation
d. Course of dealing
e. Course of performance

f. Firm offer
g. Investment security
h. Merchant
i. Open terms
j. Output contract

k. Parol evidence rule
l. Requirements contract
m. Seasonably
n. Unconscionable
o. Usage of trade

Definitions and Statements

_e_ 1. Repeated performances under a sales contract.
_f_ 2. Merchant's irrevocable offer to buy or sell goods.
_l_ 3. Contract that requires a seller to provide all of the goods that a buyer needs.
_a_ 4. Goods that are supplied for the convenience of a buyer.
_k_ 5. Rule that prohibits using prior oral or written statements to contradict the terms of a final, complete written contract.
_m_ 6. Occurring in a timely manner.
_o_ 7. Recognized and accepted practices in an industry.
_h_ 8. One who regularly deals in a particular type of goods.
___ 9. Intangible personal right, such as a claim for money under a contract.
_n_ 10. Grossly unfair.
_c_ 11. Written memorandum of an agreement.
_i_ 12. Terms that are omitted from a contract.
_j_ 13. Contract that requires a buyer to purchase all goods that a seller produces.
_d_ 14. Repeated performances by the parties under prior contracts.
_g_ 15. Investment that one expects to produce a profit primarily through the efforts of others.

COMPLETION EXERCISE

Fill in the blanks with the words that most accurately complete each statement.

1. Parties to a sales contract are required to act in __good__ __faith__.

2. When a firm offer does not state a specific time for which an offer will be kept open, then the offer is irrevocable for a __reasonable__ __time__.

3. The shipping of nonconforming goods to a buyer is not an acceptance of the buyer's purchase offer if the goods are sent as an _____.

4. An understanding in the lumber industry that a "2-by-4" piece of wood is not actually 2 inches by 4 inches is an example of a _Course_ _of_ _dealing_ .

5. The _Statute_ _of fraud_ requires contracts for the sale of goods for $500 or more to be evidenced by a writing to be enforceable.

TRUE-FALSE EXERCISE

Write **T** if the statement is true, write **F** if the statement is false.

_T_ 1. Merchants are required to cooperate in the performance of a sales contract.

_T_ 2. The UCC permits a person to accept an offer by performance.

_F_ 3. A sales agreement cannot be a legally binding contract if important terms are not stated in the parties' agreement.

_F_ 4. The shipment of nonconforming goods as an accommodation is a breach of contract.

_F_ 5. The UCC states that a contract between merchants always includes any new terms that are stated in the acceptance.

_T_ 6. As a general rule, parties may, by their conduct, create an enforceable sales contract.

_F_ 7. A firm offer may be oral or written.

_F_ 8. Under Article 2, only a formal written contract will satisfy the Statute of Frauds.

_T_ 9. If a contract includes an unconscionable term, then a court may choose to void the unfair clause and enforce the remainder of the contract.

_F_ 10. If a sales contract does not specify the place of delivery, then Article 2 states that delivery shall be made at the buyer's place of business.

```
APPLICATION OF CONCEPTS
```

MULTIPLE CHOICE QUESTIONS

_a_ 1. Jen offered to buy a truckload of Alberta peaches from Tom, requesting prompt shipment. Under the UCC, Tom can accept by:
   a. Promptly shipping the truckload of Alberta peaches to Jen.
   b. Notifying Jen that he will ship the Alberta peaches promptly.
   c. Promptly shipping a truckload of Hale Haven peaches to Jen.
   d. All of the above.

_a_ 2. When a sales contract is made between two merchants, a new term that is stated in the acceptance will not be part of the contract:
   a. If the new term is objected to by the offeror within a reasonable time.
   b. If the new term may require the offeror to do or pay anything.
   c. If the new term would materially alter the contract.
   d. a and c.

_C_ 3. Rick orally offered to sell his personal auto to Basil for $10,000 and Basil accepted. Later, Basil recanted, stating that he refused to perform the contract. In which situation would this oral contract be enforceable?

a. Rick had delivered the auto to Basil who had accepted it.

b. When Rick sued Basil to enforce the contract, Basil admitted at trial that the parties made this contract, but defended that the contract was oral.

c. In a signed writing, Rick stated that he sold the auto to Basil. Basil did not sign the writing.

d. a and b.

_C_ 4. LaDonna agreed to purchase a case of CDs from Roger. The parties did not state the price. Under these facts:

a. There is a contract and the price to be paid is whatever price LaDonna wants to pay.

b. There is a contract and the price to be paid is whatever price Roger demands.

c. There is a contract and the price to be paid is a reasonable price at time of delivery.

d. There is no contract because the agreement does not state the price for the goods.

SHORT ANSWER QUESTIONS

Answer the following questions, briefly explaining the reason for your answer.

1. Jamal offered to sell his used personal computer for $400 to his friend, Betty. Betty replied, "Let me think about it until Tuesday." Before Betty accepted, Jamal called her and stated that he revoked his offer. What law governs this transaction? Was Jamal legally entitled to revoke his offer?

UCC Article 2 governs this transaction because it is a contract of sale of good. Yes because the offeror can revoke anytime before acceptance

2. Centrex offered to sell a harvester to Carl for $50,000. The Centrex president made this offer in a signed writing. The offer stated that it would be held open for two days. Carl did not pay anything for Centrex's promise to keep its offer open. The next day, the Centrex president called Carl, stating that Centrex could not honor its offer and it was revoked. Was Centrex legally entitled to revoke its offer?

This is a firm offer (made in writing) therefore cannot be revoked for 'a reasonable time, even without consideration

3. Geneva orally contracted to buy her bridal gown from Michelle's Bridal Shoppe for $2,000. The dress was custom designed for Geneva and made from specially-ordered fabric. After the dress was partially done, Geneva called off the wedding and called Michelle's stating: "I don't need him, and I don't want the dress." Michelle's cannot resell the dress. Is the oral contract legally enforceable?

Yes. Although goods for more than $500 must be in writing, this does not apply because the goods was specially built and cannot be easily resold.

4. Shawna's Supply House orally agreed to sell Kim's Hair Salon 10 cases of shampoo for $500 per case. Shawna sent a signed, written letter to Kim, confirming the sale. Two weeks after receiving the letter, Kim wrote back, stating that she did not want the shampoo. Is the oral contract legally enforceable?

Yes. Kim did not object to the written agreement to [illegible] by Shawna within 10 days [illegible] the contract [illegible]

CASE PROBLEMS

Answer the following case problems, explaining your answers.

1. In a signed writing, Perrone's Farms agreed to supply all of the tomatoes that the Town Market needed for its two-week Harvest Festival sale. The agreement failed to state the time or place for delivery. (a) Did the parties' form a valid contract? (b) What type of agreement did the parties' enter into? (c) Determine the terms of the agreement, including price, quantity, and time and place of delivery.

a. Yes. The UCC will supply the missing part if a contract was intended
b. They entered into a valid requirement contract
c. Since the sale is open contract, UCC states that time would be a reasonable time (in time for the harvest) and the price the market forces.

2. John, a consumer, sent a purchase order for new skis to Sport Manufacturers. The order was silent regarding how disputes between the parties would be settled. Sport sent back a definite, unconditional acceptance that contained a new term not addressed in John's order. The new term stated that any disputes regarding the skis must be submitted to arbitration. John received the acceptance, but he never agreed or objected to the new term. (a) Did Sport's acceptance form a sales contract between John and Sport? (b) If a sales contract was formed, was the new term in the acceptance part of the contract? (c) What would the outcome have been if John had agreed to the new term?

a) Yes [illegible]
b) No. Since John is a non-merchant the new term is considered a proposal for him to consider [illegible]
c. If John had agreed to the new term, it would be a part of the contract.

CHAPTER 17

Performance, Title, and
Risk of Loss

```
CHAPTER REVIEW
```

PERFORMANCE OF A SALES CONTRACT: The parties must act in good faith and cooperate.

SELLER'S DUTIES: The seller's basic duty, to tender delivery of conforming goods, can be accomplished in five ways: 1) the buyer takes the goods from the seller; 2) the seller takes the goods to the buyer; 3) the seller ships the goods to the buyer; 4) a third party (bailee) has the goods and no documents of title are involved; or 5) a bailee has the goods and the seller must provide a document of title in order to get the goods.

STANDARD SHIPPING TERMS: The most commonly used shipping terms are:
- *FOB*: FOB place of shipment means the seller bears the expense and risk of loss for delivering the goods to a carrier. During shipment, the buyer bears the expense and risk of loss. FOB destination point means the seller bears the expense and risk of loss of shipping goods to the named destination.
- *FAS*: FAS means that a seller bears the expense and risk of loss for delivering goods alongside a named seagoing vessel. Title and risk of loss then pass to the buyer.
- *CIF and C & F*: CIF means the contract price includes the selling price and the cost of shipping and insurance to a named destination. C & F means that the contract price includes the price for the goods and the cost of shipping to a named destination.
- *COD*: COD requires the buyer to pay for the goods on delivery and before inspection.

INTERVENING RIGHTS: UCC § 2-513 gives the buyer the right to inspect goods. The buyer must conduct a reasonable inspection; failure to do so may operate as a waiver, requiring the buyer to perform. If the buyer notices a nonconformity, then the buyer must promptly notify the seller of the condition. If the time for performance has not expired, the seller has a right to cure the nonconformity.

BUYER'S DUTIES: A buyer must accept conforming goods; failure to do so is a breach of contract. There are four ways by which a buyer can accept goods: 1) the buyer signifies that the goods conform to the contract; 2) the buyer signifies that the goods are nonconforming, but that they will be kept and accepted; 3) the buyer fails to properly reject the goods if they are nonconforming; or 4) the buyer does any act that is inconsistent with a rejection, in other words, that is inconsistent with the seller's ownership of the goods. The buyer is allowed to pay in any normal manner, such as using a check or draft. If the seller demands cash, the seller must give the buyer a reasonable time to obtain the cash.

SPECIAL PROBLEMS: New sales techniques have created new problems including:
- *Sale on Approval*: Transaction allows a buyer to test goods for a stated time; a buyer may return the goods without obligation within this period. Title and risk of loss stay with a seller until acceptance.
- *Sale or Return*: In a sale or return contract, the buyer purchases the goods for resale; the buyer may return any unsold goods to the seller without obligation. Title and risk of loss stay with the buyer until the goods are returned.
- *Consignment*: This agreement allows a third person, the consignee, to sell goods for the owner.

- *Auctions*: An auctioneer sells goods for a third party; a sale is not complete until the auctioneer accepts a bid. In an auction "with reserve," the auctioneer may refuse to sell a good if the bids are not acceptable. In an auction "without reserve," the auctioneer must accept the highest bid.

TITLE TO GOODS: The UCC has limited the historical importance of title.
- *Modern Rule*: In a shipment contract, title passes at the time and place of shipment. In a destination contract, title passes when delivery is tendered at the destination. If the goods do not move, title passes on delivery of documents of title to the buyer; if no document exchange is required, title passes at the time and place the contract is·made.
- *Fraudulent Retention*: If after a sale the seller retains possession, the retention will be fraudulent unless the retention was made in good faith and for a commercially reasonable time.
- *Entrustment*: Entrustment is when a person gives possession of goods to a merchant who regularly buys and sells goods of that kind.
- *Insurable Interest*: Under the doctrine of insurable interest, an insurance policy on goods cannot be enforced unless the seller or buyer who purchased the policy has an insurable interest in the goods.

RISK OF LOSS: The rules vary depending on whether there is a breach of contract by either party.
- *Breach of Contract*: If the seller breaches, the risk of loss remains with the seller until the seller cures the defect or the buyer accepts the goods. If the buyer breaches, the risk of loss remains with the seller, but the buyer must compensate the seller for any loss that exceeds the seller's insurance coverage. If the buyer accepts the goods but later properly revokes acceptance of the goods, then the buyer bears the risk of loss, but the seller must compensate the buyer for any loss that exceeds the buyer's insurance coverage.
- *No Breach of Contract*: Under a shipment contract, the risk passes to the buyer when the goods are delivered to the carrier. Under a destination contract, the risk passes to the buyer when the goods are tendered at the destination.

LEASES: The concept of title is not important in determining the parties' rights under a lease of goods. Rules regarding the passing of risk of loss depend on whether the lease is a finance lease or other type of lease, whether or not the lessor is a merchant, and/or other factors.

STUDY HINTS FOR CALL-IMAGE TECHNOLOGY CASE STUDIES

The following study hints may be helpful when resolving the Call-Image Technology (CIT) case studies.

page 447	♦ Review the materials relating to concept of sale or return; especially issues relating to risk of loss. ♦ Before advising the parties, review how the law treats most consignments.

page 456	♦ Review Article 2A regarding leases of goods. In particular, focus on matters relating to warranties (covered elsewhere) and risk of loss.

MATCHING EXERCISE

Select the term or concept that best matches a definition or statement set forth below. Each term or concept is the best match for only one definition or statement.

Terms and Concepts

a. Bailee
b. CIF
c. Common carrier
d. Conclusive presumption
e. Document of title

f. Entrustment
g. Insurable interest
h. Knocking down
i. Repudiation
j. Reservation of title

k. Revests
l. Risk of loss
m. Tender
n. Unsecured creditor
o. Warehouseman

Definitions and Statements

_g_   1. Interest in goods that a buyer acquires as soon as existing goods are identified to the contract.
_h_   2. Process of acceptance of a bid by an auctioneer.
_m_   3. Offer to perform a duty.
_j_   4. Attempt by a seller to retain title until the buyer has fully performed the contract.
_n_   5. Creditor whose claim is not secured by collateral.
_o_   6. Person who is in the business of receiving and storing goods.
_l_   7. Legal responsibility for a financial loss that may result from a casualty to goods.
_k_   8. Vests again.
_a_   9. Contract price includes insurance and freight.
_____ 10. Person to whom goods are delivered with the understanding that they will be returned.
_f_   11. Delivery of goods to a merchant who regularly deals in goods of that kind.
_i_   12. Rejection of something.
_e_   13. Written evidence of ownership to goods being stored or shipped.
_____ 14. A binding inference of fact.
_c_   15. A company in the business of transporting goods or people for a fee and holding itself out as serving the general public.

COMPLETION EXERCISE

Fill in the blanks with the words that most accurately complete each statement.

1. Under a ___Consignment___, the owner of a good transfers it to another person who will try to sell the good on behalf of the owner.

2. Under a ___Sale___ ___on___ ___return___ contract, the buyer purchases goods primarily for resale, enjoying the right to return any unsold goods.

3. A seller has a right to ___cure___ a breach if the time for performance has not expired.

4. A _____ _____ _____ is a transaction whereby a buyer is allowed to test a product for a stated time, enjoying the right to return it without obligation to the seller within a stated time.

5. Identify four methods by which a buyer can accept goods:

a. by signifying that the goods conform to contract

b. " " that the goods don't conform but to retain & accept them

c. by failing to make proper rejection if they don't conform

d. By doing anything that is not consisting with the seller

TRUE-FALSE EXERCISE

Write **T** if the statement is true, write **F** if the statement is false.

_T_ 1. A buyer is generally entitled to inspect goods prior to payment unless goods are shipped COD.

_T_ 2. If a sales contract involves goods that are existing and identified at the time of contracting but a document of title is required to be delivered to the buyer, title and risk of loss do not generally pass to the buyer until the document of title is delivered to the buyer.

_F_ 3. In a CIF contract, title and risk of loss do not pass until goods are delivered at the destination.

_T_ 4. If a buyer purchases goods from a thief, then the buyer receives void (no) title, and the owner of the goods may recover the goods from the buyer.

_T_ 5. The buyer's right to reject goods on account of a minor nonconformity expires once the buyer has had a reasonable time to inspect the goods.

_T_ 6. In a FAS contract, a seller bears the expense of delivering goods alongside a named vessel.

_F_ 7. Seller owns an existing inventory of shovels, and Seller contracts to sell one unspecified shovel from this inventory. In this situation, the shovel sold is an existing and identified good.

_F_ 8. In a sale or return contract, the expense and risk of loss of returning goods is borne by the seller.

_F_ 9. In a FAS contract, title and risk of loss pass to a buyer at the time the contract is made.

_T_ 10. The fact that goods are shipped COD or that a seller retains a security interest in the goods does not affect when title or risk of loss will pass to a buyer.

APPLICATION OF CONCEPTS

MULTIPLE CHOICE QUESTIONS

_d_ 1. In which case did Buyer accept the goods in question?

a. Buyer bought a truck. During inspection, Buyer noticed that the truck was nonconforming. After using the truck for 9 months, Buyer told Seller that the truck was unacceptable.

b. Buyer bought an electric barbecue. When Buyer first attempted to use the barbecue, it did not work properly. Buyer immediately told Seller that the barbecue was unacceptable.

c. Buyer bought a computer. When the computer was delivered, Buyer discovered that the computer was nonconforming. Nonetheless, Buyer modified numerous significant internal components of the computer. Later, Buyer told Seller that the computer was unacceptable.

d. a and c.

_____ 2. On July 15, Seller contracted to sell a shipment of tools to Acme Co. The tools were not yet identified to the contract. As required by the contract, Seller duly delivered the tools to a carrier for shipment to Buyer on August 15. (Seller was Not required to deliver the tools at the destination.) On September 15, the shipment was delivered to Acme at the destination. Under these facts, when did title and risk of loss pass to Acme?
   a. July 15
   b. August 15
   c. September 15
   d. Never.

_____ 3. Art contracted to buy a sofa for $500 cash. Art is to take delivery at Seller's place of business where the sofa is located. Art has inspected and accepted the sofa. Under these facts:
   a. Art must pay for the sofa at the time of contracting.
   b. Art has the right to pay for the sofa by check, and Seller cannot demand payment in cash.
   c. Art may offer to pay by check if this is a normal method of payment. But, Seller can demand cash if Art is given a reasonable extension of time within which to obtain cash.
   d. Art must pay for the sofa in cash. Art cannot offer to pay by check even if this is a normal method of payment.

_____ 4. On May 1, John contracted to buy an existing, identified filing cabinet from Seller, a merchant. Documents of title were not involved. Seller was required to deliver the cabinet to John's place of business which was located in another city. On June 1, Seller delivered the cabinet to a carrier for shipment to John. On June 15, the cabinet was tendered to John at his place of business. Under these facts:
   a. Title passed to John on May 1.
   b. Title passed to John on June 1.
   c. Title passed to John on June 15.
   d. Title never passed to John.

SHORT ANSWER QUESTIONS

Answer the following questions, briefly explaining the reason for your answer.

1. Fran delivered her computer to Computer Traders, a merchant who regularly bought and sold used computers. Computer Traders was supposed to repair the computer. Instead, Computer Traders sold Fran's computer to Ted in the ordinary course of business. Did Ted receive title to the computer?

Yes. This was a trade of Entrustment. A merchant entrusted with goods has voidable title, and has legal power to transfer all the trustee right to a buyer in the normal course of business, in good faith

2. Jim, in Atlanta, contracted to sell peaches to Cindy in Chicago. The contract states that the peaches are sold "F.O.B. Atlanta." If the peaches are damaged during shipment, who bears the risk of loss?

The seller. The buyer bears the risk when the goods reach its destination - Atlanta

3. Kathy received an exercise bike from Seller pursuant to a sale on approval agreement. The agreement allows Kathy to test the bike for 14 days, and Kathy may return the bike at any time during this period. Kathy received the bike on June 1. Kathy shipped the exercise bike back to Seller on June 9. During shipment, the exercise bike was damaged. Does Kathy bear the risk of loss for the exercise bike?

No. This was a shipment of "sale on approval" usage, and title or risk never passed. Seller has risk

4. On May 1, Joan contracted to buy an existing, identified television from Seller, a merchant. Delivery was to be made at Seller's business. On June 1, Seller tendered delivery of the television to Joan, but Joan did not take the television. On July 1, Joan took physical possession of the television. When did Joan have an insurable interest in the television?

May 1. The buyer has an insurable interest in the goods as soon as it was in existence & identified

CASE PROBLEMS

Answer the following case problems, explaining your answers.

1. Jane delivered her car to Skweeky Kleen, a retail car wash, that does not normally buy or sell cars. Without Jane's permission, Skweeky Kleen sold her car to Buyer for $8,000, a fair price. Buyer did not know that the car belonged to Jane or that the sale was improper. Does Buyer receive title to the car?

No. The seller did not have good title therefore Buyer did not receive good title. Jane can recover her car from Buyer.

2. Tobacco Importers (TI) contracted to sell Cuban cigars to Al's Tobacco. On May 1 (the required delivery day), TI could not obtain the Cuban cigars, so they shipped a substitute cigar of similar quality. TI believed Al would be pleased with the substitutes. (a) What options does Al have with respect to the shipment? (b) What right does TI have with respect to the shipment?

a. Al has the right to accept the entire goods, reject the entire shipment, accept a commercial unit & reject the rest. If Al reject all or part of the goods, TI has the right to cure. and ship the correct cigars to Al within a reasonable time

CHAPTER 18

Warranties and Product Liability

CHAPTER REVIEW

Introduction: A warranty is a type of contractual promise that guarantees a degree of quality in the sale of goods. There are two types of warranties: express and implied.

Express warranties: An express warranty arises by virtue of the words or conduct of the seller. The promise or affirmation of fact made must also be part of the basis of the bargain.
An express warranty may be created by: 1) an affirmation of a fact or a promise about the product; 2) a description of the goods; or 3) a sample or model of the goods. The UCC does not require reliance by the buyer to create an express warranty. Express warranties focus on quantifiable (provable) facts, not opinions like "this is a good car."

Implied warranties: Implied warranties are not given by the seller. They are implied by law into a sales contract in certain cases. There are four types of implied warranties: warranty of title, warranty against infringement, warranty of merchantability, and warranty of fitness for a particular purpose.

- *Warranty of Title*: The UCC specifies that every seller of goods gives an implied warranty of title, unless this warranty is specifically excluded or the circumstances of the sale clearly indicate that the seller does not have clear title. The warranty of title assures the buyer that:
  1) the buyer will receive valid title to the goods being purchased;
  2) the seller has the legal right to transfer title to the buyer; and
  3) at the time of delivery of the goods to the buyer, the goods will not be subject to any liens that the buyer did not have actual knowledge of when entering into the contract.
- *Warranty Against Infringement*: This warranty guarantees against a rightful claim of infringement by any third person. Patent infringement is the most common type of problem in this area.
- *Warranty of Merchantability*: A merchant who regularly deals in goods of the kind being sold warrants that the goods are merchantable. The basic obligation imposed by the warranty of merchantability is that goods be "fit for the ordinary purposes for which such goods are used." This warranty assures buyers that the goods are suitable for normal and intended use.
- *Warranty of Fitness for a Particular Purpose*: This warranty obligates a seller to furnish goods that are reasonably suitable for performing a particular task intended by the buyer. This warranty arises if:
  1) a seller knows that a buyer is planning a particular use for the goods;
  2) the seller knows the buyer is relying on the seller's skill in selecting the goods; and
  3) the buyer does, in fact, rely on the seller's judgment in selecting the goods.

STATUTORY WARRANTIES: The Magnuson-Moss Warranty Act, a federal statute, provides that manufacturers must provide buyers with all warranty information prior to the sale. The manufacturer need not give any express warranties, but if a warranty is given, it must be designated as full or limited.

WARRANTY EXCLUSIONS: The seller can modify or exclude express warranties. One method of excluding express warranties is simply not to give a warranty at all. Otherwise, a seller may disclaim express warranties orally, in writing, or by conduct. When it appears that there may be both an express warranty and an attempt to exclude it, the courts try to reconcile the differences and give effect to both. When this is not possible, the express warranty is given effect.

The seller may disclaim the warranty of merchantability by following these three rules: 1) the disclaimer may be oral or in writing; 2) the disclaimer must mention "merchantability;" and 3) a written disclaimer must be conspicuous. The seller can disclaim the warranty of fitness for a particular purpose if: 1) the disclaimer is in writing and 2) it is conspicuous. Both of these implied warranties may be excluded by general language like "AS IS."

SCOPE OF WARRANTY PROTECTION: The UCC has extended warranty protection to persons who are not part of the sales contract. States may choose among three alternative provisions.

PRODUCT LIABILITY: In addition to warranty law, negligence and strict liability may provide remedies for people who are injured by defective and unreasonably dangerous products.

- *Negligence*: To establish a negligence claim against a manufacturer or seller of a product, a plaintiff must prove the basic elements of a negligence claim, namely: 1) duty, 2) breach of duty, 3) proximate cause, and 4) harm. In general, privity of contract (i.e., a direct contractual relationship between the plaintiff and defendant) is not required to sue based on negligence.

- *Strict Liability in Tort*: Strict liability is based on widely followed court cases that have adopted Rule 402A of the Restatement of Torts (Second).

    In general, Rule 402A imposes liability for personal injuries that are caused by a defective product if the following elements are established:
    1) The defendant manufactured or sold a product;
    2) The product was expected to and did reach the buyer or user in the same condition as when sold;
    3) The product had not been substantially altered or modified; and
    4) The product was defective and unreasonably dangerous.

LEASES: When goods are leased, the lessee receives certain warranties. These warranties are similar to those made in connection with the sale of goods.

STUDY HINTS FOR CALL-IMAGE TECHNOLOGY CASE STUDIES

The following study hints may be helpful when resolving the Call-Image Technology (CIT) case studies.

page 464
- ♦ When advising Tom, remember the ways in which express warranties can be created.
- ♦ Also, consider state and federal deceptive advertising laws.

page 471
- ♦ To determine the extent to which and how warranties can be excluded, you should review the Warranty Exclusions material.
- ♦ As a practical matter, CIT should also carefully monitor what competitors are doing with respect to warranties before it decides whether it wants to exclude warranties.

page 473
- ♦ Review the material dealing with negligence and strict liability as grounds for product liability.
- ♦ Consider the proper role for product warnings; particularly when they are required and the effect that they may have in sheltering a manufacturer from product liability.

REVIEW OF KEY TERMS AND CONCEPTS

MATCHING EXERCISE

Select the term or concept that best matches a definition or statement set forth below. Each term or concept is the best match for only one definition or statement.

Terms and Concepts

a. Conspicuous
b. Express warranties
c. Fungible

d. Implied warranties
e. Innately dangerous
f. Privity of contract

g. Warranty of fitness
h. Warranty of merchantability
i. Warranty of title

Definitions and Statements

_e_ 1. Product that is inherently dangerous.

_c_ 2. Goods that are interchangeable.

_b_ 3. Category of guarantees that arise due to the words or conduct of the seller.

_d_ 4. Category of guarantees that are imposed by law.

_i_ 5. Warranty that assures buyers that they will own a good free and clear of others' claims.

_h_ 6. Warranty that goods are fit for their ordinary, intended purposes.

_a_ 7. Obvious; stands out.

_f_ 8. Direct contractual relationship between two parties.

_g_ 9. Warranty that goods will fulfill a special use that is intended by the buyer.

COMPLETION EXERCISE

Fill in the blanks with the words that most accurately complete each statement.

1. Historically, buyers were not protected regarding the quality of goods. Rather, the controlling doctrine was _caveat_ _emptor_ .

2. In general, an express warranty is automatically considered to be _a basis_ _of_ _the_ _bargain_ , meaning part of the sales contract.

3. The _warranty_ _against_ _infringement_ guarantees a buyer that goods being sold do not violate others' patents.

4. The term "___as is___" will effectively exclude the implied warranties of merchantability and fitness for a particular purpose.

5. List two theories of tort law that may provide a remedy for persons who are injured by defective goods:

a. ___Negligence___.

b. ___Strict liability___.

TRUE-FALSE EXERCISE

Write **T** if the statement is true, write **F** if the statement is false.

___T___ 1. A seller's advertisement about goods can create an express warranty.

___F___ 2. An express warranty does not arise unless the buyer actually relies upon it.

___F___ 3. It is unlawful to exclude all warranties in a sale of goods.

___T___ 4. In general, it is implied that both merchants and nonmerchants make the implied warranty of title unless the sales contract specifically excludes it.

___T___ 5. A nonmerchant who sells a good does not make the implied warranty of merchantability.

___F___ 6. Under the implied warranty of merchantability, the "reasonable expectations test" is automatically breached if any foreign object is found in food.

___T___ 7. An implied warranty of fitness for a particular purpose does not arise unless the buyer actually relies on the seller's judgment in selecting goods.

___F___ 8. Only persons who are a party to the sales contract are protected by implied warranties.

___F___ 9. Whenever a person is injured by a product, the law presumes that the manufacturer liable for negligence.

___T___ 10. Under Rule 402A of the Restatement (Second) of Torts, a manufacturer may be strictly liable for injuries caused by its product, even if the manufacturer exercised all possible care in designing, manufacturing, and selling its product.

APPLICATION OF CONCEPTS

MULTIPLE CHOICE QUESTIONS

_____ 1. In which case is an express warranty made?
   a. The salesman for PainBgone aspirin states that, in his opinion, PainBgone aspirin is the best painkiller on the market.
   b. The salesman for the Belchfire 500 automobile states: "This car will go from zero to 60 miles per hour in six seconds."
   c. The salesman in the jeweler's shop states: "This diamond is one karat."
   d. b and c.

_____ 2. The warranty of merchantability is breached in which case?
   a. Juanita (a nonmerchant) sold Buyer a new toaster that Juanita had received as a gift. The toaster cannot toast bread.
   b. Seller (a merchant) sold an ordinary private airplane to Buyer. The airplane operates safely and it is fit for ordinary private use. However, the plane cannot perform acrobatic stunts.
   c. Manufacturer, a merchant, sold a portable plastic pool to Buyer. The pool leaks badly, and it cannot be repaired. However, Manufacturer was not negligent in making the pool.
   d. All of the above.

_____ 3. In which situation does Seller make an express warranty?
   a. During negotiations, Seller gave Byron a brochure regarding a ring that Byron was considering purchasing. The brochure stated that the ring was sterling silver.
   b. During negotiations for the sale of a drill, Seller stated to Buyer: "This drill is the best little drill on the market today." Seller did not say or do anything else.
   c. During negotiations for the sale of a chair to be specially manufactured, Seller showed Buyer a model of what the chair would be like. Seller did not say or do anything else.
   d. a and c.

_____ 4. Amigos Cafe sold Joe a guacamole taco. The taco had a piece of avocado pit in it. Although guacamole is made from avocados which have pits, an ordinary person would not reasonably expect to find a piece of an avocado pit in a guacamole taco. Under these facts:
   a. Amigos did not breach the warranty of merchantability; the UCC does not apply to sales of food.
   b. Under the natural substance-foreign substance test, the taco is fit (merchantable).
   c. Under the reasonable expectations test, the taco is fit (merchantable).
   d. b and c.

SHORT ANSWER QUESTIONS

Answer the following questions, briefly explaining the reason for your answer.

1. ZydiCo. manufactures accordions. It advertises in magazines that cater to accordionists. One of its advertisements states: "The ZydiCo. accordion cannot be topped." Is an express warranty created?

_____

_____

2. Brown Corp. manufactures bicycles for the national market. Brown manufactures the X-100, a mountain bike that retails for about $250, roughly the price charged for many mid-range mountain bikes. The X-100 functions fine on streets but it is unstable and unsafe to ride on unpaved terrain. Unaware of this problem, Gina bought an X-100. While riding her bike on a dirt trail, it unexpectedly flipped, throwing Gina to the ground and injuring her. Discuss Brown's potential warranty liability to Gina.

_____

_____

3. Len is an expert manufacturer of custom fly-fishing rods. Walt went to Len to purchase a rod. Walt explained his particular needs for a rod that would suit his unique fishing style, and he requested that Len make an appropriate rod. Len designed and manufactured a special rod for Walt. When Walt used the rod, he discovered that it was too stiff for his style of fishing. Has Len breached an implied warranty?

_____

_____

4. Bobbie needed a paint that could withstand unusual, prolonged heat. Bobbie developed a paint formula and furnished Acme Paints with specifications for the paint. Acme manufactured the paint in accordance with Bobbie's specifications, but the paint failed to accomplish its intended purpose. Is Acme liable for breach of the warranty of fitness for a particular purpose?

_____

_____

CASE PROBLEMS

Answer the following case problems, explaining your answers.

1. MicroView Inc., a maker of commercial microscopes, plans to sell a new microscope. MicroView is concerned about liability for implied warranties. MicroView asks you: (a) Can MicroView exclude the warranties of merchantability and fitness for a particular purpose, or are such exclusions unconscionable? (b) Can MicroView disclaim the warranty of merchantability by using a disclaimer in its contract that is the same size, type, and color of print as all other terms? (c) If MicroView's contracts conspicuously state that its microscopes are sold "AS IS," what effect would this term have on implied warranties?

_____

_____

_____

_____

2. Juan bought a new automobile. Juan drove the car for two years without any problems. However, Juan was recently rear-ended by a careless driver who was going 40 mph at the time of the impact. Juan's car burst into flames, severely injuring Juan. If Juan sues the car manufacturer for his injuries based on strict liability, what is the likely outcome of the suit? Explain.

_____

_____

_____

_____

CHAPTER 19   Remedies

```
┌─────────────────────────────────────────┐
│              CHAPTER REVIEW               │
└─────────────────────────────────────────┘
```

THE REASON FOR REMEDIES: Remedies are available because some contracts may not be performed as agreed. Remedies minimize the effects of a breach if it occurs.

SELLER'S REMEDIES: A seller's remedies may be broken down in terms of the remedies that are available if the buyer breaches before accepting the goods (preacceptance remedies) or the buyer breaches after accepting the goods (postacceptance remedies). In general, the seller may choose one or more of the remedies discussed below under each of these categories.

- *Preacceptance Remedies of the Seller*: If the buyers breach before they accept the goods, then a seller may choose one or more of the following remedies (depending on the facts of the particular case):
  1) withhold delivery of goods still in the seller's possession;
  2) stop delivery of goods in transit to the buyers;
  3) sue for incidental damages;
  4) sue for the contract price (which includes the right to identify goods to the contract and the right to complete making goods);
  5) resell goods the seller has in his or her possession (provided the sale is commercially reasonable and the buyer is given notice of the sale) and sue for the contract price minus the resale price; and
  6) sue for damages due to the breach (lost profits for volume sellers or the difference between the contract price minus market price).

     In situations 5) and 6) above, the seller may also cancel the contract and any future contractual duties that the seller may have under the contract.
- *Postacceptance Remedies of the Seller*: If the buyers breach the contract after they have accepted the goods, then remedies available to the seller are:
  1) sue for the unpaid contract price; and/or
  2) sue to reclaim (recover) the goods if: (a) the buyers are insolvent and the seller asserts the claim within ten days of delivery or (b) the buyers misrepresented their solvency in writing.

BUYER'S REMEDIES: A buyer's remedies, in the event of a breach by the seller, may also be broken down into preacceptance and postacceptance remedies.

- *Preacceptance Remedies of the Buyer*: If the seller breaches before the buyer accepts the goods, the buyer may:
  1) sue for incidental damages;
  2) claim identified goods still in the seller's possession if the seller became insolvent within ten days after receiving the buyer's payment;
  3) cancel the contract and any future contractual duties of the buyer;
  4) sue for damages equal to market price minus contract price;
  5) cover (buy substantially similar replacement goods within a reasonable time and in a commercially reasonable manner) and sue for the difference between cover price minus contract price;
  6) sue to recover the goods from the seller by suing for either specific performance (if goods are unique) or replevin (if goods are essential to the buyer's business); and
  7) resell nonconforming goods that are in the buyer's possession (in certain situations).

- *Postacceptance Remedies of the Buyer*: When the seller breaches the sales contract after the buyer has accepted the goods, then the buyer may:
  1) revoke acceptance of the goods if the nonconformity substantially impairs the goods' value; and
  2) either (a) sue for damages due to the nonconforming goods (in accordance with the rules stated above for preacceptance); or (b) deduct damages from the contract price to cover the buyer's loss.

MODIFICATIONS: In general, the parties may limit the remedies that are available if a party breaches the contract (e.g., a buyer's remedies may be limited to the seller's repairing or replacing a defective good).

The parties may also state in their contract a fixed amount of liquidated damages that are to be paid in the event of a breach. However, liquidated damages are appropriate only if: 1) they are reasonable and 2) the difficulty of setting the loss is substantial and establishing the actual loss would be inconvenient. A contract may limit consequential damages (except for personal injuries involving consumer goods).

SPECIAL PROBLEMS: Special problems associated with sales contracts include:
- *(Anticipatory) Repudiation*: Parties repudiate a contract when they indicate that they will refuse to perform a contract when the time for performance arrives. If the repudiation will substantially reduce the value of the contract, the nonrepudiating party may: 1) postpone performance for a commercially reasonable period of time; 2) treat the repudiation as an immediate breach and seek remedies; or 3) suspend performance until the problem is resolved.
- *Excused Performance*: A seller's performance may be excused if contract performance becomes impracticable. Performance is impracticable if an event has occurred which was not foreseen by either party and it renders performance unreasonably burdensome. Performance is also excused if a party must comply with a government order.
- *Adequate Assurances*: An insecure party may demand, in writing, an assurance from the other parties that they intend to perform. The insecure party may suspend performance until assurance is given, and may treat the contract as repudiated by the other parties if an assurance is not given in 30 days.
- *Duty to Particularize*: If a buyer rejects nonconforming goods, the buyer must state what the defect is. A failure to do so will preclude the use of that defect to prove breach if the seller could have cured.

STATUTE OF LIMITATIONS: A lawsuit for a breach of contract must begin within 4 years of the breach. The contract may specify a shorter period, but not less than 1 year.

LEASES: Article 2A specifies remedies in the event that the lessor or lessor breach the lease contract.

STUDY HINTS FOR CALL-IMAGE TECHNOLOGY CASE STUDIES

The following study hints may be helpful when resolving the Call-Image Technology (CIT) case studies.

page
487
♦ Review the *limited* postacceptance rights of a seller to reclaim goods from a buyer.

page
490
♦ Review the concepts of anticipatory repudiation and requests for an adequate assurance.

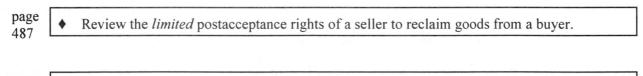

page
497
♦ Review the concept of a buyer's duty to particularize.

MATCHING EXERCISE

Select the term or concept that best matches a definition or statement set forth below. Each term or concept is the best match for only one definition or statement.

Terms and Concepts

a. Adequate assurance
b. Anticipatory repudiation
c. Consequential damages
d. Cover

e. Duty to particularize
f. Excused nonperformance
g. Liquidated damages
h. Reject

i. Remedies
j. Replevin
k. Specific performance
l. Substantially impair

Definitions and Statements

_____ 1. Promise or guarantee that a party will perform as promised.
_____ 2. Buyer's obligation to describe alleged defects so that the seller may cure.
_____ 3. Buying substitute goods from another source within a reasonable time of the breach.
_____ 4. Assortment of awards that may be granted to prevent or make up for harm resulting from a breach of contract.
_____ 5. Refusal to accept goods.
_____ 6. Definite and certain assertion that a party does not intend to perform the contract when performance becomes due.
_____ 7. Defense to performance of a contract because performance has become impracticable or impossible.
_____ 8. Court order directing a seller to perform a contract relating to unique goods.
_____ 9. Court order directing a seller to deliver contract goods that are unavailable elsewhere.
_____ 10. Significant reduction in the value of goods.
_____ 11. Damages that arise due to the particular circumstances of the parties.
_____ 12. Amount of damages stipulated in the contract.

COMPLETION EXERCISE

Fill in the blanks with the words that most accurately complete each statement.

1. A party who is reasonably insecure regarding the intent or ability of the other party to perform a sales contract may make a written demand upon the other party for an _____ _____.

2. In general, a party has _____ _____ within which to file an action for breach of a sales contract.

3. A seller may reclaim goods from a buyer if the buyer is insolvent and the seller reclaims the goods within _____ _____ after delivery of the goods to the buyer.

4. A buyer may sue for _____ of the goods being sold pursuant to a sales contract if the goods are not readily available elsewhere.

5. A buyer may revoke his or her acceptance of nonconforming goods only if the nonconformity

_____ _____ the value of the goods.

TRUE-FALSE EXERCISE

Write **T** if the statement is true, write **F** if the statement is false.

_____ 1. If a seller refuses to deliver goods, a buyer is always entitled to specific performance.

_____ 2. A nonbreaching party's cancellation of a sales contract does not release the breaching party from his or her duty to perform the contract.

_____ 3. In certain situations, buyers may resell nonconforming goods that are in their possession.

_____ 4. In general, a sales contract may limit or exclude consequential damages.

_____ 5. A party who makes an anticipatory repudiation may, in some cases, retract the repudiation.

_____ 6. A seller may be excused from performance of a contract, if such performance is made illegal.

_____ 7. The UCC forbids liquidation of damage clauses in sales contracts.

_____ 8. A sales contract can limit the remedies that will be available if a party breaches the contract.

_____ 9. A buyer may revoke acceptance of goods on the basis on any minor or major nonconformity.

_____ 10. A buyer must cover whenever the seller breaches a sales contract.

```
APPLICATION OF CONCEPTS
```

MULTIPLE CHOICE QUESTIONS

_____ 1. Stan sold his personal motorcycle to Buyer for $5,000. Prior to delivery or payment, Buyer breached the contract and refused to take the cycle. After the breach, Stan properly held a public sale and sold the cycle for $4,500. Stan had to pay a $500 commission to the auctioneer who conducted the sale. Under these facts, Stan can recover how much in damages?
   a. $0.
   b. $500.
   c. $1,000.
   d. $5,000.

_____ 2. Acme Wares sold a stove to Kitty for $600. Kitty refused to accept the oven and breached the contract. Acme would have made a profit of $300 on the sale. At the time the oven was tendered to Kitty, the oven's market price was $500. Under these facts, Acme can recover how much in damages?
   a. $0.
   b. $100.
   c. $300.
   d. $500.

_____ 3. Henry bought a power drill from Seller for $500. *Prior to paying*, Henry properly rejected the drill due to Seller's breach. Henry purchased an identical drill elsewhere for $550. Under these facts, Henry can recover how much in damages?
   a. $0.
   b. $50.
   c. $550.
   d. Nothing, Henry's only remedy was to sue for specific performance.

_____ 4. Seller sold a set of encyclopedias to Betty for $1,000. Betty accepted the encyclopedias and loves reading them, but she refuses to pay any portion of the purchase price. The market price for the encyclopedias is $900. Under these facts, Seller may sue for:
   a. $0.
   b. $100.
   c. $900.
   d. $1,000.

SHORT ANSWER QUESTIONS

Answer the following questions, briefly explaining the reason for your answer.

1. A&A Orchards agreed to sell its apple crop to Royal Grocery next month. A few days later, the Financial News reported that Royal officials had stated that Royal may soon declare bankruptcy. Discuss what A&A should do in this case.

_____

_____

2. Jake purchased two ostriches that were warranted to be a "proven breeder pair." Jake accepted the ostriches. Jake accepted the birds not knowing that they were actually both males (it is quite difficult to determine the gender of ostriches). A few months later, Jake discovered that both birds were male. Briefly discuss Jake's rights in this case.

_____

_____

3. Jodi sold Vincent a car load of Italian figurines to be delivered by train and picked up by Vincent in New York. Jodi discovered that Vincent went insolvent just after she delivered the figurines to the carrier for shipment. Discuss Jodi's rights in this case.

_____

_____

4. Alta contracted with Farmer Fred to buy a specific crop of carrots. Fred had sprayed this crop with Alart, a powerful insecticide. After the parties made this contract, the EPA passed a regulation that made it illegal to sell vegetables sprayed with Alart. Discuss the parties' rights in this situation.

_____

_____

CASE PROBLEMS

Answer the following case problems, explaining your answers.

1. Hotshot Chile Dogs has a contract to buy Cardoza chiles from Chile's Inc. Chile's has lots of Cardoza chiles but wrongfully refuses to sell them to Hotshot. Cardoza chiles are in short supply this year and Hotshot cannot replace them. Hotshot has already lost $10,000 lost profits because of Cardoza's breach and, if Hotshot does not obtain these chiles soon, it may be forced out of business. Analyze Hotshot's remedies in this case.

_____

_____

_____

_____

2. Hilda purchased a Sturtz piano from Mistro Music Store. Mistro warranted that the piano was solid cherry. The piano was to be delivered on May 1. On April 20, Mistro delivered the piano to Hilda. The next day, Hilda discovered that the piano was actually pine, stained with a cherry finish. Under these facts: (a) What should Hilda do to protect her rights in this case? (b) Discuss Mistro's right to cure its error in this case. (c) If Mistro refuses to cure its error, briefly discuss Hilda's potential remedies.

_____

_____

_____

_____

CHAPTER 20 International Sale of Goods

CHAPTER REVIEW

INTRODUCTION: There are three major legal systems in the world: 1) common law, 2) civil law, and 3) Islamic law. Historically, the existence of these different legal systems has created confusion for international traders.

THE UNITED NATIONS CONVENTION ON CONTRACTS FOR THE INTERNATIONAL SALE OF GOODS (CISG): The goal of the CISG is to provide a uniform law for international sales of goods. The CISG is the controlling law if both parties to a contract come from nations that have ratified the CISG. The CISG permits contracting parties to state that a particular nation's law governs questions relating to their contract.

OBLIGATIONS UNDER THE CISG: International business people should familiarize themselves with the CISG because it is different from U.S. contract law and the UCC. In particular, the CISG has different rules governing when an offer may be revoked and when an offer is properly accepted. Also, the CISG does not require a written agreement for the sale of goods.

- *Obligations of the Seller*: In a carriage contract, the seller must deliver goods to the carrier. Otherwise, the seller must place goods at a location known to both parties. Goods are conforming if: 1) they are fit for their normal and intended purpose; 2) they are fit for a particular purpose about which the seller knew; and 3) they are properly packaged. A buyer has two years to detect a hidden defect and reject the goods.
- *Obligations of the Buyer*: Unless the contract specifies otherwise, a buyer must pay the price generally charged for similar goods. If the price is based on weight, net weight is used. The buyer must pay the seller at the seller's place of business.

REMEDIES UNDER THE CISG: Remedies are governed by CISG Section III.

- *Remedies for Breach by the Seller*: If the seller fails to deliver conforming goods, the buyer may: 1) require the seller to perform; 2) give the seller more time to perform; 3) avoid the contract; 4) reduce the price for the goods; or 5) refuse delivery if the goods are delivered early.
- *Remedies for Breach by the Buyer*: If the buyer wrongfully fails to accept delivery or fails to pay for the goods, the seller may:
  1) require the buyer to pay the contract price, take delivery of the goods, and/or perform other obligations of the buyer;
  2) give the buyer additional time to perform; or
  3) avoid the contract.
- *Damages*: If the buyer must purchase replacement goods due to a breach by the seller, the buyer's damages equal the difference between the price of the replacement goods and the contract price. Otherwise, damages equal the difference between the current price of the goods and the contract price.

ISO 9000: The International Standards Organization (ISO) issued ISO 9000 is a comprehensive review process and guidelines to govern the quality standards of goods sold internationally. There are presently five international standards concerning quality management and quality assurance in the production process.

ETHICAL ISSUES IN THE INTERNATIONAL SALE OF GOODS: Unlike the United States and other common law nations, civil law nations require good faith during contract formation and negotiation. The CISG requires that the Convention be interpreted in "good faith." Unlike the Uniform Commercial Code, the CISG allows a party to deduct the value of an obvious defect even if the party did not give timely notice of the defect. The CISG also allows parties more time to discover hidden defects.

STANDARD SHIPPING TERMS IN INTERNATIONAL TRADE (INCOTERMS): There are four major categories of incoterms:

- *"E" Terms*: EXW requires the seller to furnish goods at the seller's place of business. EXW does not obligate the seller to load goods on a carrier or clear the goods for export. The buyer bears all risks.
- *"F" Terms*: There are three basic "F" terms: 1) FCA requires a seller to deliver goods to a carrier and clear them for export; 2) FAS requires a seller to place goods alongside a named vessel and 3) FOB requires a seller to clear goods for export; the risk of loss passes to the buyer once the goods are placed on board the carrier.
- *"C" Terms*: There are four "C" terms: 1) CFR requires the seller to clear the goods for export and pay the freight cost - the risk of loss passes to the buyer when the goods are loaded on a vessel; 2) CIF imposes the same obligations as CFR, and also requires the seller to insure the goods during transport; 3) CPT requires the seller to make shipping arrangements and pay for freight charges to the named destination; the risk of loss passes to the buyer once the goods are delivered to the carrier; and 4) CIP imposes the same duties as CPT, and also requires the seller to insure the goods to protect the buyer.
- *"D" Terms*: There are five "D" terms: 1) DAF requires the seller to clear the goods for export and make goods available at a named location, but before passing customs of the next country; 2) DES requires the seller to make the goods available for the buyer on board a ship at a named port, but before passing customs; 3) DEQ requires the seller to place goods on a dock and clear them for import; 4) DDU requires the seller to deliver goods to a named destination and the seller pays all fees except import fees; and 5) DDP requires the seller to deliver the goods to a named destination and cleared for import with all fees paid.

PROPOSED INTERNATIONAL COVERAGE: Two proposed international treaties are: 1) Convention on International Bills of Exchange and Promissory notes, which is intended to establish and govern a new international negotiable instrument (such as a promissory note); and 2) ISO 14000, which is intended to set environmental standards for goods that are internationally traded.

STUDY HINTS FOR CALL-IMAGE TECHNOLOGY CASE STUDIES

The following study hints may be helpful when resolving the Call-Image Technology (CIT) case studies.

♦ Review the scope of the CISG. In particular, contrast the applicability of the CISG when CIT is doing business with foreign firms who are from member nations and when CIT is doing business with foreign firms who are not from member nations.

page 517

♦ Review the material dealing with damages under the CISG.

116

CHAPTER 20 - INTERNATIONAL SALE OF GOODS

REVIEW OF KEY TERMS AND CONCEPTS

MATCHING EXERCISE

Select the term or concept that best matches a definition or statement set forth below. Each term or concept is the best match for only one definition or statement.

Terms and Concepts

a. CISG

b. Civil law

c. Common law

d. Convention

e. Incoterms

f. Islamic law

g. Promissory estoppel

h. UNCITRAL

i. UNIDROIT

Definitions and Statements

_____ 1. System of law that relies heavily on case law and judicial interpretation.

_____ 2. Convention that establishes uniform rules for international sales of goods.

_____ 3. Legal system based primarily on codes; case law is not a major factor.

_____ 4. U.N. Conference on International Trade.

_____ 5. Treaty or other international agreement that is accepted by two or more nations.

_____ 6. International Institute for the Unification of Private Law.

_____ 7. Contract theory that prevents a promisor from denying that a promise was made because the promisee justifiably relied on the promise.

_____ 8. System of law followed by many nations in the Middle East and other parts of the world.

_____ 9. Category of international commercial terms.

COMPLETION EXERCISE

Fill in the blanks with the words that most accurately complete each statement.

1. Civil law nations require that parties exercise _____ _____ when creating and performing a contract.

2. Many international transactions require payment by a _____ _____ _____.

3. In general, the U.S. legal system is based on the _____ _____.

4. _____ are international commercial terms that are only applied if the parties contractually agree to use them.

5. Identify the four basic categories of incoterms.

a. _____.

b. _____.

c. _____.

d. _____.

TRUE-FALSE EXERCISE

Write **T** if the statement is true, write **F** if the statement is false.

_____ 1. The provisions of the CISG are identical to those of the UCC.
_____ 2. The ISO 9000 establishes a process for creating quality standards for goods.
_____ 3. Under the CISG, an offer is irrevocable if the offeree in fact relied on the offer remaining open.
_____ 4. Under the CISG, a buyer has up to two years to notify the seller of a hidden defect.
_____ 5. Under the CISG, an offer is effective when it reaches the offeror.
_____ 6. Conduct that is considered preliminary negotiations under the UCC may be a binding contract under the CISG.
_____ 7. In general, the CISG does not apply to a sale of goods for personal or household use.
_____ 8. The CISG requires that goods be fit for a particular purpose if the seller was aware of the purpose at the time of contracting.
_____ 9. All incoterms require the buyer to pay for import costs and fees.
_____ 10. Incoterms are part of the CISG and automatically apply to all international contracts for the sale of goods.

```
APPLICATION OF CONCEPTS
```

MULTIPLE CHOICE QUESTIONS

_____ 1. Hakeem lives in a nation that has ratified the CISG. He contracted with B&E Electronics, a U.S. firm, to purchase computers. When Hakeem received the computers, he noticed a defect. At the time, he could not telephone B&E and inform them of the problem because his country's telephone system had a serious problem. Under these facts:
   a. Hakeem may reduce the price of the goods because he had a reasonable excuse for not giving B&E notice of the defect.
   b. Hakeem must fully perform the contract.
   c. Hakeem may avoid the contract because of commercial impracticability.
   d. Hakeem may avoid the contract because of *force majeure*.

_____ 2. Acme Corp., a U.S. company, made the following offer to Escabar Aircraft, a Spanish company: "Willing to sell 100 altimeters to you, but you must accept within ten days." The offer was not signed. Under these facts:
   a. Acme may revoke the offer at any time.
   b. Spain is a civil law nation. Thus, Acme can revoke the offer only for a good faith reason.
   c. The offer is irrevocable for ten days because the offer states that acceptance must be made within a certain time.
   d. The offer is irrevocable for a reasonable period of time.

_____ 3. Under the CISG, an oral contract for the sale of goods over $500 is:
   a. Enforceable.
   b. Enforceable only if made in good faith.
   c. Unenforceable because it violates the Statute of Frauds.
   d. Illegal and void.

_____ 4. Which incoterm requires the seller to deliver the goods to a named destination with all fees paid, except for import fees and costs which are borne by the buyer?
   a. DAF.
   b. DDP.
   c. DES.
   d. DDU.

SHORT ANSWER QUESTIONS

Answer the following questions, briefly explaining the reason for your answer.

1. On May 1, Roger, a U.S. merchant, sent Francois, a French buyer, an offer to sell some books. The offer was not a firm offer or option, and Roger was free to revoke the offer at any time. On May 2, Francois placed his acceptance in the mail. On May 3, Roger sold the books to another buyer. On May 6, Roger received Francois's acceptance. Under CISG rules, do Roger and Francois have a contract?

_____

_____

2. C&R, a U.S. firm, negotiated to sell a mainframe computer to Primero, a Mexican company. C&R orally offered to sell the computer for $10,000, and Primero orally accepted. The next day, C&R told Primero it could not sell the computer for the stated price and that it was revoking its offer. Under the CISG, do C&R and Primero have a contract?

_____

_____

3. FPRC, a Canadian company, purchased a data storage system from DataStor, a U.S. company. The system has been in place for 18 months, and a hidden defect has just caused the system to "crash," resulting in a major loss. Can FPRC still claim assert that the system did not conform to the contract?

_____

_____

4. Emilio, a U.S. restaurant owner, entered into a contract with La Cuccina, an Italian maker of food processors, to purchase a commercial food processor. La Cuccina assumed Emilio would use the food processor in his restaurant. Emilio actually intended to use it in his home. Does the CISG control this sale?

_____

_____

CASE PROBLEMS

Answer the following case problems, explaining your answers.

1. Jesse's Auto Parts, a U.S. company, entered into a contract for the sale of auto parts with a company in Lesotho. Jesse wants U.S. law to control the transaction and has asked for your advice. In resolving the problem, use the following analysis: (a) Are both companies located in nations that have ratified the CISG? (b) Why is it important to determine if both nations have ratified the CISG? (c) What should Jesse have done to assure that U.S. law would govern this transaction?

_____

_____

_____

_____

2. Allison, president of Household Furnishings, and Raul, a Mexican buyer, entered into negotiations for the sale of furniture. Allison orally offered to sell Raul 50 computer desks for $100 each. Raul told her that he had some commercial buyers who might be interested. He said he would talk to the potential buyers, but he needed an assurance that Allison would keep her offer open. Allison told Raul that she currently had no other buyers interested in the desks. The next day, a U.S. buyer offered Allison $150 each for the desks. Allison called Raul and told him her offer was now $150 per desk. Raul said he already had several orders for the desks at $100 each. (a) Under the UCC, would Allison's offer be irrevocable? (b) Under the CISG, is Allison's offer irrevocable?

_____

_____

_____

_____

CHAPTER 21

Introduction to Negotiables: UCC (Revised) Articles 3 and 7

```
╔══════════════════════════════════════════╗
║              CHAPTER REVIEW                ║
╚══════════════════════════════════════════╝
```

HISTORIC OVERVIEW: Commercial paper historically included 1) negotiable instruments that are used to represent obligations to pay money and 2) negotiable documents that are issued in connection with the commercial shipping and storage of goods. Today, these important types of commercial documents are governed by the UCC.

THE SCOPE OF ARTICLE 3: A negotiable instrument (instrument) is an unconditional written promise or order to pay money that satisfies the requirements for negotiability stated in UCC § 3-104. UCC Article 3 governs negotiable instruments, but does not govern money, documents of title, or securities.

USES OF NEGOTIABLE INSTRUMENTS: Generally, negotiable instruments are used as a substitute for money to pay bills and buy goods and services, and for credit transactions. Instruments include:
- *Checks*: Checks include: 1) a draft that is payable on demand and is drawn on a bank; 2) a cashier's check, which is a draft drawn by a bank on itself; 3) a teller's check, which is typically a draft drawn by a bank on another bank; 4) a negotiable money order; and 5) a traveler's check which is an instrument that is (a) payable on demand, (b) drawn on (or payable at or through) a bank, © called a "traveler's check or similar name, and (d) requires, as a condition to payment, the countersignature by the person whose signature appears on the instrument.
- *Drafts*: Drafts are instruments whereby the party issuing the instrument orders another party to pay money. Drafts include sight drafts (payable on demand) and time drafts (payable at a future date).
- *Promissory Notes*: A promissory note is an instrument that states a party's promise to pay money.
- *Certificates of Deposit*: A certificate of deposit is a note issued by a bank that: 1) acknowledges receipt of money from a customer; and 2) states the bank's promise to repay the money.

FUNCTIONS AND FORMS: Commercial paper serves as a substitute for money and as a credit instrument.

PAPER PAYABLE "TO ORDER" ("THREE-PARTY PAPER"): Drafts and checks state an order to pay money and involve three parties: 1) the drawer who originally signs a draft or check, ordering 2) the drawee to pay the amount of the draft or check to 3) the payee, the person originally named on the face of the instrument.
- *Drafts*: The drawer issues a draft to the payee, who presents the draft to the drawee, requesting payment.
- *Checks*: A check is a special type of draft and it has two features that distinguish it from other drafts; 1) it is payable on demand and 2) the drawee must be a bank or it is payable at or through a bank.
- *The Order:* Drafts and checks must generally state an order (demand) that the drawee pay the payee.
- *The Drawer*: The person who issues an instrument is called the drawer.
- *The Drawee*: The drawee does not have a legal obligation to pay a draft or check until the drawee "accepts" the instrument.
- *The Payee*: The payee is the person to whom the instrument is originally issued, and the payee may direct the drawee regarding how and to whom to make payment.

PROMISE PAPER ("TWO-PARTY PAPER"): Promise or "two-party" paper is an instrument that states a person's unconditional promise to pay money to another. There are two parties in a promise paper, the maker and the payee.

- *(Promissory) Notes*: A note is a credit instrument in which the maker promises to pay the payee a sum of money on demand or at a later time. Payment may be made in installments or in a lump-sum.
- *Certificates of Deposit*: A certificate of deposit is a special type of note that is issued by a bank acknowledging the receipt of money, and promising to pay it back at a future date with interest. Traditionally these were negotiable instruments commonly issued by banks, but they have largely been replaced by saver's certificates, which are not negotiable.
- *The Promise*: The promise to pay must be unconditional.
- *Maker*: The maker is the person who issues the promise paper and is the person who has the obligation to pay it.
- *Payee*: The payee is the person to whom the note is originally issued.

THE SCOPE OF ARTICLE 7: Article 7 of the UCC governs documents of title. The two main types of documents of title are warehouse receipts and bills of lading.

FUNCTIONS AND FORMS: A document of title is used to define the rights of the owner when goods are turned over to someone else's custody. The documents also facilitate the transfer of title to such goods. When the owner negotiates a (negotiable) document of title to another person, the owner is transferring ownership of the goods covered by the document to the other person.

- *Warehouse Receipts*: A warehouse receipt is a writing issued by a warehouseman (issuer) that 1) acknowledges receipt of goods for storage from a customer (depositor) and 2) states the terms of the parties' contract.
- *Bills of Lading*: A bill of lading is issued by a carrier who is transporting goods. The consignor is the person who arranges the transportation, the consignee is the person who will receive the goods, and the issuer is the carrier.

STUDY HINTS FOR CALL-IMAGE TECHNOLOGY CASE STUDIES

The following study hints may be helpful when resolving the Call-Image Technology (CIT) case studies.

page 536
- ♦ Before advising Tom and Anna, review the permissible uses of negotiable instruments.
- ♦ Also, bear in mind the concept of "freedom of contract."

page 544
- ♦ To the extent that your advise may relate to the negotiable instruments, review the material dealing with checks and see how credit union checks are treated.

page 549
- ♦ Whether or not to grant the requested credit terms is basically a business decision. For when the buyer receives the negotiable bill of lading, the buyer will generally be entitled to possession of the goods, whether the buyer has paid or not.

REVIEW OF KEY TERMS AND CONCEPTS

MATCHING EXERCISE

Select the term or concept that best matches a definition or statement set forth below. Each term or concept is the best match for only one definition or statement.

Terms and Concepts

a. Acceptance
b. Consignee
c. Consignor
d. Draft

e. Drawee
f. Drawer
g. Holder
h. Issuer

i. Maker
j. Note
k. Presentment
l. Warehouse receipt

Definitions and Statements

_j_ 1. Written promise to pay a sum certain in money without conditions, on demand or at a future date, payable to order or bearer.

_d_ 2. Written order directing a third person to pay a sum certain in money without conditions, on demand or at a future date, payable to order or bearer.

_g_ 3. Person to whom an instrument is negotiated.

_k_ 4. Demand for acceptance or payment of an instrument.

_a_ 5. Agreement by a drawee to accept and/or pay an instrument.

_l_ 6. Document of title acknowledging receipt of goods for storage.

_c_ 7. Party who ships goods to another party.

_b_ 8. Party to whom goods are shipped.

_h_ 9. Person who, in general, creates and originally delivers any type of instrument.

_i_ 10. Person who issues a note.

_f_ 11. Person who issues a three-party instrument.

_e_ 12. Person who is ordered to pay a three-party instrument.

COMPLETION EXERCISE

Fill in the blanks with the words that most accurately complete each statement.

1. The parties to a note are the _Maker_ and the _Payee_ .

2. A _check_ is a special form of draft which is payable on demand and is payable by, at, or through a bank.

3. When goods are turned over by the owner to another party's custody, a _Document of title_ is issued to define the parties' rights to the goods.

4. A carrier issues a _____Bills of cading_____ for goods that are received for shipment.

5. Four basic types of negotiable instruments are:
   a. ___Checks___.
   b. ___Drafts___.
   c. ___Promissory note___.
   d. ___C Ds___.

TRUE-FALSE EXERCISE

Write **T** if the statement is true, write **F** if the statement is false.

___F___ 1. Cash is one form of negotiable instrument.

___T___ 2. UCC Article 3 governs negotiable instruments and Article 7 governs documents of title.

___T___ 3. Three-party paper includes drafts and checks.

_____ 4. A preaccepted check is one that the drawee has already agreed to pay.

___T___ 5. Two-party paper states an unconditional promise to pay money.

___F___ 6. A certificate of deposit is one type of three-party paper that is be issued by a bank and contains an unconditional order to pay on demand.

___T___ 7. Notes are commonly used to evidence a debt obligation owed by the maker to the payee.

_____ 8. Credit union checks are one type of instrument that is governed by Article 3.

___T___ 9. Traveler's checks are not instruments and, therefore, they are not governed by Article 3.

___T___ 10. A party who stores goods belonging to another issues a warehouse receipt for the goods, a form of document of title governed by UCC Article 7.

APPLICATION OF CONCEPTS

MULTIPLE CHOICE QUESTIONS

_____ 1. Wilson sold goods to Brown for $1,000 on credit. Wilson issued a negotiable instrument that ordered Brown to pay the $1,000 on October 1. Brown signed the instrument, agreeing to pay as ordered. This instrument is a:
   a. promissory note.
   b. trade acceptance.
   c. check
   d. certificate of deposit

_____ 2. Myers issued a promissory note to Hays. In this case:
   a. Myers is the drawer.
   b. Myers is the maker.
   c. Hays is the payee.
   d. b and c.

_____ 3. Rankin issued a check that was drawn against his account at Last Bank. The check was issued to Douglas. In this case:
   a. Rankin is the maker.
   b. Last Bank is the drawer.
   c. Last Bank is the drawee.
   d. a and c.

_____ 4. Penny Ward issued an instrument that read: "August 1, 1999. John Haskins, you are hereby instructed to pay to the order of Steve Schwartz the sum of One Hundred Dollars ($100.00). /signed/ Penny Ward." This instrument is a:
   a. certificate of deposit.
   b. promissory note.
   c. draft.
   d. check.

SHORT ANSWER QUESTIONS

Answer the following questions, briefly explaining the reason for your answer.

1. Lites Abound Corp. sold 50 lamps to Jerry for $1,000 on credit. Lites Abound issued a document ordering Jerry to pay the $1,000 to Third Bank on July 1. What type of instrument is this document? Discuss Jerry's legal obligation, if any, to pay this document before he accepts it and after he accepts it.

A. draft. Jerry has no obligation to pay prior to acceptance. After acceptance - he will be primarily liable to pay

2. Burton issued a check drawn on his account with First State Bank. The check ordered the bank to pay Roger $100. When Roger presented the check for payment, the bank refused to pay. Discuss the bank's legal obligation, if any, to pay this check.

The bank is not obligated to the payee - unless the drawer has sufficient funds.

3. Carla Imports, located in Los Angeles, delivered goods to Bonded Carriers for shipment. The goods were to be shipped to Ajax Distributors, located in Chicago. A negotiable bill of lading for the goods was issued to the order of Ajax. Carla then forwarded the bill of lading to Ajax. Discuss the rights of the parties to the goods.

Ajax has the right to receive the goods in accordance with the terms of the document title.

4. Kendall Corp., located in Seattle, was sending a sales representative to Atlanta to make calls on customers. Kendall also owed $10,000 to a creditor who was located in Atlanta, and Kendall decided to have its sales representative deliver the payment personally. Kendall had just received a large cash payment from a customer. Kendall is trying to decide whether it should pay in cash or by check. What would you advise? Explain your answer.

Payment in check is much safer than in cash, pay to the order of the creditor

CASE PROBLEMS

Answer the following case problems, explaining your answers.

1. Smithson issued an instrument that was drawn on his account with the Old Yorker Bank. The instrument was issued to the order of Molly, a creditor of Smithson, and it ordered the Old Yorker to pay $250 to Molly. While going to the Old Yorker Bank, Molly lost the instrument. (a) What type of instrument did Smithson issue? (b) Discuss the rights and duties of Old Yorker to pay this instrument.

Check. As the Drawee, the bank has no legal obligation to Molly to pay the check prior to acceptance.

2. Transatlantic Truckers accepted 300 crates of canned crab from Connecticut Crabbers for shipment to Supermarkets Galore in Montana. Transatlantic gave Connecticut Crabbers a document listing the contents and other relevant information regarding the shipment. The document stated 300 crates were received for shipment. Inexplicably, only 270 crates arrived in Montana. (a) What type of document did Transatlantic issue? (b) What is the purpose of this document? (c) Who is liable for the shortage?

(a) Bill of lading (b) reflects ownership rights (c) Transatlantic

---

CHAPTER REVIEW

FORMAL REQUIREMENTS FOR NEGOTIABILITY: ARTICLE 3: One of the fundamental concepts of Article 3 and the law relating to negotiable instruments is the concept of holder in due course (HDC). This is because a HDC is entitled to enforce payment of an instrument without being subject to many defenses that would ordinarily allow others to escape their duty to pay. However, no one can be a HDC unless several requirements are met. The first requirement is that the paper in question must satisfy the six elements for negotiability stated in UCC § 3-104.

In general, paper is a negotiable instrument only if it meets the following six requirements: 1) the instrument is written; 2) it is signed by the drawer or maker; 3) it contains an unconditional promise to or order to pay; 4) a fixed sum of money; 5) it is payable on demand or at a definite time; and 6) it is payable to bearer or to the order of a party. If any element is missing, the paper is not a negotiable instrument and the person demanding payment cannot enjoy the rights of a HDC.

- *Writing Requirement*: An instrument must be in writing to be negotiable, but it does not have to be a formal or preprinted form; any writing may satisfy this requirement.

- *Signature Requirement*: To minimize forgery, the UCC requires an instrument to be signed by the maker or drawer, but any mark made with the intent to authenticate the writing suffices.

- *Unconditional Promise or Order Requirement*: Courts often use the "four-corner rule" to determine whether the promise or order in an instrument is unconditional. This means they look only to the instrument itself. If the instrument states that it is governed by or "subject to" terms of another writing, it is conditional and not negotiable. Also, if payment is conditioned upon some event occurring that is not absolutely certain to occur, then it is not negotiable. However, payment can be limited resort to a particular fund without rendering it nonnegotiable.

- *Sum Certain Requirement*: As long as the amount to be paid is calculable from the information on the instrument, it satisfies the sum certain requirement and is negotiable.

- *Fixed Amount of Money Requirement*: The instrument must be payable in money which is defined to be the currency of any country. The interest to be paid may be stated as an amount, or as a fixed or variable interest rate. An instrument that does not expressly require payment of interest is presumed to be interest free.

- *Determinable Time Requirement*: The payee or holder of an instrument must be able to tell from looking at the instrument when it is payable. The instrument must be either payable at a definite time or be payable "on demand." An instrument is payable on demand if it states that it is payable on sight, at presentment, or when no time for payment is stated. Language indicating that the instrument is payable after a future event of uncertain date renders the instrument nonnegotiable.

- *Words of Negotiability Requirement*: In general, an instrument must contain words of negotiability, meaning it must actually use the words either "pay to order" or "pay to bearer" or equivalent words, such as "pay to cash."

CONSTRUCTION AND INTERPRETATION: ARTICLE 3: Revised Article 3 attempts to foresee problems of interpretation that will arise frequently with negotiable instruments by setting out simple rules of interpretation. For instance UCC § 3-114 states: 1) handwritten terms control over typed or printed terms; 2) typewritten terms control over printed terms; and 3) words control over numbers.

REQUIREMENTS FOR NEGOTIABILITY: ARTICLE 7: Under Article 7, a document of title is negotiable if: 1) the document states that the goods are to be delivered to "bearer" or to "order" of a named person; and in international trade, it is negotiable if it runs to a named person or assigns.

STUDY HINTS FOR CALL-IMAGE TECHNOLOGY CASE STUDIES

The following study hints may be helpful when resolving the Call-Image Technology (CIT) case studies.

page 560
- ♦ Review the formal requirements for negotiability, including the writing requirement and the signature requirement.
- ♦ As a practical matter, consider how CIT can maintain security over a mechanical or computerized system for executing company checks.

page 536
- ♦ To answer John, review the requirements for negotiability.
- ♦ As a practical matter, consider alternatives to John's suggestion for protecting CIT, such as making payment only after the component parts have been inspected.

REVIEW OF KEY TERMS AND CONCEPTS

MATCHING EXERCISE

Select the term or concept that best matches a definition or statement set forth below. Each term or concept is the best match for only one definition or statement.

Terms and Concepts

a. Bearer
b. Fixed sum of money
c. Four-corner rule

d. Holder
e. Money
f. Order

g. Signature
h. Unconditional
i. Words of negotiability

Definitions and Statements

_i_ 1. "Pay to order" or "pay to bearer."

_g_ 2. Mark or symbol made with the intent to authenticate a writing.

_c_ 3. Doctrine requiring that a document be interpreted solely by reference to its stated terms and without reference to outside events or other documents.

_h_ 4. Absolute, without limitation.

_b_ 5. Determinable amount of money that can be calculated from the terms of an instrument.

_d_ 6. Person to whom an instrument has been negotiated.

_a_ 7. Person who possesses an instrument that is payable to bearer or cash.

_f_ 8. Written instruction to pay money signed by the person giving the instruction.

_e_ 9. Currency of any recognized country.

COMPLETION EXERCISE

Fill in the blanks with the words that most accurately complete each statement.

1. A _non-negotiable_ instrument is one that fails to satisfy one or more of the requirements for negotiability.

2. A negotiable promissory note must be signed by the _maker_ , and a negotiable draft must be signed by _drawee_ .

3. In order to be a negotiable instrument, paper must state that it is payable in some form of

Writing.

4. Under the _____ - _____ rule, negotiability of paper must be determined solely by reference to the terms of the instrument itself.

5. If the typed terms of an instrument conflict with preprinted terms, then the _Typed_ terms will generally prevail.

TRUE-FALSE EXERCISE

Write **T** if the statement is true, write **F** if the statement is false.

___F___ 1. Paper that is issued in the United States, but payable in French francs, cannot be negotiable.

___T___ 2. Paper that promises to pay "six months after my college graduation" cannot be negotiable.

___T___ 3. Paper that promises to pay "$500 on delivery of the television" cannot be negotiable.

___F___ 4. Negotiable instruments may be payable in money, goods, or services.

___T___ 5. All negotiable drafts are payable on demand.

___T___ 6. Paper that is not payable to the order of a specific person or to bearer (or cash) cannot be negotiable.

___T___ 7. If no time for payment is stated, an instrument is payable on demand.

___T___ 8. Paper that states that it is payable "with interest," without stating the amount of interest to be paid, cannot be negotiable.

___F___ 9. Paper that states that it is secured by collateral cannot be negotiable

___F___ 10. A bill of lading stating "200 boxes of macaroni to be delivered to bearer" cannot be negotiable.

APPLICATION OF CONCEPTS

MULTIPLE CHOICE QUESTIONS

_____ 1. Jason issued a check which promised to "pay to the order of Sam Turner Five Hundred Dollars ($50.00)." How much is Sam entitled to be paid?
   a. $0.
   b. $50.
   c) $500.
   d. Whatever amount Jason decides to pay.

_____ 2. Ramsey Corp. wanted to borrow $5,000 from Kim. A promissory note was written out in longhand. The note stated that Ramsey Corp. promised to pay $5,000 on demand to the order of Kim. Ron Waters, President of Ramsey Corp., was authorized to sign the note and he signed it:

Ramsey Corp.
By _____
Ron Waters, President of Ramsey Corp.

    a. The note is nonnegotiable because it is handwritten.
    b. The note is nonnegotiable because it is only signed by an agent of Ramsey Corp.
    c. The note satisfies the writing and signature requirements and it may be negotiable.
    d. a and b.

_____ 3. Which of the following terms in a promissory note would render the note nonnegotiable?
    a. Maria signed a note promising to pay $1,000 to the order of Jasmine. The duty to pay is subject to the terms of a separate loan contract made between Maria and Jasmine.
    b. Kyle signed a note promising to pay $1,000 and 100 bushels of wheat.
    c. Pete signed a note promising to pay $1,000, plus interest equal to the prime rate charged by Last Bank on January 1.
    d. a and b.

_____ 4. Bill issued paper which stated: "August 1, 1999. I promise to pay to Jane Smith the sum of $500 with 10 percent interest from date. /signed/ Bill Adams." Is this paper a negotiable instrument?
    a. No, because it does not state a time for payment.
    b. No, because it does not use words of negotiability.
    c. No, because it does not expressly state that the promise to pay is unconditional.
    d. Yes.

SHORT ANSWER QUESTIONS

Answer the following questions, briefly explaining the reason for your answer.

1. Martin purchased a gas station. Martin issued a $50,000 promissory note to the seller. The note stated that Martin's duty to pay was conditioned upon him obtaining a zoning change to expand the station. Is the promissory note negotiable?

_____

_____

2. Albert contracted to paint Johnson's house. Johnson issued and signed a promissory note to Albert that read in part, "I promise to pay to the order of Albert $2,000 on demand. This note arises out of a contract for painting services entered into by the parties on August 10, 2001." Is this a negotiable promissory note?

_____

_____

3. Harry contracted to repair Tina's car. Tina issued and signed a promissory note to Harry that read in part, "I promise to pay to the order of Harry Harrison the amount that is due pursuant to our contract dated July 1, 1999, together with 10% interest thereon until paid in full." Is this a negotiable promissory note?

_____

_____

4. Jennifer issued a check payable to the order of Acme Corp. for $100. Jennifer, however, stated on the check that it was nonnegotiable. Is the check a negotiable instrument?

_____

_____

CASE PROBLEMS

Answer the following case problems, explaining your answers.

1. Clarence Wellington III issued a promissory note to Alice stating: "I promise to pay to the order of Alice Haskins the sum of $500 on November 15, 2000. /signed/Clyde" Clarence used a pencil to write the promissory note on a piece of scratch paper. (a) Identify the six required elements of a negotiable instrument. (b) Is this promissory note negotiable?

_____

_____

_____

_____

2. Builders West, a contractor, hired Sparky, an electrician, to do the electrical work on an office project. According to their contract, Builders is obligated to pay Sparky $4,000 upon signing of the contract, with the balance payable upon completion of the project. The balance to be paid is undetermined and will be computed on an hourly rate after Sparky has completed his work. At Sparky's request, Builders issued a promissory note that stated, "Builders West promises to pay to the order of Sparky all sums due under its subcontract. Payment to be made 10 days after completion of the office project. /signed/Builders West. (a) Is the promissory note negotiable? (b) Does the promissory note represent a legal obligation to pay? (c) Does it matter whether the promissory note is negotiable or nonnegotiable?

_____

_____

_____

_____

CHAPTER 23   Negotiation and Holders in Due Course/Holders by Due Negotiation

---

CHAPTER REVIEW

TRANSFER: Negotiable instruments are transferred by assignment or negotiation.

An assignment of an instrument is fraught with uncertainties because the assignee (the person who receives the instrument) takes it subject to any claims or defenses that the obligor (the person required to pay the instrument) may be able to assert against the assignor (the person who transferred the instrument). Negotiation, on the other hand, allows the transferee to become a holder and, perhaps, a holder in due course (HDC).

NEGOTIATION: Negotiation means the transfer of an instrument by one party (other than the maker or drawer) to a second party, in such a manner that the second party becomes a holder of the instrument.

What must be done to negotiate an instrument depends on the form of the instrument at the time it is transferred from one party to a second party. Negotiation may be accomplished in the following two ways: 1) If at the time of transfer the instrument is payable to bearer or cash ("bearer paper"), it may be negotiated by the authorized transfer of possession by the person who has possession of the instrument (an indorsement is NOT required); or
2) If at the time of transfer the instrument is payable to the order of a named person, then: (a) the named person must indorse (sign) the instrument and (b) the named person must authorize its transfer.

INDORSEMENTS: In general, an indorsement is any signature on an instrument, other than that of the maker, drawer or acceptor. Any of these indorsements by a holder is sufficient to negotiate the instrument. However, the different types of indorsements may affect how the instrument is subsequently negotiated and also affect the liability of the indorser.

Types of indorsements include:

- *Special Indorsements*: A special indorsement is the signature of the indorser, together with words that specify an identified person to whom the instrument is next payable. A special indorsement: 1) passes ownership; 2) imposes liability on the indorser to pay the instrument if it is not properly paid by the maker or drawer; and 3) gives rise to certain implied warranties by the indorser. Following a special indorsement, negotiation of the instrument requires both indorsement and authorized transfer.
- *Blank Indorsements*: A blank indorsement is any indorsement that does not state an identified person to be paid. Typically, it is the indorser's signature without any other words. A blank indorsement generally has the same legal effect as a special indorsement EXCEPT that following a blank indorsement, an instrument is bearer paper and may be negotiated by transfer of possession alone.
- *Restrictive Indorsements*: A restrictive indorsement limits how the proceeds of an instrument may be applied. For instance, the restrictive indorsement "for deposit only" requires that the depository bank (first bank taking the instrument) to deposit the funds in a named account.
- *Qualified Indorsements*: A qualified indorsement is an indorsement that includes the words "without recourse" or similar language indicating that the indorser denies liability to pay the instrument.

HOLDER: A holder is a party who 1) possess a negotiable instrument, 2) that is drawn, issued, or indorsed either to the party, to bearer, or in blank.

HOLDER IN DUE COURSE: A holder in due course (HDC) is a holder who takes the instrument 1) for value, 2) in good faith, and 3) without notice of any defenses or defects.

- *For Value*: Value includes: 1) actually performing a promise for which an instrument is issued; 2) taking an instrument as security for, or in payment of, an existing debt; 3) taking an instrument in exchange for another instrument; or 4) undertaking an irrevocable obligation of a third party in exchange. An unperformed promise is not value, even if it would be consideration for a contract.
- *In Good Faith*: Good faith is honesty in fact in the transaction. A holder lacks good faith if the holder 1) actually knew of a defect in the instrument or 2) ignored facts that would show such a defect.
- *Without Notice of Defenses or Defects*: Notice is present if a reasonable person would know or have reason to know that there may be a defense, conflicting claim or ownership, or other defect.

EFFECT OF HOLDER IN DUE COURSE STATUS: On occasion, a person who has liability to pay an instrument will assert a legal defense in order to avoid this liability. Any defense, whether personal or real, can be used to negate the right to be paid of a mere holder. A HDC, however, is subject only to real defenses.

- *Personal Defenses*: Personal defenses include failure of consideration, contract defenses that render an obligation voidable, fraud in the inducement, breach of contract, breach of warranty, and nondelivery.
- *Real Defenses*: Real defenses include: 1) the contractual defense of infancy (minority); 2) other contractual defenses, such as duress or illegality, that would render a contractual obligation void under state law; 3) fraud in the execution; 4) discharge in insolvency (bankruptcy); 5) forgery of a person's signature; and 6) a subsequent material alteration of the instrument, *to the extent of the alteration*.

STATUTORY LIMITATIONS: Under FTC rules, if a transaction involves consumer credit, a holder or HDC is subject to *all* personal and real defenses that could be raised against the transferor.

HOLDER BY DUE negotiation: The holder of a duly negotiated document of title is a holder by due negotiation. A document of title has been duly negotiated if: 1) the holder purchased it in good faith and 2) without notice of any conflicting claims to the goods. Such a holder has the following rights: 1) title to the document; 2) title to the goods; 3) all rights under the laws of agency or estoppel; and 4) the right to have the goods held or delivered according to the terms of the document and free of any claims.

STUDY HINTS FOR CALL-IMAGE TECHNOLOGY CASE STUDIES

The following study hints may be helpful when resolving the Call-Image Technology (CIT) case studies.

page 583
- ◆ Before advising John, review the material dealing with restrictive indorsements.

page 586
- ◆ Review the material dealing with qualified indorsements.
- ◆ Also, Article 4, which deals with bank-customer transactions, may be relevant to this issue.

page 594
- ◆ Review the material on statutory limitations.
- ◆ Careful drafting may allow CIT to use only one form and still comply with the law.

MATCHING EXERCISE

Select the term or concept that best matches a definition or statement set forth below. Each term or concept is the best match for only one definition or statement.

Terms and Concepts

a. Blank indorsement   e. Holder in due course   i. Real defenses
b. Convert   f. Indorsement   j. Restrictive indorsement
c. Delivery (authorized)   g. Negotiation   k. Special indorsement
d. Holder   h. Personal defenses   l. Qualified indorsement

Definitions and Statements

_d_ 1. Person in possession of a negotiable instrument that is drawn, issued, or indorsed to the party, to bearer, or in blank.

_g_ 2. Transfer of a negotiable instrument in such a manner that the transferee becomes a holder.

_i_ 3. Defenses that may be asserted against a HDC.

_a_ 4. Indorsement that does not specify the party to be paid.

_j_ 5. Indorsement that limits how the proceeds shall be applied.

_e_ 6. Holder that takes an instrument free of personal defenses.

_b_ 7. Wrongfully take or hold.

_l_ 8. Indorsement that does not impose signature (contractual) liability to pay.

_f_ 9. Signature on a negotiable instrument that is made by someone other than the drawer or maker.

_k_ 10. Indorsement that specifies the next party to be paid.

_h_ 11. Defenses that cannot be asserted against a HDC.

_c_ 12. Intentional transfer of a right or physical possession of a thing to another person.

COMPLETION EXERCISE

Fill in the blanks with the words that most accurately complete each statement.

1. A check that states "pay to the order of cash" is _bearer_ paper.

2. A person to whom an instrument is negotiated is a _holder_ .

3. _Good_ _faith_ means that a holder took an instrument with no actual knowledge or reason to suspect that something was wrong with the instrument or its transfer.

4. A ___Specific___ ___Endorsement___ is made when a person merely indorses his or her name to an instrument.

5. Identify the two requirements for negotiating an instrument that is payable to the order of a named person:

a. ___authorized delivery / transfer by the holder___.

b. ___proper signature___.

Write **T** if the statement is true, write **F** if the statement is false.

___F___ 1. An ordinary holder does not have any right to demand or enforce payment of an instrument.
___F___ 2. A person has notice of a fact only if the person has actual knowledge of the fact.
___F___ 3. Under FTC rules, a HDC who has an instrument that arose out of a consumer credit transaction takes it subject to all defenses.
___T___ 4. A forgery is a real defense that may be asserted against a HDC.
___F___ 5. A holder who promises to do something has given value.
___F___ 6. A personal defense cannot be asserted against a holder or a HDC.
___T___ 7. Fraud in the inducement is a personal defense.
___T___ 8. Illegality that would render a contractual obligation void under state law is a real defense and may be asserted against a HDC.
___T___ 9. A person who takes an instrument after it has come due cannot be a HDC.
___F___ 10. It is illegal to negotiate an instrument that is overdue.

APPLICATION OF CONCEPTS

MULTIPLE CHOICE QUESTIONS

_____ 1. In which case did Bill give value sufficient to be a holder in due course?
a. Samantha issued a check to Paul. Paul indorsed the check, and delivered it to Bill as a gift.
b. Tammy issued a check to Rod. Rod indorsed the check and delivered it to Bill in payment for services Bill promised to perform for Rod. Bill has not performed these services.
c. Travis issued a negotiable note payable to Priscilla. Priscilla indorsed the note and negotiated it to Bill in payment of an existing debt that she owed Bill.
d. b and c.

_____ 2. Meg issued a negotiable note to Perry. Perry negotiated the note to Charles who paid value for the note. Which additional fact would prevent Charles from being a HDC?
a. The note was due May 1, and the note was negotiated to Charles on June 1.
b. When the note was negotiated to Charles, he knew that Meg had already refused to pay it.
c. One day after the note was negotiated to Charles, Meg told him that she refused to pay.
d. a and b.

_____ 3.   In which case does Marie have a personal defense?
   a.   Marie issued a check to Norm as payment for work that he improperly performed.
   b.   Marie issued a check to Rick due to his physical abuse. This abuse is duress and would render the obligation void under state law.
   c.   Marie's checkbook was stolen by a thief, and the thief forged her signature to a check.
   d.   All of the above.

_____ 4.   In which case does Monica have a real defense?
   a.   While mentally incompetent, Monica issued a check as payment for a car. Under state law, Monica's incompetency would render the obligation voidable.
   b.   Monica issued a check as payment for illegal drugs. Under state law, the illegal nature of the transaction would void Monica's obligation to pay.
   c.   Monica issued a check to Dean. Delivery of the check was conditioned on Dean's delivery of a stock certificate to Monica. Dean failed to deliver the certificate.
   d.   b and c.

SHORT ANSWER QUESTIONS

Answer the following questions, briefly explaining the reason for your answer.

1. Bob issued a check for $50 to Cathy as payment for cleaning services. Cathy raised the amount of the check to $500 and Steve cashed the check for Cathy. At the time Steve cashed the check, he noticed that the amount had been changed, but Cathy convinced him that it was nothing to worry about. Is Steve a HDC?

No. He had reasons to believe the check was altered.

2. Dana bought a painting while intoxicated and she issued a check to the Art Studio as payment. Under state law, Dana's lack of capacity due to intoxication would render her obligation on the check voidable. The Art Studio negotiated the check to Last Bank, a HDC. Does Dana have to pay the amount of the check to Last Bank?

Yes. Intoxication is a personal defense in this case

3. While Marie was a minor, she issued a negotiable promissory note to Todd as payment for a motorcycle. Todd negotiated the note to a HDC as payment of a debt that he owed the HDC. Marie is still a minor, but she no longer wants the cycle and she refuses to pay the note. Does Marie have to pay the HDC the unpaid balance of the note?

No. Infancy is a real defense

4. Anna, an attorney, rendered legal services for Bob. Anna was not licensed to practice law in the state where she represented Bob. Anna's failure to have the required license would void Bob's obligation to pay her. Nonetheless, Bob issued a check in the amount of $2,000 to Anna as payment for her services, and Anna negotiated the check to Harry, a HDC. Bob now refuses to pay the check to Harry. Can Bob assert his defense of illegality against Harry, thereby avoiding his obligation to pay?

Yes. Failure to have a license is illegal and a real defense

CASE PROBLEMS

Answer the following case problems, explaining your answers.

1. Samantha issued a check payable to the order of Margaret Shelf. Subsequently, the following transactions occurred: (a) Margaret negotiated the check to Rob, indorsing it "Pay to Rob Akron /signed/ Margaret Shelf;" (b) Rob then negotiated the check to Chuck, indorsing it "/signed/ Rob Akron;" (c) Chuck negotiated the check to Jill, indorsing it "/signed/Chuck Ware, Without Recourse;" and (d) Jill negotiated the check to her bank, indorsing it "/signed/Jill Weaver, For Deposit Only."
    What type of indorsement did each person make? Describe the legal effect of each indorsement.

d. Restrictive indorsement - for deposit
a. Special Indorsement
b. Blank indorsement - negotiated by transfer of possession alone
c. Qualified Endorsement - Jill can't go to Chuck for pmt if the bank does not honor it

2. Jacob issued a $50,000 negotiable note to Winston to pay for a parcel of land. Winston intentionally misrepresented to Jacob that the real estate had large oil reserves. Winston negotiated the note to Julia. Julia paid Winston $50,000 for the note, and she took it without notice of Winston's fraud. (a) Is Julia a HDC? (b) Is Jacob's defense of fraud a personal or real defense? (c) Does Jacob have to pay Julia the amount of the note?

a. Yes - She accepts the check in good faith
b. No - Fraud in the inducement is a personal defense
c. Yes - he has primary liability

CHAPTER 24   Liability and Discharge

```
┌─────────────────────────────────────────────┐
│                CHAPTER REVIEW                 │
└─────────────────────────────────────────────┘
```

BASIC CONCEPTS: Commercial paper is a substitute for money. When the holder of the commercial paper wants to convert it to money, the holder must properly present it for payment to the maker or to the drawee. Proper presentment usually results in payment and cancellation of the instrument. Sometimes, though, the instrument is dishonored (payment is refused) which may create secondary liability to pay the instrument for prior holders and/or indorsers.

THE CHAINS OF LIABILITY: Liability refers to an obligation to pay an instrument.
- *Primary liability*: A primary party is the party who is normally expected to pay an instrument. The primary liability of certain parties can be summarized as follows:
  1) The maker of a note has primary liability to pay the holder of a note. As soon as the maker of a note signs it, the maker is primarily liable to the holder or any subsequent holders;
  2) The issuer of a cashier's check or other draft drawn on the drawer has primary liability to pay; and
  3) Upon acceptance, a drawee has primary liability to pay the accepted instrument. Prior to acceptance, however, the drawee is not liable to a payee or holder to pay.
- *Secondary liability*: Secondary parties agree to pay the instrument if presentment is properly made; the primary party dishonors the instrument; and notice of the dishonor is properly given to the secondary party. The drawer of a check or draft and every indorser (except for indorsers who signed "without recourse") have secondary liability to pay the instrument, if the party with primary liability does not.

ESTABLISHING LIABILITY: The secondary (contractual) liability indorsers (and, in rare cases, also drawers) does not arise unless there is proper presentment, dishonor, and notice of dishonor of an instrument.
- *Presentment*: Presentment is a proper and timely demand for payment that is made upon the maker, drawee, or acceptor of the instrument by the holder/presenter.
- *Acceptance*: A drawee accepts a draft by writing its acceptance on the draft. However, UCC   Article 4 makes a drawee bank liable for a draft if it does not pay or return the draft, or send notice of its dishonor, until after the drawee bank's midnight deadline (midnight of the next business day after the check is presented and dishonored).
- *Dishonor*: An instrument is dishonored when proper presentment is made and acceptance is refused.
- *Notice*: Notice of dishonor may be given using any commercially reasonable means. Notice regarding an instrument taken for collection (such as a check) must be given: 1) by a bank by its midnight deadline or when it receives notice of dishonor; and 2) by anyone else within 30 days following the day on which the person receives notice of dishonor. Failure to give proper or timely notice will release all secondary parties except the drawer from liability.

LIABILITY: A negotiable instrument is a special type of contract. When a person signs an instrument (except "without recourse"), the person promises to pay it under certain circumstances.
- *Indorsement liability*: An unqualified indorsement may give rise to secondary liability to pay. Two special types of indorsements relating to this rule are ones made as an accommodation or guarantee.

1) An accommodation party is one who signs an instrument in order to benefit another person to the instrument, and the accommodation party may sign as maker, acceptor, drawer, or indorser. The accommodation party's duty to pay corresponds to the capacity in which the party signs.
2) A person who signs an instrument guaranteeing collection (as opposed to payment) may have liability to pay if certain conditions are first met.

■ *Warranty liability*: A party who transfers an instrument or presents it for payment or acceptance makes warrants that certain matters are true regarding the instrument. One set of warranties are made when the instrument is transferred, and other warranties are made when it is presented for payment or acceptance. When a warranty is breached, the person making the warranty is liable for losses caused by the breach of warranty. A warrantor may have warranty liability even if the warrantor does not have a contractual obligation to pay the instrument. (See pages 613 & 614 of the textbook for a list of warranties made upon transfer or presentment.)

SPECIAL PROBLEMS: In general, a forgery or illegal signature has no legal effect and does not impose liability on the person whose signature is forged, unless that person ratifies the unauthorized signature. However, two rules depart from this basic rule.

The "imposter rule" and the "fictitious payee rule" apply when a person is deceived into issuing an instrument to an imposter who pretends to be an intended payee, or a person is conned into issuing an instrument payable to a fictitious person. In these cases, the imposter or con artist usually forges the payee's indorsement or indorses the fictitious person's name and obtains payment of the instrument. In these cases, the issuer must pay anyone who, in good faith, subsequently pays or takes the instrument.

DISCHARGE: Discharge terminates the liability or potential liability of parties to pay an instrument. Discharge may result from the following actions:
■ *Payment*: Proper payment discharges everyone's liability; payment improperly made does not.
■ *Tender of payment*: A tender of payment that is wrongfully refused discharges secondary parties.
■ *Cancellation and renunciation*: Discharge occurs when the holder cancels the instrument or renounces his or her rights on the instrument in a signed writing.
■ *Impairment*: When a holder releases a prior party or collateral securing payment, the holder also generally discharges some or all of the secondary parties on the instrument.
■ *Other discharges*: Other acts may cause a complete or partial discharge of liability.

STUDY HINTS FOR CALL-IMAGE TECHNOLOGY CASE STUDIES

The following study hints may be helpful when resolving the Call-Image Technology (CIT) case studies.

page 607	◆ When advising Dan, review the concept of secondary liability of drawers and indorsers. ◆ Also, don't overlook the requirement that notice of dishonor must be given.

page 610	◆ Consider (revised) UCC § 3-503.

page 615	◆ Review the warranties made upon presentment of an instrument.

CHAPTER 24 - LIABILITY AND DISCHARGE

```
┌─────────────────────────────────────────────────────┐
│         REVIEW OF KEY TERMS AND CONCEPTS              │
└─────────────────────────────────────────────────────┘
```

MATCHING EXERCISE

Select the term or concept that best matches a definition or statement set forth below. Each term or concept is the best match for only one definition or statement.

Terms and Concepts

a. Accommodation   d. Midnight deadline   g. Primary liability
b. Discharge   e. Presentment   h. Secondary liability
c. Dishonor   f. Presentment warranties   i. Transfer warranties

Definitions and Statements

_d_ 1. Time by which a bank must generally give notice of a dishonored instrument.

_h_ 2. Liability to pay an instrument that is conditioned upon proper presentment, dishonor, and notice of dishonor.

_e_ 3. Request by a holder for payment or acceptance of an instrument.

_i_ 4. Guarantees that a party makes when negotiating or assigning an instrument.

_c_ 5. Refusal of a primary party to accept or pay an instrument that is properly presented.

_f_ 6. Guarantees that a party makes when demanding payment of an instrument.

_b_ 7. Termination of liability to pay an instrument

_g_ 8. Liability to pay an instrument that is NOT conditioned upon presentment, dishonor, and notice of dishonor.

_a_ 9. Act that is undertaken to benefit another.

COMPLETION EXERCISE

Fill in the blanks with the words that most accurately complete each statement.

1. The _Maker_ of a note has primary liability to pay it.

2. A drawee does not have any liability to pay a draft or check until there is an express or implied _acceptance_ of the instrument by the drawee.

3. In general, a bank must give notice of dishonor of an instrument by its _Midnight deadline_ in order to hold an indorser contractually liable on the instrument.

4. Persons who transfer or present instruments may incur contractual liability to pay the instrument and

also _____Warranty_____ to pay damages if certain matters turn out to be false.

5. Identify four common ways by which a party can be discharged from liability or potential liability to pay an instrument:

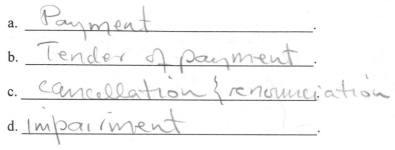

a. _____Payment_____.

b. _____Tender of payment_____.

c. _____Cancellation & renunciation_____.

d. _____Impairment_____.

TRUE-FALSE EXERCISE

Write **T** if the statement is true, write **F** if the statement is false.

_____ 1. A party who signs an instrument may incur primary or secondary liability to pay the instrument.

_____ 2. Presentment is a party's agreement to pay an instrument.

_____ 3. A drawee is not primarily liable to pay a check or draft until the drawee accepts the instrument.

_____ 4. A primary party is liable to pay an instrument even if a holder fails to present the instrument for payment when it is due.

_____ 5. If there are two or more unqualified indorsers of a draft and the drawee dishonors the instrument, the holder of the instrument can hold only the last indorser liable.

_____ 6. Parties (other than banks) must generally give notice of dishonor within 30 days following the day on which they receive notice of dishonor.

_____ 7. Parties are discharged from their liability to pay an instrument if the holder cancels the instrument.

_____ 8. A bank that issues a cashier's check has primary liability to pay it.

_____ 9. Payment, whether properly or improperly made, discharges everyone's liability on an instrument.

_____ 10. An indorser may be obligated to pay an instrument even if it is not presented for acceptance or payment when it is due.

APPLICATION OF CONCEPTS

MULTIPLE CHOICE QUESTIONS

_____ 1. In which case may Nick have secondary liability to pay if the instrument in question is subsequently dishonored?
a. Nick issued a check to Clint.
b. Nick issued a negotiable promissory note to Lonnie.
c. Ed issued a check for cash to Nick. Nick negotiated the check to Kate without indorsing it.
d. a and c.

_____ 2. In which case does Drake have primary liability to pay the instrument in question?
   a. Drake issued a check to Rhonda.
   b. Sally sold goods to Drake, and Sally issued a sales draft ordering Drake to pay the $500 purchase price to First Bank. Drake signed the draft, thereby accepting it.
   c. Dorothy issued a check to Drake. Drake indorsed the check "Drake Soren," and then negotiated the check to Frank.
   d. a and b.

_____ 3. Max issued Irene a $9,000 note. Irene sold the note to Fair Factors, indorsing it "without recourse." Max failed to pay the note because of a lack of funds. Under these facts:
   a. Irene has secondary liability to pay the note.
   b. Irene has warranty liability to pay the note.
   c. Irene has no liability to pay the note.
   d. a and b.

_____ 4. Abe issued a negotiable note to Kay. Payment of the note was secured by certain collateral. Kay indorsed the note "Kay Jones," and negotiated the note and security interest to Bart. In which situation is Kay discharged from liability on the note?
   a. Bart released Abe from liability on the note without Kay's consent.
   b. Bart accepted an early partial payment from Abe without Kay's consent.
   c. Bart terminated the security interest in the collateral without Kay's consent.
   d. a and c.

SHORT ANSWER QUESTIONS

Answer the following questions, briefly explaining the reason for your answer.

1. Pat issued a check to the order of Ken's Groceries. Ken properly indorsed the check and negotiated it to Last Bank. When Last Bank requested payment from Pat's bank, her bank refused due to insufficient funds in Pat's account. (Presentment, dishonor, and notice of dishonor were proper.) Under these facts, who has liability to pay the check to Last Bank?

_____

_____

2. Wally issued a check to Jake, and the check was drawn on Wally's bank, Peoria Bank. Jake presented the check to Peoria Bank and it accepted the check for payment. The next day, Peoria Bank discovered that Wally had no money in his account and it refused to disburse the funds to Jake. Must Peoria Bank pay the check to Jake?

_____

_____

3. Shirley issued a check payable to the order of John, and the check was drawn on Shirley's account at Third Bank. John indorsed the check in blank and negotiated it to Neil. Neil also indorsed the check in blank and presented it to Third Bank. Third Bank, however, refused to pay the check due to insufficient funds in Shirley's account. Third Bank immediately notified Neil of the dishonor, but Neil failed to inform John about the dishonor until several months later. Who has secondary liability to pay the check to Neil?

_____

_____

4. Ellen's checkbook was stolen by Lisa, and Lisa forged Ellen's signature on one of her checks and cashed it at Pizza To Go, who accepted the check in good faith and without notice that Lisa had forged Ellen's signature. Does Ellen have liability to pay this check?

_____

_____

CASE PROBLEMS

Answer the following case problems, explaining your answers.

1. Allison posed as James' landlord, Michelle. For two months, James wrote out his rent checks payable to Michelle, but gave them to Allison thinking she was Michelle. Allison indorsed and cashed these checks at Check-Rite Service. Discuss the rights of Michelle, James, and Check-Rite in this case.

_____

_____

_____

_____

2. On February 1, Mike issued a negotiable note to Patsy Bates. The note was due August 1. On June 1, Patsy indorsed the note "Patsy Bates," and negotiated the note to Noel. Noel did not present the note to Mike until November 1, and Mike refused payment due to cash flow problems. On that same day, Noel gave Patsy notice of Mike's nonpayment. (a) What is the nature of Mike's and Patsy's liability to pay the note? (b) Discuss whether the parties' respective liabilities are subject to any conditions? (c) Discuss whether Mike and/or Patsy are obligated to pay the note to Noel?

_____

_____

_____

_____

CHAPTER 25   Bank-Customer Relations/Electronic Fund Transfers

---

CHAPTER REVIEW

BASIC CONCEPTS: The bank-customer relationship is governed by Part 4 of Article 4 of the UCC. A checking account creates several relationships between the bank and the customer. First, a checking account a contract between the bank and customer. A checking account also makes the bank is an agent of the customer, and the bank must pay when a customer legally writes a check. Finally, the bank is a debtor of the customer as long as the customer's checking account is not overdrawn.

THE CUSTOMER: RIGHTS AND DUTIES: A bank customer has a duty to act with due care. UCC § 4-402 makes a bank liable to the customer for damages if the bank wrongfully dishonors a check. These damages include 1) damages due to arrest; 2) damages due to prosecution; 3) other consequential damages that can be proved. A customer may recover exemplary damages if a bank acted recklessly or with malice. To collect damages, a customer must not have contributed to his or her loss.

A customer has the right to stop payment on a check. A valid stop-payment order can be oral or written, and must contain: 1) the check number; 2) payee's name; 3) amount of check; 4) date of check; and 5) reason for the stop payment. If a bank pays a check despite a valid stop-payment order, the customer may collect damages.

A bank must send statements to its customers, and customers must examine and reconcile these statements. A customer must report any discrepancies on the statement within 30 calendar days or lose the right to assert:
1) an unauthorized customer signature;
2) a material alteration in the check; and
3) any other unauthorized signatures or alterations made by the same person. If the customer reports a discrepancy between 30 days and one year of the statement, the customer may recover only for the first unauthorized signature or alteration.

THE BANK: RIGHTS AND DUTIES: Following are some of the basic rights of a bank:
1) A bank has the right to charge the customers' accounts for their checks unless the bank has notice that a check was completed improperly or in bad faith.
2) A bank has the option of refusing to pay a stale check, which is a check more than six months old.
3) If a customer dies or becomes incompetent, the bank may pay on the customer's account until it learns of the death or incompetency.
4) If a bank learns of a customer's death or incompetency, the bank may honor checks for ten days after the date of death or incompetency, unless there has been a stop-payment order.
5) UCC § 4-407 gives the bank subrogation rights, which can give the bank the rights of: a) a holder in due course against the maker or drawer; b) a payee or any holder against the maker or drawer; or c) the drawer or maker against the payee or any holders.

SPECIAL PROBLEMS: Certified checks and unauthorized signatures present special problems.

- *Certified Checks*: A certified check makes the bank primarily liable for the check. When requesting a certified check, a customer must typically pay the amount of the check in advance.
- *Unauthorized Signatures*: UCC § 1-201 provides that an unauthorized signature (for example, a forgery) cannot impose liability on the person whose name was signed without authority. However, UCC § 3-406 imposes liability on a person who, because of negligence, contributed to the unauthorized signing of the check.

FUNDS TRANSFERS: Technology, changes in banking laws, and growth of international banking have created the need for several new banking regulations.

- *Electronic Funds Transfers*: There are four widely used methods of electronic funds transfers. The point of sale (POS) transfer uses a debit card, and the transaction looks like a credit card purchase. The automated teller machine (ATM) transaction allows customers to deposit into or to obtain money from a machine using a card and a personal identification number (PIN). Customers may authorize payments by phone if their bank is on a network. Finally, a customer may preauthorize payments or direct deposits. The Electronic Funds Transfer Act (EFTA) governs these types of transactions. EFT consumers have the same type of rights and duties as checking account customers.
- *Article 4A: Funds Transfers*: Article 4A governs wire transfers. Article 4A specifically excludes coverage of areas already governed by the EFTA.

STUDY HINTS FOR CALL-IMAGE TECHNOLOGY CASE STUDIES

The following study hints may be helpful when resolving the Call-Image Technology (CIT) case studies.

page 626
- ◆ You should consider the different types of checking accounts listed under "Basic Concepts."
- ◆ Based on your own experience with checking accounts, decide which type of account would be best for CIT as a corporation.

page 631
- ◆ You should review "The Customer: Rights and Duties" for the time limits for reconciling bank statements.
- ◆ Also check the same section of text for the consequences of failing to meet the "reasonable time" period.

REVIEW OF KEY TERMS AND CONCEPTS

MATCHING EXERCISE

Select the term or concept that best matches a definition or statement set forth below. Each term or concept is the best match for only one definition or statement.

Terms and Concepts

a. ATM
b. Certified check
c. EFT

d. Exemplary damages
e. Overdraft
f. Stale check

g. Stop payment
h. Subrogation
i.   Unauthorized signature

Definitions and Statements

_____ 1. A check written for an amount over the amount on account, and accepted by the drawee.

_____ 2. A check over six months old, which a bank may dishonor.

_____ 3. An instrument which makes the drawee primarily liable.

_____ 4. An order for a bank to not pay on a check.

_____ 5. Punitive damages.

_____ 6. Given the rights of another.

_____ 7. Electronic funds transfers.

_____ 8. Signature made without express or implied authority.

_____ 9. Automated teller machine.

COMPLETION EXERCISE

Fill in the blanks with the words that most accurately complete each statement.

1. Wire transfer are governed by UCC _____ _____.

2. An _____ _____ is inoperative against the person whose name was signed.

3. A checking account creates the following three relationships between a bank and a customer:

    a. _____.

    b. _____.

    c. _____.

4. A bank customer generally has a duty to act with _____ _____.

5. If a bank wrongfully dishonors a customer's check, the customer may sue for the following damages:

a. _____.

b. _____.

c. _____.

<u>**TRUE-FALSE EXERCISE**</u>

Write **T** if the statement is true, write **F** if the statement is false.

_____ 1. A bank is legally required to dishonor stale checks.
_____ 2. A bank is always liable if it cashes a check with an unauthorized signature.
_____ 3. The EFTA governs consumers' funds transfers that are accomplished by issuance of checks.
_____ 4. A drawer may lose the right to assert against a drawee bank a claim that a check had been altered if the drawer's negligence substantially contributed to the alteration.
_____ 5. A drawer may be criminally liable for issuing a bad check if the drawer's account has insufficient funds to pay for the check.
_____ 6. If a bank wrongfully dishonors a check, a customer may sue the bank for damages only if the customer suffered actual damages, the customer did not contribute to the damages, and the bank's actions where the proximate cause of those damages.
_____ 7. A bank must dishonor a check if it will create an overdraft on a customer's account.
_____ 8. A bank may choose not to pay a check if the bank believes in good faith that the customer's funds will go to a dishonest person or be used in a shady business deal.
_____ 9. A reasonable time in which a customer must examine his or her bank statement is one year.
_____ 10. A bank must immediately stop paying on a customer's account once it is notified that the customer has died.

APPLICATION OF CONCEPTS

<u>**MULTIPLE CHOICE QUESTIONS**</u>

_____ 1. Dan's checkbook was stolen by Milton. Milton forged Dan's signature on a check and issued it to Penny, who was unaware of the forgery. Penny presented the check to Left Bank, the drawee bank. Left Bank paid the check and charged Dan's account for the amount of the check. Under these facts:
   a. Left Bank was entitled to charge Dan's account for the check, and it has no obligation to recredit his account.
   b. Left Bank must recredit Dan's account for the amount of the check.
   c. Between Left Bank and Dan, Left Bank must bear any loss that may occur due to its payment of the check.
   d. b and c.

_____ 2. Consumer electronic fund transfers are governed by:
   a. Common law of contracts.
   b. The UCC.
   c. The Electronic Funds Transfer Act.
   d. All of the above.

_____ 3.   Cody has a checking account with State Bank. Cody has $10,000 in his checking account. Cody issued a check to Paul for $5,000. Paul properly presented the check for payment to State Bank, but the bank dishonored the check. As a result, Cody incurred $100 damages and Paul incurred $50 damages. Under these facts:
a.   State Bank is not liable to Cody or Paul.
b.   State Bank is liable to Paul for $50 damages, but it is not liable to Cody.
c.   State Bank is liable to Cody for $100 damages, but it is not liable o Paul.
d.   State Bank is liable to Cody for $100 damages, and it is liable to Paul for $50 damages.

_____ 4.   Bannock Company uses a rubber stamp with the company's name on it to sign its checks. Bannock keeps this rubber stamp, along with its company checks, securely locked in a safe. An employee broke into the safe and, using the company checks and the rubber stamp, wrote checks to himself for $10,000. Under these facts:
a.   Bannock may assert that the checks had an unauthorized signature and not be liable.
b.   Bannock will be liable for the checks because it failed to use proper measures to safeguard the checks and rubber stamp.
c.   Bannock will be liable for the checks because it is always negligent for a company to use a rubber stamp to sign its checks even if the rubber stamp is stored in a safe place.
d.   b and c.

SHORT ANSWER QUESTIONS

Answer the following questions, briefly explaining the reason for your answer.

1. Charlie had a checking account at West Bank. On May 1, Charlie wrote a check to Susan. On May 2, Charlie died in an auto accident, and West Bank was informed of his death. On May 13, Susan presented Charlie's check at West Bank for payment. May West Bank pay the check?

_____

_____

2. Maria wrote a check to Luis on April 15 from her account at Eagle Bank. On April 16, Maria gave Eagle Bank a written stop-payment order. On November 15, Luis presented the check at Eagle Bank, and the bank paid Luis. Did Eagle Bank act properly?

_____

_____

3. On June 1, Sandy wrote a check to Louis Lawyer for legal services. On June 2, Sandy realized that Louis had overcharged her, so she called her bank and requested a stop payment on her check to Louis. However, Louis had cashed the check on June 1. Can Sandy sue the bank for paying on the check?

_____

_____

4. Steve wrote a check to Robert for $500 and specifically told Robert to wait two days before depositing the check. Robert ignored Steve and deposited the check the same day in his account at North Bank. Also on the same day, Robert bought a new stereo from Al's Electronix for $520. At the time of deposit, Robert had $50 in his account. When Robert's check "bounced," Al assessed a $15 service charge against Robert and had him arrested for passing bad checks. Does Robert have any recourse against North Bank?

_____

_____

CASE PROBLEMS

Answer the following case problems, explaining your answers.

1. Jennifer, president of Jenco, hired Travis as her new secretary. Travis' responsibilities include "signing" employee paychecks twice a month by using a rubber stamp of Jennifer's signature. Jennifer always kept the rubber stamp with her signature in a locked drawer, and only she and Travis had the key. One day, Travis used the rubber stamp to sign a check, made out to himself, for $10,000. Travis left, never to be heard from again. Jennifer later learned that Travis was once convicted for embezzlement. However, she did not investigate Travis before hiring him. If the bank pays the check before Jennifer can place a stop-payment order, discuss whether Jennifer can recover her money.

_____

_____

_____

_____

2. Jeff duly issued a check to Ernie for $100. Ernie wrongfully raised the amount to $1,000, and he presented the check to Last Bank, the drawee. Last Bank paid Ernie $1,000, and it credited Jeff's account for this amount. Last Bank exercised reasonable care at all times. One week after receiving his bank statement, Jeff noticed the improper payment and informed Last Bank of the alteration. (a) Describe Jeff's duty to examine his bank statement and report alterations to Last Bank. (b) Did Jeff give timely notice of the alteration? (c) For how much, if any, can Last Bank charge Jeff's account?

_____

_____

_____

_____

CHAPTER 26   Secured Transactions: Security Interests and Perfection

CHAPTER REVIEW

CREDIT FINANCING AND ARTICLE 9: Article 9 provides a means for selling goods on credit while allowing sellers to protect themselves in case the buyer defaults on payments. The seller in a secured transaction is called the secured party; the person whose property secures payment is the debtor; and the property which secures the obligation is the collateral. Collateral can include personal property as well as general intangibles, such as patents or goodwill.

SCOPE OF ARTICLE 9: Article 9 governs any transaction that is intended to create a security interest in personal property or fixtures. The UCC categorizes collateral primarily according to their intended and actual use, although some collateral may be classified according to their nature. Types of collateral are:
1) **Consumer goods**: Goods are used or bought primarily for personal, family, or household purposes.
2) **Equipment**: Goods used or bought for use primarily in business (e.g., a company's fax)
3) **Farm products**: Crops, livestock, or supplies used or produced in farming operations. Also, products of crops or livestock in their unmanufactured states that are held by farmers.
4) **Inventory**: Goods held for sale or lease, and raw materials, work in process, and materials consumed in a business (e.g., an appliance shop's stock of TVS that are held for sale).
5) **Fixtures**: Goods that become a part of real estate (e.g., a furnace).
6) **Documents**: Negotiable documents of title to goods, such as bills of lading and warehouse receipts.
7) **Instruments**: Negotiable instruments, such as checks and negotiable promissory notes, and securities, such as stocks and bonds.
8) **Chattel paper**: Chattel paper is a writing or writings that represent: 1) a promise to pay money; and 2) either a security interest in, or a lease of, specific goods.
9) **Accounts**: Any right to payment for goods that have been sold or leased, or for services rendered, that is not represented by an instrument or chattel paper (e.g., accounts receivable).
10) **General intangibles**: Other personal property, such as goodwill of a business and trademarks.

SECURITY INTEREST: Sometimes a lease may be a security interest that secures payment of a conditional sale. It is important to distinguish between a true lease and a lease used as a security interest. This is especially true in the event the lessee files for bankruptcy.

CREATION AND ENFORCEABILITY OF THE SECURITY INTEREST: A security interest is not enforceable until it attaches to the collateral. Attachment occurs when:
1) the secured party enters into a security agreement with the debtor;
2) the secured party physically holds the collateral (a pledge) or there is a written security agreement signed by the debtor;
3) the debtor has legal rights in the collateral (ownership or a leasehold interest); and
4) the secured party gives value for the security interest (loan of money, sale on credit, or the collateral is given to secure a preexisting debt).
   Property obtained by a debtor after signing a security agreement (after-acquired property) may serve as collateral (floating lien), and collateral may secure future credit extended to a debtor (future advance).

Perfection: In order to obtain priority over other creditors or buyers who may have an interest in the same collateral, a secured party must perfect its interest. Perfection may occur in one of three ways, depending on the type of collateral involved.

■ *Filing*: Filing a financing statement gives notice to other creditors and persons who are considering purchasing the collateral that the collateral is already subject to a security interest. Depending on the type of collateral involved, the financing statement is either recorded centrally with the secretary of state or locally with the county recorder.

At a minimum, a financing statement must contain the names and addresses of the debtor and secured party, the debtor's signature, and a description of the collateral.

In general, a security interest in accounts and general intangibles can be perfected only by filing a financing statement. A security in tangible collateral, such as inventory, equipment, and consumer goods, may be perfected by filing a financing. However, some states require that a security interest in motor vehicles can only be perfected by having the security interest noted on the certificate of title.

■ *Possession*: In most cases, a security interest in instruments, such stocks and bonds, can be perfected only by the secured party taking possession of the collateral. Otherwise, a secured party may choose to perfect a security interest in tangible collateral, such as equipment or inventory, and semi-tangible collateral, such as chattel paper, by taking physical possession of the collateral. Perfection begins at the time possession begins and ends when the secured party turns the collateral over to the debtor.

■ *Automatic Perfection*: In general, a security interest in consumer goods may be perfected automatically, meaning the secured party is not required to do anything to perfect it.

RELATED TOPICS: Special topics associated with Article 9 include:

■ *Multistate Transactions*: UCC § 9-103 states where financing statements are to be filed. Security interests are generally filed in the state where the collateral is located; if the collateral is moved, the security interest must be refiled in the new state within 4 months. Goods sold for use in another state: purchase money security interest is covered under the new state's rules for 30 days. Motor vehicles: security interests are covered by the UCC and states' vehicle registration statutes.

■ *Proceeds*: A secured party's security interest, once perfected, extends to identifiable money proceeds that are realized from the sale of the collateral.

STUDY HINTS FOR CALL-IMAGE TECHNOLOGY CASE STUDIES

The following study hints may be helpful when resolving the Call-Image Technology (CIT) case studies.

page 650	◆ Review CIT's assets before responding to this question. ◆ While Article 9 allows security interests in any kind of personal property, other state laws may not (e.g., no wage assignments). Thus, you may want to review other state laws.

page 659	◆ Review the material contrasting leases of goods and security interests in goods. ◆ Find out if the "leases" are true leases or merely disguised security interests.

page 669	◆ CIT's rights and duties regarding removal of collateral to another state will primarily depend on the terms of their security agreement with the bank.

MATCHING EXERCISE

Select the term or concept that best matches a definition or statement set forth below. Each term or concept is the best match for only one definition or statement.

Terms and Concepts

a. Account
b. Chattel paper
c. Consumer good
d. Default

e. Equipment
f. Financing statement
g. Fixtures
h. General intangibles

i. Lien creditor
j. Mechanics lien
k. Pledge
l. Trustee in bankruptcy

Definitions and Statements

_____ 1. Notice of a security interest that is filed centrally or locally in order to perfect a security interest.

_____ 2. Security interest in which a secured creditor holds the collateral until the obligation is satisfied.

_____ 3. Failure to pay a debt or otherwise satisfy an obligation.

_____ 4. Type of collateral that is a monetary debt not evidenced by an instrument or chattel paper.

_____ 5. Type of collateral that includes various kinds of intangible property, except accounts.

_____ 6. Interest given by statute to secure payment to workers who repair property.

_____ 7. Court appointed administrator of a bankruptcy estate.

_____ 8. Creditor holding lien rights in property.

_____ 9. Writing that evidences both a monetary obligation and a security interest in goods.

_____ 10. Type of collateral that is primarily intended to be used to conduct a business.

_____ 11. Type of collateral that was originally personal property and has now become attached to the land or a permanent structure.

_____ 12. Type of collateral that is intended primarily for personal, family, or household purposes.

COMPLETION EXERCISE

Fill in the blanks with the words that most accurately complete each statement.

1. _____ is the process by which secured creditors protect their collateral from subsequent creditors or buyers who claim an interest in the same collateral.

2. The UCC requires a secured creditor to file a _____ _____ within ten days of written demand by a debtor who has satisfied the obligation.

3. Perfection by attachment is also known as _____ _____.

4. A security interest in stocks or bonds can be perfected only by _____.

5. List three ways that a security interest may be perfected under Article 9:

a. _____.

b. _____.

c. _____.

TRUE-FALSE EXERCISE

Write **T** if the statement is true, write **F** if the statement is false.

____ 1. Chattel paper is a form of general intangible.

____ 2. Article 9 governs secured transactions involving both tangible and intangible personal property.

____ 3. A good may simultaneously be classified as being two different types of collateral, i.e., a good may be equipment and inventory at the same time.

____ 4. Article 9 applies only to security interests created by the debtor's consent.

____ 5. In general, a bona fide lease of goods is not governed by Article 9.

____ 6. When a creditor's security interest attaches to the collateral, that creditor is assured of priority over other creditors.

____ 7. Attachment of a security interest cannot occur unless the debtor has rights in the collateral.

____ 8. A creditor may show evidence of an oral security agreement by possession of the collateral.

____ 9. A valid security agreement may, but need not, recite the price of the goods.

____ 10. Article 9 governs security interests in real property.

APPLICATION OF CONCEPTS

MULTIPLE CHOICE QUESTIONS

____ 1. Barney sold a large screen TV to Raymond on credit and required Raymond to sign a security agreement. Which of the following items must be included to make the security agreement valid?
   a. The cost of the TV.
   b. Description of the TV.
   c. Requirement that Raymond carry insurance on the TV.
   d. The length of time for Raymond to complete payments.

_____ 2. Giuseppe bought a portable fan to help cool off his restaurant. How is the fan categorized under the UCC?
   a. Inventory.
   b. Consumer goods.
   c. Fixtures.
   d. Equipment.

_____ 3. Max sold Darla a new intercom system on credit and he permanently installed it into her house. What type of collateral is the intercom system?
   a. Inventory.
   b. Consumer goods.
   c. Fixtures.
   d. Equipment.

_____ 4. Ace Finance lent $500 to Dan. Dan agreed to repay the $500 in one year, and he signed a written security agreement. The agreement granted Ace a security interest in equipment owned by Dan. Ace did not perfect the security interest. In this case:
   a. The security interest is attached.
   b. The security interest is not attached because Acc does not have possession of the collateral.
   c. The security interest is not attached because Ace did not give value.
   d. The security interest is not attached because Ace failed to perfect the security interest.

SHORT ANSWER QUESTIONS

Answer the following questions, briefly explaining the reason for your answer.

1. Peg bought a microwave from Vanessa for $300, paying her $100, promising to pay the rest in two weeks, and validly granting Vanessa a security interest in the microwave to assure payment of the balance. Vanessa filed a financing statement, perfecting her security interest. A week later, Peg sold the microwave to Bob for $200 and placed the money in a separate account. Does Vanessa have any rights in the $200?

_____

_____

2. Carter's Feed and Seed sold seed corn to Kevin on credit and Kevin granted Carter's a security interest in existing corn to secure payment of this debt. What type of collateral is involved? How can Kevin perfect its security interest in the corn?

_____

_____

3. Owen leased a $5,000 copier to Rita's Record Bar. At the end of the lease, Rita can buy the copier for $50 or return it to Owen. Is the lease a security interest covered under Article 9? Why or why not?

_____

_____

4. Acme RV sold 15 RVs to Lomax Leasing on credit, and Lomax granted Acme a security interest in the RVs to secure the unpaid purchase price. The RVs will be located at Lomax's leasing outlets in three other states. What should Acme do to assure a perfected security interest in all of the RVs?

_____

_____

CASE PROBLEMS

Answer the following case problems, explaining your answers.

1. Alice purchased a stove for her restaurant from Reliable Appliances. Alice bought the stove on credit, and she granted Reliable a security interest in the stove. Reliable filed a financing statement with the secretary of state's office. Under these facts: (a) What type of collateral is the stove? (b) Did Reliable perfect its security interest? (c) Why is perfection of the security interest important to Reliable?

_____

_____

_____

_____

2. Thomas issued a $5,000 negotiable promissory note to Helen as payment for a trailer. On May 1, Helen borrowed $2,000 from Fourth Bank and orally granted the bank a security interest in the note to secure repayment of the $2,000. The bank took possession of the note on June 1 and returned it to Helen on August 1. (a) What type of collateral is the note? (b) Did the security interest attach? (c) If a security interest attached, was it perfected? (d) If the security interest was perfected, during what period was it perfected?

_____

_____

_____

_____

CHAPTER 27   Secured Transactions: Priorities

CHAPTER REVIEW

THE CODE AND COMPETING CLAIMS FOR THE SAME COLLATERAL: The UCC provides a system for determining priority when several creditors claim the same collateral.

PRIORITIES: Generally, a perfected security interest in collateral takes priority over unsecured creditors and lien creditors who claim an interest in the same secured collateral. Only after the secured party's perfected claim is fully satisfied do other creditors receive any portion of the proceeds realized from a sale of collateral.

CONFLICTING INTERESTS IN THE SAME COLLATERAL: UCC § 9-312 sets out the rules for establishing priority to claims in the same collateral. Generally, the first secured creditor to file a financing statement or perfect a security interest, whichever comes first, has priority over other creditors. The date of filing, not the date of attachment, controls; therefore, a prudent creditor will file the financing statement as soon as possible.

If a secured creditor has a perfected floating lien in after-acquired property, then the date of perfection relates back to the original date of filing, assuring the secured party priority to the after-acquired property (with one exception relating to perfected purchase money security interests - see Exceptions below).

- ***Order of Perfection***: If filing is not required in order to perfect a security (e.g., an automatically perfected purchase money security interest in consumer goods), then the first creditor to properly perfect a security interest generally has priority.
- ***Order of Attachment***: When no creditor has perfected its security interest in the collateral, the first interest to attach has priority to the collateral. Warning: should the debtor file for bankruptcy, the trustee in bankruptcy's claim to the collateral will prevail over the unperfected security interest.

EXCEPTIONS: Although the first creditor to perfect a security interest generally has priority over other creditors, there are several exceptions. Important exceptions include:
- ***Purchase Money Security Interest***: A purchase money security interest (PMSI) is a security interest that: 1) secures payment of the unpaid purchase price for the collateral; or 2) secures repayment of a loan that was both intended to be used, and in fact used, to buy the collateral.

    A creditor holding a perfected (PMSI) in inventory has priority to the inventory over a secured party who has previously perfected an interest in the inventory as after-acquired property (i.e., the previous security interest is a floating lien). In other words, a perfected floating lien in inventory loses to a later, properly perfected PMSI in the same inventory. This exception applies only if: 1) the PMSI is perfected before the debtor gets the inventory; 2) the PMSI secured creditor gives written notice describing the inventory to those who have previously filed financing statements covering the collateral.

    A PMSI creditor in collateral other than inventory has priority over a previously perfected floating lien in the same collateral so long as the PMSI is perfected at the time the debtor gets the collateral or within 10 days afterwards.

- ***Bona Fide Purchaser of Consumer Goods***: UCC § 9-307(2) provides that a purchaser of consumer goods who (1) has no knowledge of the previously perfected security interest; (2) gives value for the goods; and (3) uses the goods for personal, family or household use, takes priority over an *automatically perfected* security interest in the same consumer goods. *Warning:* this exception does NOT apply if the prior security interest is perfected by the filing of a financing statement - in that event, the secured party and not the purchaser has priority to the consumer goods.
- ***Buyer in the Ordinary Course of Business***: UCC § 9-307(1) allows a buyer who purchases goods in the ordinary course of the seller's business to take priority over a previously perfected security interest provided that the buyer: 1) acts in good faith and 2) does not know that the sale violates the rights of a third party. *Warning:* In effect, this exception protects a good faith buyer for value who purchases an item of a merchant's *inventory*. It does not protect a buyer who purchases other types of collateral from a merchant, such as a piece of equipment or a fixture.
- ***Common Law and Statutory Liens***: UCC § 9-310 allows liens which arise through the operation of common law or statute, such as a mechanic's lien, to take priority over a perfected security interest.
- ***Fixtures***: UCC § 9-313 gives the holder of a perfected PMSI interest in fixtures priority over an encumbrancer of the real property to which the fixture is attached. In order to obtain this priority, the secured creditor must: (1) hold a PMSI in the specific fixture; (2) perfect the interest by a fixture filing within ten days of installation; and (3) the debtor must be in possession or have a recorded interest in the real property. For example, a bank that loans money to John to buy a furnace and properly records its financing statement within ten days of installation takes priority over the bank that holds a mortgage on John's house.

A secured creditor holding an interest in movable fixtures, such as office machines, has priority over the encumbrancer of real property if the interest is perfected prior to installation.

STUDY HINTS FOR CALL-IMAGE TECHNOLOGY CASE STUDIES

The following study hints may be helpful when resolving the Call-Image Technology (CIT) case studies.

page 677
- ♦ Review the priority rules stated in UCC § 9-312.
- ♦ Bear in mind a basic rule of Article 9, the first to file generally wins.

page 686
- ♦ A security interest cannot be enforced until the debtor actually defaults in performing a secured obligation.
- ♦ Regarding CIT versus the debtor's customers, review the exception dealing with buyers in the ordinary course of business.

page 690
- ♦ The discussion on Exceptions, particularly UCC § 9-307(1) and § 9-307(2), are relevant.

MATCHING EXERCISE

Select the term or concept that best matches a definition or statement set forth below. Each term or concept is the best match for only one definition or statement.

Terms and Concepts

a. Accession
b. After-acquired property
c. Buyer in ordinary course

d. Double financing
e. Encumbrancer
f. Fixture

g. Fixture filing
h. Floating lien
i. PMSI

Definitions and Statements

_____ 1. Security interest that secures payment of the unpaid purchase price for the collateral or secures repayment of a loan that was used to buy the collateral.

_____ 2. Security interest in fixtures that is perfected by filing a financing statement where the real property in question is located.

_____ 3. Person who holds a lien on real property.

_____ 4. Use of collateral to secure obligations with multiple creditors.

_____ 5. Security interest in newly-acquired (after-acquired) collateral.

_____ 6. Collateral that is acquired by a debtor after a security agreement is made.

_____ 7. Personal property that becomes so closely associated with real property that it is treated as part of the real property.

_____ 8. Person who, for value, buys goods from a merchant who regularly deals in goods of that kind, without knowledge that the sale may violate the rights of a third party.

_____ 9. Addition or improvement to a good.

COMPLETION EXERCISE

Fill in the blanks with the words that most accurately complete each statement.

1. Property that secures payment of a debt or performance of an obligation is called _____.

2. Generally, the first creditor to _____ a security interest in specific collateral has priority over other creditors who subsequently acquire an interest in the same collateral.

3. If two or more creditors have conflicting, unperfected security interests in the same collateral, then

the first interest to _____ has priority.

4. A PMSI in collateral other than inventory must file a financing statement within _____

_____ after the debtor receives the goods in order to have priority over a prior perfected security interest in the same collateral.

5. _____ is a general term that is used to describe who has a superior right to collateral.

TRUE-FALSE EXERCISE

Write **T** if the statement is true, write **F** if the statement is false.

_____ 1. A perfected security interest always takes priority over subsequent security interests in the same collateral.

_____ 2. A secured creditor's perfected claim against collateral must be fully satisfied before unsecured creditors can recover from the property.

_____ 3. The order of filing, and not attachment, determines the priority of conflicting security interests.

_____ 4. Perfection by filing may occur without attachment.

_____ 5. Filing gives priority only if the security interest attaches before another interest is perfected.

_____ 6. A PMSI need not be perfected in order to have priority over a prior perfected security interest.

_____ 7. An unperfected security interest in collateral has priority over a conflicting statutory lien.

_____ 8. A person who buys a seller's equipment is not a buyer in the ordinary course of business.

_____ 9. Anyone who buys collateral from a merchant has priority over a prior perfected security interest in the collateral.

_____ 10. The holder of a statutory lien may have priority over a prior perfected security interest.

APPLICATION OF CONCEPTS

MULTIPLE CHOICE QUESTIONS

_____ 1. Campus Cycles (CC) sold a bike to Brenda on credit. Brenda intended to use the bike for her personal enjoyment. Brenda granted CC a security interest in the bike to secure payment of the unpaid purchase price. CC did not file a financing statement. Under these facts:
a. CC's security interest is unperfected.
b. If Brenda sells the bike to Don for his personal use, and Don pays for the bike and does not know about CC's lien, then Don has priority over CC's security interest.
c. If Joe's Repair Shop obtains a common law lien on the bike for unpaid repair charges, then Joe's lien has priority over CC's security interest.
d. b and c.

_____ 2. Travis loaned $5,000 to John's Garage. John signed a security agreement granting Travis a security interest in John's existing inventory of mufflers. Travis did nothing to perfect this security interest and John kept possession of the inventory. Under these facts:
a. Travis has a perfected security interest in the mufflers.
b. Travis has an unperfected security interest in the mufflers
c. Travis does not have a security interest in the mufflers.
d. Travis has a common law lien on the mufflers.

_____ 3. On December 1, First Bank perfected a security interest in ABC Garage's inventory of tires. On February 1, Jim bought a tire from ABC for cash. On April 15, Second Bank perfected an ordinary security interest in ABC's tire inventory. Under these facts:
   a. Jim bought the tire subject to First Bank's security interest.
   b. First Bank has a security interest in the proceeds received from the sale of the tire to Jim.
   c. First Bank's security interest has priority over Second Bank's security interest.
   d. b and c.

_____ 4. J&J sold a new central air conditioning unit to Fred on credit. Fred granted J&J a security interest in the unit to secure the unpaid purchase price and J&J properly executed a fixture filing prior to delivery and installation of the unit. Last Bank had a prior mortgage recorded against Fred's house. Later, Fred defaulted on his obligations to both J&J and Last Bank. Who has priority to the air conditioning unit?
   a. J&J
   b. Last Bank
   c. J&J and Last Bank each have priority to one-half of the unit.
   d. Fred.

SHORT ANSWER QUESTIONS

Answer the following questions, briefly explaining the reason for your answer.

1. Herb borrowed $1,000 from West Bank for his store. To secure the loan, Herb granted the bank a security interest in the store's inventory, and West Bank perfected the lien on June 1. The security agreement stated that the inventory secured payment of the $1,000 loan and any future loans made to Herb. On August 1, West Bank loaned an additional $3,000 to Herb. What loans are secured by the inventory?

_____

_____

2. On March 1, Doug borrowed $2,000 from Fran, and granted Fran a security interest in his inventory. Fran did not perfect her security interest. On August 1, Doug borrowed $3,000 from Tom and granted Tom a security interest in the same inventory. Tom perfected his security interest. Later, Doug defaulted on both loans. Who has priority to the inventory: Fran or Tom?

_____

_____

3. Ken bought equipment on credit from Acme. Ken granted Acme a security interest in the equipment which Acme perfected on June 1. In August, Ken borrowed money from Commerce Bank, granting the bank a security interest in the same equipment. The bank immediately perfected its security interest. Later, Ken defaulted on both obligations. Who has priority to the equipment: Acme or Commerce Bank?

_____

_____

4. Last Bank held a perfected security interest in the inventory of Shar's Wholesale Fish Market. In the ordinary course of business, Shar sold First Catch Cafe a shipment of fish that was subject to Last Bank's security interest. Shar then defaulted on its secured debt with Last Bank. Who has priority to the fish that First Catch Cafe bought from Shar: Last Bank or First Catch?

_____

_____

CASE PROBLEMS

Answer the following case problems, explaining your answers.

1. Stan owned a hardware store and he needed a line of credit. Merchant's Bank granted him credit, secured by a lien on his current and future hardware inventory. Two months later, Stan borrowed $5,000 from Trish so that he could replenish the store's inventory of saws that had been exhausted. Stan granted Trish a security interest in the new saws, and Trish perfected her security interest one week after Stan received the saws. Stan soon defaulted on both debts. (a) What type of security interest does Merchant's Bank have? (b) What type of a security interest does Trish have? (c)Who has priority to the new inventory of saws: Merchant's Bank or Trish?

_____

_____

_____

_____

2. Buzz borrowed money from Della, his sister. To secure the loan, Buzz granted Della a security interest in some Misfit Corp. stock that he owned. Later, Buzz borrowed money from Third Bank and he granted Third Bank a security interest in the same stock. Ultimately, Buzz defaulted on the loans from both Della and Third Bank. (a) What type of borrowing technique did Buzz use in this case? (b) Were either of the security interests perfected in this case? (c) Who has priority to the stock: Della or Third Bank?

_____

_____

_____

CHAPTER 28   Secured Transactions: Default

CHAPTER REVIEW

THE CODE AND DEFAULT: The UCC does not define a default, leaving it up to the parties to provide a definition in each security agreement. Common examples of default include nonpayment of financial obligations, or permitting the collateral to be encumbered by a third party. When a default occurs, the secured party may be allowed to declare the entire due and payable immediately (acceleration clause).

Laws outside the UCC provide an array of potential remedies should a debtor default on a debt. For example, a creditor may sue and obtain a judgement, and then garnish the debtor's wages or replevy (execute on) the debtor's property and have such property to pay off the judgement.

Remedies provided under the UCC and laws outside the UCC are cumulative. In other words a creditor may pursue a combination of such remedies.

NON-CODE REMEDIES: Non-code remedies available under general civil law permit a secured creditor to file a lawsuit to foreclose on a security interest in collateral. When the court issues a judgment, the secured party may then obtain a writ of execution directing the sheriff to physically recover the collateral and sell it for the benefit of the secured party. The secured party may also use the judgment as a basis for garnishing the debtor's wages in order to obtain satisfaction of the debt.

RIGHT OF REPOSSESSION: Under the UCC, when a debtor defaults on a security agreement, the secured party may repossess the collateral without first obtaining a judgment or obtaining judicial permission, provided the action can be taken with breach of the peace. Breach of peace is not defined, but generally any action during repossession that results in physical violence is a breach of peace. The debtor may be required to assemble the collateral where the secured party can take possession.

If procedures required by the UCC are not followed in connection with the repossession and sale of collateral, the secured party may be denied a deficiency judgment for the unpaid balance of the debt and may be liable for damages to the debtor.

STRICT FORECLOSURE: Following repossession, a secured party generally has two choices: 1) the collateral may be sold and the proceeds applied to the debt, or 2) the collateral may be retained in full satisfaction of the debt.

Keeping collateral in satisfaction of the secured debt is called "strict foreclosure." In most situations, this procedure requires a secured party to:
1) send written notice to the debtor, unless the debtor has, after repossession, waived the right to require a sale of the collateral;
2) send written notice to any other secured party who has, in writing, previously claimed an interest in the collateral; and
3) wait twenty-one days for the parties to respond with any written objections.

Strict foreclosure is not permitted and the collateral must therefore be sold if:
1) any party entitled to notice objects, or
2) the debtor has paid at least 60% of the cash price of a PMSI interest in consumer goods or at least 60% of the loan for a non-PMSI security interest. If a sale of collateral is required and the seller fails to sell it within 90 days, the secured party is liable for conversion or damages.

RESALE OF REPOSSESSED COLLATERAL: If a secured creditor sells the collateral, the sale must be conducted in a commercially reasonable manner. In most cases, a sale may be public or private.

- *Notice*: The secured party must notify: 1) the debtor, unless the debtor has waived notification, or there is a threat of immediate loss of the collateral; and 2) junior secured creditors claiming an interest in non-consumer goods provided they gave written notice of their competing interest.
- ***Commercially Reasonable Sale***: A commercially reasonable sale is: 1) held in accordance with practices consistent for that type of collateral; 2) conducted in the usual manner for a recognized market; or 3) conducted pursuant to court order or approved by a creditor's committee. Failure to obtain a better price does not make a sale commercially unreasonable.

  Following a proper sale of collateral, the secured party is entitled to receive a deficiency judgment for the unpaid balance of the secured debt. If the sale is improperly carried out, then the seller may be barred from recovering any deficiency or be subject to other penalties under the Code.
- *Proceeds*: Proceeds from the sale of collateral are applied in the following order: 1) reasonable expenses of repossession and sale of the collateral, including attorney's fees if allowed under the security agreement; 2) satisfaction of the secured debt; 3) payment to eligible junior secured creditors; and 4) any surplus is paid to the debtor.

DEBTORS' RIGHTS: The debtor may redeem (reclaim) the collateral prior to sale unless this right was waived after default. Waiver of redemption cannot occur in the security agreement. To redeem, the debtor must satisfy all obligations, including the cost of repossession, sale preparation, and legal expenses prior to sale or strict foreclosure.

SECURED PARTIES' DUTIES: A secured party must: 1) take reasonable care of the collateral; 2) keep the collateral identifiable (not commingle it with other property); and 3) turn any surplus proceeds over to the debtor. UCC § 9-507 identifies the liability that secured parties incur when their noncompliance results in a loss to the debtor or junior secured creditors.

STUDY HINTS FOR CALL-IMAGE TECHNOLOGY CASE STUDIES

The following study hints may be helpful when resolving the Call-Image Technology (CIT) case studies.

page 701	♦ Repossession is generally permitted upon a default. To determine whether a default occurred, it is necessary to review the security agreement.

page 703	♦ Review the material dealing with strict foreclosure and UCC § 9-505.

page 712	♦ Review the materials on Debtor's Rights and Secured Parties' Duties. ♦ Also, revisit UCC §§ 9-501, 9-504, and 9-505.

MATCHING EXERCISE

Select the term or concept that best matches a definition or statement set forth below. Each term or concept is the best match for only one definition or statement.

Terms and Concepts

a. Conversion
b. Foreclosure
c. Fungible goods

d. Garnishment
e. Junior secured parties
f. Replevy

g. Repossession
h. Strict foreclosure
i. Writ of execution

Definitions and Statements

_____ 1. Court order allowing a party to recover personal property that is unlawfully held by another.

_____ 2. Court order allowing enforcement of a security interest in collateral.

_____ 3. Wrongful, unauthorized taking of another's personal property.

_____ 4. Court order directing a third party to pay to the court or a creditor money that the third party owes to a debtor.

_____ 5. Persons who hold security interests subordinate to those of a foreclosing party.

_____ 6. Repossession and retention of collateral as full satisfaction of a secured debt.

_____ 7. Goods that cannot be distinguished from others of the same kind; interchangeable goods.

_____ 8. Secured party's retaking of collateral upon a debtor's default.

_____ 9. Court order directing a sheriff to take and sell property belonging to a debtor in order to satisfy a judgment.

COMPLETION EXERCISE

Fill in the blanks with the words that most accurately complete each statement.

1. Default is defined by the parties in their _____ _____.

2. Under the UCC, a secured party may repossess collateral through "self-help" so long as it can be

    accomplished without committing a _____ ____ ____ _____.

3. If repossession involves a breach of the peace, the secured party may lose the right to a

    _____ _____.

4. A secured party must wait _____-_____ days after giving notice before exercising the right of strict foreclosure.

5. A sale of collateral must always be conducted in a _____ _____ manner.

TRUE-FALSE EXERCISE

T if the statement is true, write **F** if the statement is false.

_____ 1. The term "breach of the peace" is defined by the UCC.

_____ 2. An ordinary foreclosure of a security interest generally requires the filing of a lawsuit.

_____ 3. An improper repossession may subject a secured party to tort liability.

_____ 4. A secured party's right to exercise self-help repossession terminates if it requires committing physical violence.

_____ 5. There is no requirement that notice be given for a strict foreclosure.

_____ 6. If a debtor has paid any portion of the cash price for consumer goods (the collateral), then strict foreclosure is not allowed.

_____ 7. A secured party may purchase the collateral at a public sale.

_____ 8. The requirement for notice may be suspended if the collateral is perishable.

_____ 9. A sale price that is less than the market price for similar goods is not commercially reasonable.

_____ 10. A secured party may require the debtor to pay for the cost of protecting repossessed collateral.

APPLICATION OF CONCEPTS

MULTIPLE CHOICE QUESTIONS

_____ 1. Sam loaned $1,000 to Larry, who granted Sam a security interest in equipment to secure the loan. Larry later defaulted, failing to repay the loan as agreed. Under these facts:
   a. Sam can repossess the equipment using self-help.
   b. Sam can repossess the equipment using self-help even if Larry objects to the repossession.
   c. Sam can repossess the equipment using self-help only if Sam first obtains a court order permitting the repossession.
   d. a and b.

_____ 2. Gregg repossessed collateral from Dan and he properly sold the collateral for $6,000. The unpaid balance of the secured debt owing to Gregg was $5,000. The cost of the sale was $250. Jason, a junior secured creditor, had a $5,000 debt secured by the collateral. Under these facts:
   a. Gregg receives $6,000; Jason receives $0; and Dan receives $0.
   b. Gregg receives $5,250; Jason receives $750; and Dan receives $0.
   c. Gregg receives $5,000; Jason receives $1,000; and Dan receives $0.
   d. Gregg receives $2,000; Jason receives $2,000; and Dan receives $2,000.

_____ 3. Tom lent $5,000 to Jill. The loan was secured by a lien in jewelry inventory. When Jill defaulted, Tom repossessed the jewelry and properly conducted a public sale. Tom spent $500 in repossessing and selling the collateral. The jewelry sold for $4,000. Under these facts:
   a. Tom receives $4,500; $500 for expenses and $4,000 as payment on the secured debt.
   b. Tom receives $4,000 as payment on the secured debt; he cannot recover his expenses.
   c. Tom can sue Jill for a deficiency.
   d. a and c.

_____ 4. John bought a tractor on credit for $50,000, granting lien in it to secure the unpaid price. When John owed $30,000, he defaulted and the secured party repossessed the tractor, spending $750 in repossessing and storing the tractor. The tractor was sold at a properly conducted public sale for $25,000. The next day, John decided to redeem the tractor. Under these facts:
   a. John may redeem the tractor by paying the secured creditor $50,750.
   b. John may redeem the tractor by paying the secured creditor $30,750.
   c. John may redeem the tractor by paying the secured creditor $30,000.
   d. John cannot redeem the tractor.

SHORT ANSWER QUESTIONS

Answer the following questions, briefly explaining the reason for your answer.

1. Wheels Inc. sold a motorcycle to Terry on credit and Wheels had a perfected security interest in the cycle to secure payment of the purchase price. Terry defaulted and Wheels decided to repossess the cycle. When a Wheels' employee started to drive the cycle away from Terry's house, Terry jumped in front of the cycle. The employee refused to stop, crushing Terry's foot in the process. Discuss the parties' rights in this case.

_____

_____

2. Sharlene loaned Iris $2,000 to purchase a Persian rug for her new apartment. Iris signed a security agreement granting Sharlene a security interest in the rug to secure the $2,000 debt. The agreement stated that Iris waived her right to a sale in the event of default. Later, Iris failed to pay the remaining $500 owed for the rug, and Sharlene repossessed it. Can Sharlene exercise strict foreclosure in this case?

_____

_____

3. Sheldon bought a vehicle from Expo Transportation on credit for $5,000. When Sheldon defaulted on this debt, he still owed $4,000. Expo repossessed the vehicle pursuant to valid security agreement. Expo spent $400 in attorneys' fees in connection with the repossession and $60 to advertise a sale of the vehicle which is scheduled in two days. Discuss Sheldon's right, if any, to redeem the vehicle.

_____

_____

4. Thorsen's Wholesale Jewelers sold 300 gold bracelets to Ricco's Ritzy Rocks. Following default, Thorsen's repossessed the bracelets and commingled them along with 200 other bracelets. Later, Thorsen's took 300 bracelets from this commingled group of bracelets and sold them. The proceeds failed to pay off Ricco's debt. Discuss the parties' rights in this case.

_____

_____

CASE PROBLEMS

Answer the following case problems, explaining your answers.

1. Logic Inc. Lent money to Hi-Tek, taking a perfected security interest in Hi-Tek's patent for a new computer chip. Hi-Tek defaulted and Logic properly repossessed the patent in accordance with the parties' security agreement.

 Logic is considering selling the patent to MicroPro in a private sale or conducting a public sale. Three other secured creditors have a recorded security interest in the patent; however, their interests were perfected after Logic's. (a) Must Logic notify Hi-Tek of the proposed sale? (b) What action must the junior secured creditors take to protect their rights in the collateral? (c) Discuss Logic's right to choose between a public and private sale of the patent. (d) If Logic conducts a public sale of the patent, can Logic buy the patent?

_____

_____

_____

_____

2. Pursuant to a valid security agreement, A&A Appliances repossessed and sold a walk-in refrigerator unit that it had repossessed from Frank's Cafe. Prior to the sale, A&A contacted all restaurants and equipment dealers in town to notify them of the sale, and it ran ads in the newspaper for several weeks. The collateral sold for $8,000, although its market value was about $15,000.

 The unpaid balance of the secured debt owing to A&A was $10,000, and A&A incurred $500 costs in selling the collateral. Frank's argues that the sales price is not commercially reasonable. Under these facts: (a) Is the sales price commercially reasonable? (b) Assuming that the sale was properly conducted, how are the sale proceeds applied? (c) Can A&A sue for a deficiency?

_____

_____

_____

_____

CHAPTER 29 — Straight Bankruptcy

CHAPTER REVIEW

HISTORICAL BACKGROUND: The U.S. Constitution authorizes (but does not require) Congress to provide bankruptcy relief for honest debtors. There are three major type of bankruptcy proceedings: (1) Chapter 7 or liquidation; (2) Chapter 13 or personal debt reorganization; and (3) Chapter 11, generally viewed as a business or large personal debt reorganization. In addition, Chapter 12 provides relief for family farmers.

THE BANKRUPTCY REFORM ACT: The 1978 Bankruptcy Reform Act established a separate system of bankruptcy courts within in each U.S. district court. The U.S. Supreme Court declared the Act unconstitutional in a case arising from a contract dispute between two pipeline companies (one of which was in bankruptcy).

BANKRUPTCY AMENDMENTS AND FEDERAL JUDGESHIP ACT OF 1984: The Bankruptcy Amendments and Federal Judgeship Act generally corrected the constitutional problems identified by the Supreme Court, including: (1) change in appointment of bankruptcy judges; (2) providing original and exclusive jurisdiction for all bankruptcy matters to the federal District Court, giving them discretion to refer the cases to the Bankruptcy Court or to bring them back to the District Court upon showing of a good reason.

THE BANKRUPTCY REFORM ACT OF 1994: The 1994 Act created a National Bankruptcy Review Commission and increased the compensation for trustees and debt limits for Chapter 13 debtors. The Act provides for adjustments in dollar amounts based on the Consumer Price Index and also recognizes bankruptcy fraud as a crime.

STRAIGHT BANKRUPTCY A CHAPTER 7 LIQUIDATION PROCEEDING:
- *Voluntary Bankruptcy Petition*: Debtors filing under Chapter 7 must be informed of their right to file a Chapter 13 in order to encourage repayment where possible. Discharge in bankruptcy is no longer considered a "right"; however, most debtors are discharged unless a bankruptcy judge determines that the debtor has abused the system.
- *Involuntary Bankruptcy Petition*: Creditors may force a debtor into bankruptcy proceeding if: (1) the debtor appointed a receiver or is not paying debts within 120 days before the filing;; (2) a prescribed number of creditors sign the filing; and (3) the aggregate unsecured, non-contingent debt among the creditors who sign the petition is $10,000 or more. If a debtor successfully contests the bankruptcy, the petitioning creditors are liable for damages.

THE BANKRUPTCY PROCEEDING: Upon filing of a bankruptcy petition, an order for relief is issued and a trustee is appointed to administer the case
- *The Trustee*: The trustee represents the debtors estate and the interests of the unsecured creditors.
- *Automatic Stay Provisions*: Once the bankruptcy petition is filed and order for relief granted, creditors must cease any action to collect debts.
- *The Creditors' Meeting*: Within a reasonable time after filing, the trustee holds a meeting with the debtor and creditors to ask questions regarding the debtor's financial affairs. A debtor must submit detailed financial schedules listing property and debts which creditors may review.

- **Secured Creditors**: Secured creditors may retain their security interest or proceed as an unsecured creditors.
- **Exemptions**: Federal bankruptcy law provides that certain assets may be retained by the debtor to begin a fresh financial start. Some states require a resident debtor to use only the state's exemptions, while other states allow a debtor to choose state or federal. Exemptions generally allow varying amounts of cash, equity in residence, clothing, tools of debtor's trade, insurance, and certain benefits.
- **Allowable Claims**: Creditors must file their claims within six months of the creditors' meeting. Two types of claims will be barred: (1) claims which would otherwise be unenforceable against the debtor, and (2) claims including interest extending beyond the petition date (the bankruptcy filing "freezes" accrual of debt). Two other types of claims may be partially allowed or limited: (1) claims for violation or termination of a lease; and (2) claims based on breach of employment contract.
- **Recovery of Property**: A bankruptcy trustee may avoid certain transfers made by the debtor, and recover that property for the benefit of unsecured creditors. These transfers include:(1) voidable preferences or preferential payments to some creditors at the expense of others; and (2) fraudulent conveyances or transfers of property made within one year of the bankruptcy to hinder creditors.
- **Distribution of Assets**: The debtor's non-exempt assets are sold and the proceeds distributed in the priority set forth in federal bankruptcy law. Following payment of priority claims, unsecured creditors receive a pro rata distribution of the balance of proceeds from the debtor's property, if any remain..
- **The Discharge Decision**: Federal bankruptcy law contains an extensive list of non-dischargeable debts, including court-ordered alimony and child support, taxes, and student loans (with certain exceptions). The discharged debtor remains liable for non-discharged debt. A creditor or the trustee may request a revocation of the discharge if a court determines the debtor has acted wrongfully in the bankruptcy. In some cases, a debtor may reaffirm a debt in spite of the discharge.

STUDY HINTS FOR CALL-IMAGE TECHNOLOGY CASE STUDIES

The following study hints may be helpful when resolving the Call-Image Technology (CIT) case studies.

page 727

♦ To answer this question, you should review the section on Automatic Stay Provision.

page 730

♦ To answer this question, you should review the section on Secured Creditors.

MATCHING EXERCISE

Select the term or concept that best matches a definition or statement set forth below. Each term or concept is the best match for only one definition or statement.

Terms and Concepts

a. Automatic stay
b. Exempt assets
c. Fraudulent conveyance
d. General assignment for
    benefit of creditors

e. Involuntary bankruptcy
f. National Bankruptcy
    Review Commission
g. Order for relief
h. Petition in bankruptcy

I. Reaffirmation agreement
j. Receiver
k. Schedules
l. Voidable preference

Definitions and Statements

_____ 1. Listings of assets and liabilities filed by a debtor in a bankruptcy case.
_____ 2. Nine-member group created by the Bankruptcy Reform Act of 1994.
_____ 3. Assets retained by debtors under the bankruptcy law to enable a "fresh start."
_____ 4. Effect of bankruptcy filing which prohibits creditors from pursuing debtor's assets outside bankruptcy court.
_____ 5. Person appointed to manage debtor's property for benefit of a creditor outside of bankruptcy.
_____ 6. Order entered by bankruptcy court upon filing of petition.
_____ 7. Transfer of property by debtor to satisfy debts.
_____ 8. Agreement by debtor to pay a debt which would otherwise be discharged.
_____ 9. Transfer of property made by a debtor to hinder creditors' recovery of money owed.
_____ 10. Bankruptcy petition filed by creditors against a debtor against debtor's will.
_____ 11. Transfer of property or payment of debt which gives unfair advantage to some creditors.
_____ 12. Basic document which commences a bankruptcy proceeding.

COMPLETION EXERCISE

Fill in the blanks with the words that most accurately complete each statement.

1. The Bankruptcy Reform Act of 1978 was declared _____ by the U.S. Supreme Court.

2. Bankruptcy judges do not have _____ _____ jurisdiction under the Constitution.

3. Straight bankruptcy refers to a _____ of a debtor's non-exempt assets.

4. An involuntary bankruptcy requires _____ creditors out of twelve or more to sign the petition.

5. The debt limits for Chapter 13 debtors under the 1994 Bankruptcy Reform Act is _____ dollars.

TRUE-FALSE EXERCISE

Write **T** if the statement is true, write **F** if the statement is false.

_____ 1. The constitutional challenge to the Bankruptcy Act raised issues of jurisdiction.

_____ 2. Under the 1994 Act, dollar amounts for involuntary petitions, priorities, and exemptions will be tied to the Consumer Price Index.

_____ 3. Savings and loan associations may lawfully commence a Chapter 7 bankruptcy.

_____ 4. Three creditors may file an involuntary bankruptcy against a farmer.

_____ 5. Charitable corporations may not be subjected to an involuntary bankruptcy.

_____ 6. A debtor need not be insolvent to file a voluntary petition in bankruptcy.

_____ 7. If a debtor made a general assignment of property for creditors' benefit within the previous 120 days, the creditors are barred from filing an involuntary bankruptcy against the debtor.

_____ 8. Creditors may under some circumstances be liable to the debtor for damages for filing an involuntary bankruptcy petition.

_____ 9. A trustee represents the secured creditors' interests.

_____ 10. Creditors may not repossess assets of a debtor after the petition is filed.

APPLICATION OF CONCEPTS

MULTIPLE CHOICE QUESTIONS

_____ 1. PetroMine Inc. filed a petition in bankruptcy on June 1. On June 3, OfficePro, a secured creditor, attempted to repossess a copier from PetroMine's office, resulting in shouting and general disruption. Which statement best describes OfficePro's legal rights?
   a. OfficePro legally exercised its right of self-help to recover the copier.
   b. OfficePro could not legally repossess the copier because it breached the peace.
   c. OfficePro could not legally repossess the copier because it violated the automatic stay.
   d. OfficePro could not hold a secured interest under the bankruptcy proceeding.

_____ 2. Marvin is considering whether to file a petition in bankruptcy. Which of the following actions may result in denial of a discharge?
   a. Marvin transfers his stock certificates to his brother's name so that he appears to have no assets.
   b. Marvin intentionally fails to disclose his substantial lottery winnings on the bankruptcy schedules.
   c. Marvin contracts for auto repairs for which he ultimately is unable to pay.
   d. a and b.

_____ 3. Paul files a voluntary petition in bankruptcy. Which of the following claims will not be allowed by the bankruptcy trustee?
   a. A claim by Paul's friend for a loan she made to Paul which is evidenced by a promissory note.
   b. A claim by Tom who fraudulently caused Paul to enter a contract to purchase stock.
   c. A claim by Sue for wages due during the past month while she worked as Paul's assistant.
   d. All of the above.

_____ 4. Which of the following transactions may be avoided by the bankruptcy trustee as a voidable preference?
   a. Brenda pays her $750 credit card charges in full 30 days before filing bankruptcy.
   b. Tim pays $400 to each of his creditors within 60 days of filing bankruptcy.
   c. Sean gives his piano to Ursula 10 days before filing bankruptcy as security for money he borrowed two years before.
   d. a and c.

SHORT ANSWER QUESTIONS

Answer the following questions, briefly explaining the reason for your answer.

1. Santos filed a voluntary petition in bankruptcy in order to get a fresh start. Santos owns a small life insurance policy, personal clothing, a motorboat, an extensive original art collection by world-famous sculptors, and an old car. Which of these assets will most likely be allowed under the federal bankruptcy exemptions?

_____

_____

2. Three weeks before filing bankruptcy, Al borrowed $500 from Foster and gave Foster a security interest in his row boat. At the creditors' meeting George, an unsecured creditor, argues that Foster's security interest is a voidable preference and should be avoided by the trustee so that the row boat can be sold to benefit the many unsecured creditors. Is George correct?

_____

_____

3. Gordon was granted a discharge in bankruptcy on November 30. The following September one of his creditors learned that immediately prior to the bankruptcy, Gordon had transferred a large sum of money to a foreign bank account so that he would appear insolvent. What can the creditor do to correct the situation?

_____

_____

4. Martha owed Anna $5000 for money she borrowed when her daughter was ill. Shortly before receiving her discharge in bankruptcy, Martha's conscience began to bother her and she agreed in writing to pay Anna the remainder of the debt. Is such an agreement valid and enforceable?

_____

_____

CASE PROBLEMS

Answer the following case problems, explaining your answers.

1. Sara filed a voluntary petition in bankruptcy under Chapter 7. At the time she filed, she owed money to the mortgage company which had financed her house and a credit card company for various clothing purchases. Sara also owed delinquent income taxes from the previous year. The auto dealer which had financed her car held a perfected security interest in the vehicle. Sara's total bankruptcy estate was determined to be $7,000. Expenses of administering the bankruptcy were $500. (a) How much money will be available to Sara's unsecured creditors? (b) Which, if any, of Sara's assets may be exempt under federal or state exemption laws? (c) If Sara wishes to keep her car, what action can she take? (d) Are there any debts from which Sara may not be discharged?

_____

_____

_____

_____

2. Downtown Office Products has several unpaid accounts with Tim, who has indicated that he may soon file bankruptcy under Chapter 7. Among the debts owed to the company by Tim are a fax machine which is subject to a perfected security interest and miscellaneous office supplies. In addition, Tim has leased office space from the company and is liable for payment under a five year lease. If Tim does file bankruptcy: (a) May Downtown Office Products repossess the fax machine? (b) What are the company's options regarding the fax machine? (c) Will the claim for payments under the lease be wholly allowed, partially allowed, or barred by the trustee? (d) In what general order of payment will Office Products recover on its claim for the office supply purchases?

_____

_____

_____

_____

CHAPTER 30

Alternatives to Straight Bankruptcy

```
┌─────────────────────────────────────────────────┐
│                                                   │
│              CHAPTER REVIEW                       │
│                                                   │
└─────────────────────────────────────────────────┘
```

OTHER BANKRUPTCY PLANS: In addition to the liquidation proceedings under Chapter 7, the Bankruptcy Reform Act also provides for a wage earner's repayment plan for personal debts (Chapter 13); reorganization (Chapter 11), and reorganization for family farmers (Chapter 12).

- *Reorganizations: Chapter 11*: Both corporations and individuals may use reorganization plans under Chapter 11 to restructure debt without liquidation of assets. Creditors generally receive more than they would if liquidation occurred, and objecting creditors may be forced to accept the plan. Petitions may be voluntary or involuntary. A Chapter 11 debtor may fill the function as trustee ("debtor in possession"), or a trustee may be appointed upon request of an interested party. Committees of creditors, appointed by the court, meet with the trustee/debtor to discuss the restructuring. In some cases, the court may appoint an examiner to investigate the debtor's financial dealings. During the first 120 days after the petition, a debtor-in-possession retains the exclusive right to file a reorganization plan. If a trustee is appointed, or the debtor's plan is rejected within the first 180 days, other interested parties may file a plan. Small-business debtors using the "fast-track" reorganization allowed under the 1994 Act must file a plan within 100 days and plans by others must be filed within 160 days. The court must approve: 1) sale of assets; 2) mergers, consolidations or divestitures; 3) satisfaction or modification or liens or claims; 4) issuance of new stock. More than half the creditors holding at least 2/3 of the dollar amount of claims for a given class of debt must vote for the plan in order for it to be accepted by that class. If at least one class of creditors accepts the plan, the court may confirm it. A confirmed reorganization plan binds the debtor and all creditors. A court may order conversion to a liquidation if it believes the plan cannot be successfully completed. Some important companies have used Chapter 11 in recent years to restructure unforseen liabilities or relieve themselves from undesirable contracts.
- *Repayment Plans for Farmers: Chapter 12*: Neither Chapter 7, Chapter 11, nor Chapter 13 may be appropriate for family farmers. However, Chapter 12 establishes a reorganization plan for family farmers with no more than $1.5 million in debt. Involuntary Chapter 12's are not permitted. Unless there is objection, the debtor operates the farm as debtor-in-possession. The case may be converted to a Chapter 7 on request of the debtor or, if fraud is shown, on the request of an interested party.
- *Repayment Plans: Chapter 13*: Individual debtors with regular income may propose a repayment plan if: 1) they have no more than $750,000 in secured debt, and 2) $250,000 in unsecured debt. Only voluntary petitions are permitted. The repayment plan must: (1) extend for no more than three years, or five in special situations; 2) is fair to all parties; 3) is in the best interest of the creditors; 4) be feasible, that is, the debtor can conform; 5) pays at least as much as under a liquidation. As in a Chapter 11, a confirmed plan is binding on all parties and results in the debtor's discharge once the plan is completed. Under certain circumstances, a court may grant a discharge during the plan, that is, before the plan is completed.

Several changes made during the 1984 Bankruptcy Amendments include: 1) beginning payments into the court before the plan has been confirmed; 2) permitting any unsecured creditor to block confirmation unless the creditor's claim is either fully satisfied, or 100% of the debtor's disposable income is paid over for the three year period. In addition, a plan may be modified during the period to increase, as well as decrease, payments.

NON-BANKRUPTCY ALTERNATIVES: Both debtors and creditors have options for resolving disputes outside of the bankruptcy process.

- *Prejudgment Alternatives*: Before a lawsuit has been filed, a creditor may seek attachment, garnishment, or receivership of the debtor's property. In attachment, a creditor has the property seized pending the outcome of a suit. In garnishment or receivership, a third person holds the property until a judgment is entered.

- *Post-judgment Alternatives*: After the creditor has received a favorable judgment, he may seek a writ of execution against the debtor's property and have it sold to satisfy the debt, or he may file a garnishment action with the court to have wages or bank accounts turned over. The creditor may also engage in supplementary proceedings, by asking the debtor questions about various assets, to which the debtor must respond under oath.

DEBTOR-INITIATED REMEDIES ALTERNATIVES:

- *Debtor's Alternatives*: A debtor may resolve financial problems outside of bankruptcy by entering into a composition agreement with creditors, whereby all creditors agree to receive less than full satisfaction of their claims. A second possibility is an extension agreement, where creditors extend the time available for payment of the debts and agree to forego lawsuits. Both agreements are in the nature of a contract between the debtor and multiple creditors. A third alternative is an assignment for the benefit of creditors, where a debtor turns over property to a third party to satisfy claims by creditors. d trade usage, to fill in missing terms.

STUDY HINTS FOR CALL-IMAGE TECHNOLOGY CASE STUDIES

The following study hints may be helpful when resolving the Call-Image Technology (CIT) case studies.

page 753
- ◆ Remember the rights of a secured party continue in bankruptcy.
- ◆ CIT should consider whether it is an impaired creditor under the plan and respond accordingly. Review the requirements for confirmation of a reorganization plan.

page 759
- ◆ Discuss with Tom the criteria for approving a Chapter 13 plan.
- ◆ You should advise Tom to evaluate whether he would receive more in a liquidation, and review the discussion on the 1984 Bankruptcy Amendments' rights of a creditor to block a repayment plan.

page 761
- ◆ You should recommend that they consider prejudgment alternatives to bankruptcy. Review the various forms of action.

MATCHING EXERCISE

Select the term or concept that best matches a definition or statement set forth below. Each term or concept is the best match for only one definition or statement.

Terms and Concepts

a. Attachment
b. Composition agreement
c. Confirmation hearing

d. Creditors' committee
e. Debtor in possession
f. Examiner

g. Extension agreement
h. Reorganization plan
i. Supplementary proceedings

Definitions and Statements

_____ 1. A committee which reviews and assists in developing a Chapter 11 plan.

_____ 2. Person appointed by the court to investigate a debtor's affairs, similar to a trustee.

_____ 3. An agreement among a debtor and multiple creditors where the creditors all agree to a pro rata reduction in payment.

_____ 4. A plan to restructure a business or large personal debt under Chapter 11.

_____ 5. Debtor who takes on duties of trustee following a Chapter 11 bankruptcy petition.

_____ 6. A hearing before the court to approve a Chapter 11 reorganization plan.

_____ 7. Post-judgment actions to force a debtor to reveal information regarding assets.

_____ 8. Contract among debtor and multiple creditors to extend time for full payment of debts.

_____ 9. Prejudgment action to seize property of debtor to satisfy debt.

COMPLETION EXERCISE

Fill in the blanks with the words that most accurately complete each statement.

1. A Chapter 13 repayment plan may also be referred to as a _____ _____ plan.

2. Within the first 120 days (or 100 days on the "fast-track") following a Chapter 11 petition, the

_____ ____ _____ has the exclusive right to propose a reorganization plan.

3. A _____ must approve any plan to sell assets from the Chapter 11 bankruptcy estate.

4. Confirmed plans under Chapter 11 Chapter 13 repayment plan are _____ on all parties.

5. Identify the four criteria a court considers in approving a Chapter 13 repayment plan.

a. _____.

b. _____.

c. _____.

d. _____.

TRUE-FALSE EXERCISE

Write **T** if the statement is true, write **F** if the statement is false.

_____ 1. A Chapter 11 plan may be approved even if it is rejected by some creditors.

_____ 2. Successful business may file a voluntary Chapter 11 petition and obtain relief.

_____ 3. A grain company creditor may file an involuntary Chapter 12 against a family farmer.

_____ 4. A Chapter 12 plan may call for sales of land free and clear of creditors.

_____ 5. Small corporations may file Chapter 13 plans if they have a less than $1 million of debt.

_____ 6. Ordinarily, a Chapter 13 plan will not extend beyond one year.

_____ 7. A court cannot increase payments during the course of a Chapter 13 plan.

_____ 8. A creditor may seize and sell a debtor's property before judgment is entered.

_____ 9. Liens on property continue under a receivership..

_____ 10. Creditors may file an involuntary bankruptcy petition following an assignment for the benefit of creditors by a debtor.

APPLICATION OF CONCEPTS

MULTIPLE CHOICE QUESTIONS

_____ 1. Rosa filed a Chapter 13 plan to repay her creditors over time. Under what circumstances may John (a creditor) block confirmation of the plan?
   a. The plan does not require all of Rosa's disposable income during the first year.
   b. The plan does not pay 100% of John's claim..
   c. The plan does not require 100% of Rosa's disposable income.
   d. Either b or c.

_____ 2. Martino Mining filed a Chapter 11 bankruptcy proceeding. Its reorganization plan provides that several of its mining claims be sold to raise money for payment of creditors. Which of the following statements is true.
   a. The claims may be sold only if the creditors approve.
   b. The claims may be sold only if the court approves.
   c. The claims may be sold only if sufficient money is raised to pay all unsecured claims.
   d. The claims may be sold only if creditors are not impaired.

_____ 3. Fast-Track Racing Cars filed a Chapter 11 bankruptcy proceeding. It sent its reorganization plan out to several classes of creditors for a vote prior to confirmation. Which statement accurately describes the effect of the vote?
   a. The plan must be voted for by all classes of creditors to be confirmed.
   b. If the plan is voted for by at least one class of creditors, the court may confirm it.
   c. If all classes of creditors vote against the plan, the court cannot confirm it..
   d. If all classes of creditors vote for the plan, the court must confirm it.

_____ 4. Charles wishes to attach property owned by Seth to satisfy a debt. Which actions must Charles take in order to recover the debt in this manner?
   a. Charles must ordinarily post a bond with the court prior to the attachment.
   b. Charles must sell the property and turn the proceeds over to the court prior to judgment.
   c. Charles must obtain a judgment before selling the property.
   d. a and c.

SHORT ANSWER QUESTIONS

Answer the following questions, briefly explaining the reason for your answer.

1. Healthy Heart Foods fears that liability for a shipment of tainted canned goods may financially destroy the company in the future. Healthy Heart has been successful, but the potential debt from this liability may require all the company's resources. The company currently has several classes of business creditors in addition to the litigants in the product liability case. May Healthy Heart file a Chapter 11 bankruptcy?

_____

_____

2. Bart's Bakery sued the Sugar Shack over a business debt and obtained a judgment. Sugar Shack has ignored the Baker's correspondence regarding payment of the judgment. What are the Baker's options for recovering the money ordered by the Court?

_____

_____

3. Fred Grey, a family farmer, is concerned that this year's crop failure will make him unable to pay for the seed corn he purchased on credit in the spring. If he pays for the seed, he will be unable to make the mortgage payments on the land, amounting to a total obligation of $1.5 million. Can Fred's creditors file an involuntary Chapter 12 bankruptcy against him? May Fred file a Chapter 13 repayment plan, or must he proceed under another chapter?

_____

_____

4. Jackson filed a Chapter 13 bankruptcy to repay his creditors. Under the repayment plan he proposes, none of his creditors would receive full payment, but they would receive more than if he filed a Chapter 7 and all are treated fairly. It appears that Jackson can follow the proposed plan. Is Jackson's plan likely to be approved by the Court?

_____

_____

CASE PROBLEMS

Answer the following case problems, explaining your answers.

1. Carla's Greenhouse filed a Chapter 11 bankruptcy. It has several classes of creditors, some of which would rather force the Greenhouse into a liquidation. The Greenhouse has operated as debtor-in-possession and filed a reorganization plan within the 120 day period. (a) May the secured creditors repossess their interests in property necessary for the reorganization? (b) May the Court approve the reorganization plan over the objections of disgruntled creditors? (c) Must the plan provide for all claims be paid in full? (d) May some creditors force the Greenhouse into a Chapter 7 absent some wrongful action on the debtor's part?

_____

_____

_____

_____

2. Sara has serious financial problems and desperately wishes to avoid bankruptcy. Several of her creditors have indicated that they might be willing to accept a smaller payment if they could be assured of receiving it without litigation. (a) May Sara enter a composition agreement with only some, but not all, of her creditors? (b) If agreed to, is the composition binding on all parties? (c) May the agreement provide full payment for some, but not all creditors? (d) Following the agreement, may a creditor who was a party sue Sara for the original debt?

_____

_____

_____

_____

Chapter 31

The Creation and Termination of an Agency

```
┌──────────────────────────────────────────────────────┐
│                                                        │
│  ┌──────────────────────────────────────────────┐     │
│  │                CHAPTER REVIEW                  │     │
│  └──────────────────────────────────────────────┘     │
│                                                        │
└──────────────────────────────────────────────────────┘
```

AGENCY LAW AND AGENCY RELATIONSHIPS: Agency law concerns the duties and relationships that arise between employees and employers. In general, an agency is a fiduciary relationship.

RESTRICTIONS ON CREATING AN AGENCY RELATIONSHIP: Potential issues relating to the creation of an agency relationship include:
- *Capacity to be a principal*: Any person having the capacity to contract (not minors - in most states; or incompetents) can employ an agent.
- *Capacity to be an agent*: Anyone, even minors and incompetents, can be an agent.
- *Duties an agent can perform*: Agents can be authorized to do almost any legal task, unless the task involves a non-delegable duty.

TYPES OF AGENCY RELATIONSHIPS: Agents can be either general agents or special agents.
- *General and special agents*: General agents have more discretion in carrying out their employers' business than do special agents. Factors that help determine an agent's status include: 1) the number of acts an agent must complete in order to obtain an authorized result; 2) the number of people that must be dealt with; and 3) the length of time needed to obtain the desired outcome.
- *Gratuitous agents*: Agents who volunteer their services to a principal are gratuitous agents.

SERVANTS AND INDEPENDENT CONTRACTORS: The distinction between servants and independent contractors is important when determining the liability of an employer for an employee's conduct.
- *Servants*: A "servant" is a special types of agent/employee whose employer has the right to control how the employee will perform his or her duties. Importantly, employers are liable for the physical acts (torts) that are committed by their servants while acting within the scope of their employment.
- *Independent contractors*: An independent contractor is hired by employers to accomplish a task, but the employers do not have the right to control how the contractor will carry out this duty. Independent contractors who are agents of employers, (e.g., a lawyer), may owe fiduciary duties to the employers.
- *Responsibility for independent contractors*: Principals are liable for authorized contracts made on their behalf by agents, even if the agents are independent contractors. Employers are liable for damage caused by an independent contractor who was hired to perform an ultrahazardous (or, increasingly, hazardous) activity. However, an employer is generally NOT liable for the *physical acts (or physical torts) or crimes* of their independent contractors unless: 1) the employer directed the tortious or criminal activity or 2) knew about the activity and did nothing to stop it.

Note: An employer's careless hiring, selection, supervision, or retention of a servant or independent contractor may constitute a tort on the part of the employer.

DUTIES OF THE AGENT TO THE PRINCIPAL: To protect the interests of the principal the agent has the following duties: the duty of good faith (a fiduciary duty); the duty of loyalty; the duty to obey all lawful instructions (unless doing so places the agent at unreasonable risk of injury); the duty to act with reasonable care; the duty to segregate funds; the duty to account for funds; and the duty to give notice of material facts to the principal.

DUTIES OF THE PRINCIPAL TO THE AGENT: The principal has the duty to pay the agent according to their contract; the duty to provide a safe place to work; and the duty to provide safe equipment to use.

TERMINATION OF THE AGENCY RELATIONSHIP: An agency relationship may be terminated by:

- *Agreement of the parties*: An employment contract between the principal and agent may state when the agency relationship shall end.
- *Agency at will*: If the agency agreement does not state that the relationship shall last for a fixed time or until a specified event occurs, then it is terminable at any time by either party after notice. However, a principal cannot terminate for reasons that would violate an agent's legal rights.
- *Fulfillment of the agency purpose*: Fulfillment of the agency's purpose usually terminates the agency.
- *Revocation*: A principal has the absolute right to terminate an agency. If the termination violates the agent's legal rights, then the agent may sue the principal for wrongful discharge.
- *Renunciation*: When an agents notify a principal that they quit, this terminates the relationship.
- *Operation of law*: An agency can terminate by operation of law, without need for notice, if the following events occur: 1) the death of the agent; 2) either party becomes insane; 3) a bankruptcy affects the agency; 4) the agency cannot be performed; 5) unforeseen events destroy the agency's purpose; or 6) a change in the law makes the agency illegal.
- *Importance of notice*: Early termination of the agency by either party, except by operation of law, requires notice to the parties and to third parties who might be affected. Actual or constructive notice may be acceptable, depending on the facts of the case.
- *Breach of agency agreement*: If a principal wrongfully discharges an agent, the agent has a duty to mitigate his or her damages by seeking alternative employment.

SPECIAL SITUATIONS: In some agencies, the principal may owe a special duty to the agent.

- *Agency coupled with an obligation*: If the principal is obligated in some way to the agent, the agency is "coupled with an obligation."
- *Power coupled with an interest*: This type of agency arises when the agent has special powers under the agency agreement, e.g., a lender (mortgagee) has the right to sell the principal's (debtor's) property if the principal defaults. In this agency, the termination rights of the principal are usually more limited.

STUDY HINTS FOR CALL-IMAGE TECHNOLOGY CASE STUDIES

The following study hints may be helpful when resolving the Call-Image Technology (CIT) case studies.

page 775	♦ Dan needs to more carefully review the rules regarding restrictions on creating an agency.

page 784	♦ Consider the implied duties of agents to principals in general, especially the duties of good faith and loyalty.

page 786	♦ From a legal perspective, you should review the duties of a principal relating to the negligent hiring, supervision, and retention of employees.

MATCHING EXERCISE

Select the term or concept that best matches a definition or statement set forth below. Each term or concept is the best match for only one definition or statement.

Terms and Concepts

a. Agency at will
b. Agent
c. Common carrier

d. Discretion
e. Fiduciary duty
f. Independent contractor

g. Principal
h. Renunciation
I. Trust

Definitions and Statements

_____ 1. Company that transports people or goods for a fee.

_____ 2. Person who is employed to accomplish a task. The person employed has the right to control how to accomplish the assigned work.

_____ 3. Using one's judgement to determine how to accomplish a task.

_____ 4. Legal duty to act in good faith and loyally for the benefit of another.

_____ 5. Legal relationship in which legal title is held separately from beneficial ownership.

_____ 6. Person who empowers another to negotiate contracts on his or her behalf.

_____ 7. Agency relationship that may be terminated by either party at any time.

_____ 8. Person who is empowered to negotiate contracts on behalf of another.

_____ 9. Act of an agent that terminates an agency relationship.

COMPLETION EXERCISE

Fill in the blanks with the words that most accurately complete each statement.

1. A _____ _____ is hired to conduct a series of transactions over time on behalf of a principal.

2. An agency is a _____ relationship between a principal and an agent, i.e., the law will not force the parties into this relationship.

3. In a _____ _____, an agent voluntarily agrees to perform a task for a principal.

4. The _____ of _____ requires the agent to look out for the principal's best interests.

5. Identify six general methods for terminating an agency.

a. _____.

b. _____.

c. _____.

d. _____.

e. _____.

f. _____.

TRUE-FALSE EXERCISE

Write T if the statement is true, write F if the statement is false.

____ 1. Anyone can be an agent.

____ 2. A contract is not essential in order to create an agency relationship.

____ 3. A primary feature of the agency relationship is that all agents are paid for their services.

____ 4. In general, a principal has the power to terminate an agency relationship even if the termination breaches a contract between the principal and agent.

____ 5. Independent contractors who are agents can bind their principals to contracts.

____ 6. An agent breaches the duty to obey the principal's instructions when the agent refuses to do an unreasonably dangerous task.

____ 7. If the agency agreement does not specify a time limit, either party may generally terminate the relationship at any time.

____ 8. When a principal dies, the agency immediately terminates in most states.

____ 9. If the principal wrongfully discharges an agent, the agent may have the right to recover damages from the principal.

____ 10. In an agency coupled with an interest, a principal cannot unilaterally terminate the agency.

APPLICATION OF CONCEPTS

MULTIPLE CHOICE QUESTIONS

____ 1. Jane appointed Ralph as her general agent. Nonetheless, Jane cannot:
   a. Authorize Ralph to buy and sell land on her behalf.
   b. Authorize Ralph to negotiate and execute contracts on her behalf.
   c. Delegate to Ralph the legal duty to provide safe working conditions for her employees.
   d. All of the above.

____ 2. General Contractors Unlimited (GCU) hired Piper Plumbing, Inc. to install the plumbing for an apartment building. Piper is obligated to install the plumbing in accordance with certain building plans, but Piper may otherwise control its own workers, method of construction, tools, supplies, etc. In this case, Piper is an:
   a. Employee of GCU.
   b. Agent for GCU.
   c. Independent contractor for GCU.
   d. Servant for GCU.

_____ 3. Jenni owns a construction company that builds custom houses. She hired Steve as her agent to solicit new business. Steve was approached by a celebrity who wanted to have a $3 million custom house built. Steve did not disclose this information to Jenni so that he could could take advantage of this opportunity himself. Steve has breached which of the following duties?
   a. Duty of loyalty.
   b. Duty of good faith.
   c. Duty to give notice.
   d. All of the above.

_____ 4. Zsa Zsa, a circus performer, employed Eddie as her agent to find her engagements for the next five years. Under these facts, the parties' agency relationship would terminate by operation of law after one year if:
   a. Eddie declared bankruptcy (his bankruptcy does not affect his ability to perform the agency).
   b. Zsa Zsa declared bankruptcy.
   c. Zsa Zsa decided that she no longer wanted Eddie to represent her.
   d. Zsa Zsa decided to limit the number of engagements she would accept each year.

SHORT ANSWER QUESTIONS

Answer the following questions, briefly explaining the reason for your answer.

1. Juan, owner of Juan's Antiques Unlimited, Inc. hired Mary to buy antiques for him in Europe. Mary bought antiques from many dealers and had them packed and shipped back to Juan's store. Mary has been buying for Juan for the past ten years. What type of agency exists between the parties?

_____

_____

2. Norton is an explosives expert. He was hired by Acme Construction to design, place, and set off the necessary explosive charges to blast a tunnel through a mountain. Acme dictated the dimensions for the tunnel, and Norton has the right to determine how the work is to be accomplished. What is the nature of the relationship between the parties? Would Acme be liable for harm that Norton may cause to others when carrying out the blasting?

_____

_____.

3. Jodi, an adult, wanted to sell her in-line skates. Jodi asked her 17-year-old friend, Ron, to find a buyer for the skates and to negotiate their sale on her behalf. Ron agreed, and contracted to sell the skates to a third party. What is the nature of the relationship between Jodi and Ron? Can Ron lawfully serve in this capacity? Is Jodi bound by the contract that Ron negotiated on her behalf?

_____

_____

4. Argie signed a contract to sell Cuttin'-To-The-Bone cutlery to retailers located in the Western United States for two years. When will this agency relationship terminate? Can the parties later agree not to terminate the agency?

_____

_____

CASE PROBLEMS

Answer the following case problems, explaining your answers.

1. Singh and Ratou are partners in a small turban manufacturing business. In their partnership agreement, the parties agreed that they may each act on behalf of the partnership in making partnership contracts. On behalf of the partnership, Ratou contracted with California Fabrics to buy muslin that was needed for making turbans. Ratou, however, agreed to a higher price than normal because California Fabrics promised to pay her a secret commission on the sale. Under these facts: (a) What relationship exists between the individual partners and the partnership? (b) What is the nature of this relationship? (c) Did Ratou breach any duty owed to the partnership?

_____

_____

_____

_____

2. Joe, general manager of Motorworks, Inc., an automobile service center, was fired in the morning and told not to return the next day. On the same day, Kathy paid money to Joe that she owed for work that Motorworks had performed on her car. Joe kept the money. The next day, Joe went to a Motorworks' supplier and bought a set of tires on behalf of Motorworks, a transaction that he had often done in the past. However, this time Joe kept the tires and absconded. (a) Discuss the rights of Motorworks, Kathy, and the supplier in this case. (b) What should Motorworks have done differently to avoid this situation?

_____

_____

_____

_____

Chapter 32   Agency: Liability for Contracts

CHAPTER REVIEW

A FRAMEWORK FOR CONTRACTUAL LIABILITY: When agents make a contract for principals, a prime issue is whether the principal authorized the agent to enter into the contract. Principals may be disclosed, partially disclosed, or undisclosed. The status of a principal may affect the parties' legal rights and duties.

IMPOSING LIABILITY ON THE PRINCIPAL: Principals are liable on contracts made on their behalf by agents only when the agents had some type of authority to contract. Different types of authority include:
- *Express authority*: Agents have express authority when the principal tells them they can do an act.
- *Ratification authority*: When agents enter into an unauthorized contract, the agent is said to have ratification authority if the principal, knowing all of the terms of the contract, expressly or impliedly approves the entire contract.
- *Incidental authority*: Agents have the authority to do acts reasonable and necessary to complete an assigned task.
- *Implied authority*: Agents with a particular title have the authority that their position would normally suggest to third parties.
- *Emergency authority*: Agency relationships allow agents to respond to emergencies if the principal cannot be reached and the agents act reasonably under the circumstances.
- *Apparent authority*: Apparent authority exists when: 1) the principal creates an appearance that an agency exists or that an agent has broader powers than actually exist, and 2) a third party reasonably believes that the agent has such authority.
- *Authority by estoppel*: Principals who mislead third parties regarding an agent's authority cannot deny the authority of the agent after the contract is made.
- *Imputing the agent's knowledge to the principal*: Since an agent has a duty to inform the principal of important information relating to the agency, the principal is assumed to know what the agent knows and the courts will impute the agent's knowledge to the principal.

DISCLOSED PRINCIPAL: A principal whose existence is clearly disclosed is bound to the terms of a contract that is made by an agent who acted pursuant to any of the types of authority described above.
- *Liability of the agent*: Normally agents acting for a disclosed principal are not liable on the contract. However, an agent may be personally liable if: 1) the agent does not disclose that they are acting only as an agent or 2) if the agent agrees to be bound to the contract. The other contracting party may sue either the principal or agent, or both (the modern trend) in situation 1), but the other party must ultimately elect whether the principal or agent must perform the remedy.
- *Warranty of authority*: It is implied that agents warrant to the other contracting party that: 1) the disclosed principal exists; 2) the principal is competent to contract; and 3) the principal authorized the contract. If any of these warranties is false, the third party can sue the agent for any resulting losses.
- *Liability of the third party*: The third party is liable to the principal for breach of contract if the agent had any authority to act (rule does not apply to authority by estoppel). The third party is liable to the agent if the agent has a legal interest in the contract or is a party to the contract.

UNDISCLOSED PRINCIPAL: An undisclosed principal is one whose existence and/or identity is not known to the other contracting party.

- *Liability of the agent*: If a principal is completely undisclosed, the third party can sue the agent for any breach of the contract.
- *Liability of the principal*: If the other party later discovers the identity of the principal, the third party can sue the principal on the contract. The principal is liable on the contract if the agent had authority to enter into the contract.
- *Liability of the third party*: If the other contracting party breaches the contract, the other party can be sued for breach of contract.

PARTIALLY DISCLOSED PRINCIPAL: A principal is partially disclosed if the other contracting party knows that a principal exists, but does not know the principal's identity. A partially disclosed principal can be sued for breach if the agent was authorized to make the contract. However, the other contracting party must elect whether to the principal or the agent.

CONTRACT BETWEEN THE PRINCIPAL AND THE AGENT: Possible issues relating to an agency include:

- *The need for a writing*: The Statute of Frauds may require certain agency contracts to be evidenced by a writing. The equal dignities rule requires that an agency contract be written if an agent is to make a contract on behalf of the principal and that contract is required to be in writing.
- *Covenants not to compete*: Many agency contracts state that when an agent's employment is ended, the agent cannot compete against his principal. Such covenants (promises) are valid only if they are for a reasonable period of time and geographical area.

STUDY HINTS FOR CALL-IMAGE TECHNOLOGY CASE STUDIES

The following study hints may be helpful when resolving the Call-Image Technology (CIT) case studies.

page 803
- ◆ Whether CIT is bound by the order depends on whether the salesperson had authority to enter the contract in question on behalf of CIT.
- ◆ Review the different types of authority, particularly implied and apparent authority.

page 807
- ◆ The third party has the burden to prove the salesperson's authority to represent CIT.
- ◆ Before advising the salesperson regarding his or her potential liability in this case, examine the concept of "warranty of authority" and evaluate whether it applies in this case.

page 813
- ◆ Review the material dealing with the fiduciary duties of agents, particularly the duty of loyalty.
- ◆ Review the tort of unfair competition and trade secrets.
- ◆ Also, bear in mind that the fiduciary duties implied by law are minimum obligations; the CIT agency contract can generally enlarge upon these duties.

MATCHING EXERCISE

Select the term or concept that best matches a definition or statement set forth below. Each term or concept is the best match for only one definition or statement.

Terms and Concepts

a. Apparent authority
b. Assignable
c. Covenant

d. Express authority
e. Goodwill
f. Implied authority

g. Imputed knowledge
h. Partially disclosed principal
i. Undisclosed principal

Definitions and Terms

____ 1. Knowledge of one person is attributed to another person as well.

____ 2. Authority that is orally or in writing given by a principal to an agent.

____ 3. Transferable.

____ 4. Promise.

____ 5. Good name and reputation of a business.

____ 6. Principal whose existence, but not identity, is known to a third party.

____ 7. Authority that arises because a principal falsely creates the impression that an agent has authority to act.

____ 8. Principal whose existence and identity are not known to a third party.

____ 9. Authority that arises because of an agent's position.

COMPLETION EXERCISE

Fill in the blanks with the words that most accurately complete each statement.

1. _____ by _____ arises when a principal has deliberately misled a third party regarding the authority of an agent.

2. When an agent represents a _____ _____ principal, the agent does not ordinarily incur any personal liability on the contract in question.

3. When agents represent an _____ principal, the other contracting party actually believes that the agents are acting on their own behalf.

4. A covenant not to compete is unenforceable unless it is for only a reasonable _____ and a

reasonable _____ _____.

5. Describe three guarantees that are encompassed by the warranty of authority:

    a. _____ .

    b. _____ .

    c. _____ .

TRUE-FALSE EXERCISE

Write T if the statement is true, write F if the statement is false.

_____ 1. If an agent makes an unauthorized contract on behalf of a principal, the principal may choose to ratify all or only a portion of the contract.

_____ 2. A principal is liable for every contract that is made on the principal's behalf by an agent.

_____ 3. If a principal ratifies a contract, the contract is treated as if it were valid from its inception.

_____ 4. Builders Inc. hired Jim as supervisor for a building project. Jim hired, trained, supervised, and fired workmen as needed to complete the project. Jim is exercising incidental authority.

_____ 5. Emergency authority may be implied in most agency relationships.

_____ 6. When an agency relationship is terminated, a prudent principal will give third parties notice of such termination.

_____ 7. Principals are not responsible for the actions of agents unless their authority is stated in writing.

_____ 8. A principal cannot be held liable on a contract that is made by an agent who acted with only apparent authority.

_____ 9. Principals can be held legally responsible for information that is known their agents only to the extent that the agents actually communicate the information to the principal.

_____ 10. In general, agents are liable on contracts that they make on behalf of disclosed principals.

APPLICATION OF CONCEPTS

MULTIPLE CHOICE QUESTIONS

_____ 1. Niles, as agent for an undisclosed principal, entered into a contract to buy and sell land with LandHo!, Inc. Which of the following is a true statement?
    a. Niles may sue LandHo! if LandHo! breaches the contract.
    b. LandHo! may sue Niles if the contract is breached.
    c. The undisclosed principal can sue both Niles and LandHo! if the contract is breached.
    d. a and b.

_____ 2. In which situation is Pat (the principal) liable on the contract in question?
    a. Pat signed a written power of attorney, authorizing an agent to sell his house. On Pat's behalf, the agent contracted with a third party for the sale of the house.
    b. An agent signed a contract to sell Pat's car, but Pat had not authorized this sale. Later Pat decided to accept the contract as written and signed it.
    c. An agent purchased supplies from a third party on behalf of Pat, just as the agent had done many times before. Pat had never expressly authorized the agent to make these purchases, but Pat was aware that the agent had been making these acquisitions and never objected.
    d. All of the above.

_____ 3. Sue applied for a job at Paul's Cafe. When Sue arrived for her job interview, Paul was busy with other business. To avoid having to interview Sue, Paul told her: "Go see Agnes, the head cashier. Agnes is responsible for all hiring decisions." Paul lied (Agnes was not supposed to hire anyone on her own), but Sue did not know this. After the interview, Agnes hired Sue to work at the cafe. What type of authority did Agnes have in this case?
   a. Express authority
   b. Implied authority
   c. Apparent authority
   d. No authority

_____ 4. Lynn is the purchasing agent for Patty, owner of a medical supply business. Lynn was expressly authorized to buy all necessary inventory on Patty's behalf. Acting pursuant to this authority, Lynn contracted to purchase some inventory from BandageCo. Patty breached this contract and failed to pay the purchase price. In this case, BandageCo. may hold Lynn personally liable on the contract if:
   a. Patty's existence and identity were disclosed to BandageCo. at the time of contracting.
   b. Pattys' existence, but not identity, was disclosed to BandageCo. at the time of contracting.
   c. Pattys' existence and identity were undisclosed to BandageCo. at the time of contracting.
   d. b and c.

SHORT ANSWER QUESTIONS

Answer the following questions, briefly explaining the reason for your answer.

1. Ali was sales manager for Adams Co., a crate manufacturer. Ali was orally told by Adams to sell 1,000 crates to Tri-State Groceries. On behalf of Adams, Ali contracted to sell the crates to Tri-State. Who are the parties to this contract? Who is liable to perform this contract?

_____

_____

2. Nolan was authorized by Ryan to purchase up to $500 of inventory for Ryan's business. When Nolan went to the supplier's warehouse, Nolan noticed that the supplier was having an unadvertised sale of inventory items that Ryan needed in his business. Nolan was unsuccessful in reaching Ryan, so he exercised his discretion and purchased $2,000 of merchandise for Ryan. Ryan was furious, but he decided to keep the merchandise after Nolan explained to him the terms of the contract. What type of authority, if any, did Nolan initially have to make this purchase? Is Ryan liable on the contract?

_____

_____

3. Elizabeth is the manager of a large clothing store. It is customary in Elizabeth's community and in the retail clothing industry that managers can hire necessary store clerks. Without consulting with the store owner, Elizabeth hired Rachel as a cosmetics sales clerk. What type of authority did Elizabeth have to hire Rachel? Could the store owner have limited or done away with this authority?

_____

_____

4. Roger was the general manager for the Stanley Farm. Stanley had instructed Roger never to contract for more than $1,000 without first obtaining Stanley's express authority. While Stanley was out of the country, a plague of locusts invaded the farm and threatened to wipe out the farm's entire crop. In order to save the crops, Roger hired Jenni's LocustBusters to exterminate the locusts at a cost of $500. Did Roger have authority to hire Jenni's extermination company?

_____

_____

CASE PROBLEMS

Answer the following case problems, explaining your answers.

1. Alton is a clerk at Preston's Mens Store. On behalf of Preston's, Alton contracted to buy 100 ties from All-Tied-Up, a tie supplier. Preston had never told Alton that he could make any purchases on behalf of the store. When Preston learned about the contract, Preston fired Alton and refused to perform the contract. (a) Discuss the nature of Alton's authority to make the purchase contract. (b) Who is liable to perform the contract? (c) Analyze whether Alton has any liability to Preston and/or All-Tied-Up.

_____

_____

_____

_____

2. Phyllis hired Jenkins to negotiate the purchase of a patent for her, but she asked Jenkins not to disclose her identity. Jenkins told the seller that he was acting on behalf of an anonymous third party. (a) What type of principal is Phyllis? (b) Discuss whether Phyllis and/or Jenkins can be held liable on the contract. (c) Can Phyllis and/or Jenkins hold the seller liable on the contract?

_____

_____

_____

_____

Chapter 33

Agency: Liability for Torts and Crimes

CHAPTER REVIEW

AGENT'S LIABILITY: Agents who commit a tort are personally liable for their torts. The primary issue in this situation is whether the agent's employer (master) is also liable for the tort. This issue is addressed by the doctrine of *respondeat superior*.

MASTER'S LIABILITY: *RESPONDEAT SUPERIOR*:: Under the doctrine of *respondeat superior*, a master may have vicarious (i.e., derivative or imputed) liability for a tort that is committed by an employee (servant) who was acting within the scope of the agency relationship at the time that the tort was committed. The doctrine of *respondeat superior* is based on a theory of strict liability theory - since the master hired the servant, and the servant did something wrong - the master must be held accountable if the servant's actions were committed within the course and scope of the servant's employment.

To establish vicarious liability of a master under the doctrine of *respondeat superior*, a third party must establish two elements: 1) a master-servant relationship existed between the master and servant; and 2) the servant was acting within the course and scope of employment at the time the tort was committed. These two elements are generally determined by the following inquiries:

1) A master-servant relationship exists if an employer has the right to control the details of an employee's work, whether or not the employer exercises this right. Conversely, an employer-independent contractor relationship exists (a master is generally NOT liable for torts of an independent contractor) if the employer has the right to control the end result, but not the method by which the agent accomplishes the task.

2) A servant is acting within the course and scope of employment when his or her conduct: (a) is the kind for which he or she was employed to perform; (b) occurs substantially within the time and territory authorized by the master; and (c) is performed in order to further the master's interests.

Common considerations and issues that arise when applying the doctrine of *respondeat superior* include the following:

- **Factors listed in the Restatement of Agency**: The key factors are whether the conduct of the servant was within the scope of the employee's employment or, if the conduct is not authorized, was it similar or incidental to the authorized conduct so as to be within the scope of employment. Whether the acts are within the course and scope of employment depends on the facts of the particular situation.
- **Time and place of occurrence**: Two of the most important factors analyzed in the Restatement is whether the tort occurred at the work place and during work hours.
- **Failure to follow instructions**: A master can be held liable for a servant's torts even though the master forbade the servant to commit torts.
- **Failure to act**: A master can be held liable if the servant fails to act as instructed.
- **Two masters**: Sometimes masters lend or borrow servants. In such cases, it is sometimes difficult to determine which master is liable for the torts of the borrowed servant.
- **Crimes and intentional torts**: The modern trend is to increasingly hold masters liable for the intentional torts of their servants, if the servants' actions furthered or were intended to further the master's interests (e.g., a battery committed by a nightclub bouncer, while evicting a patron). Since many criminal acts are also torts, the master may sometimes be held civilly liable for such acts.

DIRECT LIABILITY OF THE PRINCIPAL: In some cases, masters have direct liability in connection with their servants' torts because the masters themselves committed a wrong, either intentionally or negligently. Direct liability of masters may be based on any of the following types of conduct:

1) A master is directly liable to a third party if the master tells an servant to commit a tort against the third party and the servant does so.

2) A master is **negligent in** hiring a servant and placing the servant in a position where the servant agent can commit a tort against others.

3) A master is **negligent in supervising** a servant who has a known problem that may expose others to danger.

4) A master is **negligent in entrusting** a servant with equipment that the servant does not know how to operate and the servant then misuses the equipment, causing damage or injury to a third party.

INDEMNIFICATION: If the principal must pay a judgment because of an agent's tort, the principal has a right to repayment from the agent. Sometimes an agent has a right to indemnification from the principal if the agent pays the injured party for his or her tort. Also, the agent can obtain indemnification from the principal if the agent is directed to do a tortious act and does it believing that it is not tortious.

INJURY ON THE JOB : At common law, an employee who is injured on the job cannot recover from the employer if:

1) the employee assumed the risk;

2) the employee was negligent and the employee's contributory negligence caused the injury; or

3) the employee was injured by another employee of the same employer.

In most states today, the foregoing issues have been rendered moot by workers' compensation statutes. These statute typically allow an employee to recover benefits for work-related injuries and the foregoing defenses can NOT be used to deny an employee his or her benefits.

STUDY HINTS FOR CALL-IMAGE TECHNOLOGY CASE STUDIES

The following study hints may be helpful when resolving the Call-Image Technology (CIT) case studies.

page 824

♦ Before answering John, review the doctrine of respondeat superior, especially material contrasting an employer's liability for torts committed by independent contractors versus those committed by servants.

page 828

♦ Consider the factors listed by the Restatement which define "scope of employment"
♦ Also , consider the issue of "time and place of occurrence" of the tort.

page 830

♦ For information dealing with CIT's potential criminal liability for such employee conduct, review the "Direct Liability of the Principal" material.
♦ For information relating to the potential forfeiture of CIT's property, it may be helpful to review specific federal and state criminal laws and precedents.

REVIEW OF KEY TERMS AND CONCEPTS

MATCHING EXERCISE

Select the term or concept that best matches a definition or statement set forth below. Each term or concept is the best match for only one definition or statement.

Terms and Concepts

a. Accessory to the crime
b. Assault
c. Battery

d. Conspiracy
e. Indemnification
f. Judgement proof

g. Personal representative
h. Vicarious liability
I. Workers' compensation laws

Definitions and Statements

_____ 1. Person who handles a deceased person's financial affairs.

_____ 2. Unable to pay a judgement, even if found liable for damages in a civil lawsuit.

_____ 3. Statutory scheme by which workers receive benefits for work-related injuries.

_____ 4. Unpermitted touching of one person by another.

_____ 5. Liability imposed on one person for wrongs committed by another.

_____ 6. Threat to imminently commit a battery against someone.

_____ 7. Agreement by two or more persons to commit a crime.

_____ 8. Person who assists another in the commission of a crime.

_____ 9. Right to be repaid.

COMPLETION EXERCISE

Fill in the blanks with the words that most accurately complete each statement.

1. The doctrine of _____ _____ generally holds masters liable for torts that their servants commit while acting within the course and scope of their employment.

2. Employers have _____ liability under respondeat superior, meaning employers are liable because their servants did something wrong, not because the employers did anything wrong themselves.

3. Two factors that courts examine when deciding whether a servant's tort was committed within the

scope of employment are the _____ and _____ that the tort occurred.

4. Masters who pay for damages caused by their servants are entitled to _____, meaning the masters are entitled to be reimbursement from the servants for the amount paid.

5. _____ _____ laws generally allow employees to recover statutory benefits for work-related injuries.

TRUE-FALSE EXERCISE

Write **T** if the statement is true, write **F** if the statement is false.

_____ 1. Employers are liable for every tort committed by their servants.

_____ 2. One justification for the doctrine of *respondeat superior* is that this doctrine makes masters more careful in supervising their servants.

_____ 3. An employer may be held vicariously liable for harm that is caused by an independent contractor while performing an inherently dangerous task for the employer.

_____ 4. Employees who commit torts within the course and scope of their employment are not personally liable for such torts - only their employers are liable.

_____ 5. A principal may be personally liable to a third party who is injured by an employee whom the principal was negligent in hiring.

_____ 6. Under the modern view, masters may be held liable for the intentional torts of their servants if the torts were committed in order to advance the masters' interests.

_____ 7. An employer is generally not liable for torts that are committed by an employee who is merely commuting to or from work.

_____ 8. Under the doctrine of *respondeat superior*, an employer is generally liable for torts that are committed by an independent contractor.

_____ 9. A principal who directs an agent to commit a crime is personally liable for the agent's criminal conduct.

_____ 10. An employer cannot be held liable for an employee's torts if the employer previously instructed the employee not to commit such wrongs.

APPLICATION OF CONCEPTS

MULTIPLE CHOICE QUESTIONS

_____ 1. In which scenario is Lupe, the owner of Lupe's Dress Shop, liable for her employee's tort?
   a. Ellen, an employee, struck her ex-husband, who had come into the store, because he told her that he was getting remarried.
   b. Ed, who was a janitor for the store and under Lupe's direction and control, failed to put away a ladder. Later, a customer was injured when the ladder fell on her.
   c. Edger, a salesperson, was driving his own car to a restaurant for lunch when he struck a pedestrian. At the time, Edger was not running any errands for Lupe.
   d. All of the above.

_____ 2. Todd was a delivery person for Kar World. While driving to deliver a part to a customer, Todd negligently damaged Kip's car. Todd was speeding at the time of the accident, a violation of a Kar World work regulation. Under these facts, who is liable to Kip?
   a. Only Todd.
   b. Only Kar World.
   c. Todd and Kar World.
   d. No one.

_____ 3. In which case would the principal be directly liable for the agent's tort?
   a. Norm, the principal, instructed Al, his agent, to assault Tim, a person who owed Norm's business a great deal of money.
   b. Zoe, owner of a lawn sprinkler firm, failed to supervise Del, foreman of the installation crew. As a result, Del incorrectly installed sprinklers, causing a customer's trees to die.
   c. Kevin, owner of Children Day Care Center, hired Carl as a staff worker. Kevin failed to do a background check on Carl, who had a string of child molestation convictions. Carl molested a child at the center.
   d. All of the above.

_____ 4. Tina slipped and fell on a piece of chalk while teaching at Elmer Elementary School. The chalk had been negligently left on the floor by a school janitor. Under these facts:
   a. At common law, Tina could not hold the school liable for her injuries.
   b. At common law, Tina could hold the school liable for her injuries.
   c. Under worker's compensation laws, Tina cannot recover benefits because her injury was caused by a fellow employee.
   d. a and c.

SHORT ANSWER QUESTIONS

Answer the following questions, briefly explaining the reason for your answer.

1. Orlando owned Orlando's Hideaway, a nightclub. Rose worked for him as a waitress. All wait staff were instructed by Orlando on how to pour hot coffee refills, so as to avoid injuring customers. Rose routinely ignored Orlando's instructions. One evening Rose, disregarding Orlando's instructions, spilled piping hot coffee on a customer, severely burning her. Who is liable for the customer's injury? Explain your answer.

_____

_____

2. Jessica is a driver for Reliable Concrete Company. After delivering a load of concrete to a customer, Jessica decided that she would visit a friend who was working at a job site about ten miles away. When she was nearing her friend's job site, Jessica negligently collided with Marilyn's car, injuring Marilyn. Under these facts, are Jessica and/or Reliable liable to Marilyn?

_____

_____

3. Orville was a temporary worker hired by LaborTemp, Inc. LaborTemp sent Orville on a two-week temporary assignment at Mann Warehouse. Mann's had the right to control what and how Orville did his work. While stacking boxes in the warehouse, Orville negligently dropped a box on a customer, injuring the customer. Who is liable for Orville's tort - LaborTemp and/or Mann Warehouse?

_____

_____

4. Bobby was driving a delivery truck for Tony's Meat Market when he negligently side-swiped Maria's car. At the time of the accident, Bobby was driving to a convenience store to get a cup of coffee. This diversion took him two blocks away from his authorized route. In this case, who is liable to Maria?

_____

_____

CASE PROBLEMS

Answer the following case problems, explaining your answers.

1. Carol hired Humboldt Remodeling Co. to remodel her house for $30,000. Humboldt was required to remodel the house in accordance with certain plans, and Humboldt was to complete the work by May 1. Humboldt had the exclusive right to control the manner and method for performing the work, including the right to select the workers and tools to be used. One day, a Humboldt employee was picking up a bathtub to be installed in Carol's house. While loading the tub into a truck, the employee negligently dropped the tub injuring Roger, a passer-by. (a) What is the relationship between Carol and Humboldt? (b) Is Carol vicariously liable for Roger's injury? (c) Is Humboldt vicariously liable for Roger's injury?

_____

_____

_____

_____

2. Sandra always spent her lunch hour out of the office, frequently driving to a nearby park to eat and nap. One day while Sandra was driving to the park to eat her lunch, she negligently ran a stop sign and struck Nora, a pedestrian. (a) Under these facts, is Sandra's employer liable for Nora's injuries? (b) Would Sandra's employer be liable for Nora's injuries if, at the time of the accident, Sandra was dropping off a package for her employer on her way to the park

_____

_____

_____

_____

CHAPTER 34   Formation of a Business

CHAPTER REVIEW

HISTORIC OVERVIEW OF PARTNERSHIPS: Today, partnerships are governed by the UPA.

PARTNERSHIPS DEFINED: You should understand the difference between general and limited partnerships.
- *Uniform Partnership Act*: The UPA defines a partnership as: 1) an association; 2) of two or more persons; 3) to carry on a business; 4) as co-owners; 5) for profit.
- *A Limited Partnership*: Must have two or more persons with at least one limited partner. A limited partner is not personally liable for partnership obligations, but cannot control the business of the partnership.
- *Revised Uniform Limited Partnership Act*: The RULPA requires profits and losses to be shared based on capital contributions, unless an agreement specifies otherwise.

PARTNERSHIP PROPERTY: The UPA defines partnership property as: 1) property contributed as capital contributions; 2) property acquired on account; 3) property acquired with partnership funds; 4) any interest in real property acquired in the partnership's name; and 5) any conveyance to the partnership in its name.

THE PARTNERSHIP AGREEMENT: A partnership is created by agreement, which may be express (oral or written) or implied.
- *Imposed Rules*: Unless an agreement states otherwise, the law imposes the following rules: 1) partners are each entitled to one vote when deciding whether the partnership should take a particular action; 2) partners are entitled to share equally in partnership profits (regardless of the amount of their contributions); 3) partners share losses in the same proportion as they share profits; and 4) books must be kept at the central office.
  Regardless of what the partnership agreement states, partners: 1) are agents of the partnership; 2) partners have unlimited personal liability to partnership creditors for partnership obligations; and 3) each partner is a fiduciary of the partnership.
- *Express Terms*: At a minimum, the partnership agreement, if there is one, should state the purpose and duration of the partnership, how profits and losses are shared, and withdrawal procedures.

LIMITED LIABILITY PARTNERSHIPS: A growing number of states recognize the limited liability partnership (LLP). With certain exceptions, a partner in an LLP is not personally liable for the malpractice, negligence, or other tort committed by a co-partner or partnership agent. But, partners remain personally liable for their own negligence and for contractual obligations of the partnership.

TAXATION OF PARTNERSHIPS: A partnership is not taxed on its profits and losses. Instead, partners are personally taxed on their share of the partnership's profits and losses.

HISTORIC OVERVIEW OF CORPORATIONS: Corporations flourish because of their ability to raise capital.

CORPORATE NATURE: Corporations are artificial entities authorized by statute.
- *Advantages of the Corporate Form*: Advantages include: 1) shareholders are protected from personal liability; 2) centralized management; 3) continuity of existence; and 4) free transferability of shares.

FORMATION OF A CORPORATION: There are several types of corporations; choose wisely.

- *Types of Corporations*: The types include: 1) public-issue private corporations; 2) close corporations; 3) professional corporations; and 4) municipal (also called public or quasi-public) corporations.
- *Promoters*: Promoters help form the corporation by procuring subscribers for stock.
- *Articles of Incorporation*: Articles create the corporation and must be filed with the secretary of state.
- *Corporate Charter/Certificate of Incorporation*: This document begins a corporation's existence.
- *Organizational Meeting*: In some states, a corporation exists only after its organization meeting.
- *Bylaws*: Bylaws regulate the internal affairs of a corporation.

DE JURE VERSUS DE FACTO CORPORATIONS: A *de jure* corporation is valid by law. If a corporation fails to comply with incorporation laws, it may qualify as a *de facto* corporation if: 1) a law under which the corporation could have been incorporated exists; 2) there was a good faith effort to comply with the statute; and 3) there was some use or exercise of corporate powers.

CORPORATE POWERS AND ULTRA VIRES ACTS: The articles set forth express powers. Corporations also have the implied power to do anything reasonably necessary to conduct business. An *ultra vires* transaction is a transaction that exceeds the purposes or powers of a corporation.

TAXATION OF CORPORATIONS: Profits and losses of a C corporation are taxed to the corporation. Profits and losses of an S corporation (Subchapter S corporation) are taxed to the shareholders.

LIMITED LIABILITY COMPANIES: LLCs are a new form of legal entity. Typical requirements include: 1) two or more members; 2) stated term of duration less than 30 years; 3) all members must have limited liability; 4) shares are not freely transferable; 5) central management is elected by the members; and 6) an indication in its name that it is an LLC. LLCs are taxed as partnerships.

OTHER TYPES OF BUSINESS ORGANIZATIONS: Partnership by estoppel; joint venture; mining partnership.

DISREGARDING THE CORPORATE ENTITY: In certain cases, such as fraud, courts may ignore the corporate form and impose personal liability on shareholders.

STUDY HINTS FOR CALL-IMAGE TECHNOLOGY CASE STUDIES

The following study hints may be helpful when resolving the Call-Image Technology (CIT) case studies.

page 858

♦ Review the material "Formation of a Corporation."

page 863

♦ When advising Tom and Anna, you should review Figure 34.1.

MATCHING EXERCISE

Select the term or concept that best matches a definition or statement set forth below. Each term or concept is the best match for only one definition or statement.

Terms and Concepts

a. Corporation
b. Estoppel
c. General partner
d. Joint venture

e. Limited liability partnership
f. Limited partner
g. Mining partnership
h. Partnership

i. Proprietorship
j. Ratification
k. Rebuttable presumption
l. Registered agent

Definitions and Statements

_____ 1. Partner in a limited partnership whose liability is limited to his or her contribution.
_____ 2. Accepting or approving an unauthorized act.
_____ 3. Partnership wherein partners are generally not liable for torts of other partners or partnership agents.
_____ 4. Partner in a limited partnership who controls the business of the partnership.
_____ 5. Legal assumption that is followed unless stronger, contrary proof is presented.
_____ 6. Partnership formed to conduct mining operations; interests can be transferred by will.
_____ 7. Person designated by a corporation to receive service of process.
_____ 8. Association of two or more persons to carry on a single business enterprise for profit.
_____ 9. Artificial legal entity whose owners are stockholders or shareholders.
_____ 10. Business owned by one person.
_____ 11. Legal bar that prevents a person from claiming or denying certain facts.
_____ 12. Association of two or more persons to carry on an on-going business for profit.

COMPLETION EXERCISE

Fill in the blanks with the words that most accurately complete each statement.

1. A corporation that is formed in strict compliance with state law is a _____

_____ corporation.

2. A _____ ____ _____ is generally issued by a state to acknowledge the legal existence of the corporation.

3. _____ are the persons who conceive the idea for a business, organize the undertaking of this business, and take steps to form the corporation to engage in this business.

4. An _____ _____ transaction is a transaction that exceeds the purposes or powers of a corporation.

5. Identify four advantages of doing business as a corporation.

a. _____.

b. _____.

c. _____.

d. _____.

TRUE-FALSE EXERCISE

Write **T** if the statement is true, write **F** if the statement is false.

_____ 1. Property may be partnership property even if title is held in the name of an individual partner.

_____ 2. If a partnership does not have a definite duration or purpose, then any partner is legally entitled to withdraw at any time.

_____ 3. The fact that parties share net profits earned by a business is strong evidence that the parties' business relationship is a partnership.

_____ 4. LLCs are generally taxed as partnerships.

_____ 5. Limited partners may exercise limited participation in the management of the partnership without becoming personally liable for partnership obligations.

_____ 6. Shares of LLCs are freely transferable.

_____ 7. For federal income tax purposes, the profits and losses of a Subchapter S corporation are taxed to the shareholders.

_____ 8. A promoter is a fiduciary of the corporation and its shareholders.

_____ 9. A partnership cannot be created unless parties specifically call their relationship a partnership.

_____ 10. In general, partnership agreements are required to be in writing to be enforceable.

APPLICATION OF CONCEPTS

MULTIPLE CHOICE QUESTIONS

_____ 1. In which situation does a partnership probably exist between Felix and Art?
   a. Felix owed $10,000 to Art. Felix agreed to pay 10 percent of his company's profits to Art as partial payment of the $10,000 debt.
   b. Felix owns an insurance company. As compensation, Felix pays Art 5 percent of the gross premiums paid on insurance policies that are sold by Art.
   c. Felix and Art co-own a grocery store. Felix and Art jointly control the business and they share the net profits and losses derived from the store.
   d. Felix and Art own a rental house. Felix and Art share the rentals earned from the property.

_____ 2. Jim and Todd are the shareholders of J&T, Inc. In which situation would a court be justified in piercing the corporate veil and imposing liability on Jim and Todd for obligations of J&T?
   a. Jim and Todd form J&T in order to obtain substantial tax benefits.
   b. Jim and Todd form J&T in order to avoid personal liability for future corporate debts.
   c. Jim and Todd form J&T in order to engage in illegal stock sales that would otherwise cause them significant personal liability.
   d. All of the above.

_____ 3. Sylvia and Janet are forming a business to engage in the high-risk business of Internet advertising. The risk is that the business will undertake large contractual debts that it may not be able to repay if enough advertising is not sold. Sylvia and Janet are willing to risk their respective investments, but neither wants to lose all of their personal assets should the business fail. In this case, what type of business entity would fulfill the parties' desire to protect their personal assets?
   a. Partnership
   b. Limited liability partnership.
   c. Corporation.
   d. b and c.

_____ 4. Polly wishes to incorporate Polly's Pets Inc. When will the corporate existence for this proposed corporation begin?
   a. The corporation will exist as soon as Polly files corporate bylaws with the secretary of state.
   b. The corporation will exist as soon as Polly commences doing business as a corporation.
   c. The corporation will exist as soon as Polly officially declares that it exists.
   d. In most states, the corporation will not exist until Polly files an appropriate application (with articles of incorporation) and the state issues a certificate of incorporation.

SHORT ANSWER QUESTIONS

Answer the following questions, briefly explaining the reason for your answer.

1. Larry and Harry have started a new business that will prove to be very profitable. Several of Larry's and Harry's friends have offered to invest. However, these friends have indicated that they may eventually want to sell their interests in the business. Suggest several strategies that Larry and Harry might use to restrict the resale of the investors' business interests.

_____

_____

2. Sean was a promoter, organizing STR, Inc. Prior to incorporation of STR, Sean entered into a contract on behalf of the corporation to buy $25,000 worth of equipment. After STR was incorporated, Sean and STR entered into a contract whereby they agreed that STR will buy the equipment from Sean. Later, the corporation failed to pay for the equipment. Is Sean liable for the $25,000?

_____

_____

3. Bruce is a limited partner in B-MER Ltd. Bruce is also a licensed attorney. On occasion, Bruce gives legal advice to B-MER. Will Bruce's conduct be considered participation in management, thereby causing Bruce to forfeit his status as a limited partner?

_____

_____

4. Lee and Mindy are partners in L&M Partnership. Prior to formation of the partnership, Lee owned a truck. Lee now regularly allows Mindy and other L&M employees to use the truck to conduct partnership business. Also, the truck is usually parked at the offices of L&M, the keys are kept in the office, and the partnership typically pays for routine maintenance on the truck. The parties never stated whether the truck was to become partnership property, and title remains in Lee's name. Is the truck partnership property?

_____

_____

CASE PROBLEMS

Answer the following case problems, explaining your answers.

1. Ted and Alice intend to form a corporation and they are trying to determine what powers the corporation may have. Ted and Alice have asked you the following questions: (a) If the articles of incorporation are silent regarding corporate powers, most states will grant a corporation the right to exercise what powers? (b) Can the corporation be formed to have perpetual succession? (c) Can the corporation be empowered to buy, sell, and mortgage real and personal property?

_____

_____

_____

_____

2. Juan and Carol are engineers who have an idea for an invention that will increase the processing speed of older computers that cannot otherwise be upgraded. Some friends have offered Juan and Carol start-up capital. However, Juan and Carol want to maintain control over management of the business. Also, Juan and Carol anticipate losses during the business's first few years, and they want to assure that they can use their share of these losses to offset other personal income on their individual tax returns. Discuss the respective advantages and disadvantages of Juan and Carol doing business as a partnership, limited partnership, or corporation.

_____

_____

_____

_____

CHAPTER 35 — Operation of a Business Organization

```
┌─────────────────────────────────────────────┐
│ ┌───────────────────────────────────────────┐ │
│ │               CHAPTER REVIEW              │ │
│ └───────────────────────────────────────────┘ │
└─────────────────────────────────────────────┘
```

OPERATION OF A BUSINESS: The terms of a partnership agreement control the partners' rights; however, if there is no agreement, each partner is considered a manager, an agent, and a principal of the other partners. In a corporation, the officers and the directors are responsible for the corporation's operations and policies.

RIGHTS OF THE PARTNERS: Rights of partners vary depending on the partnership agreement and whether the Uniform Partnership Act (UPA) governs. Unless otherwise agreed, the following rules usually apply:
- *Management*: Each partner has an equal voice in managing the partnership, but partners can define "equal." Majority votes control ordinary partnership decisions, and unanimous decisions are required to authorize extraordinary transactions.
- *Reimbursement*: Partners are entitled to a return of their capital contribution when the partnership ends if there are sufficient funds to do so.
- *Profits and Losses*: Partners are entitled to an equal share of the profits unless they agree otherwise. Partners are not entitled to salaries unless the partnership agreement provides for them.
- *Books and Records*: Each partner is entitled to review the partnership's books and records.
- *Partnership Property*: Partners are co-owners with each other of any property owned by the partnership; this is called a tenancy in partnership. This means that a partner cannot possess partnership property for personal use without the unanimous agreement of the other partners.
- *Right to an Account*: A partner may demand an accounting of the partnership's business transactions.

DUTIES OF THE PARTNERS: Each partner is an agent of the partnership, meaning he or she can bind the partnership to ordinary business contracts. Each partner is personally liable for partnership debts and is required to account for any profits. As a fiduciary of the partnership, a partner is not permitted to realize secret profits from partnership business, compete against the partnership, or engage in transactions that may involve a conflict of interest.

RIGHTS OF THIRD PERSONS WHO DEAL WITH PARTNERSHIPS: A third party is entitled to rely on a partner's apparent authority to enter into a contract, and if there is no such authority, the partner may be personally liable to the third party. Apparent authority is determined by influenced by whether the partnership is a trading or nontrading partnership, especially when borrowing money. Trading partners have broader powers. If a third party is injured by a partner's tort, the partnership (and therefore the other partners) may be liable for the partner's tort under the doctrine of *respondeat superior*.

OPERATION OF A CORPORATION: Officers are generally responsible for the day-to-day business of a corporation and the board of directors is responsible for establishing the overall policies of the corporation.

RIGHTS OF THE SHAREHOLDERS OF A CORPORATION:
- *Types of Stock Owned*: Common stock allows a shareholder to receive dividends, vote on corporate issues, and receive property upon liquidation; preferred stock confers priority as to dividends and liquidation rights - preferred stock does not vote on most matters that common stock may vote on.

- *Shareholders' Meetings*: There must be notice before a shareholder meeting, and a quorum of shareholders must be present. Shareholders vote on board members and amending bylaws. Shareholders can vote by proxy, giving their vote to someone else. Straight voting is one vote per share, and generally a majority vote is required to bind the corporation.
- *Dividends*: The board of directors has the power to decide whether to declare dividends. If dividends are declared, shareholders are entitled to them. Preferred stockholders are paid first.
- *Preemptive Stock Rights*: If a corporation issues new stock, it must make the new shares available to current stockholders first if the shareholders have preemptive stock rights
- *Inspection of Corporate Books and Records*: Shareholders are entitled to inspect a corporation's books and records, but only on a showing that it is for a "proper purpose."
- *Transfer of Shares*: Shareholders are free to transfer their shares, unless they are subject to limitations placed on the stock, such as giving current shareholders the right of first refusal to purchase the shares.

LIABILITIES OF SHAREHOLDERS: In some instances, a shareholder can be liable for corporate obligations. These exceptional situations include the following:
- *Watered Stock*: If stock is issued as fully paid but it has in fact not been fully paid, then a shareholder owns watered stock and is liable for the difference.
- *Stock Subscriptions*: These are agreements by investors to purchase shares and the corporation can enforce them by requiring the subscriber to pay the subscription price.
- *Illegal Dividends*: If a dividend that impairs the original capital structure of the corporation is paid, it is illegal and the shareholder receiving it may be liable to repay it to the corporation.
- *Dissolution*: Controlling shareholders have a fiduciary duty to minority shareholders and may be liable for a dissolution arrangement that prejudices the minority shareholders.

RIGHTS AND DUTIES OF THE MANAGERS OF A CORPORATION: Directors are fiduciaries of a corporation and they may be held personally liable to the corporation if they breach these duties, causing harm to the corporation or shareholders. Officers are agents of the corporation and can bind the corporation through any action they are expressly or implicitly authorized to perform. Directors and officers owe fiduciary duties of obedience, diligence, and loyalty to the corporation.

STUDY HINTS FOR CALL-IMAGE TECHNOLOGY CASE STUDIES

The following study hints may be helpful when resolving the Call-Image Technology (CIT) case studies.

page 878
- ♦ Review the rights and duties of partners.
- ♦ Consider the rights of third parties who deal with partnerships when answering Dan.

page 902
- ♦ To answer John, you should also consider the rights and duties of officers.
- ♦ Consider the business judgment rule discussed on pg. 900 of the textbook and *NCR v. AT&T*.

page 904
- ♦ Contrast the rules for partnerships and corporations.
- ♦ While a Subchapter S corporation must meet certain requirements to qualify for its special tax treatment, its operations and powers are basically the same as other corporations.

MATCHING EXERCISE

Select the term or concept that best matches a definition or statement set forth below. Each term or concept is the best match for only one definition or statement.

Terms and Concepts

a. Alienation
b. Capital contribution
c. Common stock
d. Constructive trust

e. Goodwill
f. Liquidation preference
g. Outsider directors
h. Preferred stock

I. Proxy
j. Par value
k. Tenancy in partnership
l. Trustees

Definitions and Statements

_____ 1. Money or assets invested by people in a business as payment for their ownership interests.
_____ 2. Form of ownership in partnership property.
_____ 3. Good reputation of a business.
_____ 4. Voting stock of a corporation.
_____ 5. Face value of stock.
_____ 6. Directors who are not shareholders or officers.
_____ 7. Written authorization to vote someone's stock.
_____ 8. Persons who are empowered to manage the business and affairs of others.
_____ 9. Priority granted to creditors or others when a business is terminated and assets are distributed.
_____ 10. Transfer of ownership to another.
_____ 11. Legal remedy imposed by law to preserve property that is wrongfully held by a party.
_____ 12. Stock that enjoys a preference to dividends and/or distributions upon dissolution of a corporation.

COMPLETION EXERCISE

Fill in the blanks with the words that most accurately complete each statement.

1. If a partner commits a tort while acting within the course and scope of partnership business, then all of

the partners have _____ and _____ liability for the tort.

2. A _____ _____ is an agreement by an investor to purchase shares in a corporation.

3. When a dividend is declared, _____ _____ stock has the right to be paid dividends for prior years that dividends were not paid and a dividend for the current year, before a dividend is paid to common stockholders.

4. List three prerequisites regarding shareholder meetings generally found in corporate bylaws:

   a._____.

   b._____.

   c._____.

5. Two lawful sources for declaring and paying dividends generally include:

   a._____.

   b._____.

TRUE-FALSE EXERCISE

Write **T** if the statement is true, write **F** if the statement is false.

_____ 1. An extraordinary partnership transaction requires unanimous consent of all partners.

_____ 2. A partner who pays a partnership obligation from personal funds is entitled to reimbursement from the partnership.

_____ 3. Unless otherwise agreed, the UPA requires payment of reasonable compensation in the form of salary for a managing partner who devotes extra time to running the business.

_____ 4. In general, a partner in a retail clothing store would not have apparent authority to sell the building in which the store is located.

_____ 5. A shareholder is absolutely liable to repay an illegal dividend if the corporation was insolvent at the time the dividend was paid.

_____ 6. Corporate property can be transferred only by the corporation, not shareholders.

_____ 7. A corporation may indemnify its directors for liabilities resulting from good faith actions that the directors took on behalf of the corporation.

_____ 8. A quorum of shareholders ordinarily consists of shareholders who own at least a majority of the outstanding shares entitled to vote.

_____ 9. Cumulative voting may enable minority shareholders to exercise greater influence in elections of directors than they could exercise under straight voting.

_____ 10. Voting trusts and pooling arrangements are less frequently used in close corporations than in large publicly-held corporations.

APPLICATION OF CONCEPTS

MULTIPLE CHOICE QUESTIONS

_____ 1. Adams is a partner in a retail clothing store. Without express authorization, Adams borrowed $5,000 on behalf of the partnership in order to purchase inventory for the store. Under these facts:
   a. The partnership is a trading partnership.
   b. The partnership is a nontrading partnership.
   c. Adams and the other partners are liable for this loan.
   d. a and c.

_____ 2.   Cooper, Tex, and Chien are the partners in CTC Partnership. Cooper contributed $50,000 to the partnership, and Tex and Chien each contributed $25,000. The partnership agreement is silent regarding management rights and allocation of profits. Under these facts:
   a.   Cooper has the exclusive right to manage the partnership.
   b.   Cooper, Tex, and Chien are each entitled to an equal vote regarding partnership matters.
   c.   Cooper is entitled to 100 percent of the partnership profits.
   d.   Cooper is entitled to 50 percent of the partnership profits.

_____ 3.   Pam was a partner in a partnership that sold office supplies. In which situation did Pam breach a duty that she owed to the partnership?
   a.   Pam purchased supplies for the partnership. Pam had express authority to act and she used reasonable judgment, but the partnership lost money due to the purchase.
   b.   Pam set up a new firm that purchased supplies from the partnership at discounted prices. Pam did not disclose her interest in the new firm, and she secretly profited from the firm's transactions with the partnership.
   c.   After termination of the partnership, Pam opened an office supply company that competed with a new business that was created by her former partners.
   d.   All of the above.

_____ 4.   Don and Rene are the partners in a partnership that owns a retail paint store. Under these facts, Don does NOT have authority to make which contract on behalf of the partnership?
   a.   Contract to purchase a case of paint.
   b.   Contract to hire a salesclerk who is needed to run the store.
   c.   Contract to sell the entire store.
   d.   Contract to purchase fire insurance for the store.

SHORT ANSWER QUESTIONS

Answer the following questions, briefly explaining the reason for your answer.

1. A partnership agreement specifies that Adams, Baker, and Campbell are to receive $12,000 a year salary with profits to be allocated 20 percent to Adams, 45 percent to Baker, and 35 percent to Campbell. Is this agreement enforceable?

_____

_____

2. ABC Inc. issued common and preferred stock. Earl owns 60,000 shares of ABC common stock and Antonio owns the remaining 40,000 shares of common stock. Trisha owns 200,000 shares of ABC preferred stock, which has typical rights and preferences. At the annual meeting, the shareholders are to vote on a proposed pay raise for corporate officers. Who can vote on this matter? As a practical matter, who has the power to determine whether the pay-raise proposal is approved?

_____

_____

3. Ed was a majority shareholder in MED Inc. In a shareholder agreement, Ed and the other shareholders agreed not to sell their stock to anyone else without first offering it to each other. This restriction was not stated on the stock certificates. In violation of this agreement, Ed sold and transferred his stock to Hank who bought it in good faith and without knowledge of the restriction. Is the stock transfer to Hank enforceable?

_____

_____

4. Roger is a minority shareholder in Neco Inc. Roger has demanded to inspect the corporation's financial records in order to compute the value of his stock. Is Roger entitled to inspect the corporations records?

_____

_____

CASE PROBLEMS

Answer the following case problems, explaining your answers.

1. Glen and Tim were the partners in a partnership that owned a store. On behalf of the partnership, Glen bought inventory from Seller on credit for $5,000. Glen had authority to make this contract. The partnership failed to pay the contract price, and the partnership was later dissolved. The partnership agreement states that Glen and Tim shall each bear 50 percent of partnership losses. (a) Is the partnership liable on the contract made by Glen? (b) Does the partnership's dissolution terminate Glen's and Tim's liability for partnership obligations? (c) Does Tim have personal liability for the contract price owed to Seller? (d) If Tim pays the entire contract price, can Tim seek reimbursement from Glen?

_____

_____

_____

_____

2. Pat is a shareholder in EagleCo. Pat bought 10,000 shares of $10 par-value common stock from EagleCo for $10 per share. Pat paid the corporation $50,000 for the stock. EagleCo later paid Pat a $5,000 dividend out of capital at a time when it was insolvent. Discuss whether Pat has any personal liability to the corporation and/or corporate creditors in this case.

_____

_____

_____

_____

CHAPTER 36

Business Terminations and Other Extraordinary Events

TERMINATION OF A SOLE PROPRIETORSHIP: The owner pays the debts and keeps any remaining assets.

PARTNERSHIP TERMINATIONS: A partnership terminates (ceases to exist) following dissolution and winding up of its business. Dissolution, winding up, and termination are three related, but separate, steps.

PARTNERSHIP DISSOLUTION: A dissolution occurs any time a partner is admitted into an existing partnership or a partner leaves a partnership. A dissolution is a change in the partners' relationship among themselves and with the partnership. Following a dissolution, the partners must either: 1) wind up and terminate the partnership and its business or 2) elect to continue the partnership business.

Actions or events that cause a partnership dissolution include:

- *Without Violation of the Agreement*: The partnership agreement may specify a time for dissolution or all the partners may agree to dissolve the partnership. Also, In a partnership at will, each partner has the legal power and right to withdraw from the partnership at any time, causing a dissolution.
- *In Violation of the Agreement*: In any partnership, even a partnership for a definite term, each partner has the legal power to withdraw at any time. A partner's wrongful withdrawal causes a dissolution, although the remaining partners may unanimously agree to continue the business and not wind up.
- *By Operation of Law*: A partnership is dissolved by law if: 1) it becomes unlawful to operate the business; 2) a partner dies; or 3) a partner or the partnership becomes bankrupt.
- *By Court Order*: A court may order the dissolution of the partnership if: 1) a partner becomes insane; 2) a partner becomes incapacitated; 3) a partner commits serious misconduct; 4) a partner repeatedly breaches the agreement; 5) the business can no longer be operated profitably; or 6) any other circumstance the court believes will justify a dissolution.

CONTINUATION OF THE PARTNERSHIP BUSINESS: The remaining partners have a right to continue the partnership if: 1) the withdrawing partner withdrew in violation of the agreement; 2) the withdrawing partner consents to the continuation; or 3) the agreement permits a continuation after a dissolution.

- *Withdrawing Partners*: Withdrawing partners must be indemnified and bought out. If the withdrawal was in violation of the agreement, the partnership may deduct damages.
- *Entering Partners*: A new partner is liable for existing debts up to the partner's capital contribution.

WINDING UP THE PARTNERSHIP: In winding up, assets are liquidated and proceeds distributed.

- *General Partnerships*: Proceeds are distributed in the following order: 1) creditors; 2) partners, acting as creditors; 3) return of capital contribution to partners; and 4) distribution of profits.
- *Limited Partnerships*: Proceeds are distributed as follows: 1) nonpartner and partner creditors; 2) amounts owed to former partners prior to their withdrawal; 3) return of capital; and 4) profits.

CHANGES IN CORPORATE STRUCTURE: Changes in corporate structure include: dissolution, merger and consolidation, sale of substantially all of the corporate assets, and stock acquisition.

LIQUIDATION OF THE CORPORATION: When a corporation liquidates, the corporation sells its assets, pays off in full its creditors, and any remaining proceeds are distributed to the shareholders in accordance with their rights and preferences. During liquidation, a corporation can sue and be sued.

DISSOLUTION OF THE CORPORATION: Dissolution terminates a corporation's existence as a legal entity.
- *Voluntary Dissolution*: Voluntary dissolution requires: 1) board authorization; 2) shareholder approval (usually two-thirds of the outstanding shares); and 3) notice to creditors.
- *Involuntary Dissolution*: The state, the shareholders, or creditors may seek an involuntary dissolution. Common reasons for involuntary dissolution include serious wrongdoing by the corporation's directors and/or officers that adversely affect the interests of shareholders and creditors.

CORPORATE MERGER AND CONSOLIDATION: A *merger* is a combination of two corporations whereby only one of the corporations continues to exist. The surviving corporation owns the assets of the original corporations, and it is also liable for their combined debts. A *consolidation* is a combination of two corporations whereby a new corporation is formed, replacing the original corporations which cease to exist. The new corporation owns the assets of the original corporations, and it is liable for their combined debts.
- *Rationales for Merger*: The most important rationales for merger include the attainment of economies of scale, acquisition of corporate "knowledge," diversification, and competition.
- *Procedure*: The board of directors must first adopt a merger plan, which must be approved by the shareholders, usually by two-third of the outstanding shares.
- *Appraisal Rights*: A shareholder who objects to a merger may be entitled to appraisal rights. To qualify, a shareholder must send a written notice of objection and make a written demand for the fair value of the shares. The corporation must then make a written offer to purchase the shares.

SALE OF SUBSTANTIALLY ALL THE ASSETS: Instead of a merger, a corporation may simply buy the assets of another corporation. However, such a sale may still require shareholder approval.

STOCK ACQUISITION: Instead of buying assets, a corporation may buy the shares of another corporation. The board of directors need not approve this transaction because a corporation may purchase stock directly from individual shareholders. However, some courts consider stock acquisitions to be de facto mergers.

STUDY HINTS FOR THE CALL-IMAGE TECHNOLOGY CASE STUDIES

The following study hints may be helpful when resolving the Call-Image Technology case studies.

page 927
- ♦ You should consider whether the family is experienced in the fast-food industry.
- ♦ You should consider the effects and problems of a merger for the purpose of diversification.

page 930
- ♦ Consider options that would make the corporation less attractive to an unwanted suitor.
- ♦ Bear in mind, however, the fiduciary duties that directors owe to the corporation.

page 932
- ♦ Contrast the advantages of a merger and a purchase of assets.
- ♦ Be careful, if the two firms merge, CIT is liable for the firms' combined liabilities.

REVIEW OF KEY TERMS AND CONCEPTS

MATCHING EXERCISE

Select the term or concept that best matches a definition or statement set forth below. Each term or concept is the best match for only one definition or statement.

Terms and Concepts

a. Appraisal right
b. At will
c. Charging order
d. Conglomerate merger

e. De facto merger
f. Economies of scale
g. Fair market value
h. Liquidate

i. Market value
j. Marshal
k. Receiver
l. Winding up

Definitions and Statements

_____ 1. Current price for which stock will sell on a national or regional stock exchange.
_____ 2. Current price that an asset will bring in a sale between two informed parties.
_____ 3. Unbiased person appointed by a court to take over, preserve, and manage the assets of another.
_____ 4. Sale of assets that, as a practical matter, effects a merger of two companies.
_____ 5. Reductions in per-unit costs resulting from a merger of companies.
_____ 6. Process for terminating a partnership that includes the marshaling and liquidation of assets.
_____ 7. Court order permitting a creditor to receive an owner's profits from the operation of a business; especially common in partnership situations.
_____ 8. Right that dissenting shareholders have to require a corporation to buy back their shares.
_____ 9. Duration of a relationship that is not expressly stated to be for a fixed period of time.
_____ 10. Mergers between noncompeting firms in different industries.
_____ 11. Settle with creditors and debtors and divide remaining assets among partners.
_____ 12. Arrangement of assets or claims in order to properly apply the assets to pay the claims.

COMPLETION EXERCISE

Fill in the blanks with the words that most accurately complete each statement.

1. In a _____, two or more existing companies combine to form a new corporate entity.

2. A _____ _____ is a merger between a subsidiary and a parent company that owns 90 percent or more of the subsidiary's stock.

3. The dissolution of a corporation may be _____ or _____.

4. Identify three instances when a partnership may be dissolved by operation of law:

   a. _____.

   b. _____.

   c. _____.

5. Identify three rationales for a merger.

a. _____.

b. _____.

c. _____.

TRUE-FALSE EXERCISE

Write **T** if the statement is true, write **F** if the statement is false.

_____ 1. Misconduct by a partner automatically dissolves a partnership.

_____ 2. Generally, shareholder approval is not required for a short-form merger.

_____ 3. Bankruptcy of a partnership causes a dissolution, but bankruptcy of only one partner does not.

_____ 4. If a partnership does not have a specified duration or purpose, then any partner is legally entitled to withdraw at any time.

_____ 5. A partnership dissolution automatically terminates the partnership.

_____ 6. A partner who withdraws in violation of an agreement has no right to demand that the partnership wind up if the remaining partners take certain steps required by the UPA.

_____ 7. The sale of a sole proprietor's business terminates the sole proprietorship.

_____ 8. Any time a partner leaves a partnership, the partnership dissolves.

_____ 9. Two-thirds of the outstanding shares must generally approve a voluntary corporate dissolution.

_____ 10. Shareholders may request a corporate dissolution if minority shareholders are oppressed.

APPLICATION OF CONCEPTS

MULTIPLE CHOICE QUESTIONS

_____ 1. Jack, Audrey, and Zoe are partners in JAZ Partnership. The agreement states that the partnership will continue until January 1, 2001. Which event does NOT cause a dissolution?
   a. On May 1, 1999, the partnership reports a loss for the preceding fiscal year.
   b. On May 1, 1999, Audrey is declared bankrupt.
   c. On May 1, 1999, Zoe withdraws in violation of the partnership agreement.
   d. On May 1, 1999, Harold is admitted as a new partner.

_____ 2. Sue and Rhonda are partners in L&M Partnership. The partnership agreement states that the partnership will continue until June 1, 2000. In which situation can Sue request a court to enter a decree dissolving the partnership prior to June 1, 2000?
   a. Rhonda made an ordinary contract on behalf of the partnership with authority to do so, but Sue now objects to the contract.
   b. Rhonda has embezzled partnership funds and she refuses to perform her partnership duties.
   c. The partnership is not as profitable as in the past.
   d. Sue cannot obtain a decree of dissolution; a court cannot dissolve a partnership.

_____ 3. The shareholders and board of directors of Acme, Inc. and Belco, Inc. have voted in favor of combining their respective corporations. Pursuant to this combination, Acme will terminate and Belco will continue to exist. This combination is a:
   a. Consolidation.
   b. Merger.
   c. Stock acquisition.
   d. Conglomerate.

_____ 4. Kendall was admitted into the Three Sons Accounting Firm, a general partnership. Kendall contributed $25,000 to the partnership. Which of the following statements is correct?
   a. Kendall has unlimited personal liability for all existing and future partnership debts.
   b. Kendall's liability to existing partnership creditors is limited to $25,000, the amount of his capital contribution, and he has unlimited liability for future partnership debts.
   c. Kendall's liability to existing and future partnership creditors is limited to $25,000, the amount of his capital contribution
   d. Kendall has no liability to existing or future partnership creditors.

SHORT ANSWER QUESTIONS

Answer the following questions, briefly explaining the reason for your answer.

1. Bob is a minority shareholder in Burgundy, Inc. Bob has been notified that Burgundy plans to merge with Chantilly, Inc., and he is opposed to this merger. What are Bob's rights in this case?

_____

_____

2. Earl, Rusk, and Aaron enter into a partnership. Ten months later, Aaron is declared insane by a court and enters a mental institution. Aaron's wife filed a petition to dissolve the partnership by court order. Earl and Roscoe object to the dissolution. Will the court dissolve the partnership?

_____

_____

3. Lightning Corp. has 20,000 shares of outstanding common stock. Pursuant to an agreement between Lightning Corp. and Blinder Corp., Lightning Corp. issued and sold 30,000 additional shares of its common stock to Blinder Corp. What type of extraordinary transaction did the parties accomplish? What is the legal effect of this transaction?

_____

_____

4. Chuck, Diane, and Bob are partners in a limited partnership, and they equally share partnership profits. The partners have agreed to dissolve the partnership. The partnership has $70,000 cash. The partnership owes $17,000 to Jim, an outside creditor, and it owes Diane $12,000 for an advance she made to the partnership. Chuck contributed $10,000 to the partnership, Diane contributed $15,000, and Bob contributed $5,000. To whom and in what order will the partnership assets be distributed?

_____

_____

CASE PROBLEMS

Answer the following case problems, explaining your answers.

1. Clay, Bonnie, and Tess were partners in a partnership, and they equally shared partnership profits. The partnership has dissolved due to Clay's death. The partnership has $90,000 cash. The partnership owes $20,000 to Roscoe, an outside creditor, and it owes Tess $10,000 for an advance she made to the partnership. Clay contributed $15,000 to the partnership, Bonnie contributed $10,000, and Tess contributed $5,000. The partnership agreement is silent regarding the partners' rights upon the death of a partner. (a) Can Bonnie and Tess indefinitely continue the partnership business or must they wind up the partnership's business? (b) In general, who is entitled to wind up the affairs of a partnership? (c) If the partnership is wound up, to whom and in what order will the partnership's assets be distributed?

_____

_____

_____

_____

2. MicroChem is a small chemical company that has just discovered a process that neutralizes some types of toxic waste. Unfortunately, MicroChem does not have the financial resources to fully develop the process, nor does it have a stable credit rating. MacroChem, a large chemical company, is looking for a new product to market. MacroChem has submitted an offer to acquire MicroChem. (a) What would be some reasons for MicroChem and MacroChem to merge? (b) What procedures must each company follow to complete the merger? (c) If the companies merge, what will be the legal effect on the two companies and their shareholders?

_____

_____

_____

_____

CHAPTER 37   Franchising

CHAPTER REVIEW

THE SIGNIFICANCE OF FRANCHISING AS A BUSINESS METHOD: Franchising has helped the United States become the world's largest market. Currently, over 2,000 U.S. companies use this business method.

DEFINITION: A franchise is an oral or written agreement, expressed or implied, in which the franchisor grants to the franchisee a license to use a trade name, service mark, trademark, logotype, or other symbol in which there is a community of interest in the business and in which the franchisee must pay a licensing fee. There are two types of franchises. Distributorships allow the franchisee to sell a product in a designated area. Chain-style businesses, or business format franchises, allow the franchisee to operate under the franchisor's trade name, subject to the franchisor's operating methods.

BENEFITS OF FRANCHISING: There are many benefits of franchising for both the franchisee and the franchisor.

The benefits to the franchisee include:
1) the opportunity to start a business with limited capital;
2) goodwill;
3) the franchisor's business expertise; and
4) assured supply of materials.

The benefits to the franchisor include:
1) the franchisee's investment capital;
2) goodwill;
3) an assured distribution network; and
4) a larger asset base.

FRANCHISING COMPARED WITH OTHER BUSINESS RELATIONSHIPS: Generally, government agencies view the franchisor-franchisee relationship as an employment relationship. It is settled law that the following are not franchises: cooperatives, concessionaires, joint ventures, general partnerships, and sales agencies. Also, franchises are not securities.

SETTING UP THE FRANCHISING RELATIONSHIP: The franchisor typically plays a large role in the set-up stage. The franchisor will choose the franchise location, train the franchisee, advertise, and set stringent guidelines. The franchisee must follow the franchisor's operating procedures, obtain liability insurance, and meet workers' compensation requirements. Legal problems frequently occur in the area of quality control and franchise termination. Typically, franchise agreements require franchisees to buy from only certain suppliers, provide factors that could cause a termination, and contain covenants not to compete. Because franchisees have limited bargaining power, case law and statutes have provided relief to franchisees from one-sided agreements.

DECISIONAL LAW AND STATUTES AFFECTING FRANCHISING: Several statutes and case law have attempted to protect franchisees against perceived abuses by franchisors. However, franchisors may still terminate the franchisee for misconduct, failure to meet sales quotas, failure to observe quality standards, and failure to maintain investment levels. Franchises are also subject to antitrust law and the UCC.

CHALLENGES TO FRANCHISING REGULATORY STATUTES: Because the laws that protect franchisees also limit the actions of franchisors, franchisors have challenged the laws on constitutional grounds. Franchisors have challenged state laws, claiming these laws: 1) impair contracts; 2) deny due process; 3) conflict with federal law; and 4) burden interstate commerce.

THE FRANCHISING ENVIRONMENT: The franchising field appears to be very stable.
- *Ownership Trends*: Increasingly, franchisees are assuming ownership of the franchise units. In the past, franchisors tended to own the units. Also, franchises are renewed 90 percent of the time.
- *International Markets*: Canada, Japan, and Australia are the three largest markets for U.S. franchisors. Increasingly, foreign franchisors are setting up in the United States.

STUDY HINTS FOR CALL-IMAGE TECHNOLOGY CASE STUDIES

The following study hints may be helpful when resolving the Call-Image Technology (CIT) case studies.

page 942
- ♦ First, consider whether CIT will be the franchisor or franchisee.
- ♦ Then, consider the benefits for franchisors and franchisees.

page 944
- ♦ You should consider the duties employers owe to employees, as well as employer liability for employee actions (you may need to review the chapter on torts).
- ♦ You should review the obligations of the franchisor in the section on "Setting Up the Franchising Relationship."
- ♦ You should review the following cases: *Brennan v. Carvel Corporation* and *Foreign Motors, Inc. v. Audi of America, Inc.*

REVIEW OF KEY TERMS AND CONCEPTS

MATCHING EXERCISE

Select the term or concept that best matches a definition or statement set forth below. Each term or concept is the best match for only one definition or statement.

Terms and Concepts

a. Chain-style
b. Concessionaires
c. Consignee
d. Cooperative

e. Distributorship
f. Franchisee
g. Franchisor
h. Logotypes

i. Royalty fee
j. Service marks
k. Stay
l. Trademark

Definitions and Statements

_____ 1. Identifying symbols.
_____ 2. Distinctive marks or symbols used to identify a particular company as the source of its products.
_____ 3. Distinctive symbols designating services offered by a particular business or individual.
_____ 4. The person or firm that grants the franchise.
_____ 5. The person receiving the franchise.
_____ 6. This franchise method allows the franchisee to sell a product in a designated area.
_____ 7. Operators of refreshment centers.
_____ 8. Franchise method that allows the franchisee to operate under the franchisor's trade name, subject to the franchisor's operating methods.
_____ 9. Person to whom goods are shipped for sale and who may return unsold goods to the consignor.
_____ 10. Groups of individuals who unite in a common enterprise and share the profits proportionately.
_____ 11. Suspend.
_____ 12. Payment made in exchange for the granting of a right or a license.

COMPLETION EXERCISE

Fill in the blanks with the words that most accurately complete each statement.

1. The two most significant legal problems in a franchise agreement are _____ and

_____ _____ .

2. Identify four benefits of franchising to franchisors.

    a. _____ .

    b. _____ .

    c. _____ .

    d. _____ .

3. Identify four benefits of franchising to franchisees.

    a. _____.

    b. _____.

    c. _____.

    d. _____.

4. _____ _____ involves choosing the court or place of jurisdiction that will be most favorable to the litigant.

5. States require the franchisor to give the franchisee _____ before terminating the franchise.

TRUE-FALSE EXERCISE

Write T if the statement is true, write F if the statement is false.

_____ 1. Government agencies tend to view the relationship between a franchisor and franchisee as that of employer and employee.

_____ 2. A franchise contract cannot permit a franchisor to terminate a franchise if a franchisee fails to meet reasonable sales quotas.

_____ 3. Franchising was not a popular method of business until after World War II.

_____ 4. A franchising agreement may meet the definition of a security under the securities laws.

_____ 5. A partnership cannot operate a franchise.

_____ 6. Franchise agreements are subject to antitrust laws.

_____ 7. Generally, it is permissible for a franchisor to suggest, but not to require, certain resale prices for the franchisee.

_____ 8. Franchisors are not subject to the UCC.

_____ 9. A distributor of a product is *clearly* a franchisee.

_____ 10. Franchisees have wide discretion in how they run their franchise.

APPLICATION OF CONCEPTS

MULTIPLE CHOICE QUESTIONS

_____ 1. Beef 'N Beer, a franchisor, wants to assure quality in its products and uniformity in its sales prices. Beef 'N Beer would like all of its franchisors to buy from a single supplier that meets its standards for quality control. It would also like to set retail prices. Under these facts, Beef 'N Beer may:

    a. Not require that franchisees buy from the supplier and set their sales prices according to its guidelines, because such action would violate antitrust law.

    b. Require that franchisees buy from the supplier and set their sales prices according to its guidelines, without violating any laws.

    c. Require that franchisees buy from the supplier and set their sales prices according to its guidelines, provided the requirements are reasonable.

    d. Not *suggest* a supplier and sales prices for its franchisees.

_____ 2. Franchisors may be subject to which of the following laws?
   a. Constitutional law.
   b. The Federal Franchise Act.
   c. The UCC.
   d. Both a and c.

_____ 3. Which of the following elements are included in the typical definition of "franchise" found in most state statutes?
   a. An agreement, a license to use a trade name, trademark, or similar characteristic in which there is a community of interest in the business of offering, selling, or distributing goods, and a license fee.
   b. A written agreement, a license to use a trade name, trademark, or similar characteristic in which there is a community of interest in the business of offering, selling, or distributing goods, and a license fee.
   c. An agreement, a license to use a trade name, trademark, or similar characteristic in which there is a community of interest in the business of offering, selling, or distributing goods, a license fee, and an intensive training program that franchisees must complete.
   d. An agreement, a license to use a trade name, trademark, or similar characteristic in which there is a community of interest in the business of offering, selling, or distributing goods, a license fee, and an employer-employee relationship between franchisor and franchisee.

_____ 4. Which of the following is typically found in franchise agreements?
   a. A covenant not to compete.
   b. A notice period, usually ninety days, before the franchisor may terminate the agreement.
   c. A covenant not to sue the franchisor.
   d. Both a and b.

SHORT ANSWER QUESTIONS

Answer the following questions, briefly explaining the reason for your answer.

1. Big Burger entered into a franchise agreement with Rhonda and chose a location for Rhonda's store. The location of the store turned out to be terrible because there was insufficient foot traffic near the store. When Rhonda began to lose money she complained to Big Burger, which did nothing. May Rhonda sue Big Burger for breach of contract?

_____

_____

2. Jethro has always wanted to start his own business. However, he does not have much money to invest, and he is not a very sophisticated business person. Would a franchise be a good way for Jethro to start a business?

_____

_____

3. Durman, Inc. is a small company, known only in a local area. It does not have a recognizable logo or trademark, and has unstable relationships with its suppliers. Would Durman make a good franchisor? Hint: Would you want to be one of Durman's franchisees?

_____

_____

4. The Taco Hut, a franchisor, wants to assure quality in its products and uniformity in its sales prices. The Taco Hut would like all of its franchisees to buy from a single supplier that meets its standards for quality control. Can The Taco Hut force all of its franchisees to buy from a single supplier without violating any laws?

_____

_____

CASE PROBLEMS

Answer the following case problems, explaining your answers.

1. Davis, president of D&D, Inc., entered into a distributor's agreement naming Graham as the sales representative of D&D for a specified territory. Graham paid Davis $10,000. Davis gave Graham detailed instructions on how to market D&D's products. Davis also gave Graham a list of customers, promotional materials, cost sheets, and purchase orders. The advertising materials all contained D&D's distinctive logo. Did Graham and Davis enter into a franchise agreement? Explain.

_____

_____

_____

_____

2. Sally has a franchise agreement with Nevus Systems, a computer manufacturer. Nevus selected a location for Sally's store in the middle of a busy business district, and hers was the only computer store in the area. Nevus also provided Sally with several months of training, as well as detailed guidelines on how to sell Nevus computers. For several months, Sally could not meet Nevus's sales quotas, which were reasonable. (a) Can Nevus terminate Sally as a franchisee? Explain. (b) Before terminating Sally, what must Nevus do to comply with most state's laws on terminating franchisees?

_____

_____

_____

_____

CHAPTER 38 | Securities Regulation

CHAPTER REVIEW

FEDERAL LAWS: Securities regulation is the "federal corporate law."

- **The Securities Act of 1933**: The Securities Act of 1933 (Securities Act) regulates the interstate sale of securities by an issuing company.

    1) **Security defined**: A security is any note, stock, treasury stock, bond, debenture, participation in any profit-sharing agreement, or investment contract. Generally, when an instrument bears one of these titles, it is considered a security. One of the most commonly litigated questions in this area revolves around the definition of an investment contract. Courts will consider an investment contract a security when it involves an investment in a common enterprise in which the investor has no managerial functions, but expects to profit solely from the efforts of others. As a practical matter, a security is a: a) passive investment whereby b) one contributes capital and c) expects to make a profit from the efforts of others.

    2) **Procedures**: Unless an exemption applies, a corporation issuing a security must: a) file a registration statement with the SEC, and b) provide a prospectus to all prospective investors.

    3) **Exempt investments**: The following classes of securities are exempt from registration: a) securities issued by federal and state governments; b) short-term commercial paper (9 months or less); c) issues by nonprofit organizations; d) issues by savings and loan associations; e) issues by common carriers; f) insurance policies and certain annuities subject to regulation by state or federal authorities; and g) intrastate offerings.

    4) **Exempt transactions**: The following transactions are exempt from the registration and prospectus requirements: private offerings; transactions by persons other than issuers; certain broker and dealer transactions; and small public issues ($5 million cap to accredited investors).

    5) **Antifraud provisions**: The Securities Act contains antifraud provisions. Section 12 prohibits oral or written misstatements of material fact, or omissions of material facts that are necessary to keep statements from being misleading. Section 17 prohibits the use of the mails or interstate commerce to further any form of fraud. Section 11 of the Securities Act imposes civil liability for any registration statement containing misstatements of material fact, or omissions of material facts necessary to keep statements from being misleading. Due diligence is the only defense to Section 11 liability. The defense is generally available to any person who, after reasonable investigation, had reasonable grounds to believe, and did believe, that the registration statement was accurate and did not omit material facts.

- **The Securities Exchange Act of 1934**: The Security Exchange Act of 1934 (Exchange Act) regulates the secondary securities market. These regulations include the following requirements:

    1) **Information and proxies**: Publicly traded companies must make public detailed information. Also, their proxy solicitations are regulated. In a proxy solicitation, management must provide shareholders with a proxy statement and a proxy form. The proxy statement must disclose all pertinent information regarding the matters under consideration, including the participants and reasons for the proxy solicitation. The Exchange Act imposes absolute liability for misleading proxy statements or for the omission of a material fact necessary to make the statement true and not misleading.

2) **Insider trading**: The Exchange Act regulates insider trading. In transactions involving material nonpublic information, an insider must publicly disclose the information or abstain from trading in the security. The parties subject to this regulation are: insiders (directors, officers, etc.); temporary insiders (outside attorneys, accountants, etc.); tippees; and misappropriators.

Section 10(b) and 10(b)-5 imposes liability for any manipulative or deceptive device used in connection with any purchase or sale of any security by any person. The elements for proving a 10(b) and 10(b)-5 violation are: a) an untrue statement of material fact or a failure to state a material fact that is needed to make a statement not misleading; b) reliance upon the statement; c) and an injury resulting from such reliance.

3) **Rule 16 (Short-swing profits)**: Insiders and persons owning more than 10 percent of a corporation's stock must file statements with the SEC disclosing the extent of their ownership and any changes that have taken place. Section 16(b) requires that insiders and persons with more than 10 percent of a company's stock pay to the corporation any short-swing profits, which is defined as any profit made by buying and selling securities in the company within a six-month period.

4) **Liabilities and Remedies**: Under 10(b) and 10(b)-5, a private action may be brought against any person who conducted a transaction in a fraudulent manner.

- *Securities and Exchange Commission Actions*: The Exchange Act empowers the SEC to conduct investigations into security transactions. The SEC generally imposes administrative remedies (censures or fines); appropriate cases are referred to the Justice Department for criminal prosecution.

STATE REGULATION: Often referred to as "blue sky laws," state jurisdiction can be concurrent with federal jurisdiction. Although state regulation varies from state to state, the typical provisions are: 1) antifraud provisions; 2) registration requirements for brokers and dealers; and/or 3) registration prerequisites for the sale and purchase of securities. State exemptions are generally similar to the federal exemptions.

THE FOREIGN CORRUPT PRACTICES ACT: The purpose of the FCPA is to stop the bribery of foreign officials. The FCPA contains both antibribery provisions and accounting standards. Criminal penalties may be imposed if an officer, director, employee, agent or stockholder acting on behalf of the business offers or pays money to foreign officials to influence foreign officials to assist the firm in obtaining or retaining business. Payments or gifts to facilitate routine governmental action are permitted.

STUDY HINTS FOR CALL-IMAGE TECHNOLOGY CASE STUDIES

The following study hints may be helpful when resolving the Call-Image Technology (CIT) case studies.

page 968
- ◆ Review the material dealing with exemptions, particularly exempt transactions.
- ◆ Review the procedures material relating to registration statements and prospectuses. Do not overlook the need to also comply with state blue sky laws.

page 976
- ◆ Review the material dealing with insider trading and section 10(b) of the 34 Act.

REVIEW OF KEY TERMS AND CONCEPTS

MATCHING EXERCISE

Select the term or concept that best matches a definition or statement set forth below. Each term or concept is the best match for only one definition or statement.

Terms and Concepts

a. Censure
b. Disgorge
c. Due diligence
d. In *pari delicto*
e. Insider trading

f. Issuer
g. Post-effective period
h. Prefiling period
i. Prospectus
j. Securities exchanges

k. Security
l. Tender offer
m. Uncollateralized
n. Underwriters
o. Waiting period

Definitions and Statements

_____ 1. Document provided to potential investors disclosing material information relating to an offering of securities.
_____ 2. Buying or selling securities on the basis of nonpublic, material information.
_____ 3. Firms that ensure the sale of corporate securities by agreeing to sell the securities to the public.
_____ 4. Unsecured; performance is not secured by property.
_____ 5. Organized markets in which investors buy and sell securities at central locations.
_____ 6. Period when issuers may begin negotiations with underwriters.
_____ 7. Company that makes its own securities available for sale.
_____ 8. Note, stock, treasury stock, bond, debenture, evidence of indebtedness, or investment contract.
_____ 9. Period when an issuer may accept oral orders for its stock and place tombstone ads.
_____ 10. Equally at fault; equally wrong.
_____ 11. Period after a registration statement becomes effective.
_____ 12. Give up ill-gotten gains.
_____ 13. Takeover bid.
_____ 14. Defense that a party made reasonable investigation, and had reasonable grounds to believe that a registration statement was accurate and did not omit material facts.
_____ 15. Formal reprimand.

COMPLETION EXERCISE

Fill in the blanks with the words that most accurately complete each statement.

1. The _____ _____ _____ _____ is the primary federal law that regulates the initial offering of securities in interstate commerce.

2. The _____ _____ _____ _____ _____ is the primary federal law that regulates the securities industry, publicly-held companies, and the resale of securities in interstate commerce.

3. A preliminary prospectus is known as a _____ _____.

4. The only advertisements that are allowed during the waiting period are called _____
_____.

5. A _____ - _____ _____ is a profit that a controlling party of a company realizes from buying and selling the company's securities within any six-month period.

TRUE-FALSE EXERCISE

Write **T** if the statement is true, write **F** if the statement is false.

_____ 1. The FCPA prohibits the payment of any thing of value to any foreign official for any purpose.

_____ 2. Under Rule 10(b)-5, the only parties barred from insider trading are traditional insiders.

_____ 3. The Exchange Act imposes reporting requirements on all companies that issue securities.

_____ 4. In a tender offer, federal securities law requires the acquiring company to inform the target company's shareholders of the purpose for the takeover.

_____ 5. A sale of stock made solely to residents of the state in which the issuing company is incorporated and primarily does business may be exempt from the Securities Act registration requirements.

_____ 6. Under the Insider Trading Sanctions Act of 1984, a court may impose a penalty of up to three times the unlawful gain that a party made from insider trading.

_____ 7. The Securities Act may impose both civil and criminal penalties for its violation.

_____ 8. A proxy is an assignment by the shareholder of the right to vote his or her shares.

_____ 9. The fact that a company's securities are exempt from registration does not necessarily mean that they are exempt from the antifraud rules of federal securities laws.

_____ 10. In general, federal securities laws apply only if a transaction involves a security.

APPLICATION OF CONCEPTS

MULTIPLE CHOICE QUESTIONS

_____ 1. Mayfield Corp. is selling a variety of instruments and property in order to raise capital. Which instrument or property would not be a security within the meaning of the federal securities laws?
   a. A share of common stock in Mayfield Corp.
   b. A ten-year corporate bond issued by Mayfield Corp. that bears 15 percent annual interest.
   c. A 100-acre parcel of land.
   d. Investment interests in a shrimp farm operated by Mayfield Corp., with investors sharing in the profits made by the farming enterprise.

_____ 2. R&V Limited Partnership is planning to issue limited partner interests and to publicly offer these securities for sale in interstate commerce. What must R&V do to comply with the 1933 Act?
   a. R&V has no duties under the 1933 Act. R&V is only required to comply with blue sky laws in the states in which the securities are offered.
   b. R&V is only required to file a registration statement with the SEC.
   c. R&V is only required to provide a prospectus to prospective investors.
   d. R&V must file a registration statement and provide a prospectus to prospective investors.

_____ 3. Pepco Inc. has just received a conclusive, secret medical report that establishes that Pepco's only product causes cancer. As a result, the company may be liable to thousands of persons who may have contracted cancer by using this product. Under these facts, which party is engaging in insider trading in violation of Rule 10(b)-5?
   a. Tom, a Pepco director, sells his Pepco stock without disclosing the report.
   b. Bonnie, an outside financial analyst who was retained by Pepco to assess the financial impact of this report, sells all of her Pepco stock without disclosing the report.
   c. Faye, a receptionist, saw the report and sold her Pepco stock without disclosing the report.
   d. All of the above.

_____ 4. Frye Co. is subject to all provisions of the 1934 Act. Dick is a director of Frye Co. and he owns 5 percent of the company's common stock. Bonnie owns 15 percent of the company's common stock. Sally owns 4 percent of the company's common stock. Under Rule 16 of the 1934 Act:
   a. If Dick buys and sells stock in Frye Co. within a six-month period thereby earning a profit, Dick must pay the profit to the company even if he did not trade on inside information.
   b. Dick, Bonnie, and Sally must each file disclosure statements with the SEC.
   c. Dick, Bonnie, and Sally are each exempt from filing disclosure statements with the SEC.
   d. a and b.

SHORT ANSWER QUESTIONS

Answer the following questions, briefly explaining the reason for your answer.

1. Nassau Inc. plans to issue and sell $4 million worth of preferred stock. The stock will be sold to 45 banks, investment companies, and other accredited investors. There will be no general solicitation or public offering of the stock. Is this offering exempt from the registration requirements of the 1933 Act?

_____

_____

2. Kathy needed a visa to travel to the country of Ruritania on business. When she spoke with a low-level embassy employee, he told her it would take two months to get the visa. Kathy offered the employee $50 if he could speed up the process. Is Kathy's bribe prohibited under the FCPA?

_____

_____

3. Margaret is the president of Duffy Toys, a publicly-held corporation, and she purchased 2,000 shares of its stock in September. Duffy came out with the Goober Doll which proved extremely popular. After a huge Christmas season, Duffy's stock increased by $5 per share. Margaret sold her stock in January and realized a $10,000 profit. What duty, if any, does Margaret owe Duffy regarding the $10,000 profit?

_____

_____

4. Randolph is a janitor at GeoTech. While cleaning the CEO's office, Randolph notices a confidential corporate report on the CEO's desk marked "For Release to the Public Tomorrow." Randolph likes to dabble in the stock market, and he thinks the information will make him some money. If Randolph trades GeoTech securities based on this information before it is released to the public, is he guilty of insider trading?

_____

_____

CASE PROBLEMS

Answer the following case problems, explaining your answers.

1. Midas Inc. owns several gold mines. Unknown to the public, Midas engineers have just discovered a massive new gold deposit. After this discovery, the Midas board of directors made several public announcements denying that the company had made any new discoveries. Without knowledge of the secret discovery, Tom sold his Midas stock for $10 a share. One week later, Midas stock went to $20 per share when the Midas board announced the new discovery. (a) What federal securities act governs this case? (b) What must Tom prove in order to establish a securities violation by the Midas board of directors? (c) In all likelihood, did the board violate federal securities law?

_____

_____

_____

_____

2. CryoTech is in the waiting period after filing a registration statement with the SEC. CryoTech's underwriter, Penton & Thorton, sent the following notice to its best customers: "CryoTech produces an environmentally safe coolant for air conditioners that will not harm the ozone layer. CryoTech will offer 1 million shares of newly issued common stock to the public. Interested parties may contact Penton & Thorton, underwriter." (a) Does this notice violate the Securities Act? (b) When may CryoTech begin to sell the offered shares?

_____

_____

_____

_____

CHAPTER 39

Constitutional Regulation of Business

CHAPTER REVIEW

A HISTORICAL PERSPECTIVE: Government regulation emerged after a time of abuse by big business. Businesses routinely mistreated workers, and the rule was "let the buyer beware."

SHOULD GOVERNMENT REGULATE BUSINESS?: Regulation takes two forms: social regulation concerns such issues as workplace safety and consumer protection; economic regulation concerns such issues as prices and industry conditions. A regulation's benefits should be weighed against its costs.

THE COMMERCE CLAUSE: The commerce clause allows the federal government broad regulatory power.
- *Exclusive Federal Power*: The federal government has exclusive power to regulate commerce:
    1) with foreign nations;
    2) with Native American tribes; and
    3) between states (interstate commerce).
The power to regulate interstate commerce also allows the federal government to regulate commerce originating in one state that has a national economic effect.
- *Concurrent State Power*: States may regulate commerce if the regulations:
    1) serve a state interest;
    2) do not impose an undue burden on interstate commerce;
    3) do not conflict with federal law; and
    4) do not discriminate against out-of-state businesses.
- *Exclusive State Power*: States have exclusive regulatory power over purely local activities that have remote effects on other states.

EQUAL PROTECTION: The equal protection clause protects individuals from invidious discrimination that arises from governmental (not private) action. Equal protection applies to federal and state governments.
- *Level 1: The "Rational Basis" Test*: This test applies to most social and economic regulation; courts presume that such regulations are valid. This test allows the government to discriminate against similarly situated persons if the regulation is rationally related to a legitimate purpose.
- *Level 2: The "Compelling State Interest" Test*: This test applies to regulations based on suspect classifications (race or ethnic origin); courts presume that such regulations are invalid. A regulation based on a suspect classification is valid only if it furthers a compelling state interest, and there is no less burdensome way of accomplishing this interest. Affirmative action programs are judged using this test.
- *Intermediate Level: The "Substantially Important State Interest" Test*: This test applies to gender-based classifications. A regulation based on gender is valid if it furthers a substantially important state interest.

DUE PROCESS: The due process clause protects against deprivations of life, liberty, and property.

- *Procedural Due Process*: Before the government (state or federal) can deprive a person of life, liberty, or property, the government must provide some type of hearing. A fair hearing requires notice to the aggrieved party, an opportunity for the person to be heard, and an impartial decision maker.
- *Substantive Due Process*: A regulation is invalid under substantive due process if it fails to advance a legitimate government interest or is an unreasonable way of advancing a legitimate interest. Substantive due process applies to all persons, regardless of race, sex, or ethnicity. However, courts will defer to legislatures and uphold regulations unless they are clearly irrational.

THE "TAKINGS" CLAUSE: The takings clause prevents the government (federal or state) from taking property for public use without just compensation. A taking has occurred if the governmental action destroys the property's current use or unreasonably impairs the value of the property and the owner's reasonable expectations regarding it. In some cases, land use regulations may constitute a taking.

THE FIRST AMENDMENT/COMMERCIAL FREE SPEECH: Laws regulating the content of speech (what you say) are valid only if they are narrowly written to advance a compelling state interest. Courts start with the presumption that laws regulating the content of speech are invalid. However, government may validly regulate the time, place, or manner of speech. Protection of commercial speech is more limited than protection of individual speech.

ADMINISTRATIVE AGENCIES: Administrative agencies have legislative and judicial powers. Congress has the power to create and abolish agencies, and limits their power and authority by statute. Agencies are subject to substantive and procedural due process requirements. Courts have the power to review agency decisions.

STUDY HINTS FOR CALL-IMAGE TECHNOLOGY CASE STUDIES

The following study hints may be helpful when resolving the Call-Image Technology (CIT) case studies.

page 1005
- ◆ Review the material on The Equal Protection Clause and consider which test would be used to determine the constitutionality of the law.

page 1011
- ◆ Tom and Anna should review their state's laws regarding covenants not to compete.
- ◆ Whether Lindsay and Dan sign a legal covenant is a matter to be negotiated by the parties.

page 1015
- ◆ You should consider the procedural due process clause.
- ◆ You should also consider the takings clause.

MATCHING EXERCISE

Select the term or concept that best matches a definition or statement set forth below. Each term or concept is the best match for only one definition or statement.

Terms and Concepts

a. Caveat emptor
b. Delegated
c. Disenfranchised
d. Due process clause
e. Equal protection clause

f. Insular
g. Interstate
h. Intrastate
i. Invidious
j. Laissez-faire

k. Plenary
l. Quasi-judicial
m. Quasi-legislative
n. Taking
o. Transportation

Definitions and Statements

_____ 1. Carrying or conveying from one place to another; the removal of persons or goods from one place to another.

_____ 2. Between two or more states; between a point in one state and a point in another state.

_____ 3. Begun, carried on, and completed wholly within the boundaries of a single state.

_____ 4. Partly judicial; empowered to hold hearings but not trials.

_____ 5. A term meaning *hands-off*; the belief that business operates best when uninhibited by the government.

_____ 6. Partly legislative; empowered to enact rules and regulations but not statutes.

_____ 7. A term meaning *let the buyer beware*.

_____ 8. Full; complete; absolute.

_____ 9. Governmental action that destroys the property's current use or unreasonably impairs the value of the property and the owner's reasonable expectations regarding it.

_____ 10. Constitutional provision that generally prohibits unreasonable government actions.

_____ 11. Constitutional provision that guarantees all persons and classes the same protection of the law.

_____ 12. Repugnant; discrimination stemming from bigotry or prejudice.

_____ 13. Assigned responsibility and/or authority by the person or group normally empowered to exercise the responsibility or authority.

_____ 14. Isolated from others.

_____ 15. Restricted from enjoying certain constitutional or statutory rights; burdened by systemic prejudice or bigotry.

COMPLETION EXERCISE

Fill in the blanks with the words that most accurately complete each statement.

1. _____ _____ _____ have quasi-judicial and quasi-legislative functions.

2. Regulations are either _____ or _____.

3. The takings clause prohibits government from taking property without _____

   _____.

4. The two types of due process are _____ and _____.

5. Identify the three tests used in an equal protection analysis.

   a. _____.

   b. _____.

   c. _____.

TRUE-FALSE EXERCISE

Write **T** if the statement is true, write **F** if the statement is false.

_____ 1. The Constitution prohibits a state from adopting a law that directly discriminates against interstate commerce, such as imposing special restrictions on only interstate commerce.
_____ 2. Subject to certain limits, a matter may be regulated by both the federal government and a state.
_____ 3. A state that discriminates against nonresidents is violating the equal protection clause.
_____ 4. Courts cannot review the actions of an administrative agency.
_____ 5. The government may never regulate the content of speech.
_____ 6. If a state government fires an employee, it has deprived the employee of a property right.
_____ 7. Commercial speech receives less protection than individual speech.
_____ 8. Interstate commerce is narrowly interpreted and includes only activities that directly involve the movement of goods or services across state boundaries.
_____ 9. A state may regulate commerce with foreign nations if it directly affects state residents.
_____ 10. Congress may regulate activity originating in a single state if the activity will affect the national economy.

APPLICATION OF CONCEPTS

MULTIPLE CHOICE QUESTIONS

_____ 1. Wood, Inc. manufactures and sells furniture in interstate commerce. Wood's manufacturing plant is located in Phoenix, Arizona. Under these facts:
   a. The federal government has the power to regulate Wood's business.
   b. Subject to limits, Arizona has the power to regulate Wood's business.
   c. Arizona does not have the power to regulate any aspect of Wood's business; states do not have the power to regulate any matters that the federal government regulates.
   d. Both a and b.

____ 2. Federal law generally requires that certain private employers must pay time-and-a-half for hours worked in excess of 40 hours per week. Assume that a state law directly conflicts with this federal law by requiring payment of time-and-a-half for only those hours worked in excess of 50 hours per week. Under these facts:
   a. Federal law controls.
   b. State law controls.
   c. Neither federal nor state law controls; conflicting federal and state laws cancel each other.
   d. A court will decide which law to apply.

____ 3. Which of the following actions may violate the constitutional guarantee of due process?
   a. Amy is fired by her private employer without a hearing.
   b. A government agency imposed a fine on Dill Corp. for violating federal law. Dill Corp. was not given a hearing to determine whether it actually violated the law.
   c. Congress adopts a law. Key Co., which is subject to this law, asserts that the law violates due process because the law is only of marginal value.
   d. The State of Michigan intends to criminally prosecute Paul for an alleged crime. Paul is notified of the charges and action, and he is given an opportunity to defend himself in court.

____ 4. A state adopts a law forbidding the sale of products in plastic containers. This law does not prohibit the sale of products in glass containers. Assume that this law is rationally and reasonably related to accomplishing a legitimate environmental goal. The class of manufacturers that sell products in plastic containers asserts that this law violates equal protection. Does it?
   a. No, because equal protection only prohibits laws that discriminate on the basis of race, religion, or national origin.
   b. No, because equal protection does not prohibit laws that distinguish between classes of businesses if the classification is related to accomplishing a valid governmental interest.
   c. Yes, because equal protection prohibits the government from adopting a law that may treat any class of persons or businesses differently from other classes.
   d. Both a and b.

SHORT ANSWER QUESTIONS

Answer the following questions, briefly explaining the reason for your answer.

1. Roscoe owns a small diner in a very small southern town. He serves primarily to local customers, but occasionally, travelers from other states stop in to have a meal. Is Roscoe engaged in interstate commerce?

_____

_____

2. Kathy has graduated from law school but has not yet passed the bar examination. She lives in a state that prohibits persons from placing the phrase "Attorney-at-Law" after their names unless they have passed the bar. This law is designed to protect the public from unqualified lawyers. Kathy feels she has worked hard in law school and deserves to have "Attorney-at-Law" after her name. She claims the state is violating her right to free speech. Is it?

_____

_____

3. The government has constructed a dam along a river. The dam caused the river to flood onto Sam's land. Because of the flood, he cannot use the land, and its value has substantially decreased. Is this a "taking?"

_____

_____

4. A state legislature passed a law prohibiting state residents from owning cars more than ten years old. The purpose of the law is to "improve the overall appearance of the state." The legislature believes it is a legitimate state interest to have a modern-looking state, and requiring state residents to own new cars is rationally related to that goal. Does this law violate substantive due process?

_____

_____

CASE PROBLEMS

Answer the following case problems, explaining your answers.

1. Amax Corp.'s manufacturing plant is located in Missouri. Amax Corp. sells its goods in several states, and it conducts a significant portion of its business in Colorado. (a) Is Amax Corp. engaging in interstate commerce? (b) Does the federal government have the right to regulate Amax Corp.'s business? (c) In general, does Colorado have the constitutional power to regulate business conducted by Amax Corp. in Colorado? (d) What restrictions will apply if Colorado regulates Amax Corp.'s business activities?

_____

_____

_____

_____

2. A state has just passed a law prohibiting Purple-Americans, a race of people, from serving on the police force. According to the state, Purple-Americans tend to be short and not very muscular. Because police officers may need to defend themselves in a fight with dangerous criminals, they need to be tall and muscular. The state claims that the law serves a compelling state interest because it promotes a physically strong police force, which is necessary to protect the public. Using an equal protection analysis, determine whether this law violates the equal protection clause.

_____

_____

_____

_____

CHAPTER 40

Antitrust Law

CHAPTER REVIEW

THE BASIS OF REGULATORY REFORM: Government regulation emerged because of business's irresponsible behavior during the 1800s.

THE SHERMAN ACT: Passed in 1890, the purpose of the Sherman Act is to preserve competition. The Sherman Act prohibits 1) combinations that unreasonably restrain trade and 2) attempts to monopolize.

Whether conduct violates the Sherman Act is evaluated under one of two rules. Under the per se rule, certain conduct is so harmful to competition that it is an automatic antitrust violation. It is not necessary to prove that a firm intended to restrain competition or that competition was in fact restrained. Under the rule of reason, a court examines the 1) purpose and 2) effect of conduct to determine whether it is an unreasonable restraint of trade and, therefore, a violation of the Sherman Act. In other words, it is not the conduct itself, but its effect in a given industry that makes conduct legal or illegal.

- *Section 1*: Section 1 prohibits "contracts, combinations, or conspiracies" that unreasonably restrain interstate commerce. Section 1 also prohibits the following actions (*per se* violations): 1) horizontal price fixing; 2) vertical price fixing; 3) horizontal market divisions; and 4) group boycotts. Courts generally infer violations from the actions of companies.

- *Section 2*: Under Section 2, monopolizing is illegal, that is, conduct whereby one or more persons attempt to gain a monopoly or maintain a monopoly if they already have one. Illegal monopolizing generally requires proof of two things: 1) possessing monopoly power in the relevant market or attempting to possess this power, and 2) intentionally acquiring or maintaining this power.

  Generally, if a firm controls 70 percent or more of a relevant market, the firm has monopoly power. The relevant market may include the market for the goods produced by the firm and substitute goods. The courts then look at the elasticity of demand between the challenged product and the substitute. If the product controls 70 percent of this market, the company has monopoly power. Defenses to a charge of illegal monopolization include: 1) the company did not consciously try to retain this power; 2) the power was legally acquired; or 3) the company was thrust into this position.

- *Remedies*: The Sherman Act has both civil and criminal remedies. An individual may be fined up to $100,000 and be sentenced to three years in jail. A corporation can be fined up to $1 million. Injured parties may recover treble (triple) damages and attorneys' fees.

THE CLAYTON ACT: The Clayton Act is designed to *prevent* antitrust violations, not just remedy them.

- *Section 2: Price Discrimination*: Section 2, as amended by the Robinson-Patman Act, prohibits buyers from knowingly accepting a discriminatory price. Section 2 also prohibits dummy brokerage fees and promotional kickbacks. Section 2 is violated if a competitor is hurt. Defenses to a § 2 violation are: 1) the price offered meets, but does not beat, a competitor's price; or 2) a different price is being charge for goods because they are obsolete.

- *Section 3: Exclusive Dealings and Tying Arrangements*: In an exclusive dealing contract, one party requires another party to do business only with them. In a tying arrangement, the seller refuses to sell one product unless the buyer also purchases another product. One defense to a charge of an illegal tying arrangement is that the tying arrangement is necessary to preserve the safety or performance of the product. Harm is not required to find a § 3 violation; the mere likelihood of harm is sufficient.
- *Section 7: Antimerger Provisions*: Section 7, as amended by the Cellar-Kefauver Act, prohibits the acquisition of stock or assets of another firm that may tend to have a negative effect on any line of commerce. A violation typically involves showing that a "concentration trend" has been established. As a defense, a company might show that without the merger, one of the companies would have failed.
- *Section 8: Interlocking Directorates*: In some situations, Section 8 prohibits a person from sitting on the board of directors of two or more competing companies.

THE FEDERAL TRADE COMMISSION ACT: The FTC Act created the Federal Trade Commission (FTC) to enforce antitrust laws. Section 5 of the Act prohibits unfair methods of competition and deceptive trade practices. Conduct need not actually deceive to be unfair and deceptive; it need only have a "fair possibility" of deception. A statement is considered deceptive if it is ambiguous, with one honest meaning and one deceptive meaning. Currently, the FTC primarily focuses on bait-and-switch and deceptive ads.

UNFAIR TRADE PRACTICES: Common law unfair trade practices include palming off goods and violating trade secrets. Palming offs goods involves advertising, designing, or selling goods so they appear to be goods made by someone else. Trade secrets are any special processes or formulas that are guarded by the holder of the trade secret. Employees who reveal trade secrets may be liable in tort. A person or company who receives the trade secret is guilty of misappropriating the trade secret, and a court can prevent the person or company from using the information obtained. Illegal use of a trade secret may also subject the user to liability for damages. Other protections are found in patent, copyright, and trademark law. A utility patent grants an inventor the exclusive right to use the invention for 20 years (formerly, it was 17 years). A copyright protects writers, artists, and composers. A copyright grants a creator the exclusive right to profit from a work for the creator's life plus 50 years. A trademark is a mark used to identify a product.

EXEMPTIONS: Labor unions are exempt from the Sherman and Clayton Acts. Farm cooperatives are also exempt from these laws as long as they are engaged in the sale of farm produce.

STUDY HINTS FOR CALL-IMAGE TECHNOLOGY CASE STUDIES

The following study hints may be helpful when resolving the Call-Image Technology case studies.

page 1030	♦ Review the concept of relevant markets to determine whether CIT has monopoly power. ♦ Also, consider the three defenses to a § 2 action and the Kleenzall example on page 1031.

page 1035	♦ You should consider § 3 of the Clayton Act.

MATCHING EXERCISE

Select the term or concept that best matches a definition or statement set forth below. Each term or concept is the best match for only one definition or statement.

Terms and Concepts

a. Antimerger provision
b. Bait-and-switch
c. Clayton Act
d. Copyright

e. Exclusive dealing
f. Group boycott
g. Horizontal market division
h. Horizontal price fixing

i. Patent
j. Trademark
k. Sherman Act
l. Vertical price fixing

Definitions and Statements

_____ 1. Agreement on price among competitors.
_____ 2. Agreement on price between a supplier and customer.
_____ 3. Agreement among competitors dividing territories in which they will each sell.
_____ 4. Agreement among competitors not to sell to a particular buyer or not to buy from a particular seller.
_____ 5. Exclusive right to use, make, or sell an invention for 20 years.
_____ 6. Prohibits the acquisition of stock or assets in another firm that may tend to have a negative affect on any line of commerce.
_____ 7. Exclusive right to use, reproduce, or sell a creative work.
_____ 8. Advertising a product at an enticing price to get a customer into the store and then talking the customer into buying a more expensive item.
_____ 9. Arrangement that requires one party to deal only with one other party.
_____ 10. Federal antitrust law that prohibits combinations that restrain trade and prohibits attempts to monopolize an industry.
_____ 11. Mark or symbol that is used to identify the source of a product.
_____ 12. Federal antitrust law that is designed to prevent antitrust violations, not just remedy them.

COMPLETION EXERCISE

Fill in the blanks with the words that most accurately complete each statement.

1. _____ _____, which is prohibited by the Robinson-Patman Act, may result when a manufacturer charges different customers different prices for the same goods.

2. The Sherman authorizes injured private parties to recover _____ _____.

3. _____ _____ _____ is indicated when a company captures 70 percent or more of a relevant market.

4. _____ _____ involves advertising, designing, or selling goods as if they were the goods of another.

5. Identify the two rules that are used to evaluate whether conduct violates the Sherman Act:

a. _____.

b. _____.

TRUE-FALSE EXERCISE

Write **T** if the statement is true, write **F** if the statement is false.

_____ 1. It is a per se violation of the Sherman Act for a company to have a monopoly in any market.

_____ 2. Section 1 of the Sherman Act requires an action by two or more people in order to find a violation, whereas one person, acting alone, may violate Section 2.

_____ 3. Mergers between two large companies are not permitted.

_____ 4. The FTC Act protects patents, trademarks, and copyrights.

_____ 5. Trade secrets are protected for up to 50 years, after which time they become available for use by all persons and companies.

_____ 6. Exclusive dealing arrangements are a per se violation of federal antitrust laws.

_____ 7. Price fixing is a per se violation of the Sherman Act.

_____ 8. The relevant market for purposes of antitrust law includes the goods in question and any substitute goods.

_____ 9. Actual harm is required to show a violation of the Clayton Act.

_____ 10. Traditionally, a tying arrangement is a per se violation of the Clayton Act.

APPLICATION OF CONCEPTS

MULTIPLE CHOICE QUESTIONS

_____ 1. Which of the following actions violates the federal antitrust law?
   a. Oilco, Inc. is a large business that owns 50 percent of the oil refinery business in the United States.
   b. Manufacturer gives Ollie the exclusive right to sell Manufacturer's products in a certain area. This agreement does not substantially lessen competition in this case.
   c. Digger, Inc. manufactures earth-moving equipment. Digger and its distributors agree that the distributors will not resell Digger's equipment below certain minimum prices.
   d. San Francisco imposes certain residential rent limitations.

_____ 2. Heffer, Inc. and other meat producers agree to fix prices that they charge for their competitive meat products that are sold in interstate commerce. Under these facts:
   a. Heffer may be liable for three times the actual damages caused by its price fixing.
   b. Heffer may be subject to fines up to $10 million.
   c. Individuals who are guilty of this price fixing may be fined, but they cannot be imprisoned.
   d. No one can be sued, fined, or imprisoned for their conduct because price fixing is generally legal under the Sherman Act.

_____ 3. Vectra and Spectra market their products in Georgia and Arkansas. Both agree that Vectra should market only in Georgia, and Spectra should market only in Arkansas. Under these facts Vectra and Spectra:

    a. Have violated the prohibition against horizontal market divisions, a per se violation of § 1 of the Sherman Act.

    b. Have violated the prohibition against horizontal market divisions, but their agreement may be legal if it did not actually hurt competition.

    c. Have violated the prohibition against horizontal market divisions only if it can be shown that they had an actual agreement.

    d. Have violated the prohibition against horizontal market divisions, but their agreement may be legal if it did not actually hurt an individual or company.

_____ 4. Which of the following does not create a potential antitrust merger problem?

    a. ManCo, the sole manufacturer of gizmos, wants to merge with I&C, the sole user of gizmos.

    b. ManCo, the sole manufacturer of gizmos, wants to merge with I&C., one of four users of gizmos.

    c. ManCo, one of four manufacturers of gizmos, wants to merge with I&C, one of four users of gizmos.

    d. ManCo, one of 20 manufacturers of gizmos, wants to merge with I&C, one of 30 manufacturers of widgets, a product unrelated to gizmos.

SHORT ANSWER QUESTIONS

Answer the following questions, briefly explaining the reason for your answer.

1. LubeTech manufactures 1Lube, a universal lubricant that works on all engines and moving parts, in any temperature, and in all conditions. 1Lube is also cheaper than comparable lubricants. Because of 1Lube, LubeTech controls 80 percent of the lubricant market. Has LubeTech violated § 2 of the Sherman Act?

_____

_____

2. CyberFun manufactures the Dude! portable video game. CyberFun has invented a portable virtual-reality video game that is comparable in price to current portable video games, and is sure to make regular portable video games obsolete. In an effort to clear its inventory of Dude!'s, CyberFun has offered to sell the games at a substantially reduced price to one of its distributors. Is CyberFun guilty of price discrimination?

_____

_____

3. Joe, Moe, and Doe manufacture widgets and are located in three different states. Recently, a fourth competitor, Shmoe, has dominated the widget market. Joe, Moe, and Doe agree that each would be better off if they sold only in their own state. Is this agreement a violation of § 1 of the Sherman Act?

_____

_____

4. Big Muscle, which manufactures vitamins for body builders, is in severe financial difficulty. VitaHealth, a vitamin manufacturer that sells its products in all fifty states, offered to acquire Big Muscle when no other company offered to merge with Big Muscle. The merger may reduce competition somewhat in the muscle-building vitamin industry. Does this merger violate § 7 of the Clayton Act?

_____

_____

CASE PROBLEMS

Answer the following case problems, explaining your answers.

1. LeatherTech has designed a process to make synthetic leather. It is virtually impossible to tell the difference between LeatherTech's product and real leather. LeatherTech's product is soft and pliable, it stretches, and it even smells like leather. LeatherTech uses this synthetic leather to manufacture coats, and it currently has a 90 percent share of the market for synthetic leather coats. However, it only has a 25 percent share of the winter coat market. (a) What is LeatherTech's relevant market? (b) Has LeatherTech violated the Sherman Act?

_____

_____

_____

_____

2. CompuTron makes the Micro Data Storage Unit (MiDSU) The MiDSU compresses data from a computer and transfers it to a 1.5 inch "minidisk." Currently, no other company manufactures a mini-disk that is compatible with the MiDSU. In fact, using any other mini-disk will destroy the MiDSU because only the CompuTron mini-disk has a secret patented processor that can protect the MiDSU from harm. Consequently, CompuTron will not sell its MiDSU to retailers unless they also buy its minidisk. (a) What type of arrangement is this? (b) Has CompuTron potentially violated any antitrust laws? (c) What defense is available to CompuTron?

_____

_____

_____

_____

CHAPTER 41

Consumer Protection

```
┌─────────────────────────────────────────────┐
│                                               │
│               CHAPTER REVIEW                  │
│                                               │
└─────────────────────────────────────────────┘
```

INTRODUCTION: Federal consumer protection laws have been adopted to provide uniformity and to correct abuses in commercial practices.

CONSUMER CREDIT: The large volume of credit transactions in the United States has led to a giant industry involving the sale of credit reports and has led to government regulation.

THE CONSUMER CREDIT PROTECTION ACT: The Truth in Lending Act (TILA), which is Title I of the Consumer Credit Protection Act of 1968, is a landmark consumer protection law. The TILA is primarily a disclosure statute, requiring creditors to inform consumers of the actual costs of credit. The statute carries civil, criminal, and statutory liabilities for a creditor's failure to comply. The TILA allows for a three-day period in which consumers who use their homes as collateral for loans can cancel those loans.

Lobbying efforts by lenders led to passage of the Truth in Lending Simplification and Reform Act in 1980. This Act relaxed the TILA's requirements for detailed disclosures by creditors.
In response to numerous class action lawsuits, the TILA was amended in 1995 to provide retroactive and prospective relief from liability for certain creditor finance charges.

The Federal Reserve Board enacted Regulation Z to cover persons who regularly offer credit to consumers for personal, family, or household use and the transactions have a finance charge or, by written agreement, are payable in four or more installments. This regulation requires detailed disclosures in a meaningful sequence in the initial statement, and it requires periodic statements containing specified disclosures. Regulation Z specifies procedures and time limits for consumers and creditors in dealing with billing errors. Regulation Z covers both open-ended credit (e.g., credit card purchases) and closed-end credit (e.g., credit purchases of cars).

THE FAIR CREDIT REPORTING ACT: The Fair Credit Reporting Act of 1970 (FCRA) regulates practices by companies that *regularly* engage in credit reporting. The FCRA requires consumer-reporting agencies to maintain reasonable procedures to avoid violations of the Act. Agencies must report only accurate and up-to-date information, and must report the information only to those eligible to receive it. Consumers, however, have little recourse against agencies that report irrelevant information that arguably invades their privacy. Consumers have no right under the FCRA to see their files, but consumers do have the right to be notified if adverse actions have been taken based on a credit report. Consumers must be informed of the identity and address of the reporting agency that compiled a report that led to adverse action, and the consumer has a limited right to correct erroneous information contained in a report.

THE EQUAL CREDIT OPPORTUNITY ACT: The Equal Credit Opportunity Act prohibits discrimination based on sex, marital status, race, religion, national origin, age, receipt of public assistance, and exercise of consumer protection rights.

THE FAIR DEBT COLLECTION PRACTICES ACT: The Fair Debt Collection Practices Act (FDCPA) regulates the activities of those who collect bills owed to others. The FDCPA prohibits certain acts which harass or intimidate debtors or which coerce payment through false statements. The FDCPA provides for civil and criminal penalties.

THE UNIFORM CONSUMER CREDIT CODE: Few states have adopted the Uniform Consumer Credit Code (UCCC); most states rely on their own laws.

THE CONSUMER PRODUCT SAFETY ACT: The Consumer Product Safety Act of 1972 established the Consumer Product Safety Commission (CPSC). The Consumer Product Safety Commission may set safety standards for consumer products, collect information on consumer injuries, require corrective action for hazardous consumer products, and ban unsafe products.

STUDY HINTS FOR CALL-IMAGE TECHNOLOGY CASE STUDIES

The following study hints may be helpful when resolving the Call-Image Technology (CIT) case studies.

page 1050
- ◆ Review the discussion of the Fair Credit Reporting Act before answering this question.
- ◆ Consider what steps need to be followed to make sure any information provided is accurate and up-to-date.

page 1054
- ◆ Review the section on The Equal Credit Opportunity Act.

page 1060
- ◆ Review the section on the Fair Debt Collection Practices Act, including the *Bentley v. Great Lakes Collection Bureau* case.
- ◆ Consider whether different restrictions would apply to a collection agency than to CIT itself.

MATCHING EXERCISE

Select the term or concept that best matches a definition or statement set forth below. Each term or concept is the best match for only one definition or statement.

Terms and Concepts

a. Closed-end credit
b. Cooling-off period
c. CPSC
d. Debt collector

e. ECOA
f. FCRA
g. FDCPA

h. Open-ended credit
I.   Regulation Z
j.   TILA

Definitions and Statements

_____ 1. Federal act that requires disclosure of actual costs of credit.
_____ 2. Credit transaction for a fixed term, such as a credit purchase of a refrigerator payable in 12 monthly installments.
_____ 3. Business that collects accounts or debts for someone else who has given credit.
_____ 4. Credit transactions available for an indefinite time period, such as credit card transactions.
_____ 5. Federal act that regulates the activities of those who collect bills owed to others.
_____ 6. Federal agency created to help protect the public from injuries from consumer products.
_____ 7. Federal Reserve Board's enactment summarizing the scope of the Truth in Lending Act.
_____ 8. Time allowed under the Truth in Lending Act for consumers to cancel loans which use their homes as collateral.
_____ 9. Federal act requiring consumer-reporting agencies to adopt reasonable procedures for collecting and disseminating consumer information.
_____ 10. Federal act prohibiting certain discriminatory practices in the extension of credit.

COMPLETION EXERCISE

Fill in the blanks with the words that most accurately complete each statement.

1. The _____ _____ _____ ____, Title I of which is known as the Truth in Lending Act, was a landmark consumer protection law passed in 1968.

2. Remedies available to individuals under the Truth in Lending Act include _____

_____, _____ _____ of twice the finance charges, and

_____ _____.

3. The Federal Reserve Board's _____ ____ implements the Equal Credit Opportunity Act.

4. The Truth in Lending Act requires _____ and _____ disclosure of credit terms.

5. Potentially hazardous consumer products are regulated by the _____ _____

_____ _____.

TRUE-FALSE EXERCISE

Write **T** if the statement is true, write **F** if the statement is false.

____ 1. The Truth in Lending Act is part of the Equal Credit Opportunity Act.
____ 2. Regulation B is the implementing regulation for the Truth in Lending Act.
____ 3. Regulation Z is the implements the Equal Credit Opportunity Act.
____ 4. A consumer must notify a creditor of a billing error within 60 days of the creditor's transmitting the bill to the consumer.
____ 5. The Fair Debt Collection Practices Act does not apply to persons or businesses collecting their own bills.
____ 6. The UCCC has brought uniformity to state laws governing consumer credit because of its adoption by all of the states.
____ 7. The Truth in Lending Act regulates only credit disclosure.
____ 8. The FCRA requires a credit bureau to allow consumers to see their files.
____ 9. Lenders may not discriminate against recipients of public assistance.
____ 10. Sales of tobacco and tobacco products are governed by the Consumer Product Safety Commission.

APPLICATION OF CONCEPTS

MULTIPLE CHOICE QUESTIONS

____ 1. Ms. Kim borrowed $20,000 from Lone Sharx Associates, using her house as collateral. Which of the following consumer protection statutes provides Ms. Kim with a three day "cooling off" period to rescind the loan agreement?
   a. The Fair Credit Reporting Act
   b. The Uniform Consumer Credit Act
   c. The Truth in Lending Act
   d. The Equal Credit Opportunity Act

____ 2. Burt believes that he did not incur a $200 charge reflected on his credit card. If Burt contacts the credit card company within the applicable time frame to dispute the charge, what action may the credit card company take against Burt?
   a. The credit card company may apply the disputed charge against Burt's credit limit.
   b. The credit card company may attempt to collect the disputed $200 from Burt.
   c. The credit card company may close Burt's account if Burt continues to dispute the charge.
   d. The credit card company may report Burt's failure to pay the $200 to a credit reporting agency.

_____ 3. Paula attempted to open a charge account at Marston's Department Store. The store denied her application based on an unsatisfactory credit report. What may Paula do to correct the situation?
a. Paula may obtain a copy of the credit report by contacting the credit reporting agency.
b. Paula may obtain information regarding the adverse information contained in the credit report.
c. Paula may demand that the adverse information be removed from the credit report.
d. All of the above.

_____ 4. Marty applied for a loan from First Bank. The Bank denied the loan, but failed to notify Marty regarding the reasons for its action. Under the ECOA, what are Marty's options regarding the Bank's failure to follow federal law?
a. Marty may sue the Bank and seek attorneys fees and costs.
b. Marty may sue the bank for actual and punitive damages.
c. Marty may ask the U.S. Attorney General to impose civil penalties against the Bank.
d. All of the above.

SHORT ANSWER QUESTIONS

Answer the following questions, briefly explaining the reason for your answer.

1. Terence reviews loan applications for The Friendly Loan Company. Karen has filed an application for a loan to buy a new car. Terence knows that Karen is planning to marry a college student and believes that Karen may have difficulty making the car payments. May Terence deny the loan based upon Karen's future wedding plans?

_____

_____

2. The Consumer Product Safety Commission has noted an unusually high incidence of injuries to children who use a certain brand of in-line skates. What actions may the CPSC take regarding the particular brand of skates?

_____

_____

3. Grace was denied credit for the purchase of a new home based upon erroneous information in her credit file. If Grace disputes the information and the credit agency's investigation fails to resolve the dispute, what action may Grace take to tell potential creditors her side of the dispute?

_____

_____

4. After several attempts between 8 a.m. and 7 p.m., the Moore Collection Agency was unable to reach Zach about his overdue account with Acme Rental. Moore then tried to call Zach at 7 a.m., hoping to reach him before he left for work. Did Moore's actions violate any laws?

_____

_____

CASE PROBLEMS

Answer the following case problems, explaining your answers.

1. On August 2, a representative of Vaughn Home Improvement came to Maurice's home to give him an estimate on replacement windows. While the representative was there, Maurice signed a contract to make a credit purchase of the windows for $12,000. Maurice's home was to be used as collateral. On August 3, Maurice decided he had made a bad choice by ordering the windows. (a) Does Maurice have any recourse? (b) What legislation covers Maurice's situation? (c) What factor triggers the application of this legislation? (d) How soon must Maurice take action?

_____

_____

_____

_____

2. Stuart owns the Quik-Serv Collection Agency. He instructs all employees to recover debts for their customers within thirty days. He also recommends that the employees aggressively pursue debtors by calling their employers and talking with their neighbors and thereby embarrass them into making quick payments. (a) Which consumer protection law regulates the collection agency? (b) May the agency contact debtors' employers and neighbors? (c) What kinds of penalties or other adverse actions might the agency face if it violates the law? (d) What additional action might Stuart face, if he includes the words "federal", "national", or "the United States" on written collection communications?

_____

_____

_____

_____

CHAPTER 42

CHAPTER REVIEW

THE ENVIRONMENTAL PROTECTION AGENCY: The EPA, a federal administrative agency, enforces federal environmental laws, conducts research, and adopts regulations covering air, water, and waste products.

THE NATIONAL ENVIRONMENTAL POLICY ACT: NEPA requires all federal agencies to analyze the environmental impact of their policies and actions to avoid environmental degradation.

- *Environmental impact statement*: A federal agency must prepare an environmental impact statement (EIS) whenever the agency proposes legislation, recommends any actions, or undertakes any activity if the following three elements are present: 1) the activity involves a proposed federal action 2) that is "major" and 3) has a significant impact on the environment.

    An EIS examines the proposed action, possible alternatives including no action, long-term and short-term impacts, commitment of resources, and unavoidable adverse consequences.

- *Council on environmental quality*: NEPA established the Council on Environmental Quality to advise the president regarding developing and recommending federal environmental regulations.

Air Pollution: Particulates, carbon monoxide, nitrogen oxides, sulfur oxides, and hydrocarbons are five categories of air pollution that are regulated under the Clean Air Act.

- *The Clean Air Act*: This Act sets standards for air pollution emissions and establishes time tables for the reduction of air pollutants.

- *The 1970 amendments*: Amendments to the Act gave the EPA responsibility for establishing national ambient air standards (standards relating to mobile air emissions, such as automobile pollution). States must submit to the EPA a state implementation plan (SIP) setting out how the state plans to meet the federal standards.

- *The 1977 amendments*: These amendments delayed compliance with federal standards.

- *The 1990 amendments*: These amendments set new compliance dates. It also sets up a permit system aimed at controlling pollution at major stationary points. In addition, it increased the civil and criminal penalties for violating federal clean air laws. Penalties include administrative fines of up to $25,000 per day, and other fines up to $1 million for each violation and up to 15 years imprisonment.

Water Pollution: The Clean Water Act (CWA) establishes goals and timetables for cleaning up the nation's waterways.

- *The Clean Water Act*: Water pollution sources are classified as either point sources or nonpoint sources. A point source is: 1) any type of physical structure or device, such as pipes, tubes, ditches, or tunnels 2) that is regularly used to convey pollutants from an industrial source to waterways. Nonpoint sources are such things as farms, mining, and forestry operations.

    Point sources are regulated through a discharge permit system (NPDES). Nonpoint sources are exempt from having to comply with the CWA. Effluent limits are set for the amount and kinds of pollutants that may be discharged into streams or rivers through point sources. Individual states classify waters within their state and administer the permit program with EPA oversight.

    Companies are forbidden from discharging pollutants through a point source unless they have a discharge permit that allows such discharge. Discharge of pollutants through a point source is illegal if: 1) the discharging party does not have a discharge permit or 2) more pollutants are discharged than is allowed by a permit. A party who violates the CWA may suffer both civil and criminal liability.

- *Safe Drinking Water Act*: The Safe Drinking Water Act (SDWA) regulates water delivered through the public water supply systems, establishing maximum contaminant levels (MCL's) for various pollutants. States administer and enforce the federal law.

NOISE POLLUTION: Before passage of the Noise Control Act in 1972, nuisance laws provided the sole basis for protection from excessive noise. Federal law now preempts state laws in setting standards for major noise sources, such as construction equipment, transportation equipment, motors, and engines. Nonetheless, the states continue to bear the primary responsibility for enforcing noise pollution laws.

LAND CONSERVATION AND POLLUTION: Numerous laws prohibit pollution of public domain, meaning land owned or controlled by the federal government, and private land.

- *The Toxic Substances Control Act (TSCA)*: The TSCA screens (evaluates) chemicals before they are manufactured and marketed to the public in order to assess the risk that they may pose to humans and to the environment. The EPA is required to test and regulate only those chemicals that pose an "unreasonable risk."
- *The Federal Insecticide, Fungicide, and Rodenticide Act (FIFRA)*: FIFRA regulates the sale and use of pesticides and establishes civil and criminal penalties.
- *The Resource Conservation and Recovery Act (RCRA)*: This Act provides assistance to states for establishing programs for disposing of solid, nonhazardous waste programs. It also establishes a system for regulating the generation, transportation, storage and disposal of hazardous waste.
- *The Comprehensive Environmental Response, Compensation, and Liability Act (CERCLA)*: CERCLA, also known as the "Superfund," imposes strict liability on an owner or operator of a facility where emergency response actions must be taken to protect public health and environment. Sites may be cleaned up with federal funds with costs later recovered from potentially responsible parties (PRPs).

WILDLIFE CONSERVATION: The Endangered Species Act protects threatened or endangered species of wildlife both in the United States and abroad. Habitats are also protected.

ENFORCEMENT AND REMEDIES: Environmental laws are enforced by fines and/or imprisonment.

INTERNATIONAL ASPECTS: While many foreign countries are plagued by pollution, the European Union has adopted environmental protection measures.

.

STUDY HINTS FOR CALL-IMAGE TECHNOLOGY CASE STUDIES

The following study hints may be helpful when resolving the Call-Image Technology (CIT) case studies.

page 1077	◆ Review the discussion of environmental self-audits before answering this question. ◆ Also, review the discussion of the Clean Air Act.

page 1085	◆ CIT should explore obtaining an appropriate permit for its effluents. ◆ Also, since penalties may depend on the good faith compliance efforts of a company, CIT should immediately undertake to bring its operations into compliance with the law.

MATCHING EXERCISE

Select the term or concept that best matches a definition or statement set forth below. Each term or concept is the best match for only one definition or statement.

Terms and Concepts

a. Ambient air standards
b. Aquifer
c. CERCLA
d. Citizen suit

e. CWA
f. Effluent
g. EIS
h. Leachings

I. Manifest
j. NEPA
k. Nuisance
l. Public domain

Definitions and Statements

_____ 1. Federal act that requires federal agencies to analyze environmental impact of their actions.
_____ 2. Standards set for surrounding air in atmosphere.
_____ 3. Legal action that may be brought by private persons for others' violations of environmental laws.
_____ 4. Liquid draining or percolating through substances.
_____ 5. Report that analyzes an action's potential impact on the environment.
_____ 6. Federal statute that provides for correcting serious hazardous waste pollution.
_____ 7. Use of one's property that impairs use or enjoyment of property held by another person.
_____ 8. Subsurface accumulations of water held in rock, gravel, or sand.
_____ 9. Discharge of fluids.
_____ 10. Lands held by the federal government for public use.
_____ 11. Federal statute that is intended to preserve the water quality of the nation's navigable rivers and streams.
_____ 12. A list, such as that required for the transportation of hazardous wastes.

COMPLETION EXERCISE

Fill in the blanks with the words that most accurately complete each statement.

1. The Environmental Protection Agency was created by _____ _____ in 1970.

2. The Safe Drinking Water Act sets _____ _____ _____ or MCLs for pollutants to drinking water supplies.

3. Most federal environmental laws provide both _____ and _____ penalties for violations.

4. NEPA requires federal agencies to prepare an environmental impact statement prior to undertaking

any _____ federal action.

5. The Resource Conservation and Recovery Act (RCRA) generally regulates the disposal of

_____.

TRUE-FALSE EXERCISE

Write **T** if the statement is true, write **F** if the statement is false.

_____ 1. Federal environmental laws are often enforced by the states.
_____ 2. Violators of most environmental laws face only civil penalties.
_____ 3. Environmental laws often provide for the issuance of permits that allow companies to discharge certain amounts and kinds of pollutants into the air and water.
_____ 4. Under CERCLA, landowners are sometimes held liable for the cleanup of hazardous substances even if they did not personally dump these substances on their land.
_____ 5. The Endangered Species Act protects the habitat of a species as well as the species itself.
_____ 6. Environmental protection laws are unique to the United States.
_____ 7. In general, states can adopt water pollution laws that conflict with the Clean Water Act.
_____ 8. The federal Superfund is designed to aid in cleaning up inactive hazardous waste sites.
_____ 9. Under certain environmental laws, a private citizen can sue a polluter only if the citizen suffers a special harm, meaning harm that is different from the harm suffered by the general public.
_____ 10. The CWA regulates the discharge of pollutants from point sources, but not from nonpoint sources.

APPLICATION OF CONCEPTS

MULTIPLE CHOICE QUESTIONS

_____ 1. The government brought an action against Martin Co. for using pipes to illegally discharge residue wastes into the Roaring River in violation of the CWA. Martin had a permit that allowed it to discharge wastes, but the amount it discharged exceeded its allotted exemption. However, Martin did not intentionally violate its permit, and it did not discharge more wastes than other similar companies. Is Martin liable in this case?
   a. Yes.
   b. No, because it did not intend to violate the law.
   c. No, because it did not discharge more wastes that other similar companies.
   d. No, because the CWA does not apply to discharges from nonpoint sources, such as the discharge pipes in this case.

_____ 2. The U.S. Army Corps of Engineers (a federal agency) proposes building a large dam. The dam will affect the environment, and it will require abandonment of several towns. In this case:
   a. The U.S. Army Corps of Engineers must prepare an EIS before it builds the dam.
   b. An EIS must consider the impact that the dam may have on residents and businesses in the towns that must be abandoned if the dam is built.
   c. An EIS must consider feasible, practical alternatives to the dam.
   d. All of the above.

_____ 3. In the manufacturing of super-balls at its Pittsburgh plant, Orbit Inc. produces a toxic chemical waste that may cause lung cancer. Orbit plans to dispose of these wastes by burying them in a disposal area located in Nevada. Under these facts:
   a. RCRA regulates the production, transportation, and disposal of the waste in this case.
   b. RCRA forbids production of any toxic wastes, such as the waste in this case.
   c. RCRA forbids transporting any toxic wastes, such as the waste in this case.
   d. All of the above.

_____ 4. Olivia leased ten acres of her property to Brexus Corp. Brexus operated a hammer factory where hazardous chemicals are used in the manufacturing process. Some of these hazardous chemicals escaped from the Brexus factory, damaging the surrounding land. Who is liable in this case?
   a. Only Olivia.
   b. Only Brexus Corp.
   c. Olivia and Brexus Corp.
   d. No one.

SHORT ANSWER QUESTIONS

Answer the following questions, briefly explaining the reason for your answer.

1. Donald intends to build homes on property he recently purchased. When he purchased the property, Donald was aware that the prior owner had abandoned leaking tanks of hazardous waste on the property. As it turns out, the property is highly toxic, requiring massive clean-up. What federal law applies in this case? Who is liable for the cost of cleaning up this property?

_____

_____

2. Cows, Inc. owns a feedlot and meat processing plant. When it rains, water from the feedlot runs into a nearby river. Also, Cows Inc. discharges acid from its plant directly into the river, using pipes. Cows, Inc. does not have any permits that sanction its activities. Analyze whether Cows, Inc. is violating the CWA.

_____

_____

3. CleanOil has dumped hazardous waste into the Green River for five years, hurting its fish population. Fred has fished this river for ten years, but can no longer do so because of CleanOil's pollution. Does Fred have standing to bring a citizen suit against CleanOil for violating the CWA?

_____

_____

4. Acme Disposal Company transported a shipment of hazardous waste. Foster, Acme's employee, improperly disposed of this waste, contaminating the city's drinking water. What law applies in this case? Who violated the law in this case?

_____

_____

CASE PROBLEMS

Answer the following case problems, explaining your answers.

1. The Ski Corp. wants to build a new ski resort on Forest Service land and has filed for a permit allowing it to do so. The project will require clearing trees along numerous ski runs, and using large quantities of public river water for snowmaking and drinking purposes. (a) Does the proposed project involve a major federal action? (b) Must an EIS be prepared? (c) If an EIS is prepared, what matters must it address?

_____

_____

_____

_____

2. Tony wants to build a shopping mall next to an undeveloped expanse of land that is inhabited by the black-footed ferret. This type of ferret is an endangered species. (a) What federal environmental law may apply in this case? (b) What must Tony do in order to comply with this law?

_____

_____

_____

_____

CHAPTER 43

Labor and Fair Employment Practices

```
┌─────────────────────────────────────┐
│            CHAPTER REVIEW             │
└─────────────────────────────────────┘
```

LABOR: In the 1800s and the early 1900s federal courts saw union activities as criminal conspiracies.

- *Federal Statutes*: A series of federal statutes establish, protect, and define the rights of employees to collectively bargain with their employers. These laws include:

  1) **The Norris-LaGuardia Act (1932)**: The Norris-LaGuardia Act removed barriers that had hindered union organization, permitting unions to organize and collectively bargain. In addition, this Act: a) authorizes boycotts and picketing,, and b) outlaws yellow dog contracts, that is, agreements by which workers promise not to join a union.

  2) **The Wagner Act (1935)**: Also called the National Labor Relations Act (NLRA), the Wagner Act encourages organizing activities and collective bargaining by allowing workers the freedom to: a) join unions, b) collectively bargain with an employer, and 3) engage in mutually beneficial activities. It also requires employers to bargain with unions in good faith. The Wagner Act established the National Labor Relations Board (NLRB), which is charged with administering and interpreting the unfair labor practice provisions of this law.

  3) **The Taft-Hartley Act (1947)**: Also called the Labor Management Relations Act, the Taft-Hartley amended the Wagner Act to forbid certain union practices. Among other things, this Act: a) protects the employers' rights to express their opinions about unionization so long as they do not take reprisals against employees who are attempting to unionize; b) preserves the employees' rights to engage in informational picketing (picketing intended to inform the public that workers are receiving wages and benefits below what other employers in the area are providing); c) prohibits closed shops (workers cannot be hired unless they already have joined the union), while still permitting union shops (all workers in the bargaining unit must join the union after being hired, usually after a thirty-day grace period); d) mandates a "cooling-off" period in certain circumstances before employees can strike; and e) preserved the rights of states to enact right-to-work laws (right-to-work laws prohibit employers from requiring workers to join a union or to pay dues and initiation fees as conditions of employment, even if an employer's workers are represented by a union).

  4) **The Landrum-Griffin Act (1959)**: Also called the Labor Management Reporting and Disclosure Act, this Act provides for civil and criminal penalties for union leaders who are corrupt. It also mandates democratic procedures in union affairs and a "bill of rights" for members.

  5) **Further issues**: Some common issues include the following:

     a) Decertification - Employers can contest the validity of a certification election by requesting the NLRB to decertify the union, i.e., determine that the union does not represent the employees.

     b) Soliciting - Employers can generally forbid soliciting unionization on the employers' premises and during working hours.

- *State law*: State law regulating labor is preempted by federal law. Activities peripheral to federal law or of deep state concern are subject to state regulation.

EMPLOYMENT:

- *Fair Employment Practices Laws*: Federal antidiscrimination laws include the following:

1) **Civil Rights Act of 1964**: Title VII of this Act applies to employers with 15 or more employees, unions with 15 or more member or who operate a hiring hall, and employment agencies. This law forbids any form of employment discrimination on the basis an employee's race, color, religion, sex, or national origin.

Title VII forbids the following types of practices: a) disparate treatment (employer intentionally discriminates against a job applicant or employee because of the person's race, national origin, color, religion, or sex); b) disparate impact (employer adopts a neutral employment qualification that has a significantly different, unfavorable effect on a protected class and the qualification is not a business necessity); and c) harassment (verbal, nonverbal, written, and/or physical conduct in the workplace that causes an employee to suffer ridicule, humiliation, or physical injury due to the person's race, national origin, color, religion, or sex).

The Pregnancy Discrimination Act mandates that pregnancy be treated as any other disability protected by law, it expressly states that sex discrimination under Title VII includes discrimination on the basis of pregnancy, childbirth, or related medical conditions

2) **The Immigration Reform and Control Act**: This Act bans discrimination against persons because they are not U.S. citizens.

3) **The Equal Pay Act** This Act prohibits discrimination in wages between men and women if they are both performing the same work under substantially the same working conditions.

4) **The Age Discrimination in Employment Act**: This Act prohibits discrimination against job applicants or employees because they are 40 years of age or older.

5) **The Rehabilitation Act of 1973**: This executive order directs federal contractors to reasonably accommodate "otherwise qualified" handicapped individuals in connection with employment.

6) **The Americans with Disabilities Act**: Among other things, this Act requires employers to make a reasonable accommodation in employment for qualified persons with disabilities.

7) **Other laws**: Other important employment laws include The Civil Rights Act of 1991; the Family and Medical Leave Act; the Occupational Safety and Health Act; the Social Security Act; and state workers' compensation statutes.

STUDY HINTS FOR CALL-IMAGE TECHNOLOGY CASE STUDIES

The following study hints may be helpful when resolving the Call-Image Technology (CIT) case studies.

page 1112

♦ Review the *Lechner, Inc. v. NLRB* case on page 1111.
♦ Review the discussion regarding the Taft-Hartley Act.

page 1116

♦ John should understand "disparate impact" interpretations of employment requirements, but should also understand "business necessity" as justification for differential treatment.

page 1117

♦ Tom should review the material dealing with harassment under Title VII.
♦ It would also be instructive to review the Harris v. Forklift Systems, Inc. case.

MATCHING EXERCISE

Select the term or concept that best matches a definition or statement set forth below. Each term or concept is the best match for only one definition or statement.

Terms and Concepts

a. Bona fide occupational qualification   d. Informational picketing   g. Severance pay
b. Boycott   e. Reverse discrimination   h. Unfair labor practice
c. Family and Medical Leave Act   f. Secondary boycott   i. Wildcat strike

Definitions and Statements

_____ 1. Refusal to do business with a supplier of an employer.
_____ 2. Strike by a minority group of workers that is not authorized by the union.
_____ 3. Picketing that is intended to inform the public that an employer does not employ union workers and/or does not pay the same as other employers.
_____ 4. Wages paid when a worker is terminated from a job.
_____ 5. Discrimination against white employees that may result from affirmative action programs.
_____ 6. Characteristic or skill that is required because it is essential for the performance of a job.
_____ 7. Act by an employer or union that violates federal labor laws.
_____ 8. Federal law that entitles some employees to take up to 12 weeks unpaid leave.
_____ 9. Refusal to do business with the employer.

COMPLETION EXERCISE

Fill in the blanks with the words that most accurately complete each statement.

1. _____ occurs when workers walk or stand in front of an employer's place of business.

2. A _____ _____ agreement is a contract between an employer and union that establishes the basic terms of employees who are represented by the union.

3. Title VII of the Civil Rights Act of 1964 prohibits discrimination against employees on

the basis of _____ , _____ _____ , _____ ,

_____ , and _____ .

4. The _____ _____ ____ _____ _____ is a federal law that is intended to prevent accidents in the workplace and to provide a safe working environment.

5. The _____ _____ _____ _____ prohibits employment discrimination against qualified persons with disabilities.

TRUE-FALSE EXERCISE

Write **T** if the statement is true, write **F** if the statement is false.

_____ 1. Wildcat strikes are unlawful.

_____ 2. The National Labor Relations Board has the power to punish employers and unions who engage in unfair labor practices.

_____ 3. Good faith bargaining that is required under federal labor law means that each side must continue to make concessions during negotiations until an agreement is reached.

_____ 4. The EEOC enforces most federal antidiscrimination laws, including Title VII.

_____ 5. An employer who intentionally pays Hispanic employees less than other employees has committed a disparate treatment violation of Title VII.

_____ 6. An employer must take any steps necessary in order to accommodate employees' religious beliefs.

_____ 7. The Age Discrimination in Employment Act forbids employers from firing anyone who is 40 or older.

_____ 8. An employee generally has 2 years within which to file a discrimination complaint under Title VII.

_____ 9. The Family and Medical Leave Act only applies to certain employers who have 50 or more employees.

_____ 10. When employees are involuntarily laid off due to a lack of work, the employees may be entitled to receive unemployment benefits.

APPLICATION OF CONCEPTS

MULTIPLE CHOICE QUESTIONS

_____ 1. Niles was concerned about the unsafe working conditions in his employer's factory and he contacted OSHA. OSHA inspectors came to the factory and asked to inspect the plant. Under these facts, the Occupational Safety and Health Act provides for which of the following:
   a. OSHA inspectors may inspect the plant without first obtaining a warrant.
   b. OSHA can issue a citation and fine the employer if it is in violation of OSHA regulations.
   c. Niles can be discharged for filing the complaint with OSHA.
   d. All of the above.

_____ 2. In most states, which individual would be eligible for unemployment benefits?
   a. Niya was laid off of her job as a computer programmer because of a recession in the industry.
   b. Jay is a full-time student and not available for work.
   c. Steve was fired because he was drunk on the job and pilfered tools from his employer.
   d. a and b.

_____ 3. Shari was injured in an accident at work. Both Shari and employer were negligent. Under these facts, in a state with a typical Workers' Compensation statute:
  a. Shari can recover workers' compensation benefits.
  b. Shari cannot recover workers' compensation benefits because she was negligent.
  c. Shari can sue her employer under tort law because her employer was negligent.
  d. a and c.

_____ 4. Marlene has been a full-time employee of Garland Corp. for two years. Marlene recently became pregnant and gave birth to a son. Garland Corp. is subject to the Family and Medical Leave Act of 1993. Under these facts:
  a. Marlene is entitled to receive one year of paid leave so she can care for her son.
  b. Marlene is entitled to receive twelve weeks of paid leave so she can care for her son.
  c. Marlene is entitled to receive twelve weeks of unpaid leave so she can care for her son.
  d. Marlene is not entitled to receive any paid or unpaid leave so she can care for her son.

SHORT ANSWER QUESTIONS

Answer the following questions, briefly explaining the reason for your answer.

1. Dr. Kathy Payne advertised for an "experienced receptionist, females preferred." Payne is a gynecologist and she believes that her patients feel more comfortable when greeted by a female receptionist than when greeted by a male receptionist. Bill, a highly qualified job applicant applied for the advertised job, but was rejected because of his gender. Has Payne violated Title VII in this case?

_____

_____

2. Julio was born in Mexico and currently lives in the United States. Julio is not yet a U.S. citizen. He applied for an analyst position at the Intelligence Research Center (IRC), a private company that provides intelligence analysis for the government. Analysts must have a top secret security clearance, which is impossible to obtain without U.S. citizenship. IRC refused to hire Julio because he did not have the required clearance. Has IRC violated any federal antidiscrimination law in this case?

_____

_____

3. Ames Fire Department requires its firefighters to be able to lift 250 pounds because, on rare occasion, a firefighter may have to lift this amount of weight. Chris applied for a job as fire fighter and she was qualified to perform the duties of the job. Chris and all other female applicants were rejected, however, because they could not lift this weight. Fifty percent of the qualified applicants were women. Has the Ames Fire Department violated Title VII?

_____

_____

4. St. Leo University, a Catholic college, refused to hire Mohammed as a professor because he is a Muslim. Instead it hired Paul, who is Catholic, even though he was less qualified. Has St. Leo violated Title VII?

_____

_____

CASE PROBLEMS

Answer the following case problems, explaining your answers.

1. Joe Wiper, the head custodian at Blinker High School, often makes crude sexual remarks in the presence of Maria and other male custodians. Maria complained to the assistant principal in charge of custodians, Dave Dingle. Dingle told her to "lighten up" and refused to do anything about Joe's constant comments and sexual innuendo. Joe recently told Maria that her job may be in jeopardy because of cutbacks in the janitorial force, but that he can protect her if she agrees to have sex with him. Has Joe and/or Blinker High School violated Title VII?

_____

_____

_____

_____

2. Kim Pak was born in Korea and she recently became a U.S. citizen. Kim speaks fluent English, but she has a mild Korean accent. Her accent does not interfere with her ability to communicate with others. Kim applied for the job of manager at the Jasper Hotel, for which she was qualified. However, Kim was not hired for this position because: (a) Kim speaks with a Korean accent; (b) Kim is fifty years old and she may not work for as many years as someone younger; and (c) Kim has a hearing disorder and the hotel would have to spend $300 to purchase a special telephone for her. Separately discuss the validity of each of these reasons for not hiring Kim.

_____

_____

_____

_____

CHAPTER 44

Real Property and Joint Ownership

PROPERTY RIGHTS: Property is both an object subject to ownership and a group of rights and interests.

REAL PROPERTY DEFINED: You should understand the difference between fixtures and nonfixtures.
- *Definition of Real Property*: Land and things permanently attached to land, like structures and roads.
- *Definition of a Fixture*: Property that at one time was movable and independent of real estate but became attached to it. Common examples include water heaters, built-in ovens, installed dishwashers.
- *The Nature of Plants*: Generally, plants are real property. The UCC classifies plants based on who will remove them. If the seller removes plants, then they are goods; if the buyer removes, then real estate.
- *State Governance*: The laws of the state where the property is located govern the land.
- *Federal Regulation*: The federal government, through the Americans with Disabilities Act (ADA), regulates property open to the public so that it can accommodate handicapped persons.

ACQUISITION OF REAL PROPERTY: Land ownership is a society-based concept.
- *Original Occupancy*: Occurs when the government allows private occupancy of land that was previously government owned.
- *Voluntary Transfer by the Owner*: Transfer is accomplished by a written deed, which contains key information. The three type of deeds are 1) warranty, 2) grant, and 3) quitclaim. It is prudent, but not necessary, to record a deed.
- *Transfer by Will or Intestate Succession*: A valid will can pass property to a named beneficiary.

PROTECTION OF REAL PROPERTY: Real property can be lost by operation of law or government action.
- *Involuntary Transfer by Operation of Law*: A lender may foreclose if a person is in default on a mortgage. Property may be attached to satisfy a legal judgment. Failure to pay for labor or materials for the premises will create a mechanic's lien.
- *Involuntary Transfer by Government Action*: Under the doctrine of eminent domain, the government may take land for public use, but it must provide compensation. The government may also enact zoning ordinances.
- *Private Restrictions on Land Use*: Restrictive covenants, which are private agreements between landowners, may limit how land can be used.
- *Adverse Possession*: A person who has open, notorious, continuous, and actual possession of property will acquire title to it after the expiration of a holding period (ranging from five to thirty years).
- *Easements*: An easement is the right to use land in a particular manner. An express easement is stated. An easement by prescription arises when a person starts to use land openly. After a period of time, the person will gain an easement. An easement by necessity arises when there is no means of access to the servient estate. An easement by implication arises when someone needs to use land, but the need is not as great as in an easement by necessity. An easement may also be created by contract.

RENTAL OF REAL PROPERTY: Understand the types of tenancies and the duties of landlord and tenant.

- *Types of Tenancies*: A tenancy for a fixed term automatically expires after a set period of time. A periodic tenancy continues for successive periods (such as a month) until terminated. Notice must be given before termination. A tenancy at will can be terminated at any time by the landlord or tenant. A tenancy at sufferance arises when a tenant wrongfully remains on the property.
- *Rights and Duties of Tenants*: A tenant has the right of quiet enjoyment, and some courts recognize the warranty of habitability. Assignments and subleases are allowed unless prohibited by the lease.
- *Rights and Duties of Landlords*: A landlord has the right to rent and to collect for damage. A landlord does not warrant that premises are safe, but must warn tenants of latent defects.
- *Legislative Trends*: The Fair Housing Act prohibits discrimination by landlords.

JOINT OWNERSHIP OF REAL PROPERTY: Exists when two or more people have concurrent title.

- *Tenancy in Common*: Exists when two or more people have an undivided interest in property.
- *Joint Tenancy with Rights of Survivorship*: Each tenant has an undivided interest, and the property passes to the other tenants upon the death of a tenant. A will has no effect on this type of tenancy.
- *Tenancy by the Entireties*: The tenants must be husband and wife, and each has an undivided interest with right of survivorship.
- *Community Property*: This law, recognized in eight states, provides that each spouse owns one-half of most property accumulated *during* marriage. Property acquired before marriage, inherited, received by gift, or purchased with separate funds remains separate property.
- *Distinguishing Among the Forms of Joint Ownership*: The words used on a deed are controlling. If the deed does not specify the form of joint ownership, then: 1) If the tenants are married, most states presume community property or tenancy by the entireties. If the state does not recognize these forms, then the law presumes joint tenancy with right of survivorship. 2) If the tenants are not married, most states presume a tenancy in common.

STUDY HINTS FOR CALL-IMAGE TECHNOLOGY CASE STUDIES

The following study hints may be helpful when resolving the Call-Image Technology (CIT) case studies.

page 1150	♦ Tom and Anna should understand mechanics' liens.

page 1151	♦ Review the sections on "Involuntary Transfers by Government Action" and "Private Restrictions on Land Use."

page 1158	♦ You should consider notice provisions required in periodic tenancies. ♦ Also consider tenants' rights with regard to installed fixtures and renovations.

MATCHING EXERCISE

Select the term or concept that best matches a definition or statement set forth below. Each term or concept is the best match for only one definition or statement.

Terms and Concepts

a. Community property
b. Constructive eviction
c. Decedent
d. Easement

e. Escrow
f. Fixture
g. Nuisance
h. Periodic tenancy

i. Separate property
j. Tenancy at will
k. Tenancy for a fixed term
l. Title

Definitions and Statements

____ 1. Rights to the access and use of someone else's real estate.
____ 2. Unlawful interference with the use of public or private property.
____ 3. Starts at a fixed time and continues for successive periods until terminated.
____ 4. Normally includes property: a) owned by either spouse before marriage; b) given to a spouse by gift or will; and c) acquired with separate funds.
____ 5. Property that at one time was movable and independent of real estate but became attached to it.
____ 6. Legal doctrine providing that one-half of property that is acquired during marriage belongs to each spouse.
____ 7. Tenancy for a set period of time.
____ 8. A person who has died.
____ 9. Legal ownership of property.
____ 10. Tenancy that can be terminated any time at the desire of either the landlord or the tenant.
____ 11. Process of preparing for the exchange of real estate.
____ 12. Occurs when a landlord materially interferes with a tenant's right to quiet enjoyment.

COMPLETION EXERCISE

Fill in the blanks with the words that most accurately complete each statement.

1. _____ _____ includes land, buildings, fixtures, and rights in land.

2. In some states, the law provides to tenants an implied _____ _____ _____, which states that a landlord impliedly warrants that the premises will be fit for living.

3. A _____ _____ contains a number of implied promises by the grantor to the effect that a good and marketable title is being conveyed.

4. A party may acquire title to property by _____ _____ if the party takes possession of the property, and such possession is actual, visible, notorious, exclusive, hostile, and continuous for the legally required period of time.

5. _____ proceedings are the means by which a lender can take possession of property in the event of _____.

TRUE-FALSE EXERCISE

Write **T** if the statement is true, write **F** if the statement is false.

_____ 1. An easement by prescription can be considered to be an "easement by adverse possession."
_____ 2. A landlord has a duty to inform the tenant of all latent defects on the premises.
_____ 3. In determining whether property is a fixture, courts will look at the reasonable expectations and understandings of most people.
_____ 4. In general, movable machinery and equipment are fixtures.
_____ 5. A deed is not valid unless consideration is given for the deed.
_____ 6. In general, a deed is not effective and does not transfer title unless the grantor effectively delivers the deed to the grantee.
_____ 7. In general, a deed must be recorded to be effective.
_____ 8. Statutes commonly hold that a grantor who conveys land by a quitclaim deed warrants that the grantor owns the land and that the land is not subject to any liens.
_____ 9. In some instances, government regulation may constitute a taking of property.
_____ 10. The Fair Housing Act requires landlords to act in good faith when leasing property.

APPLICATION OF CONCEPTS

MULTIPLE CHOICE QUESTIONS

_____ 1. Joseph owns a farm. In a signed writing, Joseph granted Fran the irrevocable right to use a road on his farm so that Fran could more easily reach her own property. What kind of interest in land did Joseph grant to Fran?
   a. Express easement.
   b. Easement by implication.
   c. Easement by prescription.
   d. Lease for a fixed term.

_____ 2. Shanti leased a building. Shanti installed a stove and a boiler in the building. Upon expiration of the lease, Shanti intends to remove the stove, but not the boiler. The stove can be easily removed without harming anything. Removal of the boiler, however, will seriously damage both the building and the boiler. Are the stove and boiler fixtures?
   a. The stove and boiler are both fixtures.
   b. The stove is not a fixture, but the boiler is a fixture.
   c. The stove is a fixture, but the boiler is not a fixture.
   d. Neither the stove nor the boiler is a fixture.

_____ 3. Margaret contracted to sell a seaside cottage to Lex. Margaret executed a deed to convey title to Lex, three witnesses signed the deed, and the deed was acknowledged. Pursuant to the contract, Margaret delivered the deed to an escrow company, with instructions to deliver the deed to Lex when he delivered the purchase price to the escrow company. Under these facts:
   a. Title passed to Lex when Margaret signed the deed.
   b. Title passed to Lex when Margaret delivered the deed to the escrow company.
   c. Title will pass to Lex when he pays and the escrow company delivers the deed to him.
   d. Title will not pass to Lex until he makes the required payment, the escrow company delivers the deed to Lex, and Lex records the deed.

_____ 4. Select the correct answer.
   a. A person who owns an interest in property by joint tenancy can generally transfer the interest by a will.
   b. In states recognizing community property, any property received by an inheritance becomes community property if the property was received during the marriage.
   c. Persons who own property as tenants in common may not transfer their interest by a will.
   d. Persons owning property as tenants in common do not need to have equal interests.

SHORT ANSWER QUESTIONS

Answer the following questions, briefly explaining the reason for your answer.

1. Landlord inspected an apartment and noticed a rotted staircase. The defect could not have been noticed by someone with no experience in inspecting wood. Tenant moved into the apartment, fell through the rotted staircase, and was injured. Landlord never told Tenant about the rotted staircase. Is Landlord liable for Tenant's injuries?

_____

_____

2. Samantha purchased land adjacent to Stan's. One way for Samantha to get to a road is to cross Stan's driveway. The other way is to cross through a trail, which is rocky and usually muddy. Samantha could use the trail if she purchased a four-wheel drive vehicle. Can Samantha claim an easement over Stan's driveway?

_____

_____

3. Murray leased office space for three years. After three years, he remained in the office. Murray's landlord then told him to leave immediately, without giving Murray any notice. Was the landlord required to give Murray notice before evicting him?

_____

_____

4. Anna gave Bob a quitclaim deed to some property. Bob later discovered that the property had a lien on it. Can Bob sue Anna for breach of implied covenants?

_____

_____

CASE PROBLEMS

Answer the following case problems, explaining your answers.

1. Humphrey granted Karen an easement to use his driveway to get to her house. The easement stated that Karen was the only person who could use the easement. After several months, Karen opened a day care in her home. Every morning and afternoon, several cars drove on Humphrey's driveway. Humphrey was greatly annoyed by the increased number of cars using his driveway. (a) What type of easement did Humphrey grant to Karen? (b) Is Karen properly using the easement?

_____

_____

_____

_____

2. Steve had a one-year lease for an apartment in Sleepy Hollow. The lease provided that a tenant must give one month's notice before termination. Steve's neighbor liked to play his stereo late into the night, which interferes with Steve's sleep. Steve complained to the building manager several times, but the neighbor continued to play his stereo. With six months remaining on his lease, Steve moved out.
(a) What type of tenancy was this? (b) Was it proper for Sleepy Hollow to require a tenant to give notice before termination? (c) Under the laws of most states, what doctrine can Steve use to justify his leaving without notice? (d) Is Steve required to pay Sleepy Hollow for the remainder of his lease?

_____

_____

_____

_____

CHAPTER 45

Personal Property and Bailments

OWNERSHIP OF PROPERTY: Personal property is anything that can be owned or possessed, except land and anything attached to the land. Classifications of property and various interests in property include:

- *Classifications of Property*: All property that is not classified as real property is considered personal property. Personal property is made up of tangible and intangible property. Tangible property is property that can be moved, while intangible property cannot be physically possessed.
- *Components of Ownership*: Ownership of personal property includes all rights related to the property. Possession of personal property includes only the right to control the property.

ACQUISITION OF PERSONAL PROPERTY BY INDIVIDUALS: There are several ways by which an individual can acquire personal property, including:

- *Original Possession*: The first person to possess certain property, such as a wild animal, has original possession. Another example of this form of ownership is an original painting or other creation.
- *Voluntary Transfers of Possession*: A voluntary transfer from a previous owner to another is one method of acquisition. Examples include transfers by purchase, gift, gift causa mortis, inheritance, and intestate succession. Three requirements for a valid gift are: 1) the donor intends to make a gift; 2) the donor delivers the property to the donee; and 3) the donee accepts the gift. A gift causa mortis is a gift that is made while the donor is alive, but the gift is made in contemplation of immediate death. The requirements for a valid gift causa mortis are: 1) the donor intends to make a gift; 2) the gift is made in contemplation of death; and 3) the donor actually dies from the contemplated cause.
- *Involuntary Transfers of Possession*: Personal property may be involuntarily transferred.
    1) **Accession**: Accession occurs when a person adds value to property that the person does not own.
    2) **Innocent trespasser**: Generally, title to the property remains with the original owner. However, an innocent trespasser may acquire title in the following situations: a) due to work performed on the property, it has lost its original identity; b) a great difference in value exists between the original property and the improved property; or c) a completely new type of property has been created and the innocent trespasser added a major portion of the new property. If the original owner retains title to the property, the innocent trespasser can recover the value of the improvement. However, a willful trespasser cannot acquire title to the improved property. Also, a willful trespasser is subject to liability for any damages caused and cannot recover for the value of any improvements.
    3) **Confusion**: Confusion occurs when personal, fungible property of two or more individuals is mixed together and cannot be separated. If confusion occurs without any misconduct, the parties each receive an undivided interest. However, if misconduct is involved, different rules apply. If the new mixture cannot be divided, title passes to the innocent party, but if it can be divided, the wrongdoer is entitled to receive a portion of the new mixture.

PROTECTION OF PERSONAL PROPERTY:

- *Conversion*: Conversion occurs when a person wrongfully takes or interferes with the property of another. The rightful owner may recover the property and sue for damages.

265

- *Escheat*: If the rightful owner of property cannot be found, the subject property escheats to the state.
- *Judicial Sale*: A judicial sale may take place in order to enforce a civil judgment. If a losing party does not pay a judgment ordered by a court, the prevailing party may execute upon the judgment and have the sheriff seize property of the losing party. A sheriff's sale, or judicial sale, is then held and the proceeds are applied towards satisfaction of the judgment.
- *Repossession of Property*: A secured party may repossess (retake) personal property if a debtor has defaulted on a secured obligation.

BAILMENTS OF PERSONAL PROPERTY: A bailment is a relationship that occurs when one person temporarily possesses personal property owned by another with the consent of the owner, and for a specific purpose. The person who holds the property is bailee, and the owner is the bailor.
- *Bailee's Duty of Care*: There are three bailment categories that determine the bailee's liability.
- *Classifications of Bailments*: The three types of bailments are:
  1) **A bailor benefit bailment**: This bailment solely benefits the bailor. The bailee is responsible for gross negligence in caring for the bailment property.
  2) **Mutual benefit bailment**: When both the bailor and bailee benefit, a mutual benefit bailment is established. In this situation, the bailee is liable for ordinary negligence.
  3) **Bailee benefit bailment**: This type of bailment is one that benefits only the bailee. Here, the bailee is liable for slight negligence.
- *Limitations on a Bailee's Liability*: State laws place limits on a bailee's liability or, conversely, limit disclaimers of liability. Otherwise, the bailment contract may either increase or decrease liability, subject to any statutory limitations.
- *Termination of a Bailment*: A bailment terminates at the end of the period specified by the parties. If no ending point is discussed, the bailment relationship is terminable at will by either the bailor or the bailee. The bailment also terminates if the subject property is destroyed.
- *Bailee's Duty to Return the Property*: As a general rule, the bailee is required to return the bailment property to the bailor. Exceptions to this rule include: 1) the subject property is lost or stolen through no fault of the bailee; 2) the subject property is taken by legal process; 3) the property is claimed by someone with better legal title; or 4) the bailee takes a lien on the property.

STUDY HINTS FOR CALL-IMAGE TECHNOLOGY CASE STUDIES

The following study hints may be helpful when resolving the Call-Image Technology case studies.

page 1176
- ◆ Review the concept of transfer of title by purchase.
- ◆ Since Donna owns the software, she had the exclusive right to use and protect it. Analyze whether the client violated this right.

page 1182
- ◆ Review the material on classifications of bailments, focusing on the duty of care of the bailee under bailment law.

page 1184
- ◆ Review the material on contractual limitations of liability.

REVIEW OF KEY TERMS AND CONCEPTS

MATCHING EXERCISE

Select the term or concept that best matches a definition or statement set forth below. Each term or concept is the best match for only one definition or statement.

Terms and Concepts

a. Accession   e. Confusion   i. Judicial sale
b. Bailee   f. Conversion   j. Negotiable instruments
c. Bailment   g. Escheat   k. Possessory lien
d. Bailor   h. Gift causa mortis l. Transfer tax

Definitions and Statements

_____ 1. Transferable documents used as credit instruments and as substitutes for money, including checks, drafts, promissory notes, and certificates of deposit.
_____ 2. Tax on the ability to transfer assets.
_____ 3. Security interest granted by law which allows a bailee to keep property if the bailor fails to pay for a bailment or for work performed on the property.
_____ 4. Owner of property that is the subject of a bailment.
_____ 5. Person who has possession of property under a bailment.
_____ 6. Wrongful taking or interference with the personal property of another.
_____ 7. Transfer of possession of personal property to another, with an understanding that the property shall be returned.
_____ 8. Gift made in expectation of immediate death.
_____ 9. Transfer of ownership of property to the government.
_____ 10. Improvement to the property of another.
_____ 11. Court-ordered sale of property.
_____ 12. Commingling of fungible property of two or more people .

COMPLETION EXERCISE

Fill in the blanks with the words that most accurately complete each statement.

1. A(n) _____ _____ _____ for value is a person who buys property in good faith, for a reasonable value, and without actual or constructive knowledge that there are problems with the transfer.

2. A valid transfer of a gift requires _____, _____, and _____ .

3. In a bailor benefit bailment, the bailee is liable for only _____ _____ .

4. In a mutual benefit bailment, the bailee is liable for _____ _____.

5. In a bailee benefit bailment, the bailee is liable for _____ _____.

TRUE-FALSE EXERCISE

Write **T** if the statement is true, write **F** if the statement is false.

_____ 1. The law treats mislaid property the same as abandoned property.

_____ 2. A hunter kills a wild animal. The hunter has original possession of the animal.

_____ 3. A willful trespasser cannot acquire title to property by accession.

_____ 4. The finder of lost property is generally entitled to keep the property unless a statute requires that the property be given to the police.

_____ 5. Once property escheats to the state, the rightful owner cannot reclaim it.

_____ 6. A bailee generally forfeits a possessory lien by willingly returning the property to the bailor.

_____ 7. A bailment cannot be implied from the conduct of parties.

_____ 8. A valid gift requires that the donor presently intend to make the gift.

_____ 9. A bailment for the sole benefit of the bailor is created when a person gratuitously keeps and takes care of the property of another.

_____ 10. A bailee receives only possession of bailed goods; a bailee does not receive title to the goods.

APPLICATION OF CONCEPTS

MULTIPLE CHOICE QUESTIONS

_____ 1. Grandma, who was in good health, intended to make a present gift of her car to Mindy. Grandma wrote: "I give my Porsche to Mindy," and she gave Mindy the keys to the car, which was located 150 miles away. Prior to Mindy's taking possession of the car, Grandma died. Under these facts:
   a. Grandma did not make a valid inter vivos gift of the car to Mindy.
   b. Grandma made a valid inter vivos gift of the car to Mindy.
   c. Grandma made a valid gift causa mortis of the car to Mindy.
   d. Grandma only promised to make a gift, which promise was revoked when she died.

_____ 2. Dirk rented a tuxedo from Dapper Dan for $50 per night. This bailment is a:
   a. Bailment for the benefit of the bailor.
   b. Bailment for the benefit of the bailee.
   c. Mutual benefit bailment.
   d. Gratuitous bailment.

_____ 3. Select the correct answer.
   a. Rosie rented a locker at the Airport and she put a bag in the locker. Rosie kept the locker key. In this case, the bag has been delivered and accepted by Airport, and Airport is a bailee.
   b. Hill rents a boat to Dan. The boat is located at a lake 30 miles away. Hill gives Dan keys to the boat. Dan drives to the lake and takes possession of the boat. In this case, the boat has been delivered to and accepted by Dan, and Dan is a bailee.
   c. Unknown to Lon, Jeff left a bike at Lon's house. In this case, the bike has been delivered to and accepted by Lon, and Lon is a bailee.
   d. Ken parked a car in a self-service lot and Ken kept the keys. The parking lot is a bailee.

_____ 4. Roxie agreed to repair Tom's TV for $100. Pursuant to their contract, Tom delivered the TV to Roxie and Roxie properly repaired the TV. Under these facts:
   a. If Tom refuses to pay the repair charge, Roxie has a lien on the TV and she can keep the TV until Tom pays the $100 charge.
   b. Roxie is obligated to insure the TV while it is in her possession.
   c. Roxie has a duty only to exercise slight care for the TV, and she will be liable for damage to the TV only if it results from her gross negligence.
   d. Roxie is entitled to use the TV for her personal use.

SHORT ANSWER QUESTIONS

Answer the following questions, briefly explaining the reason for your answer.

1. Uncle Rich promised to give his niece, Cindy, $10,000 for her birthday. Cindy was so excited that she ran up $10,000 on her credit card. Outraged by Cindy's irresponsible behavior, Uncle Rich told Cindy that he would not give her anything. Can Cindy sue Uncle Rich for the money?

_____

_____

2. Mary brought her car to Fred's Garage for repairs. When Fred charged Mary $500 for the repairs, Mary thought it was too much and refused to pay. Fred told Mary that he would not give her the car until she paid. Did Fred act properly?

_____

_____

3. Ralph asked Judy to take his Ferrari to the garage for him. While driving to the garage, Judy could not help herself and drove the car at 100 mph when the posted speed limit was only 45 mph. Under state law, driving 30 miles above the speed limit is considered reckless (grossly negligent) driving. Judy wrecked the car. Is Judy liable to Ralph for the damage to his car?

_____

_____

4. Jethro was in the hospital and he believed he would die. He told Sally May, his girlfriend, that he wanted her to have his car when he died. Sally May immediately took possession of the car. Jethro recovered. However, two weeks after being released from the hospital, Jethro was struck by a hit and run driver and he died shortly afterwards. Who is entitled to the car - Sally May or Jethro's estate?

_____

_____

CASE PROBLEMS

Answer the following case problems, explaining your answers.

1. Acme Rentals rents equipment. Its lease contract states that it is not liable for any injuries or property loss that may be caused by its equipment. The contract also states that any person renting equipment is liable for any damage or loss to the equipment, regardless of the reason for the casualty or loss. Harry rented two cement mixers from Acme. One was stolen by a third party. The other mixer tipped over and fell on Harry's foot, breaking it. It tipped over because an Acme employee had negligently failed to replace a brace that had previously broken off. (a) What type of bailments are involved in this case? (b) Is Harry liable for the stolen mixer? (c) Is Acme liable for Harry's broken foot?

_____

_____

_____

_____

2. Jake wanted to go water skiing, but he did not have any skis. Jake's friend, Luis, lent Jake a pair of skis. While Jake was skiing, a defective foot support on one ski accidentally tore loose, causing Jake to fall and break his arm. Luis did not know that the foot support was defective. However, Luis did not inspect the skis before lending them to Jake. (a) What type of bailment is involved in this case? (b) Describe the duty that Luis owed to Jake. (c) Is Luis liable to Jake for Jake's injuries? (d) Is Jake liable to Luis for damage to the skis?

_____

_____

_____

_____

CHAPTER 46   Wills, Estates, and Trusts

CHAPTER REVIEW

THE TRANSFER OF AN ESTATE: Everyone has an estate, no matter how small. States govern the transfer of estates under probate codes, which may vary greatly from state to state.

WILLS: A will specifies who should inherit property, can appoint a personal representative, and can name a guardian for minor children.
- *Formal Wills*: Formal wills are written, signed by the testator, and witnessed by at least two people.
- *Holographic Wills*: Holographic wills are valid if written and signed in the testator's own handwriting.
- *Nuncupative Wills*: Nuncupative wills are oral, and can usually dispose of only personal property.
- *Matching Wills*: Mutual wills are separate wills with matching provisions. These are appropriate for a husband and wife. In joint wills, two people sign the same document.

REQUIREMENTS FOR A VALID WILL: To execute a will a person must have testamentary capacity. This requires that a person; 1) understand the nature of his or her assets; 2) know who his or her close relatives are; and 3) understand the purpose of a will.

TESTAMENTARY DISPOSITIONS AND RESTRICTIONS: Generally, a will may exclude family members; however, spouses have the right to a share of the estate. There are limits on giving to charity and the duration of trusts. A will can be ignored if it was signed under fraud, duress, or undue influence.

INTESTATE SUCCESSION: Intestacy statutes govern the distribution for people who have no will, have an invalid will, or whose will does not completely dispose of their property.

PROBATE AND ESTATE ADMINISTRATION: Probate determines the validity of a will and ensures that estates are properly administered. Personal representatives administer the estate and owe fiduciary duties to the beneficiaries. The representative must notify creditors, pay debts, pay any estate taxes, and distribute the remaining assets according to the will.

AVOIDING PROBATE: Advantages: May reduce time and costs, and provides privacy. Disadvantages: The estate will still pay taxes, there may be more paperwork, and creditors will not be discharged for failing to file a claim against the estate.

TRANSFER TAXES: The federal government taxes the transfer of property by an estate tax, gift tax, and generation-skipping transfer tax. States have gift and estate or inheritance taxes.

RETIREMENT PLANS: Pension plans have both income tax and transfer tax consequences. Employer plans may be defined-benefit or defined-contribution plans.

LIVING WILLS AND DURABLE POWERS OF ATTORNEY: A living will states a person's wishes concerning life-prolonging medical treatment. A durable power of attorney appoints a person to make medical decisions.

TRUSTS DEFINED: A fiduciary relationship where specific property is transferred to the care of a trustee.

EXPRESS TRUSTS: A trust must have a creator, a trustee, and one or more beneficiaries.
- *Private Trusts*: Trusts created for an individual and having a limited duration.
- *Charitable Trusts*: Trusts where money is given to a charity tax-free.
- *Additional Types of Express Trusts*: Other trusts include accumulation (reinvests income), sprinkling (trustee determines which beneficiary receives income and how much), spendthrift (protects the beneficiary from imprudent spending), and discretionary (trustee has discretion to pay or not pay the beneficiaries).

ADVANTAGES OF TRUSTS: Trusts are flexible, and payments to the trust may be spread out over time.

DISADVANTAGES OF TRUSTS: If the trust is irrevocable, the creator cannot withdraw money for emergencies.

SELECTION OF TRUSTEES AND EXECUTORS: Corporate fiduciaries (trustees and executors) do not die, and generally have the expertise to serve in these capacities. However, corporate fiduciaries charge fees.

DUTIES OF TRUSTEES: Trustees must preserve trust property and make it productive. As fiduciaries, trustees must act with the care, skill, and prudence of a businessperson managing his or her own property.

IMPLIED TRUSTS: Implied trusts are created by operation of law or imposed by courts.
- *Resulting Trusts*: Arise when an owner fails to make a complete disposition of property or places title to property in the name of another without intending to make a gift.
- *Constructive Trusts*: An equitable remedy to redress a wrong and prevent unjust enrichment.

STUDY HINTS FOR CALL-IMAGE TECHNOLOGY CASE STUDIES

The following study hints may be helpful when resolving the Call-Image Technology (CIT) case studies.

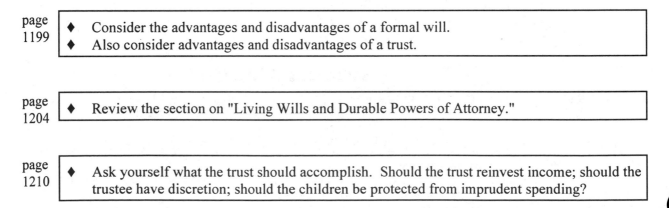

page 1199
- ◆ Consider the advantages and disadvantages of a formal will.
- ◆ Also consider advantages and disadvantages of a trust.

page 1204
- ◆ Review the section on "Living Wills and Durable Powers of Attorney."

page 1210
- ◆ Ask yourself what the trust should accomplish. Should the trust reinvest income; should the trustee have discretion; should the children be protected from imprudent spending?

MATCHING EXERCISE

Select the term or concept that best matches a definition or statement set forth below. Each term or concept is the best match for only one definition or statement.

Terms and Concepts

a. Affidavit

b. Codicil

c. Community property

d. Decedent

e. Domicile

f. Honorary trust

g. Intestate share

h. Personal representative

I. Probate

j. Probate codes

k. Residuary clause

l. Testamentary capacity

m. Testator

n. Testatrix

o. Trust

Definitions and Statements

_____ 1. A clause that disposes of the remainder of an estate.

_____ 2. The procedure for verifying that a will is authentic and should be implemented.

_____ 3. Portion of the estate that a person is entitled to inherit if there is no valid will.

_____ 4. State statutes that deal with the estates of incompetents, people who have made wills, and people who have died.

_____ 5. An arrangement in which one person or business holds property and invests it for another.

_____ 6. A special form of joint ownership between husband and wife.

_____ 7. A man who makes a will.

_____ 8. A woman who makes a will.

_____ 9. Written statement made under oath.

_____ 10. A person who manages the financial affairs of the estate.

_____ 11. A person who has died.

_____ 12. An arrangement that does not meet trust requirements and thus is not enforceable as a trust, although it may be carried out voluntarily.

_____ 13. One's permanent legal residence.

_____ 14. Sufficient mental capability or sanity to execute a valid will.

_____ 15. A separate written document that modifies an existing will.

COMPLETION EXERCISE

Fill in the blanks with the words that most accurately complete each statement.

1. _____ are persons who actually inherit property from the decedent.

2. The _____-_____ doctrine permits a court to modify a trust in order to follow the creator's charitable wishes as closely as possible.

3. The legal document that specifies the recipients of a trust, their interests, and how the trust should be

managed is called a _____ _____.

4. Lineal descendants, such as children and grandchildren, are called _____.

5. The legal document that specifies how a person feels about life-prolonging medical treatment if the

person should become very ill with no hope of recovery is called a _____ _____.

TRUE-FALSE EXERCISE

Write **T** if the statement is true, write **F** if the statement is false.

____ 1. In most states, a will must leave assets to the testator's family members and other relatives.
____ 2. In most states, a formal will must be witnessed by two disinterested persons.
____ 3. Probate of a will is an optional procedure; a will is generally effective without probate.
____ 4. Property of a person who dies without a will or with an invalid will is distributed according to intestate succession.
____ 5. A constructive trust arises by operation of law and serves to prevent unjust enrichment or redress a wrong.
____ 6. If a person is severely ill, a living will allows that person's property to be distributed before the person dies.
____ 7. In many states, a creditor forfeits the right to be paid if the creditor fails to file a claim with a decedent's probate estate within the time required by law.
____ 8. Courts generally will award intestate shares to pretermitted heirs on the grounds that the omission was a mistake.
____ 9. A decedent's debts must be paid by an estate prior to distributions to beneficiaries.
____ 10. A personal representative must be a family member.

APPLICATION OF CONCEPTS

MULTIPLE CHOICE QUESTIONS

____ 1. Arthur used drugs heavily for years. Due to his drug use, Arthur suffered permanent mental impairment, and he could not recall to whom he was related or what he owned. Nonetheless, Arthur executed a properly signed and witnessed will. The will left everything to Joe, a recent acquaintance. Nothing was left to Arthur's daughter, about whom Arthur had forgotten. Under these facts:
    a. The will is invalid because a testator cannot disinherit a child.
    b. The will is invalid because Arthur did not have testamentary capacity.
    c. The will is valid. A testator may disinherit a child, and a will is valid if it is properly signed and witnessed.
    d. a and b.

_____ 2.   Niles is trustee of a trust. The trust beneficiaries are Niles's nieces. The trust has $100,000 cash. In most states, what would Niles be permitted to do as trustee?
a.   Niles may invest the cash in U.S. Treasury bonds and corporate stocks.
b.   Niles may make an interest-free loan of the trust's cash to his business.
c.   Niles may delegate all of his duties under the trust to his wife.
d.   Both a and c.

_____ 3.   While single, Murray executed a will, leaving his estate to his parents. Several years later, Murray married Nancy. Two years later, Nancy gave birth to Murray's son. During that same year, Murray mistakenly tore his will in half, thinking it was waste paper. Under the laws of at least some states, which event may have revoked Murray's will (in whole or in part)?
a.   Murray's marriage to Nancy.
b.   The birth of Murray's son.
c.   Murray's tearing of the will.
d.   Both a and b.

_____ 4.   Select the correct answer.
a.   Testator typed a will, signed it, but no one witnessed his signature. In most states, the will is a valid formal will.
b.   Testator wrote out a will in his own handwriting, signed it, but no one witnessed his signature. In most states, the will is a valid holographic will.
c.   Testator typed a will, signed it, and had two persons witness his signature. Under the will, both witnesses were to receive substantial amounts of money on Testator's death. In most states, the will is a valid formal will.
d.   Both a and c.

SHORT ANSWER QUESTIONS

Answer the following questions, briefly explaining the reason for your answer.

1. Roger is married to Paula. Their marriage has been on the rocks, and Roger decides not to leave anything to Paula in his will. If Roger dies while still married to Paula, can Paula claim anything against Roger's estate? (Assume Roger died in a common-law state.)

_____

_____

2. Ted's will states that his estate should be divided equally between his two children, Marcy and Leslie. Marcy and Leslie have since died. Marcy has left two children, and Leslie has left four. How will the estate be divided using per capita with representation?

_____

_____

3. Mike, a rich and successful writer, would like to leave money to his nephew, Mark. However, Mike is concerned that Mark is financially irresponsible. Advise Mike on how he should structure the gift to Mark.

_____

_____

4. Jake is rich and eccentric. He has $10 million that he would like to place in a trust to benefit all of his descendants forever. Can Jake create a trust that will last forever?

_____

_____

CASE PROBLEMS

Answer the following case problems, explaining your answers.

1. Abe died intestate, leaving an estate of $200,000. He is survived by a wife, three children, and a cousin. Assume Abe died in a state that follows the Uniform Probate Code procedure for intestate succession. How much will each of the following persons receive: (a) Abe's wife? (b) Abe's three children? (c) Abe's cousin?

_____

_____

_____

_____

2. Luis created a trust and named Mary as trustee. The trust deed does not specify whether it is revocable or irrevocable. While Mary served as trustee, she irresponsibly made speculative investments that caused the trust to lose money. (a) Under the law of *most* states, is the trust revocable or irrevocable? (b) Did Mary breach any duty? (c) What remedies are available for Mary's conduct?

_____

_____

_____

_____

CHAPTER 47

Intellectual Property, Computers, and the Law

CHAPTER REVIEW

INTRODUCTION: Intellectual property is intangible property that is the product of human creativity.

COPYRIGHTS: Copyright law protects original works of authorship fixed in any tangible medium of expression that can be perceived, reproduced, or otherwise communicated, such as literary works, paintings, and films. Copyright law only protects the expression of ideas; not the ideas themselves.

- *Protection and Infringement*: A copyright entitles its owner to reproduce the work, prepare derivative works, distribute copies of the work, and perform and publicly display the work. Infringement of a copyright is shown by evidence that the defendant had access to the work and the defendant's work shows substantial similarities to the owner's work. "Fair use" is the most common defense to an infringement action, since it is permissible to use copyrighted work for certain limited purposes.
- *Remedies*: If infringement is proven, the court may order an injunction, the destruction of infringing items, and payment of damages.
- *International Dimensions*: Under the Berne Convention, each member nation must extend its laws to protect citizens of other members nations and works originally published in a member nation must be protected in all member states without having to comply with any additional formalities.
- *Computers*: The 1980 Computer Software Copyright Act allows computer programs to be copyrighted.

PATENTS: Patent law protects inventions, and gives inventors the exclusive right to their inventions. Patentable inventions include a process, machine, manufacture, composition of matter, and useful improvements thereof. To be patented, an invention must be 1) original, 2) useful, and 3) nonobvious. Utility patents last for 20 years and design patents last for 14 years. After expiration of a patent, others can use the previously patented invention in any way they wish.

- *Protection and Infringement*: There are three types of patent infringements: direct, indirect, and contributory. A direct infringement involves a person who makes, uses, or sells a patented invention. An indirect infringement involves inducing others to infringe. A contributory infringement occurs when a party sells a component of a patented invention knowing the component is specially made for use with the patented item.
- *Remedies*: If infringement is proven, the court may order an injunction and payment of damages.
- *International Dimensions*: Under the Paris Convention, like the Berne Convention, member nations must honor the patent laws of other member nations.
- *Computers*: The Supreme Court has held that some types of computer programs are patentable.

TRADEMARKS: Trademarks are used to identify goods, and trademark law prevents others from using the same or deceptively similar name to identify their goods.

- *Protection and Infringement*: A trademark can be any word, name, symbol, device, or a combination thereof that is used to identify and distinguish the services or goods of one party from those of another. A trademark can be protected only if it is distinctive, meaning that it is arbitrary, fanciful, or suggestive. Generic or descriptive marks or marks using people's surnames cannot be protected unless

they have acquired a "secondary meaning." Trademarks are protected from uses that bear a "likelihood of confusion" for consumers. "Fair use" is a defense to a trademark infringement claim.
- *Remedies*: Remedies include injunction, return of profits, damages, and punitive damages.
- *International Dimensions*: Under the Paris Convention, as with patents, member nations must honor the trademark laws of other member nations.

TRADE SECRETS: A trade secret is: 1) secret business information that gives its owner a competitive advantage 2) because the information is not known to competitors and is difficult or costly to acquire.
- *Protection*: Factors considered when deciding whether material is a trade secret include: 1) extent to which the information is known outside the owner's business; 2) extent it is known by employees; 3) steps taken to guard the information's secrecy; 4) value of the information to the owner and competitors; 5) money expended in developing the information; and 6) difficulty of others acquiring the information.
- *Liability*: Liability for misappropriating trade secrets may be based on either a breach of contract theory and or wrongful acquisition theory.
- *Remedies*: If misappropriation is proven, the court may order an injunction and payment of damages.
- *Computers*: Trade secret law protects computer programs. Employers should keep software developments secret and ensure that employees sign noncompetition and confidentiality agreements.

UNFAIR COMPETITION: Some extreme forms of competition (and infringements) are considered unlawful under the common law and/or statutes. "Palming-off," false advertising, and product disparagement are considered unfair competition. Remedies generally include injunctions and damages. Unfair competition laws may protect particularly strong marks from being used by others for a noncompetitive use if this use may lessen (dilute) the value or distinctiveness of the mark over time, (e.g., using a strong product mark to identify sexually-explicit products or services).

THE SEMICONDUCTOR CHIP PROTECTION ACT OF 1984: This law prohibits "reverse engineering" that seeks to copy computer chips or their protected components.

ADDITIONAL LEGAL PROTECTIONS FOR COMPUTERS: Contract law, the UCC, and tort law all provide additional protections against the misuse of various computer hardware and software. Invasion of privacy also provides protection against unwarranted dissemination of computer programming information. Finally, antitrust law and criminal law are other sources of relief.

STUDY HINTS FOR CALL-IMAGE TECHNOLOGY CASE STUDIES

The following study hints may be helpful when resolving the Call-Image Technology (CIT) case studies.

page 1221	◆ Review the material on copyrights and copyright infringement. ◆ Also, consider the issue of unfair competition and antidilution.
page 1229	◆ Contrast the duration for utility patents versus the potentially unlimited duration for protection of trade secrets under unfair competition law.
page 1234	◆ Review the law relating to trademarks (including secondary meaning) and unfair competition (including palming off).

CHAPTER 47 - INTELLECTUAL PROPERTY, COMPUTERS, AND THE LAW

MATCHING EXERCISE

Select the term or concept that best matches a definition or statement set forth below. Each term or concept is the best match for only one definition or statement.

Terms and Concepts

a. Contributory infringement   e. Indirect infringement   i. Proprietary
b. Copyright   f. Infringement   j. Trademark
c. Direct infringement   g. Misappropriation   k. Trade secret
d. Fair use   h. Patent   l. Unfair competition

Definitions and Statements

_____ 1. Protection for creative works, such as books, movies, and theatrical productions.
_____ 2. Unauthorized use of a patent, trademark, or copyright.
_____ 3. Protection for novel, useful, and nonobvious inventions.
_____ 4. Making, using, or selling a patented invention without the holder's permission.
_____ 5. Sale of a material component of a patented invention, knowing that the component was specially made or adapted for use with the invention.
_____ 6. Inducing others to infringe upon a patent.
_____ 7. Word or symbol that identifies the source of a particular product.
_____ 8. Confidential business information that gives a party a competitive advantage over others.
_____ 9. Unauthorized use or appropriation of a trade secret.
_____ 10. Private, exclusive ownership.
_____ 11. Wrongful activities including palming-off, false advertising, and product disparagement.
_____ 12. Limited, permissible use of copyrighted and trademarked material.

COMPLETION EXERCISE

Fill in the blanks with the words that most accurately complete each statement.

1. International uses of copyrighted material are protected by the _____

_____.

2. Utility patents last for _____ years and design patents last for

_____ years.

3. An _____ may be ordered by the court to stop an infringement.

4. Trademark holders are protected from uses of their material that would cause a _____ _____ _____ for consumers.

5. List four factors that courts consider in order to determine whether information is a trade secret:

a. _____.

b. _____.

c. _____.

d. _____.

TRUE-FALSE EXERCISE

Write **T** if the statement is true, write **F** if the statement is false.

____ 1. Trademarks protect inventions, such as a new machine or tool.
____ 2. Patents may be used to protect certain artificially created life forms.
____ 3. Software may be protected by copyright law or unfair competition law.
____ 4. A new cartoon cannot be copyrighted because it is not a serious literary work.
____ 5. The U.S. Constitution gives the states the right to regulate copyrights.
____ 6. Under the Paris Convention, member nations must honor the patent laws of other member nations.
____ 7. Ideas may be copyrighted so long as they are original.
____ 8. "Fair use" may be a defense to a trademark infringement claim.
____ 9. There are no international treaties that protect copyrights. Therefore, a person in the United States is free to copy works created by others in foreign countries.
____ 10. Trade secrets are protected for only 20 years.

APPLICATION OF CONCEPTS

MULTIPLE CHOICE QUESTIONS

____ 1. Ken invented a new type of mathematical calculator that he called "Wiser Guyser." Under these facts, the name "Wiser Guyser":
   a. Can be protected by registration for a patent.
   b. Can be protected by registration for a copyright.
   c. Can be protected by registration for a trademark.
   d. Cannot be protected.

_____ 2. Carl invented a new eating instrument for people who like to eat fast: a five-pronged fork. (Normal forks have only four prongs). Under these facts, can Carl patent his new fork?
a. Yes, it is novel.
b. Yes, it is useful.
c. Yes, it is both novel and useful.
d. No, it is an obvious derivative of an existing product, the four-pronged fork.

_____ 3. Which of the following names can be registered for trademark protection?
a. "Motor oil," the name of a product that is used to lubricate engines.
b. "Hot sauce," the name for a spicy food additive.
c. "DuraBond," the name for a new type of glue.
d. "Southern food," the name for food from the southern part of the United States.

_____ 4. Benders, a bar and grill, has been in business for many years, and it has an excellent reputation. John wanted his restaurant to be a success, so he remodeled his restaurant so the storefront looked the same as the unique design of Benders' establishment and he erected a sign over his restaurant reading "Benters." In this case, John is liable for:
a. Patent infringement.
b. Copyright infringement.
c. Theft.
d. Unfair competition.

SHORT ANSWER QUESTIONS

Answer the following questions, briefly explaining the reason for your answer.

1. Bill purchased a copy of a copyrighted computer program for $350. Bill made a copy of the program and gave it to Kim. Has Bill violated the law?

_____

_____

2. Selma wrote a computer program and copyrighted it under U.S. copyright law. Selma allowed a German to review the program, but the German firm stated that they were not interested in the program. Unknown to Selma, the German firm duplicated the program and is selling it in Germany. Discuss Selma's legal rights.

_____

_____

3. For many years, Wowee Corp. has manufactured and sold high-quality toy slot cars known as "Wowee Toys." Wowee has registered this trademark. One year ago, Waui Enterprises, a travel agency, commenced business and started marketing cruise packages called "Waui Cruises." Has Waui Enterprises violated Wowee Corp.'s trademark?

_____

_____

4. Jesse created a fictional tale about the life of a squirrel who became king of the animal world. He did not write it down, but instead told it neighborhood children. His tale was so popular with little children that he then wrote it down. Could Jesse have copyrighted his original tale? Can Jesse copyright the written version of this tale?

_____

_____

CASE PROBLEMS

Answer the following case problems, explaining your answers.

1. Over a five-year period, Jackson Corp. spent considerable time and money to develop a private list of 200,000 area homeowners. This list tracks home values, year of construction, and last home-repair project. This list has proven invaluable for marketing its home-improvement services. (a) Can Jackson protect its exclusive right to this list? (b) What is the best way for Jackson to protect this list? (c) If a competitor stole this list from Jackson and used it in the competitor's business, what remedies would Jackson have?

_____

_____

_____

_____

2. In 1984, Hillary Thompson began selling enormous pieces of sour ball candy called "Thompson's Giant Sour Ball Candies." By the 1990s, Hillary's candies had become nationally known, and people thought only of her candy when they heard the words "Thompson's Giant Sour Ball Candies." (a) Was Hillary entitled to trademark protection for the name of her candy when she first began to sell it? (b) Was Hillary entitled to trademark protection for the name of her candy by the 1990s? (c) What would be the best way for Hillary to protect her trademark?

_____

_____

_____

_____

CHAPTER 1 - INTRODUCTION TO LAW

MATCHING EXERCISE

1. l	6. a	11. e
2. h	7. d	12. c
3. i	8. g	13. f
4. k	9. m	14. o
5. n	10. b	15. j

COMPLETION EXERCISE

1. Enforceability
2. preventive law
3. police power
4. order
5. Commutative justice, distributive justice

TRUE-FALSE EXERCISE

1. F	2. T	3. T	4. T	5. T
6. F	7. T	8. T	9. F	10. T

MULTIPLE CHOICE QUESTIONS

1. b	2. c	3. d	4. d

SHORT ANSWER QUESTIONS

1. Yes. Under the doctrine of *stare decisis*, lower courts are generally obligated to follow existing precedents.
2. The Jacksons can sue under the civil law. They should request an injunction.
3. Senator Adams' position represents the theory of natural law. Senator Bend's perspective reflects the sociological theory of law.
4. Lexington may search out an attorney by checking the state bar association directory of *Matindale-Hubbell*. Also talking to friends or business associates who have had similar problems may be helpful.

CASE PROBLEMS

1. (a) This law is an example of commutative justice - everyone is treated the same. (b) This law serves the needs to be reasonable, definite, and practical. (c) This law in not flexible.
2. (a) Attorney fee arrangements may be hourly (fee is based on an hourly rate); contingent fee (fee is equal to a percentage of what the attorney recovers); or a flat fee (a one-time fee). (b) An hourly fee would be appropriate. A flat-rate fee would be difficult to determine and a contingent fee would similarly tend to either over compensate or inadequately compensate the attorney.

CHAPTER 2 - BUSINESS ETHICS

MATCHING EXERCISE

1. k
2. i
3. c
4. f

5. g
5. j
7. e
8. h

9. l
10. d
11. a
12. b

COMPLETION EXERCISE

1. Ethics
2. Morals
3. veil of ignorance
4. amoral
5. different from

TRUE-FALSE EXERCISE

1. T   2. F   3. T   4. T   5. T
6. T   7. T   8. F   9. T   10. F

MULTIPLE CHOICE QUESTIONS

1. d   2. b   3. a   4. d

SHORT ANSWER QUESTIONS

1. *Caveat emptor*, "let the buyer beware."
2. Egoism. From a financial perspective, not recalling the jack hammer is perceived to be in the company's best financial interests.
3. Rule utilitarianism. Pal's wants to produce the most good for its universe, its employees. Complying with all laws is perceived to be the best way to do this.
4. The general manager is choosing to be loyal to his employer which is generally considered to be moral conduct in our society. However, it is doubtful that this loyalty accomplishes a morally right consequence in this situation.

CASE PROBLEMS

1. (a) Gordon acted morally because he acted in accordance with his individual belief's regarding what is right and wrong. (b) However, Gordon's acted unethically, as measured by society's views regarding what is proper or improper conduct. (c) In any event, Gordon acted illegally; the legal system had declared it unlawful to sell cigarettes to minors and Gordon was legally bound to obey this rule.
2. (a) The companies in this case acted solely in a reactive manner; they undertook to change only after their legal problems arose. (b) Clearly, the companies could have taken a more proactive approach; curtailing their activities, conducting tests to discover or verify harm. (c) The companies acted unethically in this case. Society does not condone this type of behavior.

CHAPTER 3 - INTERNATIONAL LAW

MATCHING EXERCISE

1. j
2. a
3. o
4. d
5. e

6. b
7. c
8. n
9. i
10. m

11. f
12. l
13. g
14. h
15. k

COMPLETION EXERCISE

1. Foreign Corrupt Practices Act
2. International Court of Justice
3. European Commission
4. Council of Ministers
5. Any three of the following: agent; distributor; franchise; foreign subsidiary.

TRUE-FALSE EXERCISE

1. F   2. T   3. F   4. T   5. F
6. T   7. F   8. F   9. T   10. F

MULTIPLE CHOICE QUESTIONS

1. c   2. d   3. b   4. b

SHORT ANSWER QUESTIONS

1. Gill should be concerned with the EU competition laws. Gill can obtain a negative clearance (exemption) from the EC Commission.
2. Two approaches are: a) cash in advance, and b) require a letter of credit as payment.
3. ArmorTech must obtain an appropriate export license from the U.S. government. Because of the product's military significance, its export may be limited or banned.
4. NAFTA, a trade agreement between the United States, Mexico, and Canada. The World Trade Organization that can issue binding regulation relating to the international trade of 117 countries.

CASE PROBLEMS

1. (a) Bill should study the laws and culture of Ruritania. For instance, his style of negotiations would be considered rude and offensive in Ruritania and many other countries. Also, the possibility of nationalization and political unrest should never be overlooked.
2. (a) No. U.S. antitrust laws do not generally apply to the foreign conduct of foreign companies.
(b) Yes. U.S. antitrust laws may be enforced against the Abuk companies in U.S. courts if their conduct violates U.S. law and their conduct has a substantial impact on U.S. domestic commerce.

CHAPTER 4 - THE AMERICAN LEGAL SYSTEM AND COURT JURISDICTION

MATCHING EXERCISE

1.	o	6.	c	11.	a
2.	m	7.	g	12.	j
3.	h	8.	d	13.	b
4.	l	9.	e	14.	n
5.	k	10.	I	15.	f

COMPLETION EXERCISE

1. case, controversy
2. standing
3. jurisdiction
4. *in personam*
5. long-arm

TRUE-FALSE EXERCISE

1. F	2. T	3. F	4. T	5. F
6. F	7. F	8. F	9. F	10. T

MULTIPLE CHOICE QUESTIONS

1. b   2. c   3. c   4. c

SHORT ANSWER QUESTIONS

1. No. Unless authorized by statute for violation of a particular law, persons do not have standing to sue for violation of a law unless they establish that they have been personally harmed by the law's violation.
2. No. This is a political question which the legislature, not the courts, must decide.
3. (a) Substantive law - it involves a question of the parties' legal rights and duties. (b) Procedural law - it involves how the lawsuit must be initiated.
4. It is an invalid ex post facto law to the extent that it seeks to retroactively criminalize past conduct. It is a valid exercise of the state's police power to the extent that it applies prospectively.

CASE PROBLEMS

1. (a) Yes. Both parties are "doing business" in Nebraska. They are conducting an on-going business, taking advantage of Nebraska law. (b) Yes. The plaintiff can use the Nebraska long-arm statute, if necessary, to serve process on TWC and Ramon outside of the state. They allegedly committed a tort in Nebraska which is generally sufficient grounds for invoking the long-arm statute. Service on the defendants will give the Nebraska court *in personam* jurisdiction over the defendants.
2. Yes. Janet and Carson are residents of different states, establishing diversity jurisdiction. In addition, the lawsuit involves more than $75,000, second element necessary invoking the jurisdiction of U.S. district courts based on diversity.

CHAPTER 5 - TORTS

MATCHING EXERCISE

1.	f	5.	h	9.	g
2.	k	6.	e	10.	c
3.	b	7.	d	11.	j
4.	a	8.	l	12.	i

COMPLETION EXERCISE

1. private (civil); public (criminal)
2. Intentional
3. material fact
4. false imprisonment
5. duty, breach, proximate (legal) causation, harm/injury

TRUE-FALSE EXERCISE

1. F	2. T	3. T	4. T	5. T
6. T	7. T	8. T	9. T	10. F

MULTIPLE CHOICE QUESTIONS

1. d	2. d	3. c	4. d

SHORT ANSWER QUESTIONS

1. Defamation (slander). Requirements include a false statement of fact, intentional communication to a third person, harm to reputation.
2. No. Although Fran and Northern would have committed the tort of false imprisonment under the common law, states have statutes that shield them from liability in situations such as this.
3. Yes. Dan committed an unlawful, offensive touching of Jessie.
4. Yes. She has committed the tort of trade disparagement. She wrongfully injured the reputation of the Blue Bull Cafe.

CASE PROBLEMS

1. Will has committed fraud. Will intentionally misstated a material fact, intending for persons such as Lilly to rely upon his misstatements, and Lilly did reasonably rely on the untruths to her detriment.
2. (a) In this case, WDC owed three duties in particular to the homeowners: not to expose them to an unreasonable risk of harm (negligence); not to use its land in such a way that it would unreasonably interfere with the homeowners' right to enjoy their homes (nuisance); and not to come upon the property of the homeowners (or put into motion things that would come upon the homeowners property (trespass).
(b) WDC has liability under nuisance law. Its liability for negligence and trespass is likely, but not certain. Foreseeability and proximate causation are the most difficult issues for all of these torts.

CHAPTER 6 - ANATOMY OF A CIVIL SUIT

MATCHING EXERCISE

1. c	6. g	11. m
2. b	7. j	12. o
3. n	8. a	13. f
4. d	9. l	14. i
5. k	10. e	15. h

COMPLETION EXERCISE

1. Discovery
2. judgment
3. cross-examination
4. appeal
5. depositions, interrogatories, production of documents and things, physical or mental examination, request for admissions

TRUE-FALSE EXERCISE

1. F	2. F	3. T	4. T	5. F
6. F	7. T	8. T	9. T	10. F

MULTIPLE CHOICE QUESTIONS

1. b	2. d	3. c	4. a

SHORT ANSWER QUESTIONS

1. Hin should review the facts relating to the occurrence, writing down important points, including the names and addresses of witnesses etc. Also, he should bring with him any potentially relevant documents.
2. The fee agreement for the living will is a flat-free, meaning a fixed fee. The second fee is a contingent fee. In the first arrangement, the attorney will receive $120, and in the second the attorney will receive 40% of the amount, if any, that is awarded to Chad.
3. The jury will determine questions of fact, including whether there was a contract and whether the vegetables were tainted. The jury will also determine the amount of damages, if any.
4. The judgment of a trial court is not a final judgment. If the judgment is upheld on appeal, the doctrine of *res judicata* will bar the parties from again litigating the same claims.

CASE PROBLEMS

1. (a) The purpose of summary judgement is to resolve a lawsuit before trial when there are no genuine issues of material fact to be decided. (b) Summary judgment is not appropriate in this case because the issue of who ran the red light is an important, disputed fact. (c) Under the restated facts, summary judgment would be appropriate because there are no factual issues, only legal issues.
2. (a) When a court affirms a judgment, it upholds the judgment. Suiter Corp. wins. (b) When a court reverses a judgment, without more, the judgment is voided and judgment is awarded for the other party. Pizza Man Corp. wins. (c) When a case is reversed and remanded, the judgment is set aside and the case is returned to the lower court, often for an entirely new trial. Thus, it is not certain who wins.

CHAPTER 7 - ALTERNATE DISPUTE RESOLUTION

MATCHING EXERCISE

1. c
2. e
3. g

4. b
5. f
6. a

7. d
8. i
9. h

COMPLETION EXERCISE

1. mediator
2. Uniform Arbitration Act
3. facilitate; evaluate
4. Advisory arbitration
5. fast; relatively inexpensive; experts determine parties' rights.

TRUE-FALSE EXERCISE

1. F
6. F

2. F
7. T

3. T
8. T

4. F
9. T

5. F
10. T

MULTIPLE CHOICE QUESTIONS

1. c
2. a
3. c
4. a

SHORT ANSWER QUESTIONS

1. Neuron and BioMed will jointly select an arbitrator. The arbitrator should be familiar with the law and arbitration, and also have an expertise in this area of science.
2. The mediator could use caucusing (meeting separately with each party) or shuttle mediation (going back and forth between the parties, carrying proposals and comments).
3. In a minitrial, a neutral party, such as a retired judge, is hired to hear the matter outside of court. Each side presents their side of the story, using experts if appropriate. Executives from each company attend the minitrial and, following its conclusion, the executives meet to try to resolve the matter.
4. In most states, Gina can sue her former landlord in small claims court.

CASE PROBLEMS

1. (a) Mediation would allow the parties to avoid litigation, saving both time and money. This approach would also allow the parties to potentially work out a compromise solution. (b) One possible solution would be to restrict the hours during which the grinder is used.
2. (a) The parties must arbitrate the dispute. Arbitration is required by the contract, and federal law makes this agreement legally enforceable. (b) Yes. In binding arbitration, the award is legally binding on both parties. (c) No. Errors of fact or law are generally not sufficient grounds to appeal an award.

CHAPTER 8 - CRIMES AND BUSINESS

MATCHING EXERCISE

1. h
2. d
3. o
4. n
5. m

6. k
7. g
8. f
9. j
10. c

11. a
12. b
13. i
14. l
15. e

COMPLETION EXERCISE

1. persons; property
2. act; mental state
3. RICO
4. individual rights
5. Duress; insanity; intoxication; justification

TRUE-FALSE EXERCISE

1. T
6. F

2. T
7. F

3. F
8. F

4. T
9. F

5. T
10. T

MULTIPLE CHOICE QUESTIONS

1. c

2. d

3. d

4. a

SHORT ANSWER QUESTIONS

1. Norma will be charged with arson. If she set the fire she did a criminal act with the requisite mental state of intent.
2. Samuel committed burglary because he forcibly entered the building with the intent to steal.
3. Since the crime in question is a strict liability crime, all that must be proven is that Cal committed the prohibited act; a criminal mental state is not required. Cal is guilty.
4. Roland committed criminal fraud (theft by deception). He made a false statement of a material fact, knowing that it was false and with the intent that Roland rely upon it, and Roland did reasonably rely on the statement resulting in a financial loss.

CASE PROBLEMS

1. (a) The Acme supervisors are probably guilty of some form of manslaughter, such as involuntary or negligent manslaughter. (b) Acme would also be held criminally accountable for this crime since it was committed by its agents who were acting within the scope of their employment.
2. (a) Allen committed criminal fraud (and also federal crimes such as mail fraud). (b) Allen may be fined and/or imprisoned. (c) Mrs. Hinton can sue to rescind the contract, restitution (return of her money) and probably punitive damages (damages to punish Allen and to deter others from similar conduct).

CHAPTER 9 - INTRODUCTION TO CONTRACT LAW AND CONTRACT THEORY

MATCHING EXERCISE

1. e
2. g
3. b

4. d
5. i
6. a

7. h
8. f
9. c

COMPLETION EXERCISE

1. legally enforceable
2. consideration
3. legal capacity
4. genuine assent
5. legal

TRUE-FALSE EXERCISE

1. T	2. F	3. T	4. T	5. F
6. F	7. T	8. T	9. T	10. T

MULTIPLE CHOICE QUESTIONS

1. d   2. b   3. d   4. b

SHORT ANSWER QUESTIONS

1. Yes. The parties have an implied contract.
2. A legally enforceable contract was never formed, only a social obligation arose.
3. Jason may rescind (terminate) the contract and recover his money (restitution). Alternatively, Jason may affirm the contract and sue for damages for the decreased value of the car.
4. No. A court would likely find that the contractual term in question is unenforceable because it violates public policy. (Also, under the UCC, such a term is presumably unconscionable).

CASE PROBLEMS

1. (a) This contract is a secured transaction that is governed by the Uniform Commercial Code (Article 9). (b) This contract is a contract for the sale of goods and it is also governed by the Uniform Commercial Code (Article 2). (c) This is a service contract and it is governed by the common law of contracts.
2. (a) The parties did not enter into a contract. There was never a valid agreement (offer and acceptance) for painting the car. (b) Ken is legally obligated under quasi contract to pay for the reasonable value of the painting. He received a benefit and, under the facts of the case, he would be unjustly enriched if he did not pay for the work rendered.

CHAPTER 10 - CONTRACTUAL AGREEMENT: MUTUAL ASSENT

MATCHING EXERCISE

1. k
2. g
3. d
4. f
5. b

6. i
7. o
8. c
9. e
10. h

11. m
12. n
13. l
14. a
15. j

COMPLETION EXERCISE

1. mutual assent
2. invitations to deal
3. offer, acceptance
4. counteroffer
5. revocation; counteroffer; rejection; lapse of time

TRUE-FALSE EXERCISE

1. F	2. T	3. T	4. F	5. T
6. T	7. F	8. T	9. T	10. T

MULTIPLE CHOICE QUESTIONS

1. b   2. d   3. c   4. b

SHORT ANSWER QUESTIONS

1. No. The circumstances indicate that Kelly was not serious about making an offer, so Kelly never made an offer that Lorenz could have accepted. Contractual intent is lacking in this case.
2. Yes. This offer was sufficiently definite and objectively indicated the required contractual intent.
3. Yes. Tricia's first offer was terminated by Jason's counteroffer, but Tricia accepted Jason's counteroffer, thereby forming a contract.
4. Yes. Unlike the common law "mirror image" rule, the UCC does not require that an acceptance be identical to the terms of the offer.

CASE PROBLEMS

1. (a) No. Sally's advertisement was an invitation to deal; advertisements are generally not offers.
(b) Yes. Measured by the objective standard, Bryan clearly indicated an intent to be bound by the terms of his offer if it were accepted. Moreover, he never communicated to Sally that his acceptance was conditional. (c) Yes. Sally's acceptance formed a contract with Bryan.
2. (a) Bess must communicate her acceptance. (b) Fred's offer will lapse after a reasonable amount of time has passed. (c) Bess may communicate an acceptance in any reasonable commercial manner.
(d) Under the mail-box rule, Bess' acceptance will be effective when she places it in the mail.

CHAPTER 11 - CONSIDERATION: THE BASIS OF THE BARGAIN AND CONTRACTUAL CAPACITY: THE ABILITY TO AGREE

MATCHING EXERCISE

1. k	6. n	11. m
2. o	7. b	12. f
3. h	8. e	13. c
4. j	9. l	14. a
5. i	10. g	15. d

COMPLETION EXERCISE

1. composition agreement
2. Legal (contractual) capacity
3. unconscionable
4. preexisting duty
5. firm offer

TRUE-FALSE EXERCISE

1. T	2. T	3. F	4. F	5. F
6. F	7. T	8. F	9. T	10. F

MULTIPLE CHOICE QUESTIONS

1. c   2. d   3. b   4. a

SHORT ANSWER QUESTIONS

1. Yes. Stacy was a minor at the time of contracting and, therefore, she may disaffirm the contract.
2. Yes. A party need not suffer a hardship to give consideration. Consideration simply requires a party to undertake a new legal obligation that they did not previously have.
3. No. Ina had a preexisting duty to paint and prep the house.
4. Yes. Linda may have entered into a bad bargain, but the bargain was not unconscionable. The law does not evaluate the adequacy of the considerations exchanged.

CASE PROBLEMS

1. (a) Not legally enforceable. Sandy's prior, voluntary work is only past consideration. Past consideration is not sufficient to support a later promise to pay for the benefit already freely given.
(b) Legally enforceable. Ralph made two promises. One promise was only to perform a preexisting duty, which is not consideration. However, his second promise, to perform new work, is consideration and renders the agreement a legally enforceable contract.
2. (a) No. In general, a person is not legally entitled to rely on another's promise. (b) CompuTech's promise is not legally enforceable under promissory estoppel since Ralph's reliance was not reasonable.
(c) Ralph should have entered into a contract with CompuTech before moving to Wyoming.

CHAPTER 12 - LEGALITY OF SUBJECT MATTER AND REALITY OF CONSENT

MATCHING EXERCISE

1.	h	6.	a	11.	b
2.	i	7.	e	12.	d
3.	n	8.	k	13.	g
4.	m	9.	c	14.	l
5.	f	10.	j	15.	o

COMPLETION EXERCISE

1. *mala in se*
2. price-fixing agreement
3. Usury
4. unilateral
5. bilateral

TRUE-FALSE EXERCISE

1. T	2. T	3. F	4. F	5. T
6. T	7. F	8. T	9. F	10. T

MULTIPLE CHOICE QUESTIONS

1. a	2. a	3. c	4. a

SHORT ANSWER QUESTIONS

1. No. Slick Larry never deprived Angela of her ability to exercise her free will. Being "pushy" is not duress.

2. No. This statute is only intended to raise revenue for the government and it is not designed to protect the public.

3. Yes. Alvin had a fiduciary relationship with Sandy. His conduct violated his duty of upmost loyalty, and his duty to make full disclosure to Sandy.

4. No. This was just a bad bargain. Earl was sophisticated in antique cars and simply made an error in judgment about the car's actual value.

CASE PROBLEMS

1. (a) Protective (regulatory). (b) This contract is void and unenforceable because it violated a licensing statute that was designed to protect the public. (c) Jim will be denied any recovery. In general, when an agreement is declared illegal and void, the court will deny any remedy.

2. (a) Yes, both parties were mistaken regarding the same material fact. (b) Dynamic must prove that the mistake was mutual, the mistake was factual in nature, and the matter was material, meaning an important consideration in deciding whether or not to contract.

CHAPTER 13 - PROPER FORM AND INTERPRETATION OF CONTRACTS

MATCHING EXERCISE

1. b	6. l	11. e
2. m	7. h	12. c
3. k	8. i	13. o
4. a	9. d	14. g
5. j	10. n	15. f

COMPLETION EXERCISE

1. totally integrated
2. partially integrated
3. (any two or three of the following) undue influence, fraud, duress, mistake, or lack of consideration
4. general usage
5. contracts to answer for the debt of another; contracts for interests in land; contracts not to be performed within one year; contracts made in consideration of marriage; contracts of executors and administrators of estates; contracts for the sale of goods for $500 or more

TRUE-FALSE EXERCISE

1. F	2. F	3. T	4. T	5. F
6. F	7. T	8. T	9. F	10. F

MULTIPLE CHOICE QUESTIONS

1. a	2. d	3. b	4. d

SHORT ANSWER QUESTIONS

1. No. It is possible that Steve may fully perform within one year because he may die during this time.
2. The court can look at Al's and Pete's course of dealing, meaning their repeated, prior acts in carrying out the contract in question.
3. No. TSRC's contractual obligation to employ Ivan was subject to a condition precedent that was not satisfied (Ivan did not pass the security check). Thus, TSRC's duty was discharged (terminated).
4. This contract is legally enforceable. Under the UCC, the writing requirement is satisfied if one merchant to a contract sends to the other merchant contracting party a sufficient written confirmation and the merchant receiving the confirmation does not object, in writing, within 10 days of receipt.

CASE PROBLEMS

1. (a) Yes. This is a contract for the sale of land. (b) Yes. The paper states the material terms of the contract and it is signed by Jim, who is refusing to perform. (c) Since the paper satisfies the writing requirement under the Statute of Contracts, the oral agreement is legally enforceable.
2. (a) This is a totally integrated contract because it states the entire agreement of the parties. (b) Yes. Because the term "computer system" is ambiguous, Ralph may use parol evidence to explain the intended meaning of this term. (c) Ralph can present evidence of usage of trade and general usage.

CHAPTER 14 - THE RIGHTS OF THIRD PERSONS

MATCHING EXERCISE

1. k		5. e		9. f	
2. c		6. d		10. b	
3. l		7. h		11. j	
4. i		8. g		12. a	

COMPLETION EXERCISE

1. Intent
2. first in time
3. waiver of defense
4. warranties
5. An assignment is forbidden when it may: (a) materially change the duty of the promisor, (b) materially impair the chance of return performance, or (c) materially increase the burden or risk to the other party.

TRUE-FALSE EXERCISE

1. F	2. F	3. F	4. T	5. F
6. F	7. T	8. T	9. T	10. F

MULTIPLE CHOICE QUESTIONS

1. a	2. b	3. a	4. d

SHORT ANSWER QUESTIONS

1. No. Last Bank knew about and accepted the assignment and, therefore, its rights are vested.
2. Yes, the assignment was valid. Nonetheless, FTC regulations allow Laurie to assert her defense against Third Bank because the transaction is a consumer credit transaction.
3. No. The assignment will materially increase the burden and risk for Mike and, therefore, Air Freight cannot assign its contractual rights without Mike's consent.
4. Juan must pay Rosa $2,700. Yes. Rosa has only the same right to enforce the contract that Jasper has. Therefore, her right to be paid is subject to a $300 set-off, for the breach by Jasper.

CASE PROBLEMS

1. (a) Harry's is a third-party beneficiary of the contract because it may receive a benefit from performance of the contract. However, Harry's is only an incidental beneficiary because neither the city nor Virgil's intended to directly benefit Harry's. (b) Because Harry's is only an incidental beneficiary, it cannot sue Virgil's to enforce its proper performance of the contract.
2. (a) This is a delegation. (b) JobFinders was entitled to delegate its typing duties because these are standardized duties that anyone can properly perform. (c) JobFinders, as delegator, remains liable to Trina for the improper performance. A delegation of duties does not generally terminate the delegator's legal obligation to make sure that the work is properly performed.

CHAPTER 15 - CONTRACTUAL DISCHARGE AND REMEDIES

MATCHING EXERCISE

1. g	6. i	11. m
2. k	7. o	12. d
3. e	8. l	13. f
4. n	9. b	14. c
5. h	10. a	15. j

COMPLETION EXERCISE

1. Discharge
2. duty to mitigate
3. Consequential
4. Punitive
5. Specific performance

TRUE-FALSE EXERCISE

1. T	2. T	3. T	4. F	5. T
6. F	7. T	8. T	9. T	10. F

MULTIPLE CHOICE QUESTIONS

1. c	2. a	3. a	4. d

SHORT ANSWER QUESTIONS

1. No. It is not impossible to do the work, only Theo cannot do it. This type of personal inability does not establish the defense of impossibility. Theo must hire someone else to do the work.
2. Josh's must mitigate its damages, i.e., it must take reasonable steps to avoid/minimize its damages.
3. No. This contract is a personal-satisfaction contract. Moreover, it does involve Albert's personal taste and, therefore, he has the right to personally determine whether the work is satisfactory or not.
4. Craftsman committed a material breach of contract. Todd may recover $3,500, the amount necessary to put him in the same financial position he would have been in had Craftsman properly performed.

CASE PROBLEMS

1. (a) A contract may be discharged if an unforeseeable event makes it impossible for anyone to perform the contract. (b) A contract may be discharged when an unforeseeable event frustrates the essential purpose for the contract. (c) No. The fluctuation in prices for natural gas was foreseeable. This is a risk that Mark implicitly took on, and he cannot now escape from his contractual duties.
2. (a) Wainwright has substantially performed the contract, meaning, it completed its duties with a small, unintentional deviation. (b) Wainwright can enforce the contract. (c) The Johnsons must pay the contract price ($100,000) minus damages for Wainwright's nonmaterial breach ($500), that is, a total of $99,500.

CHAPTER 16 - FORMATION OF THE SALES CONTRACT:
CONTRACTS FOR LEASING GOODS

MATCHING EXERCISE

1. e	6. m	11. c
2. f	7. o	12. i
3. l	8. h	13. j
4. a	9. b	14. d
5. k	10. n	15. g

COMPLETION EXERCISE

1. good faith
2. reasonable time (not to exceed three months)
3. accommodation
4. usage of trade
5. Statute of Frauds

TRUE-FALSE EXERCISE

1. T	2. T	3. F	4. F	5. F
6. T	7. F	8. F	9. T	10. F

MULTIPLE CHOICE QUESTIONS

1. d	2. d	3. d	4. c

SHORT ANSWER QUESTIONS

1. UCC Article 2 governs this transaction because it is a contract for the sale of goods. Yes. As a general rule, an offeror can revoke an offer at anytime and for any reason prior to acceptance.
2. No. As an exception to the general rule stated above, a merchant who makes a firm offer cannot revoke it for the time stated, and consideration is not required to make this promise legally binding.
3. Yes. Although a sales contract for $500 or more is generally required to be evidenced by a writing to be enforceable, this rule does not apply if the goods are to be specially made, they cannot be readily resold, and the seller has substantially begun to make or acquire the goods.
4. Yes. Shawna sent Kim a written confirmation of their agreement and Kim did not object to the confirmation, in writing, within ten days.

CASE PROBLEMS

1. (a) Yes. (b) The parties entered into a valid requirements contract. (c) Since the sales contract has open terms, the UCC implies that the price shall be a reasonable price at time and place of delivery, quantity shall be the Town Market's reasonable requirements, and the good shall be delivered within a reasonable time (but in time for the festival) at Perrone's place of business.
2. (a) Yes. The acceptance appears to be definite and seasonable (timely). (b) No. Since John is a nonmerchant, the new term is treated merely as a proposal for him to consider. (c) If John had agreed to the new term, then it would be part of the contract.

CHAPTER 17 - PERFORMANCE, TITLE, AND RISK OF LOSS

MATCHING EXERCISE

1. g	6. o	11. f
2. h	7. l	12. i
3. m	8. k	13. e
4. j	9. b	14. d
5. n	10. a	15. c

COMPLETION EXERCISE

1. consignment
2. sale or return
3. cure
4. sale on approval
5. Signifying that goods conform; signifying that goods do not conform, but accepting the goods despite the nonconformity; failing to properly reject; doing anything inconsistent with the seller's ownership

TRUE-FALSE EXERCISE

1. T	2. T	3. F	4. T	5. T
6. T	7. F	8. F	9. F	10. T

MULTIPLE CHOICE QUESTIONS

1. d   2. b   3. c   4. c

SHORT ANSWER QUESTIONS

1. Yes. This was an entrustment and Ted received good title.
2. Cindy. This was a shipment contract and, therefore, the risk of loss during transportation fell on Cindy.
3. No. This is a sale on approval transaction. The risk of loss never passed to Kathy because she never accepted the bike.
4. May 1. A buyer has an insurable interest in goods as soon as they are existing and identified.

CASE PROBLEMS

1. (a) No. As a generally rule, a buyer receives only the same title to goods as the seller possessed. In this case, Skweeky Kleen had no title (void title) to Jane's car and, therefore, it could pass nothing but a void title to Buyer. Jane may recover the car from Buyer.
2. (a) Al has the right to accept the entire shipment, reject the entire shipment, or accept a commercial unit and reject the remainder. (b) If Al rejects all or a portion of the shipment, TI has a right to cure (correct) its nonconforming performance by shipping the correct cigars to Al within the original contract time or within an additional reasonable period of time.

CHAPTER 18 - WARRANTIES AND PRODUCT LIABILITY

MATCHING EXERCISE

1. e
2. c
3. b

4. d
5. i
6. h

7. a
8. f
9. g

COMPLETION EXERCISE

1. *caveat emptor*
2. a basis of the bargain
3. warranty against infringement
4. AS IS
5. negligence; strict liability

TRUE-FALSE EXERCISE

1. T	2. F	3. F	4. T	5. T
6. F	7. T	8. F	9. F	10. T

MULTIPLE CHOICE QUESTIONS

1. d   2. c   3. d   4. b

SHORT ANSWER QUESTIONS

1. No. This is not a statement of fact that can be proven; it is sales puffing.
2. Brown Corp. is liable for breach of the warranty of merchantability. Its X-100 model is not fit for the ordinary purposes that mountain bikes are used, and it is also doubtful that it would be without objection in the trade as it is described.
3. Yes. Len has breached the implied warranty of fitness for a particular purpose. Len knew that Walt was contemplating a particular use for the rod and that Walt was relying on Len to furnish a suitable rod.
4. No. In this case Bobbie was relying on her own judgment, not Acme's judgment. Therefore, the warranty of fitness for a particular purpose did not arise.

CASE PROBLEMS

1. (a) In general, MicroView can disclaim all implied warranties. Disclaimers made in accordance with Article 2 are not unconscionable. (b) MicroView cannot disclaim the warranty of merchantability by including an inconspicuous disclaimer in its contracts. To exclude this warranty, a disclaimer must be conspicuous and mention "merchantability." (c) The statement "AS IS" would exclude the warranties of merchantability and fitness for a particular purpose.
2. The outcome of this case would be somewhat uncertain. All elements for strict liability are present, except the requirement that the goods be unreasonably dangerous is problematic in this case. In many states, the question is whether the automobile would meet the reasonable expectations of the consumer.

CHAPTER 19 - REMEDIES

MATCHING EXERCISE

1. a
2. e
3. d
4. i

5. h
6. b
7. f
8. k

9. j
10. l
11. c
12. g

COMPLETION EXERCISE

1. adequate assurance
2. four years
3. ten days
4. replevin
5. substantially impairs

TRUE-FALSE EXERCISE

1. F	2. T	3. T	4. T	5. T
6. T	7. F	8. T	9. F	10. F

MULTIPLE CHOICE QUESTIONS

1. c   2. c   3. b   4. d

SHORT ANSWER QUESTIONS

1. A&A should make a written demand for assurance from Royal Grocery. It may also choose to suspend its performance until an adequate assurance is provided.
2. Jake can revoke his acceptance of the ostriches and recover the amount paid. In addition, he would be entitled to sue the seller for any damages he suffered due to the seller's breach.
3. Jodi would be entitled to stop shipment of the figurines.
4. The parties' contractual obligations are discharged by operation of law (justification).

CASE PROBLEMS

1. Hotshot basically has two remedies in this case: replevin and damages. Because the goods are not available elsewhere and are essential to Hotshot's business, Hotshot may replevin them from Chile's. In addition, Hotshot is entitled to sue Chile's for any damages resulting from its breach.
2. (a) In order to protect her rights, Hilda should immediately give notice of breach of contract to Mistro. This notice should also identify all nonconformities. If she wishes to reject, she should do so, subject to Mistro's right to cure. (b) Mistro may cure by delivering a conforming piano within the original contract time or within an additional reasonable time. (c) If Mistro fails to cure, then Sally may reject the piano, cancel the contract, and sue Mistro for damages.

CHAPTER 20 - INTERNATIONAL SALE OF GOODS

MATCHING EXERCISE

1. c
2. a
3. b

4. h
5. d
6. i

7. g
8. f
9. e

COMPLETION EXERCISE

1. good faith
2. letter of credit
3. common law
4. Incoterms
5. "E" terms; "F" terms; "C" terms; "D" terms

TRUE-FALSE EXERCISE

1. F
6. T

2. T
7. T

3. T
8. T

4. T
9. F

5. T
10. F

MULTIPLE CHOICE QUESTIONS

1. a

2. c

3. a

4. d

SHORT ANSWER QUESTIONS

1. Yes. Under the CISG, an acceptance is not effective until it reaches the offeror. Nonetheless, the offeror cannot revoke the offer once the acceptance has been sent, as in this case. Thus, a contract was made on May 6 when Francois's acceptance was received.
2. Yes. The CISG provides that all oral contracts for the sale of goods are enforceable.
3. Yes. The CISG allows buyers up to two years to discover hidden defects.
4. Yes. Although the CISG does not normally apply to a sale of goods for personal or household use, it will apply if the seller neither knew nor should have known that the goods would be used such purposes. This exception applies in this case and, therefore, the CISG controls.

CASE PROBLEMS

1. (a) Yes. (b) If both nations have ratified the CISG, then the CISG will generally govern the rights and duties of the parties under the sales contract. (c) Jesse may specify in the contract that U.S. law will control.
2. (a) No. Allision did not make a firm offer or an option contract. (b) Yes. Allison told Raul that she had no other buyers in response to his inquiry whether she would keep the offer open. Thus, it can be forcibly argued that Raul reasonably and actually relied on the offer being irrevocable, which in turn does render it irrevocable.

CHAPTER 21 - INTRODUCTION TO NEGOTIABLES:
UCC (REVISED) ARTICLES 3 AND 7

MATCHING EXERCISE

1. j
2. d
3. g
4. k

5. a
6. l
7. c
8. b

9. h
10. i
11. f
12. e

COMPLETION EXERCISE

1. maker; payee
2. check
3. document of title
4. bill of lading
5. drafts, checks, promissory notes, certificates of deposit

TRUE-FALSE EXERCISE

1. F	2. T	3. T	4. T	5. T
6. F	7. T	8. T	9. F	10. T

MULTIPLE CHOICE QUESTIONS

1. b   2. d   3. c   4. c

SHORT ANSWER QUESTIONS

1. This instrument is a draft, also known as a trade acceptance or sales draft. Jerry has no obligation to pay it prior to acceptance. After he accepts it, he will have primary liability to pay.
2. The bank has no duty to pay Roger prior to its acceptance of the check. If Burton has sufficient funds in his account to pay, then the bank owes Burton a duty to pay based on the parties' depositary contract.
3. Ajax has the right to receive the goods in accordance with the terms of the document of title.
4. Pay by check. If the check is payable to the order of the creditor, then Kendall will be protected from liability if the check is lost or stolen in route.

CASE PROBLEMS

1. (a) Smithson issued a check. When issued, the check was order paper. (b) As the drawee of the check, the Old Yorker Bank has no legal obligation to Molly to pay the check prior to acceptance. After acceptance, the bank has primary liability to pay.
2. (a) The document is a bill of lading. (b) It reflects the ownership rights to the goods being shipped and a contract between Transatlantic Truckers and Connecticut Crabbers. (c) Transatlantic is liable for the loss.

CHAPTER 22 - NEGOTIABILITY

MATCHING EXERCISE

1.	i	4.	h	7.	a
2.	g	5.	b	8.	f
3.	c	6.	d	9.	e

COMPLETION EXERCISE

1. nonnegotiable
2. maker; drawer
3. money
4. four corner
5. typed

TRUE-FALSE EXERCISE

1. F	2. T	3. T	4. F	5. F
6. T	7. T	8. T	9. F	10. F

MULTIPLE CHOICE QUESTIONS

1. c	2. c	3. d	4. b

SHORT ANSWER QUESTIONS

1. No. The obligation is not unconditional; it is conditioned upon the occurrence of an event that is not certain to occur.
2. Yes. It meets all six requirements for a negotiable instrument.
3. No. It is not payable for a sum certain. The amount of principal cannot be determined from the face of the paper.
4. Yes. Checks are negotiable and their negotiability cannot be taken away by writing on them that they are nonnegotiable.

CASE PROBLEMS

1. (a) To be negotiable, an instrument must be: 1) written; 2) signed by the drawer or maker; 3) state an unconditional promise to or order to pay; 4) a fixed sum of money; 5) payable on demand or at a definite time; and 6) payable to bearer or to the order of a party. (b) This instrument fulfills all six requirements when issued and, therefore, it is negotiable.
2. (a) No. The sum to be paid is not for a certain amount, and the obligation to pay is conditioned upon completion of the project. (b) Even though the note is nonnegotiable, it still establishes a contractual obligation to pay. (c) Yes. Since it is a nonnegotiable instrument, subsequent transferees who take the note cannot be a HDC and, therefore, they take the note subject to all defenses, both personal and real.

CHAPTER 23 - NEGOTIATION AND HOLDERS IN DUE COURSE/HOLDERS BY DUE NEGOTIATION

MATCHING EXERCISE

1. d
2. g
3. i
4. a

5. j
6. e
7. b
8. l

9. f
10. k
11. h
12. c

COMPLETION EXERCISE

1. bearer
2. holder
3. Good faith
4. blank indorsement
5. authorized delivery by the holder; proper indorsement by the holder

TRUE-FALSE EXERCISE

1. F	2. F	3. T	4. T	5. F
6. F	7. T	8. T	9. T	10. F

MULTIPLE CHOICE QUESTIONS

1. c   2. d   3. a   4. b

SHORT ANSWER QUESTIONS

1. No. Bob had notice that the document had possibly been altered.
2. Yes. Last Bank is a HDC and, therefore, it takes the check subject only to real defenses. Dana's defense of intoxication is only a personal defense and, therefore, it cannot be used to avoid liability.
3. No. The contractual defense of infancy (minority) is a real defense. Marie may raise this defense and avoid her liability to pay the note.
4. Yes. The defense of illegality is a real defense in this case and, therefore, Bob may raise this defense in order to avoid his liability to pay the check.

CASE PROBLEMS

1. (a) Special indorsement. (b) Blank indorsement. (c) Qualified indorsement. (d) Restrictive indorsement.
2. (a) Yes. The instrument is negotiable, and Julia was a holder who took the note by negotiation for value, in good faith, and without notice of any defect or defenses. (b) Jacob's defense of fraud in the inducement is a personal defense. (c) Jacob must pay the note to Julia because he has primary liability to pay it (as maker) and he cannot assert his defense against Julia because she is a HDC.

CHAPTER 24 - LIABILITY AND DISCHARGE

MATCHING EXERCISE

1. d
2. h
3. e

4. i
5. c
6. f

7. b
8. g
9. a

COMPLETION EXERCISE

1. maker
2. acceptance
3. midnight deadline
4. warranty liability
5. payment; tender of payment; cancellation and renunciation; impairment

TRUE-FALSE EXERCISE

1. T
6. T

2. F
7. T

3. T
8. T

4. T
9. F

5. F
10. F

MULTIPLE CHOICE QUESTIONS

1. a
2. b
3. c
4. d

SHORT ANSWER QUESTIONS

1. Pat has secondary liability as drawer of the check. Ken's Groceries has secondary liability as an indorser.
2. Yes. Peoria Bank accepted the check, thus incurring primary liability to pay whether or not Wally has sufficient money in his account to cover the check.
3. Shirley has secondary liability as the drawer of the check. John does not have any signature liability to pay because notice of dishonor was not given to him in a timely fashion.
4. No. A person does not have signature (contractual) liability to pay an instrument unless the person or an authorized agent signs it. Here, the forgery is a real defense that can be raised avoiding any claimed liability.

CASE PROBLEMS

1. James must pay the amount of the checks to Check-Rite. Under the "imposter rule," when a person is deceived into issuing an instrument to an imposter who pretends to be an intended payee and the imposter forges the payee's indorsement, then the issuer must pay anyone who, in good faith, subsequently pays or takes the instrument, in this case Check-Rite. Michelle still has a contractual right under its lease to demand James to pay her the rent for the two months in question.
2. (a) Mike is a primary party, and Patsy is a secondary party. (b) Mike's obligation is not subject to any conditions, whereas Patsy's liability is subject to proper presentment, dishonor, and notice of dishonor.
(c) Mike must pay the note. Since presentment was not made in a timely fashion, she has no secondary liability to pay.

CHAPTER 25 - BANK-CUSTOMER RELATIONS/ELECTRONIC FUND TRANSFERS

MATCHING EXERCISE

1. e
2. f
3. b

4. g
5. d
6. h

7. c
8. i
9. a

COMPLETION EXERCISE

1. Article 4A
2. unauthorized signature
3. contract; agent; and debtor (also acceptable: agent, debtor, creditor)
4. due care
5. damages due to arrest; damages due to prosecution; other consequential damages that can be proven

TRUE-FALSE EXERCISE

1. F
6. T

2. F
7. F

3. F
8. F

4. T
9. F

5. T
10. F

MULTIPLE CHOICE QUESTIONS

1. d

2. c

3. d

4. a

SHORT ANSWER QUESTIONS

1. No. A bank may honor a check up to ten days after a customer's death; here, Susan presented Charlie's check 18 days after his death and the bank may not honor it.

2. Yes. Stop-payment orders are effective only for six months, so Maria's stop-payment order had expired in October. Although this check was stale, a bank may honor a stale check if it chooses.

3. No. A bank must be given a reasonable time to process a stop-payment order. Because Louis cashed the check before Sandy gave the bank the stop-payment order, the bank had no time to act.

4. No. The bank properly dishonored the check.

CASE PROBLEMS

1. If the bank can show that Jennifer acted negligently when she gave Travis important responsibilities without checking his background, Jennifer could have contributed to the unauthorized signature. If the bank is successful, Jennifer could be liable for the loss.

2. (a) Jeff has 30 days in which to examine his statement and report any errors. (b) Jeff gave timely notice because he reported the error in one week. (c) Last Bank may properly charge Jeff's account for $100.

CHAPTER 26 - SECURED TRANSACTIONS: SECURITY INTERESTS AND PERFECTION

MATCHING EXERCISE

1. f	5. h	9. b
2. k	6. j	10. e
3. d	7. l	11. g
4. a	8. i	12. c

COMPLETION EXERCISE

1. Perfection
2. termination statement
3. automatic perfection
4. possession
5. possession by secured creditor; filing of financing statement; automatic perfection

TRUE-FALSE EXERCISE

1. F	2. T	3. F	4. T	5. T
6. F	7. T	8. T	9. T	10. F

MULTIPLE CHOICE QUESTIONS

1. b	2. d	3. c	4. a

SHORT ANSWER QUESTIONS

1. Yes. Vanessa has a perfected interest in the identifiable cash proceeds.
2. Farm products. Carter's should file the financing statement in the county where the farm is located.
3. Yes. The copier lease is a disguised sale, with the seller retaining a security interest.
4. Reva should file financing statements in all of the states where the leasing outlets are located and/or take such other steps as may be required by those jurisdictions to perfect the security interest.

CASE PROBLEMS

1. (a) The stove is equipment. (b) Yes. A security interest in equipment may be perfected by filing a financing statement centrally, which is typically with the secretary of state or comparable government office. (c) Perfection is important because it will help Alice ensure priority to the collateral over most subsequent secured parties who may claim an interest in the collateral.
2. (a) The note is an instrument. (b) Yes. There was an oral security agreement, value was given, the debtor has an interest in the note, and the secured party has possession of the note. (c) Yes. Possession of the instrument by the secured party perfects the interest. (d) June 1 until August 1.

CHAPTER 27 - SECURED TRANSACTIONS: PRIORITIES

MATCHING EXERCISE

1. i
2. g
3. e

4. d
5. h
6. b

7. f
8. c
9. a

COMPLETION EXERCISE

1. collateral
2. file (perfect)
3. attach
4. ten days
5. Priority

TRUE-FALSE EXERCISE

1. F
6. F

2. T
7. F

3. T
8. T

4. F
9. F

5. F
10. T

MULTIPLE CHOICE QUESTIONS

1. d

2. b

3. d

4. a

SHORT ANSWER QUESTIONS

1. The security interest secures both debts.
2. Tom's perfected security interest wins over Fran's unperfected security interest even though Fran's interest was the first one to attach.
3. Acme wins. The first to perfect generally wins.
4. First Catch. The buyer in the ordinary course exception applies in this case.

CASE PROBLEMS

1. (a) Merchant's has a perfected floating lien. (b) Trish has a perfected PMSI. (c) Merchant's wins. The perfected PMSI exception does not apply in this case because Trish did not perfect the PMSI prior to the debtor receiving the inventory collateral, as required by the Code.
2. (a) Buzz engaged in double financing. (b) Neither of the security interests were perfected. In general, the only way to perfect in instruments is for the secured party to take possession. (c) Della wins. Between two unperfected security interests, the first to attach has priority.

CHAPTER 28 - SECURED TRANSACTIONS: DEFAULT

MATCHING EXERCISE

1. f
2. b
3. a

4. d
5. e
6. h

7. c
8. g
9. i

COMPLETION EXERCISE

1. security agreement
2. breach of the peace
3. deficiency judgment
4. twenty-one
5. commercially reasonable

TRUE-FALSE EXERCISE

| 1. F | 2. T | 3. T | 4. T | 5. F |
| 6. F | 7. T | 8. F | 9. F | 10. T |

MULTIPLE CHOICE QUESTIONS

1. d   2. b   3. d   4. d

SHORT ANSWER QUESTIONS

1. A secured creditor can use self-help to repossess collateral only if it can be done without committing a breach of the peace. Wheels violated this limit and is liable for damages.
2. No, Iris can waive her right to sale only after default occurs.
3. Sheldon may redeem prior to a sale of the collateral by paying $4,460, the amount of the outstanding debt plus costs of repossession and sale.
4. Thorsen's may be liable to Ricco because it commingled the bracelets in violation of the UCC. The bracelets were not fungible and Thorsen's had a duty to keep them separate and identifiable.

CASE PROBLEMS

1. (a) Logic must notify Hi-Tek unless Hi-Tek has waived its notice of sale. (b) Junior secured creditor must notify Logic that they claim an interest in the collateral. (c) Logic may choose either a private or public sale, so long as each is conducted in a commercially reasonable manner. (d) If a public sale is conducted, Logic is free to bid on the patent at such sale.
2. (a) The sales price is commercially reasonable. A&A took all reasonable steps possible to obtain the best price. The fact that it sold for less than its market value does not automatically make the sale commercially unreasonable. (b) Proceeds of the sale are first applied to the cost of the repossession and sale, second applied to payment of the balance of the secured debt owed to A&A.

CHAPTER 29 - STRAIGHT BANKRUPTCY

MATCHING EXERCISE

1. k		5. j		9. c	
2. f		6. g		10. e	
3. b		7. d		11. l	
4. a		8. i		12. h	

COMPLETION EXERCISE

1. unconstitutional
2. Article III
3. liquidation
4. three
5. $1 million

TRUE-FALSE EXERCISE

1. T	2. T	3. F	4. F	5. T
6. T	7. F	8. T	9. F	10. T

MULTIPLE CHOICE QUESTIONS

1. c	2. d	3. b	4. d

SHORT ANSWER QUESTIONS

1. The life insurance policy, personal clothing, and the old car will likely be allowed as exemptions which Santos may keep for a "fresh start."
2. George is incorrect; the security interest in the boat was given for new value (Foster's $500 loan to Al.)
3. The creditor may seek to have the discharge revoked during the one year period following the discharge because of Gordon's fraudulent behavior in transferring the money.
4. The agreement is valid and enforceable if filed with and approved by the court.

CASE PROBLEMS

1. Sara's creditors will have $6500 because the expenses of the proceeding are paid first. Sara will be permitted to keep her personal clothing and a specified amount of equity in her house under federal or most state exemption laws. If Sara wishes to keep the car, she can enter into a reaffirmation agreement with the dealer to continue the payments. The income taxes from the previous year may not be discharged.
2. The company may not repossess the fax machine after the bankruptcy is filed because that would violate the automatic stay; the company may retain its security interest. The lease payments will be partially allowed. Office Products will receive a pro rata portion with other general unsecured creditors after payment of expenses and taxes.

CHAPTER 30 - ALTERNATIVES TO STRAIGHT BANKRUPTCY

MATCHING EXERCISE

1. d
2. f
3. b

4. h
5. e
6. c

7. i
8. g
9. a

COMPLETION EXERCISE

1. wage earner's
2. debtor in possession
3. court
4. binding
5. (a) is in the best interest of the creditors (b) is feasible (c) pays at least as much as liquidation (d) is fair to all creditors

TRUE-FALSE EXERCISE

1. T
6. F

2. T
7. F

3. F
8. T

4. T
9. T

5. F
10. T

MULTIPLE CHOICE QUESTIONS

1. d

2. b

3. b

4. d

SHORT ANSWER QUESTIONS

1. Yes, Healthy Heart may use Chapter 11 to restructure its debt in order to provide for the future claims arising from the product liability action.
2. The Bakery may obtain a writ of execution and sell Sugar Shack's property to satisfy the debt. If the writ of execution is unsatisfied, the bakery could use a supplemental proceeding to discover assets. Possibly Sugar Shack's bank account could be garnished.
3. Creditors may not file an involuntary Chapter 12; Fred cannot file a Chapter 13 because the amount of debt is too high, but he may file a voluntary Chapter 12.
4. Yes, Jackson's plan meets the criteria for confirmation of a Chapter 13 plan.

CASE PROBLEMS

1. No, they may not repossess, but they retain their security interest. The court may approve the plan notwithstanding the objections of some creditors. A plan may be confirmed even if some claims are not paid in full. Conversion to Chapter 7 is usually granted only for wrongful acts by the debtor-in-possession.
2. If Sara wishes to enter a composition agreement, all creditors must participate. The composition agreement serves as a contract, and thus is binding. Creditors generally all take a similar reduction in their claims which serves as consideration for the agreement. No, the binding nature of the composition agreement releases Sara from obligation on the original debt, and substitutes only the new, restructured debt.

CHAPTER 31 - THE CREATION AND TERMINATION OF AN AGENCY

MATCHING EXERCISE

1. c
2. f
3. d

4. e
5. i
6. g

7. a
8. b
9. h

COMPLETION EXERCISE

1. general agent
2. consensual
3. gratuitous agency
4. duty of loyalty
5. agreement of the parties; notice by either party in an agency at will; fulfillment of purpose; revocation, renunciation, operation of law.

TRUE-FALSE EXERCISE

1. T
6. F

2. T
7. T

3. F
8. T

4. T
9. T

5. T
10. T

MULTIPLE CHOICE QUESTIONS

1. c

2. c

3. d

4. b

SHORT ANSWER QUESTIONS

1. Mary is a general agent. She handles many transactions over a long period of time on behalf of Juan.
2. Norton is an independent contractor. Although Acme would not normally be liable for Norton's torts, it would be in this case since he was retained to engage in an ultrahazardous activity on Acme's behalf.
3. The parties have a gratuitous, principal-agent relationship. Ron may serve as an agent even though he is a minor, and Jodi would be bound by a contract made on her behalf by Ron.
4. The agency will end in two years, as agreed. However, the parties can, by mutual agreement, agree to extend the agency for a further period of time.

CASE PROBLEMS

1. (a)The partners are agents of the partnership. (b) The partners are fiduciaries of the partnership, meaning they must act with loyalty and good faith in all partnership dealings. (c) Ratou clearly violated his fiduciary duty to the partnership. He was obligated to negotiate the best price he could obtain for the partnership, he should not have taken secret profits, and he should have disclosed his conflict of interest.
2. (a) Motorworks must bear the loss resulting from Joe's improper behavior. At the time Kathy paid Joe, he still had implied authority to accept her payment. When Joe purchased the tires from the supplier, he had apparent authority to do so, obligating Motorworks on the purchase contract. (c) Motorworks should have dismissed Joe on the spot to avoid problems like it has with Kathy, and it should have given actual and constructive to all others that Joe was no longer its agent.

CHAPTER 32 - AGENCY: LIABILITY FOR CONTRACTS

MATCHING EXERCISE

1. g
2. d
3. b

4. c
5. e
6. h

7. a
8. i
9. f

COMPLETION EXERCISE

1. Authority by estoppel
2. disclosed principal
3. undisclosed principal
4. time; geographical area
5. principal exists and is competent; agent is the agent for the principal; agent is authorized to enter into this type of contract on behalf of the principal

TRUE-FALSE EXERCISE

1. F
6. T

2. F
7. F

3. T
8. F

4. F
9. F

5. T
10. F

MULTIPLE CHOICE QUESTIONS

1. b

2. d

3. c

4. d

SHORT ANSWER QUESTIONS

1. The parties to the contract are Adams Co. And Tri-State Groceries. These same parties are liable to perform the contract. Ali has no liability on the contract.
2. Originally, Nolan had no authority to purchase the extra inventory. However, Ryan ratified the contract. Therefore, Ryan, not Nolan, is liable on the contract.
3. Elizabeth had implied authority to hire Rachel. Her authority is implied from her position. Yes, the store could have limited or even done away with Elizabeth's implied authority.
4. Yes. Roger had emergency authority to hire Jenni's LocustBusters.

CASE PROBLEMS

1. (a) Alton had no authority to purchase the ties on behalf of Preston's. (b) Because Alton had no authority to make the contract, no one is liable on the contract. (c) Alton is liable to All-Tied-Up for breach of warranty of authority. He is liable for any profits that All-Tied-Up would have made.
2. (a) Phyllis is a partially disclosed principal. (b) The patent holder must elect whether to hold Phyllis or Jenkins liable on the contract. (c) Phyllis can hold the third party liable on the contract since the third party knew there was a principal involved.

CHAPTER 33 - AGENCY: LIABILITY FOR TORTS AND CRIMES

MATCHING EXERCISE

1. g
2. f
3. i

4. c
5. h
6. b

7. d
8. a
9. e

COMPLETION EXERCISE

1. *Respondeat superior*
2. vicarious
3. time, place
4. indemnification
5. Workers' compensation

TRUE-FALSE EXERCISE

1. F
6. T

2. T
7. T

3. T
8. F

4. F
9. T

5. T
10. F

MULTIPLE CHOICE QUESTIONS

1. b

2. c

3. d

4. a

SHORT ANSWER QUESTIONS

1. Rose is personally liable for her own tort. Orlando is vicariously liable for Rose's tort because it occurred within the course and scope of her employment duties.

2. Jessica is liable for her own negligence. Under the facts, Reliable is not vicariously liable for Jessica's negligence because it did not occur within the scope of her employment. When the accident occurred, Jessica was acting only with the intent to benefit herself, not Reliable.

3. Under the facts stated, it would appear that Mann Warehouse would be vicariously liable for Orville's tort. Mann had the right to control Orville's conduct, making Orville a servant, albeit a temporary one.

4. Bobby is liable for his own tort. Under the doctrine *respondeat superior*, Tony's is also liable since Bobby was acting within the course and scope of his duties. The deviation in terms of time and distance was small, and it was foreseeable. Thus, most courts would hold Tony liable despite this minor detour.

CASE PROBLEMS

1. (a) The relationship between Carol and Humboldt is that of employer-independent contractor.
(b) Under the general rule, Carol is not liable for the tort of an independent contractor, here Humboldt.
(c) On the other hand, Humboldt is liable to Roger under the doctrine of *respondeat superior*.
2. Sandra's employer is not vicariously liable to Nora. The time and place where the accident occurred and Sandra's activities (personal lunch and nap) do not fall within the course or scope of employment.
(b) If Sandra had also been running an errand for her employer at the time of the accident, most courts would impose vicarious liability on the employer.

CHAPTER 34 - FORMATION OF A BUSINESS

MATCHING EXERCISE

1. f
2. j
3. e
4. c

5. k
6. g
7. l
8. d

9. a
10. i
11. b
12. h

COMPLETION EXERCISE

1. *de jure*
2. certificate of incorporation
3. Promoters
4. *ultra vires*
5. insulation from unlimited personal liability; centralization of management; continuity of existence; free transferability of shares

TRUE-FALSE EXERCISE

1. T
6. F

2. T
7. T

3. T
8. T

4. T
9. F

5. T
10. F

MULTIPLE CHOICE QUESTIONS

1. c   2. c   3. c   4. d

SHORT ANSWER QUESTIONS

1. Doing business as a partnership, a limited partnership, or a limited liability company will effectively prevent investors from selling their interests to others without Harry's and Larry's consent. Also, in a corporation, the parties could restrict the transfer of investors' stock by an appropriate agreement.
2. Yes. This was neither a novation nor a release, merely an assumption by the corporation. Sean remains liable on the contract with the seller.
3. No. limited partners who advise general partners are not considered to be involved in management.
4. Probably not. There is insufficient evidence to indicate an intent that the truck is partnership property. Title remains in Lee's name and partners often use their own property when doing partnership business.

CASE PROBLEMS

1. (a) The corporation would be allowed to do what is reasonably necessary to conduct its business and, in many states, it can do anything that natural persons can do. (b) Yes. (c) Yes.
2. (a) Partnership: advantage - flow through taxation; disadvantage - all owners have equal control and unlimited personal liability. (b) Limited partnership: advantage - flow through taxation and, as general partners, control of business; disadvantage - as general partners, unlimited personal liability.
(c) Corporation: advantage - as majority shareholders, effectively control business and limited liability; disadvantage - losses taxed to corporation (unless make Subchapter S election).

CHAPTER 35 - OPERATION OF A BUSINESS ORGANIZATION

MATCHING EXERCISE

1. b
2. k
3. e
4. c

5. j
6. g
7. i
8. l

9. f
10. a
11. d
12. h

COMPLETION EXERCISE

1. joint; several
2. subscription agreement
3. cumulative preferred
4. notice to shareholders; quorum requirement; time and place for meetings
5. current net profits (retained earnings); (unrestricted) earned surplus

TRUE-FALSE EXERCISE

1. T
6. T

2. T
7. T

3. F
8. F

4. T
9. T

5. T
10. F

MULTIPLE CHOICE QUESTIONS

1. d

2. b

3. b

4. c

SHORT ANSWER QUESTIONS

1. Yes. A partnership agreement can provide for the payment of salaries to partners and it may specify how profits are to be divided.

2. Earl and Antonio may vote since they are common stockholders. As majority common stockholder, Earl has the ability to determine whether the proposal passes or not.

3. Yes. Although Ed violated the shareholder agreement and may be liable to the other shareholders, Hank was unaware of this fact and may enforce the agreement. The result would have been different had the restriction been conspicuously stated on the stock certificates.

4. Yes. Shareholders generally have a right to inspect corporate books for proper purposes. Determining the value of one's shares is a proper purpose.

CASE PROBLEMS

1. (a) The partnership is liable on the contract since Glen had authority to make it. (b) No. A dissolution does not eliminate partners' liability for partnership obligations. (c) Tim and Glen both have unlimited personal liability to the seller of the inventory if the partnership fails to pay this debt. (d) Yes. A partner who pays more than his or her share of a partnership obligation is entitled to indemnification (contribution) from the other partners for their portion of the debt that was paid.

2. Pat is liable to the corporation (and in some states to the corporation's creditors) for: (a) watered stock - $50,000 and (b) illegal dividend - $5,000.

CHAPTER 36 - BUSINESS TERMINATIONS AND OTHER EXTRAORDINARY EVENTS

MATCHING EXERCISE

1.	i	5.	f	9.	b
2.	g	6.	l	10.	d
3.	k	7.	c	11.	h
4.	e	8.	a	12.	j

COMPLETION EXERCISE

1. consolidation
2. short-form merger
3. voluntary or involuntary
4. unlawful for business to continue; a partner dies; a partner or the partnership becomes bankrupt
5. economies of scale; enhanced knowledge; diversification

TRUE-FALSE EXERCISE

1. F	2. T	3. F	4. T	5. F
6. T	7. T	8. T	9. T	10. T

MULTIPLE CHOICE QUESTIONS

1. a	2. b	3. b	4. b

SHORT ANSWER QUESTIONS

1. First, Bob can vote against the merger. If the merger is properly authorized, then Bob has the right, as a dissenting shareholder, to exercise his appraisal rights and have the corporation purchase his stock.
2. The court has the discretion to decide whether to grant the request for dissolution or not. Although insanity of a partner is grounds for requesting dissolution, dissolution is not automatic. In this situation, the court will likely grant the request if the insane partner's interest cannot be adequately protected.
3. A form of stock acquisition. The legal effect of this transaction is a sale of Lightning Corp. To Blinder Corp., i.e., a modified form of de facto merger.
4. First, Jim and Diane receive $17,000 and $12,000 respectively. Next, the partners each receive repayment of their contributions. Finally, the remaining $11,000 is shared equally by the three partners.

CASE PROBLEMS

1. (a) They may continue the partnership business, if Clay's estate agrees. Otherwise, they must wind up. (b) The surviving partners are entitled to wind up the partnership. (c) Assets are distributed in the following order: Roscoe - $20,000; Tess - $10,000; the partners are repaid their capital contributions; the remaining $30,000 is split three ways among the partners and estate (same manner profits are shared).
2. (a) Knowledge: MicroChem has a process that MacroChem wants. Also, MacroChem has more experience and better access to capital. (b) The directors of each company must adopt a plan of merger; two-thirds of the outstanding shares of each corporation must approve. (c) MicroChem will cease to exist; MacroChem will survive, owning the firms' combined assets and taking on the firms' combined debts.

CHAPTER 37 - FRANCHISING

MATCHING EXERCISE

1.	h	5. f		9.	c
2.	l	6. e		10.	d
3.	j	7. b		11.	k
4.	g	8. a		12.	i

COMPLETION EXERCISE

1. termination, quality control
2. franchisee's investment capital, goodwill, assured distribution network, larger asset base
3. can start a business with limited capital, goodwill, franchisor's business expertise, assured supply
4. Forum shopping
5. notice

TRUE-FALSE EXERCISE

1. T	2. F	3. T	4. F	5. F
6. T	7. T	8. F	9. F	10. F

MULTIPLE CHOICE QUESTIONS

1. a	2. d	3. a	4. d

SHORT ANSWER QUESTIONS

1. Yes. According to the *Brennan* case, failing to provide a suitable location may be a breach of contract.
2. Yes, because a person can start a franchise with limited capital and can benefit from the franchisor's business expertise.
3. No. Durman does not have enough goodwill and name recognition to make a good franchisor.
4. No. This would probably violate the antitrust laws.

CASE PROBLEMS

1. Yes. This case is like *Blankenship*. The parties' conduct conformed to the statutory definition of a franchisee - - Davis trained Graham, provided him with sales material, and allowed him to use D&D's logo (at least there was implied permission to use the logo, because the sales material contained the logo), and in return Graham paid Davis a fee.

2. (a) Yes. Failing to meet reasonable quotas is adequate grounds to terminate a franchise. (b) Nevus should provide notice, generally around 90 days.

CHAPTER 38 - SECURITIES REGULATION

MATCHING EXERCISE

1.	i	6.	h	11.	g
2.	e	7.	f	12.	b
3.	n	8.	k	13.	l
4.	m	9.	o	14.	c
5.	j	10.	d	15.	a

COMPLETION EXERCISE

1. Securities Act of 1933
2. Securities Exchange Act of 1934
3. red herring
4. tombstone advertisements
5. short-swing profits

TRUE-FALSE EXERCISE

1. F	2. F	3. F	4. T	5. T
6. T	7. T	8. T	9. T	10. T

MULTIPLE CHOICE QUESTIONS

1. c   2. d   3. d   4. a

SHORT ANSWER QUESTIONS

1. Yes. The offering is less than $5 million and is made only to accredited investors.
2. No. "Grease payments" to low-level officials are allowed.
3. This is a short-swing profit and Margaret must pay the $10,000 to the corporation.
4. Yes. While the Supreme Court has yet to rule directly on the validity of the misappropriation theory, the SEC and lower federal courts would hold Randolph liable for misappropriating this information.

CASE PROBLEMS

1. (a) The Securities Exchange Act of 1934. (b) Tom must show that the Midas board of directors made a misleading statement or omitted a material fact that made the statement misleading. (c) Yes. The board's statement was more than misleading; it was untrue.
2. (a) Yes. Advertisements during the waiting period are limited to tombstone advertisements.
(b) CryoTech may begin to sell offered shares in the posteffective period.

CHAPTER 39 - CONSTITUTIONAL REGULATION OF BUSINESS

MATCHING EXERCISE

1. o	6. m	11. e
2. g	7. a	12. i
3. h	8. k	13. b
4. l	9. n	14. f
5. j	10. d	15. c

COMPLETION EXERCISE

1. Administrative agencies
2. economic; social
3. just compensation
4. substantive; procedural
5. rational basis; compelling state interest; substantially important state interest

TRUE-FALSE EXERCISE

1. T	2. T	3. F	4. F	5. F
6. T	7. T	8. F	9. F	10. T

MULTIPLE CHOICE QUESTIONS

1. d	2. a	3. b	4. b

SHORT ANSWER QUESTIONS

1. Yes. The diner is serving to out-of-state customers and thus has an impact on the national economy.
2. No. The law is narrowly tailored to protect the government's substantially important goal of protecting people from unqualified lawyers.
3. Yes. The government has deprived the landowner of the property's present use.
4. Yes. This law is an unreasonable and irrational way of advancing a legitimate government interest.

CASE PROBLEMS

1. (a) Yes, because Amax does business in several states. (b) The commerce clause allows the federal government to regulate interstate activities. (c) Colorado may regulate Amax in those areas where it has concurrent power with the federal government. (d) Colorado may not pass laws that discriminate against Amax because it is an out-of-state company.
2. This is a government regulation that results in invidious discrimination. The Level 2 Test applies because the law implicates a suspect classification. This law does not pass this test because there are less burdensome ways of accomplishing this objective.

CHAPTER 40 - ANTITRUST LAW

MATCHING EXERCISE

1. h
2. l
3. g
4. f

5. i
6. a
7. d
8. b

9. e
10. k
11. j
12. c

COMPLETION EXERCISE

1. price discrimination
2. treble damages
3. Monopoly power
4. Palming off
5. Per se; rule of reason

TRUE-FALSE EXERCISE

| 1. F | 2. T | 3. F | 4. F | 5. F |
| 6. F | 7. T | 8. T | 9. F | 10. F |

MULTIPLE CHOICE QUESTIONS

1. c   2. a   3. a   4. d

SHORT ANSWER QUESTIONS

1. No. LubeTech's market position has been "thrust upon it" because it produces a quality product.
2. No. Charging a lower price is permissible if a product is obsolete.
3. Yes. This is a horizontal market division, a per se violation of § 1 of the Sherman Act.
4. No. Under the "failing company" doctrine, this merger will be permitted because it will keep Big Muscle from going out of business.

CASE PROBLEMS

1. (a) The relevant market is winter coats. (b) LeatherTech has not violated § 1. It controls less than 70 percent of the relevant market, i.e., winter coats.
2. (a) This is a tying arrangement. (b) Under the facts stated, CompuTron has not violated § 3 of the Clayton Act. (c) Although CompuTron is selling its products pursuant to a tying arrangement, it can defend its action because no competitor produces a disk that is compatible with the MiDSU and its disks are necessary to protect the MiDSU from harm.

CHAPTER 41 - CONSUMER PROTECTION

MATCHING EXERCISE

1. j
2. a
3. d
4. h

5. g
6. c
7. i

8. b
9. f
10. e

COMPLETION EXERCISE

1. Consumer Credit Protection Act
2. Actual damages; statutory damages; attorney's fees
3. Regulation B
4. clear, conspicuous
5. Consumer Product Safety Commission

TRUE-FALSE EXERCISE

1. F
6. F

2. F
7. F

3. F
8. F

4. T
9. T

5. T
10. F

MULTIPLE CHOICE QUESTIONS

1. c

2. a

3. b

4. d

SHORT ANSWER QUESTIONS

1. Terence may not discriminate against Karen on the basis of marital status or future marital plans.
2. The CPSC may require a study of the injuries, issue warnings, require a recall, and ban future sales.
3. She may require the credit agency to include her statement regarding the information in the file.
4. Yes. Moore, a debt collector, violated the Fair Debt Collection Practices Act by telephoning Zach before 8 a.m.

CASE PROBLEMS

1. Maurice may choose to rescind or cancel his contract based on the Truth in Lending Act. This law applies because Maurice used his home as collateral. Maurice has a 3-day cooling off period in which to decide to cancel, although the power of rescission potentially lasts for three years from the consummation of the transaction or the sale of his property, whichever occurs first.

2. The agency is regulated by the Fair Debt Collection Practices Act. The agency may not contact third persons regarding payment of the debt. Civil (damages, costs, attorney's fees) and criminal penalties may be imposed.

CHAPTER 42 - ENVIRONMENTAL PROTECTION

MATCHING EXERCISE

1.	j	5.	g	9.	f
2.	a	6.	c	10.	l
3.	d	7.	k	11.	e
4.	h	8.	b	12.	i

COMPLETION EXERCISE

1. Executive Order
2. maximum contaminant levels
3. civil; criminal
4. major
5. waste (sometimes referred to as "solid waste")

TRUE-FALSE EXERCISE

1. T	2. F	3. T	4. T	5. T
6. F	7. F	8. T	9. T	10. T

MULTIPLE CHOICE QUESTIONS

1. a   2. d   3. a   4. c

SHORT ANSWER QUESTIONS

1. CERCLA. Under the facts, both Donald and the prior owner may be held liable.
2. Cows, Inc.'s discharges through pipes violate the CWA; the run-off does not.
3. Yes. Fred has standing because he has personally suffered a special damage that is greater than that suffered by the general public.
4. RCRA applies in this case since the conduct involves the transportation and disposal of wastes. Both Foster, the employee, and Acme, Foster's employer, are liable for violating the law.

CASE PROBLEMS

1. (a) Yes. The proposed project involves a major federal action. The action involves a potentially significant impact on the environment and the Forest Service indirectly has control over the project. (b) Yes, an EIS must be prepared to determine the environmental impact of the proposed ski resort. (c) The EIS must, among other things, evaluate the potential impact on the forest, water, and wildlife. It must also consider alternatives to the project.

2. (a) The Endangered Species Act applies in this case. (b) Among other things, Tony must assure that his project does not harm, wound, or kill any of the protected black-footed ferrets, or harm any significant habitats that may in turn harm or kill members of the species.

CHAPTER 43 - LABOR AND FAIR EMPLOYMENT PRACTICES

MATCHING EXERCISE

1.	f	4.	g	7.	h
2.	i	5.	e	8.	c
3.	d	6.	a	9.	b

COMPLETION EXERCISE

1. Picketing
2. collective bargaining
3. race; national origin; religion; color; sex (gender)
4. Occupational Safety and Health Act
5. Americans with Disabilities Act (of 1990)

TRUE-FALSE EXERCISE

1. T		2. T		3. F		4. T		5. T	
6. F		7. F		8. F		9. T		10. T	

MULTIPLE CHOICE QUESTIONS

1. b		2. a		3. a		4. c	

SHORT ANSWER QUESTIONS

1. Yes. The fact that Dr. Payne's patients prefer a female receptionist does not justify discriminating against Bill on the basis of his gender.
2. No. The top secret security clearance is a BFOQ and, therefore, Julio may be denied employment even if this requirement may have a disparate impact on some ethnic minorities.
3. Yes. The requirement that firefighters be able to lift the weight in question constitutes a disparate impact violation of Title VII. Further, it is not a BFOQ because it is not necessary for employees to carry out the normal, essential functions of their job.
4. No. Religious educational institutions may make religion a BFOQ.

CASE PROBLEMS

1. Yes. Joe's actions constitute sexual harassment, a violation of Title VII. His conduct may constitute an "abusive work environment," although the further findings would be needed to fully establish this violation. However, his proposal for protecting her job is clearly a "quid pro quo" violation. The school would be liable for his conduct since he is, in effect, a supervisor in the school's employ.
2. (a) Jasper's refusal to hire Kim because of her accent would violate Title VII - it is discrimination based on her national origin. (b) The refusal to hire Kim because she is 50 is a clear violation of the Age Discrimination in Employment Act. (c) The refusal based on Kim's hearing difficulty violates the Americans with Disabilities Act. Jasper has a duty to reasonably accommodate this disability.

CHAPTER 44 - REAL PROPERTY AND JOINT OWNERSHIP

MATCHING EXERCISE

1. d	5. f	9. l
2. g	6. a	10. j
3. h	7. k	11. e
4. i	8. c	12. b

COMPLETION EXERCISE

1. Real property
2. warranty of habitability
3. warranty deed
4. adverse possession
5. Foreclosure; default

TRUE-FALSE EXERCISE

1. T	2. T	3. T	4. F	5. F
6. T	7. F	8. F	9. T	10. F

MULTIPLE CHOICE QUESTIONS

1. a   2. b   3. c   4. d

SHORT ANSWER QUESTIONS

1. Yes. A landlord has a duty to disclose latent defects.
2. Yes. This is an easement by implication.
3. No. Murray's lease for a fixed term required him to move out after three years; by staying, he became a tenant at sufferance.
4. No. A quit-claim deed only transfers what the grantor owned.

CASE PROBLEMS

1. (a) This was an express easement. (b) No, Karen is not properly using the easement. This is an excessive use that will extinguish the easement.
2. (a) Tenancy for a fixed term. (b) Yes; it is common for leases to require notice before termination. (c) Steve can use the doctrine of constructive eviction to get out of his lease. (d) No.

CHAPTER 45 - PERSONAL PROPERTY AND BAILMENTS

MATCHING EXERCISE

1.	j	5.	b	9.	g
2.	l	6.	f	10.	a
3.	k	7.	c	11.	i
4.	d	8.	h	12.	e

COMPLETION EXERCISE

1. bona fide purchaser
2. intent; delivery; acceptance
3. gross negligence
4. ordinary negligence
5. slight negligence

TRUE-FALSE EXERCISE

1. F		2. T		3. T		4. T		5. F
6. T		7. F		8. F		9. T		10. T

MULTIPLE CHOICE QUESTIONS

1. a	2. c	3. b	4. a

SHORT ANSWER QUESTIONS

1. No. A promise to make a gift is generally not enforceable.
2. Yes, this was a valid possessory lien.
3. Yes. This was a bailor benefit bailment, making Judy liable for gross negligence. Driving at 100 mph (55 mph above the speed limit) is gross negligence.
4. Jethro's estate. There was no valid gift made to Sally May. Present intent was lacking for a valid inter vivos gift and Jethro did not die as expected, negating any gift causa mortis argument.

CASE PROBLEMS

1. (a) The bailments are mutual benefit bailments. (b) Harry is liable for the stolen mixer because he contractually agreed to take on this risk. (c) Acme is liable to Harry for his broken foot. Acme is liable for injuries resulting from its ordinary negligence.
2. (a) This is a bailee benefit bailment. (b) Luis owed Jake only a limited duty and would be liable only for gross negligence. (c) Luis' failure to inspect the skis is not gross negligence and, therefore, he is not liable to Jake. (d) Jake, on the other hand, owes a duty of great care. Nonetheless, there is no evidence that he was negligent at all. Thus, he is not liable to Luis for damage to the ski.

CHAPTER 46 - WILLS, ESTATES, AND TRUSTS

MATCHING EXERCISE

1.	k	6.	c	11.	d
2.	i	7.	m	12.	f
3.	g	8.	n	13.	e
4.	j	9.	a	14.	l
5.	o	10.	h	15.	b

COMPLETION EXERCISE

1. Heirs
2. cy pres
3. trust deed
4. issue
5. living will

TRUE-FALSE EXERCISE

1. F		2. T		3. F		4. T		5. T
6. F		7. T		8. T		9. T		10. F

MULTIPLE CHOICE QUESTIONS

1. b		2. a		3. d		4. b

SHORT ANSWER QUESTIONS

1. Yes. Paula may claim her elective share (or forced share), which allows a disinherited spouse to elect to take a portion of the estate.
2. Each child will receive one-sixth of the estate.
3. Mike should create a spendthrift trust for Mark.
4. No. Under the Rule Against Perpetuities, trusts cannot last forever.

CASE PROBLEMS

1. (a) Abe's wife will receive the first $50,000 plus one-half of the remaining estate or $75,000. (b) The children will receive the remainder of the estate distributed equally, which would be $25,000 each.
(c) Abe's cousin will receive nothing because Abe's wife and children have first claim to the estate.
2. (a) Most states presume that a trust is irrevocable. (b) A trustee must manage the trust as a reasonably prudent businessperson would manage his or her own business. Mary breached her fiduciary duty to safeguard the principal and make prudent investments. (c) Mary will be personally liable for the loss to the trust.

CHAPTER 47 - INTELLECTUAL PROPERTY, COMPUTERS, AND THE LAW

MATCHING EXERCISE

1. b
2. f
3. h
4. c

5. a
6. e
7. j
8. k

9. g
10. i
11. l
12. d

COMPLETION EXERCISE

1. Berne convention
2. twenty years; fourteen years
3. injunction
4. likelihood of confusion
5. extent that information is known outside of the business; extent that information is known by employees; measurers taken to guard the information's secrecy; value of the information to the owner and competitors; money spent in developing the information and the difficulty that others may have in producing the same information.

TRUE-FALSE EXERCISE

1. F
6. T

2. T
7. F

3. T
8. T

4. F
9. F

5. F
10. F

MULTIPLE CHOICE QUESTIONS

1. c

2. d

3. c

4. d

SHORT ANSWER QUESTIONS

1. Yes.
2. Since Selma copyrighted her program under U.S. law, she is entitled under the Berne Convention to protection from infringement in Germany. Thus, she can sue the German firm for infringement.
3. No. Although the names sound the same or substantially similar, there is little likelihood that consumers will be confused regarding who is furnishing the cruise packages.
4. Jesse could not copyright his original, unwritten tale - at that point it was, in essence, merely an idea. Once Jesse transcribed the tale, then he could copyright it.

CASE PROBLEMS

1. (a) Yes. This list is an original, creative work that is entitled to protection. (b) Jackson could protect it by copyrighting it or it could rely upon common law protection for it as a trade secret. The best way is the latter, because then this information will not be publicly disclosed and there is no limit on how long it may be protected. (c) Injunction, damages, destruction of the infringing material.
2. (a) Initially, Hillary was not entitled to trademark protection because the name was merely descriptive. (b) By the 1990s, the name had acquired a secondary meaning and was entitled to protection. (c) The best way to protect her trademark would be to register it with the federal government.

EXERCISES TO ACCOMPANY THE QUICKEN BUSINESS LAW PARTNERS PROGRAM CD-ROM

Welcome to the application portion of business law and the legal environment of business! It is often painless to sit and memorize laws and elements of crimes and then repeat them back to your instructor through a test. But real thinking is required when you must understand when you have rights as a debtor or what to do when you can't get the other side to a contract to make good on a promise. Do you have the right to request a credit report? How would you do it? What if you wanted to file a suit to collect your damages? What language would you use and what would the form for a complaint look like?

With the help of Quicken software, you can now work through the following exercises to understand how law and rights look when you put them into action. You will gain the first-hand experience of drafting a letter of complaint to a breaching contract party. You can learn how to make requests for information from the federal government. You will even learn how to exercise your right under federal law to obtain a copy of your own credit report.

In the following scenarios you might be able to find help in solving a dispute with your landlord. You could discover a way to have your business handled for you if you must be out of town. With these exercises you bring together your own questions, your knowledge of the law, and your skills for critical thinking in solving individual problems.

Most of the exercises include answers so that you can check your application skills. Some exercises are more comprehensive and may be assigned by your instructor. Just remember to read the assignment carefully, review the Quicken forms, and apply your knowledge to the circumstances to find a solution. You will gain valuable knowledge and skills in resolving the inevitable legal issues that cross every business person's and consumer's desk.

EXERCISES

EXERCISE 1
POWERS OF ATTORNEY

Text References: Chapters 31, 32, and 33

Review the materials on agency in Chapters 31, 32, and 33. Then, with the Quicken Business Law Partners Program, review documents for the power of attorney.

1. What authority does a general power of attorney give?

2. According to the agreement, is the person with this authority entitled to compensation?

3. Can a person serve under the power of attorney without compensation?

4. Can a person who has requested another to serve under power of attorney revoke this power of attorney?

Refer to the special power of attorney in the Quicken business law partners documents.

5. What is the distinction between this document and the general power of attorney? Is the agent entitled to compensation?

EXERCISE 2
BREACH OF CONTRACT AND WITHHOLDING PAYMENT
(NOTE: Exercises 2 through 8 are based on the following fact pattern)

Text References: Chapters 5, 15 and 25

David and Joan Woods contracted with Tolleson Carpet for the purchase and installation of carpet in their home for a total price of $4281. While the installers were moving the furniture in the Woods' family room in order to remove the old carpet and install the new, one worker swung a roll of carpet around in such a way that it hit the screen of the Woods' wide-screen television. Joan Woods witnessed the screen being scraped by the roll of carpet but could not get close enough to inspect the television screen when it happened.

After the carpet installation was complete, both David and Joan noticed a scratch on their wide-screen television. Joan told David, "That's just where that worker scraped the roll of carpet when they were moving the furniture." The Woods' television was two months old at he time of the carpet installation. The Woods had a repair service examine the screen. Replacement cost for the screen, including labor, was estimated at $671.

Joan called Tolleson's manager, Frank Fairbanks and explained the problem with the television screen. "Look," Fairbanks responded, "you can't prove we did that. That's not our problem. Besides, read your contract, it says right in there that we have no liability for any damages to your house or furniture that occurs while we're installing your carpet." Joan hung up and told David, "I guess I could put it all in writing and maybe the company could respond.

Refer to the BBB/Attorney General Letter of Complaint provided in the Quicken Business Law Partner documents.

1. What details will Joan and David need to fill in to draft the complaint?

2. What documents do you think they should attach to their complaint?

3. Can you think of means of alternative dispute resolution that might help Joan and David and Tolleson to resolve their differences?

EXERCISE 3
STOP PAYMENT ORDERS

Text Reference: Chapter 25

David has just given Tolleson a check for $2,281, the balance due on the carpet contract. "I wonder if there is anything I can do to get my money back until this issue with the television screen is resolved," wondered David.

Review Chapter 25 in the text and determine whether David can take any action with the check to Tolleson. Refer to the Quicken Business Law Partner credit documents, the stop payment on a check form, and answer the following questions:

1. Can the Woods rightfully stop payment on the check to Tolleson?

2. Must the drawer give a reason for the stop payment?

3. According to the stop payment form, who will pay the costs and fees for stopping payment?

4. Will the bank be held liable if the stop payment order should not have been requested by the drawer?

5. Who will be held liable if the stop payment order was wrongfully issued?

EXERCISE 4
NOTICE OF DISHONOR

Text Reference: Chapter 25

After Tolleson deposited the Woods' check, it is notified that the check has been dishonored by the Woods' bank. Review Chapter 25 and determine Tolleson's rights. Answer the following questions:

1. Is Tolleson required to notify the Woods of the bank's dishonor of the check?

Turn to the Quicken Bad Check Notice under the credit document section, and answer the following questions:

2. According to the notice, what will happen if payment is not made immediately?

3. Is interest accruing?

EXERCISE 5
COLLECTION ACTIVITIES

Text Reference: Chapter 41

With no response from the Woods, Tolleson has referred the matter to a collection agency. The collection agency has contacted the Woods and demanded payment. The letter from the collection agency includes the following paragraph:

Tolleson Carpet has made repeated demands for payment on your carpet contract. Please pay the amount due ($2281.00) today so that your credit rating is not affected by your non-payment of this binding obligation.

If payment is not received within 10 days, we shall proceed with all rights and remedies afforded Tolleson by law.

Review Chapter 29 and the Quicken Business Law Partners Credit Documents and answer the following questions:

1. Has the collection agency violated any laws with it demand letter?

2. What rights could Woods assert?

EXERCISE 6
CREDIT REPORTS

Text Reference: Chapter 41

The Woods are concerned that their problems with Tolleson may have resulted in a blemish on their previously flawless credit report. Review Chapter 29 and the Quicken Business Law Partner Credit Documents. Refer to the request for a credit report and answer the following:

1. What must be included with a request for a credit report in order for the report to be furnished?

2. Why would the inclusion of a social security number be important?

EXERCISE 7
SMALL CLAIMS COURT

Text References: Chapters 1 and 15

Suppose that the Woods still have not paid the remaining balance for the carpet and Tolleson wishes to proceed with a suit to recover the amount due from the Woods. Refer to the Quicken Business Law Partners Credit Documents and the small claims worksheet and answer the following questions:

1. Go to the list of state small claims limits in the document. Does the claim against the Woods qualify for small claims court in your state? Suppose that the Woods have paid all but the $671 for the television screen, would the Tolleson suit then qualify for small claims court in your state?

2. What additional information do you need to complete the checklist?

3. Who is the plaintiff in this suit? Who is the defendant?

4. Which state has the highest small claims court maximum?

EXERCISE 8
FILING A LAW SUIT

Textbook Reference: Chapters 1 and 15

Suppose that the Woods make the $2,281 payment to Tolleson and then file suit against Tolleson to collect the $671 for the repair of their television screen. Refer to the Quicken Business Law Partners Credit Document and the portion on Defending A Lawsuit - Business and answer the following questions:

1. In this situation, who is the plaintiff? Who is the defendant?

2. What additional information do you need to complete the form?

EXERCISE 9
CREDIT APPLICATIONS AND DENIAL

Text References: Chapter 41

Assume you have been denied a loan for the purchase of a car. Refer to Chapter 41 and the Challenge to a Denial of Credit in the Quicken Business Law Partners program.

1. What requests for information are made in the letter?

EXERCISE 10
LANDLORD-TENANT RELATIONS

Textbook Reference: Chapter 44

Assume that the heating in your apartment does not work, and it is very cold outside. Refer to Chapter 44 and the Complaint to the Landlord in Quicken Business Law Partners.

1.   What two things does the note to the landlord accomplish?

2.   What rights do tenants have generally regarding the conditions of their leased premises?

EXERCISE 11
COMMERCIAL REAL ESTATE LEASES

Textbook References: Chapter 44

Refer to Chapter 44 and the Real Estate Lease-Commercial in the Quicken Business Law Partners and answer the following questions:

1.   When is the rent due under the lease?

2.   Who is responsible for insurance on the property?

3.   How does either party give notice to the other according to the lease?

4.   What happens if a portion of the lease agreement is unenforceable?

EXERCISE 12
RESIDENTIAL LEASES

Textbook Reference: Chapter 44

Refer to the Residential Lease in the Quicken Business Law Partner and Chapter 44. Answer the following questions:

1.   What provisions do you see in the residential lease that are not found in the commercial lease?

2.   What is the habitability clause and what does it do for the tenant?

EXERCISE 13
RENTAL APPLICATION

Textbook Reference: Chapter 44

Refer to the Rental Application in the Quicken Business Law Partner and answer the following questions:

1. What happens if a tenant submits an application and is approved by the landlord and then fails to rent the premises?

2. Will the landlord be permitted to do a credit check?

3. List the grounds on which the landlord can't discriminate.

4. What rights does the tenant have if rejected by the landlord?

EXERCISE 14
RENTAL PROPERTY INSPECTION

Textbook Reference: Chapter 44

Refer to the Renter's's Inspection Worksheet in the Quicken Business Law Partners and answer the following questions:

1. What are the general standards for the condition of the premises that the parties confirm through sign-off on this inspection sheet?

2. What effect does this checklist have on termination rights of the tenant?

3. What defects does the tenant assume the risk for?

4. What does the tenant agree to do with respect to the smoke detector?

EXERCISE 15
BILL OF SALE

Textbook References: Chapters 17 and 18

Refer to the Bill of Sale in the Quicken Business Law Partner and answer the following questions:

1. What does property sold "AS IS" mean?

2. What does a bill of sale do?

3. Is a bill of sale different from a document of title?

EXERCISE 16
BILL OF SALE FOR MOTOR VEHICLES

Textbook References: Chapters 17, 18 and 41

Refer to the Bill of Sale-Motor Vehicles in the Quicken Business Law Partner and answer the following questions:

1. What differences are there between the bill of sale and the bill of sale for motor vehicles?

2. What happens if the seller makes a false statement regarding the vehicle's mileage?

3. What promise does the seller make in the bill of sale about the vehicle's odometer?

EXERCISE 17
EQUIPMENT LEASE

Textbook Reference: Chapter 45

Refer to the Equipment Lease in the Quicken Business Law Partner and answer the following question:

1. When is the rent due?

2. Who has the risk of loss or is responsible for damage to the equipment?

3. Can the lessee make alterations to the equipment?

4. Who pays for repairs to the equipment?

5. Can the lessor see the equipment during the term of the lease?

6. What options are given to the lessee when the lease ends?

7. Does the lessor make any warranties about the property?

8. Is the lessor's disclaimer valid?

9. Can the lessee assign the lease?

10. How will disputes be settled?

EXERCISE 18
A LICENSE AGREEMENT

Textbook Reference: Chapter 47

Refer to Chapter 47 and the License Agreement in Quicken Business Law Partner and answer the following questions:

1. What types of arrangements would this agreement cover?

2. What is the compensation under the agreement?

EXERCISE 19
PROMISSORY NOTES

Text Reference: Chapter 21

Refer to the Promissory Note in the Quicken Business Law Partner documents and answer the following questions:

1. How are payments applied?

2. In what currency is the note payable?

EXERCISE 20
ARTICLES OF INCORPORATION

Text References: Chapters 34, 35, and 36

Review the Articles of Incorporation in the Quicken Business Law Partner and answer the following questions:

1. List the information needed for incorporation using this document.

2. Is this same information required under the Model Business Corporation Act?

3. Will the corporation provide indemnity for its officers and directors?

4. What does indemnity for officers and directors mean?

EXERCISE 21
CORPORATE BYLAWS

Text References: Chapters 34, 35, and 36

Review the Corporate Bylaws in the Quicken Business Law Partner and answer the following:

1. How often will meetings of shareholders be held?

2. Who can call a special meeting?

3. When must notice of a meeting be given?

4. What constitutes a quorum for meetings?

5. Can a quorum be met with proxy representation?

6. Can a director be removed without cause?

7. List the offices provided by the bylaws.

8. Who elects the officers?

9. How are the bylaws amended?

10. Can you own shares in the corporation without actually having stock certificates?

EXERCISE 22
CORPORATE PROXY

Text Reference: Chapter 35

Review the corporate proxy in the Quicken Business Law Partner and answer the following:

1. Does this proxy revoke prior proxies?

2. Review Chapter 35 and explain why a proxy might be necessary.

3. Is there a provision for designating votes?

EXERCISE 23
EMPLOYMENT/AGENCY CONFIDENTIALITY AGREEMENT

Text References: Chapters 31 and 47

Review the Confidentiality Agreement in the Quicken Business Law Partner and answer the following:

1. What is the definition of confidential information given?

2. What kinds of information would you list as being confidential? Refer to Chapters 31 and 47.

EXERCISE 24
EMPLOYMENT/AGENCY--CONSULTING AGREEMENT

Textbook References: Chapters 31, 32, 33, and 43

Review the Consulting Agreement in the Quicken Business Law Partner and answer the following:

1. Will the consultant be an independent contractor or an employee?

2. Why is this distinction important? What differences exist between hiring an independent contractor and hiring an employee? Refer to Chapters 31, 32, 33, and 43.

EXERCISE 25
EMPLOYMENT/AGENCY--EMPLOYMENT AGREEMENT

Text References: Chapters 31 and 43

Review the Employment Agreement in the Quicken Business Law Partner and answer the following:

1. How long will the employment last?

2. Is an employment of this length legal?

3. How are the parties to the agreement to give notice?

EXERCISE 26
EMPLOYMENT/AGENCY--LETTER OF ACCEPTANCE

Text References: Chapters 10 and 31

        Review the Quicken Business Law Partner Letter of Acceptance under Employment and answer the following:

1. Prior to the time of the use of this document, what interaction had the parties had regarding employment?

2. How would a letter like this help the employee? Be sure to review Chapters 10 and 31.

EXERCISE 27
NON-COMPETE AGREEMENT--ANTITRUST AND EMPLOYMENT

Text References: Chapters 31, 39, and 47

        Review the Non-Compete Agreement in the Quicken Business Law Partner and answer the following:

1. What types of activities does the agreement prohibit?

2. What remedies are given for violation of the agreement?

3. Discuss why and when this type of an agreement would be necessary.

EXERCISE 28
CONSIGNMENT AGREEMENT—SALES, UNIFORM COMMERCIAL CODE (UCC) ARTICLE 2

Text References: Chapters 17 and 45

Review the Consignment Agreement in the General Business document section of Quicken Business Law Partner and answer the following:

1. What is a consignment arrangement?

2. Who is the consignee?

3. Who is the consignor?

4. How will the consignee be compensated for the sale of the goods?

5. Who has title to the goods during the consignment?

6. Who has the risk of loss during the consignment?

7. What is the difference between a bailment and a consignment?

EXERCISE 29
COPYRIGHT APPLICATION--INTELLECTUAL PROPERTY

Text References: Chapter 47

Review the Copyright Application in the Quicken Business Law Partner and answer the following:

1. List the types of works that can be copyrighted.

2. If a book is written by an employee during the course of employment, who has the right to the copyright?

EXERCISE 30
GENERAL CONTRACT - PRODUCTS AND SALES, UCC ARTICLE 2

Text References: Chapters 16-19

Review the General Contract-Products in the General Business documents of Quicken Business Law Partner and answer the following:

1. What happens in the buyer fails to make a payment?

2. What is the time given for delivery?

3. Who pays the costs if improper packaging produces damages to the goods?

4. Who pays the taxes in this transaction?

5. What are the inspection rights under the contract?

6. Are these inspection rights different from those given under the UCC?

7. What is force *majeure*?

8. Give examples listed as force *majeure*.

9. What do the parties agree to do in the event there is a dispute between them?

10. What is the pledge of confidentiality?

11. Is an assignment of this contract permitted?

EXERCISE 31
TRADEMARK VIOLATION--INTELLECTUAL PROPERTY/TRADEMARKS

Text References: Chapter 47

Review the Trademark Violation letter in the Quicken Business Law Partner and answer the following:

1.   What is the demand made in the letter?

2.   If the recipient of the letter complies with its demands, what will happen?

EXERCISE 32
GOVERNMENT RECORDS

Text References: Chapters 4 and 39

Review the Request for FBI and CIA Records in the Government section of the Quicken Business Law Partner and answer the following:

1.   If you used this letter request, what would you obtain?

2.   If the agency indicates it will withhold the records you have requested, what information must the agency give?

EXERCISE 33
EMPLOYMENT LAW--REGULATION OF EMPLOYMENT

Text Reference: Chapter 43

Review the Social Security-Earnings Benefit Request in the Quicken Business Law Partner and answer the following:

1.   What information is this request designed to obtain for you?
2.   What are the penalties for making a request to obtain this information on someone other than yourself without their permission?

ANSWERS

EXERCISE 1

1. A general power of attorney gives Jake full authority to run Nancy's business affairs. He can open, maintain and close bank accounts and securities accounts. He is given full access to safe deposit boxes. He can sell, exchange, buy, invest, and reinvest assets. He can purchase insurance and collect debts. He can enter into binding contracts on Nancy's behalf. He can exercise her stock options, employ help and sell, mortgage and lease property. If Nancy had any kind of business operations, he could run them with full authority. He can prepare, sign and file government documents on Nancy's behalf.

    This general power of attorney is an enormously broad one that gives Jake full and complete authority over any of Nancy's property and legal issues. In this case, a general power of authority may be more than Nancy wishes to give to Jake.

2. Yes, Jake is entitled to reasonable compensation plus reimbursement for expenses.

3. Yes, Jake could serve as a gratuitous agent but this form entitles him to compensation. Because jake is helping Nancy as a friend, they will need to change this portion of the form. Remember, forms are not customized for individual needs and there are legal issues and implications for each clause.

4. Yes, Nancy can revoke the power of attorney at any time. Nancy may want to put a time limitation on the power of attorney. Nancy could also put a transaction limitation on it in that she could direct the transactions for which Jake has authority.

5. The special power of attorney in the Quicken Business Law Partner requires that the specific matters for which there is authority be spelled out; the power of attorney is limited in scope in that transactional limitations are placed on the delegated authority.

6. Yes, Jake is again entitled to compensation. Jake can serve as a gratuitous agent but the clause on compensation would need to be deleted from the document.

EXERCISE 2

1. Joan and David will need to tell their story in their letter as it is reflected in the facts. They will need to spell out their issues about the carpet layers and the television screen.

2. Copies of the documents Joan and David should attach are: the carpet contract; the purchase contract for the television (to show it was a relatively new purchase at the time of the carpet problem); and the estimate for the repair. Joan and David could attach affidavits from people who had seen the screen before the installation (including themselves) that attest to the fact the screen was not scratched prior to the installers' conduct.

3. Joan and David and the Tollesons could sit with a mediator and try and work out a fair solution such as perhaps at least splitting the cost of the screen repair. They could also try arbitration in which the arbitrator could propose a solution.

EXERCISE 3

1. Yes, the Woods can stop payment on the check. Stopping payment on the check is not a final determination for the contract rights that might exist between the parties. Stopping payment on the check is simply a means for the Woods to gain leverage in terms of resolution of the dispute. By stopping payment, they are not in the position of having to seek money from Tolleson. Tolleson will be forced to deal with the issues the Woods have raised in order to obtain payment.

2. Yes, the drawer must give a reason for the stop payment order. In this case, the Woods would simply explain that they are stopping payment because of a contract dispute.
3. The drawer bears the cost of stopping payment on a check.
4. No, the bank is not liable because the bank has no way of knowing whether the contract complaint is legitimate. The bank puts a clause in its stop payment forms to protect it — the bank stops the payment at the customer's direction but does not agree to assume the liability if the bank is wrong.
5. The drawer has full liability to the payee for a wrongful stop payment order. This liability rests where it should because the stop payment order is the result of a dispute between the drawer and the payee. To the extent the drawer is wrong, the parties' contractual liability will take over and determine damages.

EXERCISE 4

1. Yes, Tolleson is required to notify the Woods because the primary party, or at least the first party for presentment of the instrument, the bank, has refused to pay. In order to attach liability of the secondary party (the drawer), the payee must give notification of dishonor.
2. If payment of the amount of the check is not made immediately, Tolleson will make an additional charge and there will be no further credit extended to the Woods.
3. Yes, interest does accrue during the entire time that Tolleson attempts to collect the amount due from the Woods.

EXERCISE 5

1. The collection agency has not violated any of the provisions of the Fair Debt Collections Practices Act assuming that the notice is given privately. The notice contains a classic collector's hedge in that it does not threaten a suit directly in case the creditor or the agency decides not to proceed with such action. The notice is broad enough that any additional action could be taken, but not so specific that the agency would be making a threat it would not carry out which is a violation of the FDCPA.
2. The Woods could respond that they wish to have no further contact from the collection agency and the contact would have to stop. If the Woods do assert their rights to no further contact, the issue about the scratched screen will come to a head because it is intertwined with the issue of payment and any legal action by Tolleson to collect the amount due will enable the Woods to respond with their claim for damages to their TV.

EXERCISE 6

1. Personal ID (copy), the appropriate fee, social security number and addresses for the last five years.
2. The social security number is included because mix-ups between individuals with the same names can be avoided when the SS# is used. Also, phony requests are at least reduced because the SS# is more difficult to come by than a name and address. The additional information on addresses is also requested to match persons with reports correctly. Because of numerous lawsuits over the past few years of mix-ups in identification, credit reporting agencies take additional precautions with respect to data and the released of credit reports.

EXERCISE 7

1. Simply review the chart provided in the Quicken small claims worksheet and match it to your state. In most states the $671 qualifies for small claims court.
2. To complete the small claims checklist, you will need an address for Tolleson as well as its business status, i.e., is it a corporation or sole proprietorship, etc.

3. Tolleson is the plaintiff and the Woods would be the defendants.
4. Florida and Delaware, with a maximum of $15,000 have the highest small claims court jurisdiction.

EXERCISE 8
1. In this factual situation, the Woods will be the plaintiffs and Tolleson will be the defendant.
2. Tolleson will need to check with its employees or contractors who installed the carpeting to see what happened. Tolleson will need to find and provide any documentation it has with respect to the incident.

EXERCISE 9
1. The information requested in the Quicken form is whether a consumer reporting agency was used, and, if so, which one. The letter also requests a description of the nature of the investigation conducted. An important tip in checking a credit denial is to be certain that the creditor had the information on you--did they have the right credit report and the right person?

EXERCISE 10
1. The letter serves two very important purposes: the landlord is put on notice of a heating problem in the apartment: and the landlord is given a time within which to solve the problem.
2. Most states gives residential tenants a warranty of habitability which means that the premises are fit and habitable at the time of the lease. The Uniform Residential Landlord Tenant Act (URLTA) also provides tenants with rights in the event the basic essentials of habitation (such as heat, water, and, in some circumstances, air conditioning) cease to work. Those rights include the right to make a demand for repair (which is what this Quicken letter is designed to do), and then the right to self-help or making the repairs themselves and then billing the landlord or deducting that amount from their rent. However, all these rights begin with the notice to the landlord of the problem.

EXERCISE 11
1. The rent is due on the first day of each month.
2. Both the landlord and the tenant are responsible for carrying insurance on their respective properties. Tenants would have to carry their own insurance, for example, on their furniture. Landlords would carry an owner's policy on the property.
3. Notice must be given in writing.
4. If one portion of the lease is unenforceable, it is to be struck from the lease so that the remainder can be enforced.

EXERCISE 12
1. Some of the provisions in the residential lease not found in the commercial lease include the condition of the dwelling unit, absences for extended periods of the tenant from the property, and the rights and obligations with respect to the keys.
2. The habitability clause simple puts into the official language of the lease the rights most tenants have in most states: that the premises are in habitable condition at the commencement of the lease.

EXERCISE 13
1. The tenant whose application is approved by the landlord and who fails to enter into a lease agreement will lose his or her application fee. The reason for such damages is that the landlord does expend time and effort (and in some cases fees for the credit report) in processing an application.
2. Yes, the application form authorizes the landlord to do a credit check.

3. The grounds on which a landlord can't discriminate are race, religion, national origin, age, and disability.
4. If the applicant makes a written request for the reason for rejection of the application, the landlord has 60 days within which to respond to the applicant.

EXERCISE 14

1. The general standards that the checklist is intended to confirm are that the premises are in good, clean, sanitary order and in good condition and repair.
2. The tenant, by signing off on the inspection sheet, agrees to return the premises to the landlord in the same condition as when the inspection occurs.
3. The tenant assumes the risk for any defects in the rental property that he knew of or should have known of through inspection of the property.
4. The tenant agrees to test the smoke detector at least every other week and to be certain that it has an alkaline battery that is in working order.

EXERCISE 15

1. When the phrase "AS IS" appears in a contract it means that both the implied warranty of merchantability as well as the implied warranty of fitness for a particular purpose are disclaimed. The goods are sold with all their defects and the buyer assumes the risk of those defects. Subsequently discovered defects cannot be a basis for suit or liability against the seller.
2. A bill of sale is evidence of a transfer of title.
3. A bill of sale is evidence of a transfer of title. It is not, however, a document of title.

EXERCISE 16

1. A bill of sale for motor vehicles has more details including a description of the car (make, model, etc) as well as the mileage.
2. A false statement about the mileage on the car is a federal offense and can result in fines and/or imprisonment.
3. The seller promises that the odometer is in good working order and that it has not been tampered with so as to affect the recorded mileage on the car.

EXERCISE 17

1. The rent on the leased equipment is due when the equipment is returned.
2. The lessee agrees to assume the risk of loss and responsibility for damage to the property.
3. No, the lessee is not permitted to make alterations to the equipment.
4. The lessee is responsible for repairs to the equipment.
5. Yes, the lessor retains the rights of inspection of the equipment during the term of the lease.
6. When the lease agreement ends, the lessee is given the option of renewing the lease agreement or purchase the leased property according to stated financial terms
7. No, the lessor specifically disclaims any warranties about the leased equipment.
8. This disclaimer may create problems since it is, in essence, an exculpatory clause that permits the lessor to lease defective property that could injure the lessee and others. It is against public policy to hold oneself immune from liability for one's own negligence. While many lease agreements contain such provisions, they can be successfully challenged on the grounds of unconscionability.

9. No, assignment by the lessee is prohibited.
10. The lease agreement provides that any disputes between the parties will be settled through binding arbitration.

EXERCISE 18

1. This license agreement would cover any type of use of intellectual property such as the right to use a song or software.
2. The compensation to the owner of the intellectual property will be payment of royalties which is a percentage of total sales as when a songwriter is given a percentage of record sales in exchange for the artist's right to record the song.

EXERCISE 19

1. Payments under the note are applied first to accrued interest and then to principal.
2. The note is payable in U.S. currency.

EXERCISE 20

1. Under these sample incorporation documents, the information needed is the total # of shares, the registered agent for the corporation, the purpose of the corporation and the directors.
2. No, the MBCA does not require all the information noted in these articles of incorporation. These articles require more information which is permitted and possibly desirable from the standpoint of the parties' rights.
3. Yes, the corporation's officers and directors will enjoy the protection of indemnity from the corporation.
4. Indemnity means that the officers and directors can be reimbursed for the expenses they incur in defending their conduct with respect to the corporation. There can be some exceptions such as when the directors and officers engage in fraud.

EXERCISE 21

1. The shareholders will hold meetings at least once each calendar year.
2. A special meeting of shareholders can be called by the president, the board or a majority of the outstanding shareholders of voting shares.
3. Notice of a meeting must be given no later than 10 days prior to the meeting. The time can be measured from the time the notice is mailed and not when it actually is received by the shareholders.
4. A quorum is the majority of the outstanding voting shares.
5. Yes, proxies can be used to make up a quorum.
6. Yes, a director can be removed with or without cause.
7. The offices provided in these bylaws include the president, vice president, secretary and treasurer. More than one office can be held by a single person.
8. The officers are elected by the directors.
9. The bylaws can be amended by the directors or the shareholders by a majority of a quorum of voting shares.
10. Yes, you can own shares in the corporation without having to have certificates as evidence.

EXERCISE 22

1. Yes, all prior proxies are revoked.
2. Proxies are needed because the majority of shareholders are unable to attend the annual meeting yet they want to have a voice in corporate governance. They designate a representative as well as their voting choices.
3. Yes, a segment of the proxy allows the shareholder to dictate how votes should be made.

EXERCISE 23

1. The definition of confidential information given in the document is proprietary information not generally known to the public.
2. Information about customers including customer lists, new products, strategies, supply chain management techniques, planned ad campaigns, etc.

EXERCISE 24

1. The consultant will be an independent contractor.
2. This distinction is important because of wage tax issues and liability issues and worker's compensation coverage issues. For an employee, an employer must pay wage taxes, if fully liable for acts within the scope of employment and subjects the employee to worker's compensation system rules. An independent contractor pays his or her own wage taxes and is not covered by worker's compensation. The employer would also not be liable for the torts of an independent contractor.

EXERCISE 25

1. It is an "at will" agreement — it can be terminated at any time.
2. Yes, it is legal. There are some exceptions such as terminating a whistle-blower that would prevent termination because such a termination would be retaliatory in nature.
3. Notices must be given in writing.

EXERCISE 26

1. From the document, we can conclude that the parties had a conversation about a contract for employment.
2. A letter such as this would help the employee prove that some type of a contract exists. It would be contemporaneous evidence of discussions of employment. It also serves as a formal acceptance of an oral offer. Further, the failure of the employer to correct any misunderstandings about the conversation and offer of employment would allow the employee to rely on the oral promise and begin the process of terminating another job or moving.

EXERCISE 27

1. The types of activities prohibited under the agreement are: competing directly' competing indirectly; soliciting customers for business; inducing employees to leave; revealing confidential business information.
2. Monetary remedies as well as injunctive relief are afforded under the agreement.
3. This type of an agreement is necessary to prevent employees from obtaining proprietary information and then using it to start their own businesses or taking it to other employers who are competitors.

EXERCISE 28

1. A consignment is an arrangement whereby the property owner transfers property to a consignee for purposes of selling that property in exchange for a fee or a commission. For example, a consignment furniture store is filled with the used furniture of others that can be sold for a price below new and in exchange for a percentage to the consignee.
2. The consignee is the party who has possession of the property and agrees to sell it for a fee.
3. The consignor is the owner of the property who transfers possession.
4. The consignee is entitled to a fee or percentage for the sale of the goods.
5. The consignee.
6. The consignee.
7. A bailment is a temporary transfer of possession. A consignment is the transfer of possession for purposes of sale with the authority to transfer title to another. Until the terms of the consignment arrangement end, the title is held by the consignee. A bailee does not hold title in any type of bailment.

EXERCISE 29

1. The types of works that can be copyrighted are music, books, movies, television shows, magazines, newspapers, periodicals and software.
2. The employer has the right to the copyright because the employer provided the resources for its development.

EXERCISE 30

1. The failure of the buyer to make a payment is considered a material breach.
2. "Time is of the essence" is the time given for delivery — ASAP would be the standard.
3. The seller absorbs the loss if the goods are damaged due to improper packaging.
4. The buyer is to pay the taxes.
5. The inspection rights include the right to open, test and view.
6. The inspection rights afforded under the contract are about the same as those given under Article 2 with the exception that the buyer must give written notice of rejection and the reasons for such rejection.
7. A force majeure is an event that interferes with the performance of the contract that is beyond the parties' control and was not anticipated by them.
8. Examples of force majeure in the contract include: acts of God; fire; explosion; vandalism; storms; riots; military action; wars, insurrections.
9. If the matter has not been resolved in five days, they agree to go to binding arbitration.
10. A pledge of confidentiality is an agreement not to disclose the terms of the agreement or any proprietary information regarding the product.
11. No, assignment of the contract is not permitted.

EXERCISE 31

1. The demand is that the use of the trademark stop.
2. If the recipient complies, the owner of the trademark will take no further action and will not seek any damages.

EXERCISE 32

1. All information about you held by the FBI and CIA with certain exceptions such as information related to any ongoing investigations.
2. The agency must disclose why the information is being withheld.

EXERCISE 33
1. The requestor must provide what documents he/she is looking for and for what period.
2. That the request be forwarded to the proper agency.

EXERCISE 34
1. Your history of wages and applicable social security withholding as well as what benefits you could expect under SS programs.
2. Making a request for another without their permission is a violation of federal law that carries fines and/or imprisonment.

Internet Resources for Business Law Students

Each chapter highlights the most helpful and relevant resources available on the Web. Because Internet addresses change, often frequently and usually unexpectedly, all of the resources listed here are repeated and updated on the Business Law Web Site (http://davidson.westbuslaw.com/).

Chapter 1, Introduction to Law	
'Lectric Law Library's™ Lawcopedia™ The Lawcopedia's 'Lectric Legal Lexicon defines legal words, terms and phrases.	http://www.lectlaw.com/ref.html
Electronic Legal Source Electronic Legal Source, maintained by CyberNation, provides a searchable legal dictionary, legal forms, news, and information.	http://www.e-legal.com/
International Constitutional Law (ICL) ICL provides hypertext constitutions and legal information for over sixty countries.	http://www.uni-wuerzburg.de/law/index.html
The Multilaterals Project The Multilaterals Project, maintained by Tufts University, includes a variety of multilateral treaties, including the GATT and NAFTA.	http://www.tufts.edu/fletcher/multilaterals.html
The Legal Information Institute (LII) LII, maintained by the Cornell Law School, provides opinions of the Supreme Court and the New York Court of Appeals, a the full U.S. Code and Uniform Commercial Code, treaties, and statutes.	http://www.law.cornell.edu/
Thomas: Legislative Information on the Internet The U.S. Congress, via Thomas (for Thomas Jefferson) provides news and information on Congress, bills before Congress (text, summary, and status), the Congressional Record, and committee information.	http://thomas.loc.gov/
FedLaw FedLaw, maintained by the U.S. General Services Administration (GSA), includes federal laws and regulations.	http://www.legal.gsa.gov/
Federal Judicial Center The Federal Judicial Center, the federal courts' agency for research and education, provides publications on a variety of judicial issues.	http://www.fjc.gov/
StateLaw StateLaw, maintained by the Washburn School of Law, provides links for state legislative and governmental information--including court cases and statutes--as well as local information.	http://lawlib.wuacc.edu/washlaw/uslaw/statelaw.html
West's Legal Directory West's Legal Directory, updated daily, offers over 800,000 profiles of lawyers and law firms in the United States and Canada, including International offices.	http://www.wld.com/

Chapter 2, Business Ethics	
Depaul University Institute for Business and Professional Ethics The Depaul University Institute for Business and Professional Ethics maintains materials on ethics, including articles, professional papers, an online journal, and book reviews.	http://condor.depaul.edu/ethics/
Ethics Connection Ethics Connection, maintained by the Markkula Center for Applied Ethics at Santa Clara College, provides current and past issues of Issues in Ethics, case problems for ethics, and other ethics materials.	http://www.scu.edu/Ethics/
Centre for Applied Ethics The University of British Columbia's Centre for Applied Ethics provides working papers, research projects, and links for applied ethics sites.	http://www.ethics.ubc.ca/
KPMG Business Ethics KPMG Business Ethics, maintained by KPMG Peat Marwick, LLP, a global accounting and consulting firm, provides ethics information, including a free newsletter and interactive ethics cases.	http://www.us.kpmg.com/ethics/
Students for Responsible Business SRB, a network of business students dedicated to integrating social responsibility into business schools, provides a newsletter, media resources, press releases, and association information.	http://www.srbnet.org
Ethics Update Ethics Updates provides updates on current ethics literature, both popular and professional.	http://www.acusd.edu/ethics/
The Institute for Global Ethics The Institute For Global Ethics, a independent, nonsectarian, and nonpolitical organization, provides general resources on ethics.	http://www.globalethics.org/
Corporate Conduct Quarterly (CCQ) CCQ provides news concerning corporate ethics and compliance, as well as information on conferences, major decisions, and changes in the field.	http://camden-www.rutgers.edu/~ccq/

Chapter 3, International Law	
International Trade Law (ITL) ITL, hosted by the University of Tromso, Norway, provides international trade conventions and documents.	http://itl.irv.uit.no/trade_law/
Legal Information Institute (LII)--International Law LII, maintained by the Cornell Law School, provides links to international agreements and organizations, journals, and other resources.	http://www.law.cornell.edu/topics/torts.html
The Multilaterals Project The Multilaterals Project, maintained by Tufts University, provides texts of multilateral treaties, including GATT and NAFTA.	http://www.tufts.edu/fletcher/multilaterals.html
Pace University School of Law Institute of International Commercial Law (IICL) IICL provides the full text of the United Nations Convention for Contracts on the International Sale of Goods (CISG), its legislative history, cases, and commentaries.	http://www.cisg.law.pace.edu/
Foreign Corrupt Practices Act--15 USC §78dd-2 LII provides a hypertext and searchable version of 15 USC §78dd-2, popularly known as the Foreign Corrupt Practices Act.	http://www.law.cornell.edu/ uscode/15/ 78dd-2.html
Europa (European Union) Europa, maintained by the European Commission, provides official documents, press releases, publications, and statistics on the European Union.	http://europa.eu.int/
World Trade Organization (WTO) The WTO provides economic research and analysis, dispute settlement material, international trade policy, and publications.	http://www.wto.org/
United Nations (UN) The UN provides material on The International Court of Justice, the report of the International Law Commission, materials from the UN Commission on International Trade Law (UNCITRAL), and access to the UN Treaty Database.	http://www.un.org/law/
International Court of Justice (ICJ) The ICJ provides official judgments, advisory opinions, and orders.	http://www.law.cornell.edu/icj/
U.S. Department of State The U.S. Department of State maintains information regarding trade policy and law, diplomatic initiatives, business and travel services, and career information.	http://www.state.gov/

Chapter 4, The American Legal System and Court Jurisdiction	
U.S. Constitution Emory Law School maintains a hypertext and searchable version of the U.S. Constitution.	http://www.law.emory.edu/FEDERAL/usconst.html
U.S. Federal Judiciary The U.S. Federal Judiciary site, maintained by the Administrative Office of the U.S. Courts, provides a clearinghouse for information from and about the Judicial Branch of the U.S. Government.	http://www.uscourts.gov/
U.S. Federal Courts Finder Emory Law School maintains links to recent court decisions from the 13 U.S. Circuit Courts of Appeals and the Supreme Court.	http://www.law.emory.edu/FEDCTS/
StateLaw StateLaw, maintained by the Washburn School of Law, provides links for state and local legislative and governmental information--including court cases and statutes.	http://lawlib.wuacc.edu/washlaw/uslaw/statelaw.html
Local Government Home Page The Local Government Home Page provides information for city, county, and state governments.	http://www.localgov.org/
The Legal Information Institute (LII) Guide to Legal Citation LII, maintained by the Cornell Law School, provides a brief primer on legal citation.	http://www.law.cornell.edu/citation/citation.table.html
Law Journal EXTRA! (LJX!) LJX!, sponsored by the New York Law Publishing Company, provides daily legal news, case law, and legal analysis.	http://www.ljextra.com/
Court TV Law Center Court TV Law Center provides highlights from Court TV's broadcasts, news, and reference information.	http://www.courttv.com/
'Lectric Law Library 'Lectric Law Library provides links and materials for legal research, news, and professional activities.	http://www.leclaw.com/
Legal History and Philosophy Legal History and Philosophy, created by attorney Thomas P. Vincent, is mostly relevant quotes from readings and historical documents. The site is modified at least monthly.	http://www.commonlaw.com/

Chapter 5, Torts	
Legal Information Institute (LII)--Tort Law Materials LII, maintained by the Cornell Law School, provides an overview of tort law, including the Federal Torts Claim Act (28 U.S.C § 2671-80), recent Supreme Court tort decisions, and other information.	http://www.law.cornell.edu/topics/torts.html
The U.S. House of Representatives Internet Law Library--Tort Law The U.S. House of Representatives Internet Law Library for tort law provides links to cases, essays, statutes, and organizations concerned with tort law.	http://law.house.gov/110.htm
American Bar Association's Tort and Insurance Practice Section (TIPS) TIPS, a national professional group of plaintiff attorneys, defense attorneys, and insurance company counsel, provides information and links addressing tort law and insurance.	http://www.abanet.org/tips/home.html
American Tort Reform Association (ATRA) ATRA provides information on tort reform issues, press releases, *The Reformer Newsletter*, "horror stories" about tort law abuse, and contact information.	http://www.atra.org/atra/

Chapter 6, Anatomy of a Civil Suit

The RAND Institute for Civil Justice The RAND Institute for Civil Justice provides "objective, empirically based, analytic research [to] facilitate change in the civil justice system." The Institute disseminates its work to the legal, business, and research communities, and to the general public.	http://www.rand.org/centers/icj/
Federal Rules of Civil Procedure (1996) LII, maintained by the Cornell Law School, provides the Federal Rules of Civil Procedure in a hypertext and searchable format.	http://www.law.cornell.edu/rules/frcp/overview.htm
The Internet Directory of Expert Witnesses The Internet Directory of Expert Witnesses allows expert witnesses to be located quickly and for free for anyone to browse. Experts can be contacted directly via phone, fax or e-mail.	http://www.expertwitness.com/
The Experts Pages The Expert Pages, a unit of Advice & Counsel Corporation, is a directory of experts, expert witnesses, consultants, and service providers to lawyers.	http://expertpages.com/
The National Registry of Experts The National Registry of Experts is a professional organization established to provide support, recognition, training and continuing education to expert witnesses.	http://www.expert-registry.com/
Trial Behavior Consulting, Incorporated Trial Behavior Consulting, Incorporated, provides mock trials, case strategy, *voir dire* questions, community surveys, focus groups, witness preparation, and jury selection, among other services.	http://www.lawinfo.com/biz/tbci/
The Wilmington Institute The Wilmington Institute helps lawyers forecast the probable outcome of their litigation and trials.	http://www.wilmington-institute.com/
Carolyn Robbins Jury Simulations, Inc. Carolyn Robbins Jury Simulations, Inc., provides lawyers with jury research services.	http://www.crjury.com/
American Bar Association's Center for Professional Responsibility The American Bar Association's Center for Professional Responsibility provides standards and scholarly resources in legal ethics and professional responsibility.	http://www.abanet.org/cprhome.html
West's Legal Directory West's Legal Directory, updated daily, offers over 800,000 profiles of lawyers and law firms in the United States and Canada, including International offices.	http://www.wld.com/

Chapter 7, Alternate Dispute Resolution	
American Arbitration Association (AAA) The American Arbitration Association provides membership information, rules and procedures, education and research, publications, a directory of its members, and information on ADR law. AAA also maintains the Uniform Arbitration Act.	http://www.adr.org/
International Academy of Mediators International Academy of Mediators provides membership information and a directory of members, as well as other information on mediation.	http://www.iamed.org/
Society of Professionals in Dispute Resolution (SPIDR) Society of Professionals in Dispute Resolution (SPIDR) provides membership information, publications, and current events in ADR.	http://www.igc.apc.org/spidr/
Private Judges in Los Angeles Private Judges in LA provides the services of retired judges for dispute resolution.	http://www.privatejudgesla.com/
The Program On Negotiation at Harvard Law School The Program On Negotiation at Harvard Law School includes program and publication information.	http://www.law.harvard.edu/groups/pon/
Federal Arbitration Act—9 USC § 1 Legal Information Institute, maintained by the Cornell Law School, provides a hypertext and searchable version of 9 USC §1, popularly known as the Federal Arbitration Act.	http://www.law.cornell.edu/uscode/9/ch1.html
International Chamber of Commerce—Dispute Resolution The International Chamber of Commerce provides an index of international arbitration and alternative dispute resolution services, including information on the International Court of Arbitration.	http://www.iccwbo.org/arb/index.htm

Chapter 8, Crimes and Business	
Legal Information Institute (LII)—Criminal Law LII, maintained by the Cornell Law School, provides links to federal and state criminal statutes, organizations, journals, and other resources.	http://www.law.cornell.edu/topics/criminal.html
American Bar Association's Criminal Justice Section American Bar Association's Criminal Justice Section provides information and links addressing criminal law.	http://www.abanet.org/crimjust/home.html
U.S. Department of Justice The U.S. Department of Justice provides links to its many agencies, including the Federal Bureau of Investigation, as well as cases, statutes, and other materials relating to criminal justice.	http://www.usdoj.gov/
The National Criminal Justice Reference Service (NCJRS) NCJRS is a collection of clearinghouses supporting the U.S. Department of Justice, with domestic and international materials.	http://www.ncjrs.org/
United Nations Crime and Justice Information Network (UNCJIN) UNCJIN, maintained by the United Nations, provides an international clearinghouse for criminal justice statistics and information.	http://www.ifs.univie.ac.at/~uncjin/uncjin.html
Federal Bureau of Investigation The Federal Bureau of Investigation provides information, publications, and history.	http://www.fbi.gov/
Bureau of Justice Statistics (BJS) The BJS provides statistics and information for federal crimes, prosecution, sentencing, and corrections.	http://www.ojp.usdoj.gov/bjs/
Counterfeit Access Device and Computer Fraud and Abuse Act of 1984, 47 USC § 1001 The Legal Information Institute (LII), maintained by the Cornell Law School, provides a hypertext and searchable version of 47 USC § 1001, popularly known as the Counterfeit Access Device and Computer Fraud and Abuse Act of 1984	http://www.law.cornell.edu/uscode/18/1001.html
Racketeer Influenced and Corrupt Organizations Act (RICO), 18 USC § 1961 LII provides a hypertext and searchable version of 18 USC § 1961, popularly known as the Racketeer Influenced and Corrupt Organizations Act (RICO).	http://www.law.cornell.edu/uscode/18/1961.html
U.S. Sentencing Commission The U.S. Sentencing Commission provides publications and guidelines, statistics, reports to Congress, and links to state sentencing commissions.	http://www. ussc.gov/

Chapter 9, Introduction to Contract Law and Contract Theory	
Commission on European Contract Law The Commission on European Contract Law, a body of lawyers drawn from all the Member States of the European Community, drafted the *Principles of European Contract Law*. Includes here is Part I-- Performance, Non-performance, Remedies.	http://ananse.irv.uit.no/trade_law/documents/ lex-mercatoria/eu/txt/eu.principles.lando. commission.html
Uniform Commercial Code (UCC) The Legal Information Institute (LII), maintained by the Cornell Law School, provides a hypertext and searchable version of Articles 1-9 of the Uniform Commercial Code. As well, LII maintains links to the UCC as adopted by particular states, as well as proposed revisions.	http://www.law.cornell.edu/ucc/ucc.table.html
Legal Information Institute--Contract Law Materials LII provides an overview of contract law, links to federal government statutes, treaties, and regulations; federal and state judicial decisions regarding contract law (including Supreme Court decisions); state statutes; and other materials.	http://www.law.cornell.edu/topics/contracts. html
The American Law Institute The American Law Institute, publisher of Restatements of the Law, Model Codes, and other proposals for law reform, provides press releases, its newsletter, and other publications.	http://www.ali.org
The National Conference of Commissioners on Uniform State Laws The National Conference of Commissioners on Uniform State Laws (NCCUSL), the drafters of the UCC, provides drafts and revisions of its uniform and model acts.	http://www.law.upenn.edu/library/ulc/ulc.htm

Chapter 10, Contractual Agreement: Mutual Assent	
Uniform Commercial Code §2-204 The Legal Information Institute (LII), maintained by the Cornell Law School, provides a hypertext and searchable version of UCC §2-204, Formation in General.	http://www.law.cornell.edu/ucc/2/2-204.html
Uniform Commercial Code §2-205 LII provides a hypertext and searchable version of UCC §2-205, Firm Offers.	http://www.law.cornell.edu/ucc/2/2-205.html
Uniform Commercial Code §2-206 LII provides a hypertext and searchable version of UCC §2-206, Offer and Acceptance in Formation of Contract.	http://www.law.cornell.edu/ucc/2/2-206.html
Uniform Commercial Code §2-207 LII provides a hypertext and searchable version of UCC §2-207, Additional Terms in Acceptance or Confirmation.	http://www.law.cornell.edu/ucc/2/2-207.html
Uniform Commercial Code §2-305 LII provides a hypertext and searchable version of UCC §2-305, Open Price Term.	http://www.law.cornell.edu/ucc/2/2-305.html
Uniform Commercial Code §2-309 LII provides a hypertext and searchable version of UCC §2-309, Absence of Specific Time Provisions; Notice of Termination.	http://www.law.cornell.edu/ucc/2/2-309.html
Uniform Commercial Code §2-310 LII provides a hypertext and searchable version of UCC §2-310, Open Time for Payment or Running of Credit; Authority to Ship Under Reservation.	http://www.law.cornell.edu/ucc/2/2-310.html
Uniform Commercial Code §2-328 LII provides a hypertext and searchable version of UCC §2-328, Sale by Auction.	http://www.law.cornell.edu/ucc/2/2-328.html

Chapter 11, Consideration: The Basis of the Bargain	
Uniform Commercial Code (UCC) §2-302 The Legal Information Institute (LII), maintained by the Cornell Law School, provides a hypertext and searchable version of UCC §2-302, Unconscionable Contract or Clause.	http://www.law.cornell.edu/ucc/2/2-302.html
Uniform Commercial Code §2-209 LII provides a hypertext and searchable version of UCC §2-209, Modification, Recission, and Waiver.	http://www.law.cornell.edu/ucc/2/2-209.html
Legal Information Institute--Contract Law Materials LII provides an overview of contract law, links to federal government statutes, treaties, and regulations; federal and state judicial decisions regarding contract law (including Supreme Court decisions); state statutes; and other materials.	http://www.law.cornell.edu/topics/contracts.html
The American Law Institute The American Law Institute, publisher of Restatements of the Law, Model Codes, and other proposals for law reform, provides press releases, its newsletter, and other publications.	http://www.ali.org

Chapter 12, Contractual Capacity, Legality of Subject Matter, and Reality of Consent	
Uniform Commercial Code §2-302 The Legal Information Institute (LII), maintained by the Cornell Law School, provides a hypertext and searchable version of UCC §2-302, Unconscionable Contract or Clause.	http://www.law.cornell.edu/ucc/2/2-302.html
Sherman Antitrust Act--15 U.S.C. §1-7 LII provides a hypertext and searchable version of 15 U.S.C. §1-7, popularly known as the Sherman Antitrust Act.	http://www.law.cornell.edu/uscode/15/1.html
Clayton Act--15 U.S.C. §12-27 LII provides a hypertext and searchable version of 15 U.S.C. §12-25, popularly known as the Clayton Antitrust Act.	http://www.law.cornell.edu/uscode/15/12.html
Federal Trade Commission Act, 15 U.S.C. §41-58 LII provides a hypertext and searchable version of 15 U.S.C. §41-58, popularly known as the Federal Trade Commission Act.	http://www.law.cornell.edu/uscode/15/41.html
National Fraud Information Center National Fraud Information Center, a project of the National Consumers League, provides a daily report and other information on fraud, as well as the opportunity to report fraud.	http://www.fraud.org/

Chapter 13, Proper Form and Interpretation of Contracts	
Uniform Commercial Code (UCC) §2-201 The Legal Information Institute (LII), maintained by the Cornell Law School, provides a hypertext and searchable version of UCC §2-201, Formal Requirements; Statute of Frauds.	http://www.law.cornell.edu/ucc/2/2-201.html
Uniform Commercial Code §2-202 LII provides a hypertext and searchable version of UCC §2-202, Final Written Expression: Parol or Extrinsic Evidence.	http://www.law.cornell.edu/ucc/2/2-202.html
Uniform Commercial Code §2-208 LII provides a hypertext and searchable version of UCC §2-208, Course of Performance or Practical Construction.	http://www.law.cornell.edu/ucc/2/2-208.html

Chapter 14, The Rights of Third Persons	
Uniform Commercial Code (UCC) §2-210 The Legal Information Institute (LII), maintained by the Cornell Law School, provides a hypertext and searchable version of UCC § 2-210, Delegation of Performance; Assignment of Rights.	http://www.law.cornell.edu/ucc/2/2-210.html
Uniform Commercial Code §9-104 LII provides a hypertext and searchable version of UCC §9-104, Transactions Excluded From Article.	http://www.law.cornell.edu/ucc/9/9-104.html
Uniform Commercial Code §9-201 LII provides a hypertext and searchable version of UCC §9-201, General Validity of Security Agreement.	http://www.law.cornell.edu/ucc/9/9-201.html
Uniform Commercial Code §9-203 LII provides a hypertext and searchable version of UCC §9-203, Attachment and Enforceability of Security Interest; Proceeds; Formal Requisites.	http://www.law.cornell.edu/ucc/9/9-203.html
Uniform Commercial Code §9-206 LII provides a hypertext and searchable version of UCC §9-206, Agreement Not to Assert Defenses Against Assignee; Modification of Sales Warranties Where Security Agreement Exists.	http://www.law.cornell.edu/ucc/9/9-206.html
Preservation of Consumers' Claims and Defenses--16 C.F.R. 433 The law firm of Arent Fox Kintner Plotkin & Kahn maintains a collection of advertising law resources, including relevant C.F.R. sections.	http://www.webcom.com/~lewrose/trr/holder.html

Chapter 15, Contractual Discharge and Remedies	
Uniform Commercial Code (UCC) §2-209 The Legal Information Institute (LII), maintained by the Cornell Law School, provides a hypertext and searchable version of UCC §2-209, Modification, Rescission and Waiver.	http://www.law.cornell.edu/ucc/2/2-209.html
Uniform Commercial Code §2-308 LII provides a hypertext and searchable version of UCC §2-308, Absence of Specified Place for Delivery.	http://www.law.cornell.edu/ucc/2/2-308.html
Uniform Commercial Code §2-609 LII provides a hypertext and searchable version of UCC §2-609, Right to Adequate Assurance of Performance.	http://www.law.cornell.edu/ucc/2/2-609.html
Uniform Commercial Code §2-610 LII provides a hypertext and searchable version of UCC §2-610, Anticipatory Repudiation.	http://www.law.cornell.edu/ucc/2/2-610.html
Uniform Commercial Code §2-615 LII provides a hypertext and searchable version of UCC §2-615, Excuse by Failure of Presupposed Conditions.	http://www.law.cornell.edu/ucc/2/2-615.html
Uniform Commercial Code §2-703 LII provides a hypertext and searchable version of UCC §2-703, Seller's Remedies in General.	http://www.law.cornell.edu/ucc/2/2-703.html
Uniform Commercial Code §2-710 LII provides a hypertext and searchable version of UCC §2-710, Seller's Incidental Damages.	http://www.law.cornell.edu/ucc/2/2-710.html
Uniform Commercial Code §2-711 LII provides a hypertext and searchable version of UCC §2-711, Buyer's Remedies in General; Buyer's Security Interest in Rejected Goods.	http://www.law.cornell.edu/ucc/2/2-711.html
Uniform Commercial Code §2-715 LII provides a hypertext and searchable version of UCC §2-715, Buyer's Incidental and Consequential Damages.	http://www.law.cornell.edu/ucc/2/2-715.html
Uniform Commercial Code §2-718 LII provides a hypertext and searchable version of UCC §2-718, Liquidation or Limitation of Damages; Deposits.	http://www.law.cornell.edu/ucc/2/2-718.html
Uniform Commercial Code §2-719 LII provides a hypertext and searchable version of UCC §2-719, Contractual Modification or Limitation of Remedy.	http://www.law.cornell.edu/ucc/2/2-719.html
Uniform Commercial Code §2-725 LII provides a hypertext and searchable version of UCC §2-725, Statute of Limitations in Contracts for Sale.	http://www.law.cornell.edu/ucc/2/2-725.html

Chapter 16, Formation of the Sales Contract: Contracts for Leasing Goods

Uniform Commercial Code (UCC) Articles 2, Sales The Legal Information Institute (LII), maintained by the Cornell Law School, provides Articles 2, Sales.	http://www.law.cornell.edu/ucc/2/overview.html
Uniform Commercial Code §2-105 LII provides UCC §2-105, Definitions	http://www.law.cornell.edu/ucc/2/2-105.html
Uniform Commercial Code §2-106 LII provides UCC §2-106, Definitions	http://www.law.cornell.edu/ucc/2/2-106.html
Uniform Commercial Code §2-201 LII provides UCC §2-201, Formal Requirements; Statute of Frauds.	http://www.law.cornell.edu/ucc/2/2-201.html
Uniform Commercial Code §2-204 LII provides UCC §2-204, Formation in General.	http://www.law.cornell.edu/ucc/2/2-204.html
Uniform Commercial Code §2-206 LII provides UCC §2-206, Offer and Acceptance in Formation of Contract.	http://www.law.cornell.edu/ucc/2/2-206.html
Uniform Commercial Code §2-207 LII provides UCC §2-207, Additional Terms in Acceptance or Confirmation.	http://www.law.cornell.edu/ucc/2/2-207.html
Uniform Commercial Code §2-302 LII provides UCC §2-302, Unconscionable Contract or Clause.	http://www.law.cornell.edu/ucc/2/2-302.html
Uniform Commercial Code §2-305 LII provides UCC §2-305, Open Price Term.	http://www.law.cornell.edu/ucc/2/2-305.html
Uniform Commercial Code §2-306 LII provides UCC §2-306, Output, Requirements and Exclusive Dealings.	http://www.law.cornell.edu/ucc/2/2-306.html
Uniform Commercial Code §2-307 LII provides UCC §2-307, Delivery in Single Lot or Several Lots.	http://www.law.cornell.edu/ucc/2/2-307.html
Uniform Commercial Code §2-308 LII provides UCC §2-308, Absence of Specified Place for Delivery.	http://www.law.cornell.edu/ucc/2/2-308.html
Uniform Commercial Code §2-309 LII provides UCC §2-309, Absence of Specific Time Provisions; Notice of Termination.	http://www.law.cornell.edu/ucc/2/2-309.html
Uniform Commercial Code §2-310 LII provides UCC §2-310, Open Time for Payment or Running of Credit; Authority to Ship Under Reservation.	http://www.law.cornell.edu/ucc/2/2-310.html
Uniform Commercial Code Article 2A, Leases LII provides UCC's Article 2A, Leases.	http://www.law.cornell.edu/ucc/2A/overview.html
The National Conference of Commissioners on Uniform State Laws	http://www.law.upenn.edu/library/ulc/ulc.htm
The American Law Institute	http://www.ali.org

Chapter 17, Performance, Title, and Risk of Loss	
Uniform Commercial Code (UCC) §2-301 The Legal Information Institute (LII) provides UCC §2-301, General Obligations of Parties.	http://www.law.cornell.edu/ucc/2/2-301.html
Uniform Commercial Code §2-303 LII provides UCC §2-303, Allocation or Division of Risks.	http://www.law.cornell.edu/ucc/2/2-303.html
Uniform Commercial Code §2-304 LII provides UCC §2-304, Price Payable in Money, Goods, Realty, or Otherwise.	http://www.law.cornell.edu/ucc/2/2-304.html
Uniform Commercial Code §2-319 LII provides UCC §2-319, F.O.B. and F.A.S. Terms.	http://www.law.cornell.edu/ucc/2/2-319.html
Uniform Commercial Code §2-320 LII provides UCC §2-320. C.I.F. and C. & F. Terms.	http://www.law.cornell.edu/ucc/2/2-320.html
Uniform Commercial Code §2-322 LII provides UCC §2-322. Delivery "Ex-Ship"	http://www.law.cornell.edu/ucc/2/2-322.html
Uniform Commercial Code §2-324 LII provides a hypertext and searchable version of UCC §2-324. "No Arrival, No Sale" Term.	http://www.law.cornell.edu/ucc/2/2-324.html
Uniform Commercial Code §2-326 LII provides UCC §2-326, Sale on Approval and Sale or Return; Consignment Sales and Rights of Creditors.	http://www.law.cornell.edu/ucc/2/2-326.html
Uniform Commercial Code §2-327 LII provides UCC §2-327. Special Incidents of Sale on Approval and Sale or Return.	http://www.law.cornell.edu/ucc/2/2-327.html
Uniform Commercial Code §2-328 LII provides UCC §2-328, Sale by Auction.	http://www.law.cornell.edu/ucc/2/2-328.html
Uniform Commercial Code §2-401 LII provides UCC §2-401, Passing of Title; Reservation for Security	http://www.law.cornell.edu/ucc/2/2-401.html
Uniform Commercial Code §2-402 LII provides UCC §2-402, Rights of Seller's Creditors Against Sold Goods.	http://www.law.cornell.edu/ucc/2/2-402.html
Uniform Commercial Code §2-503 LII provides UCC §2-503, Manner of Seller's Tender of Delivery	http://www.law.cornell.edu/ucc/2/2-503.html
Uniform Commercial Code §2-509 LII provides a hypertext and searchable version of UCC §2-509, Risk of Loss in the Absence of Breach.	http://www.law.cornell.edu/ucc/2/2-509.html
Uniform Commercial Code §2-513 LII provides UCC §2-513, Buyer's Right to Inspection of Goods.	http://www.law.cornell.edu/ucc/2/2-513.html
Uniform Commercial Code Article 7, Warehouse Receipts, Bills of Lading and Other Documents of Title LII provides UCC's Article 7, Warehouse Receipts, Bills of Lading and Other Documents of Title.	http://www.law.cornell.edu/ucc/7/overview.html

Chapter 18, Warranties and Product Liability	
Uniform Commercial Code (UCC) §2-209 The Legal Information Institute (LII), maintained by the Cornell Law School, provides UCC §2-209, Modification, Rescission and Waiver	http://www.law.cornell.edu/ucc/2/2-209.html
Uniform Commercial Code §2-312 LII provides UCC §2-312, Warranty of Title and Against Infringement; Buyer's Obligation Against Infringement.	http://www.law.cornell.edu/ucc/2/2-312.html
Uniform Commercial Code §2-313 LII provides UCC §2-313, Express Warranties by Affirmation, Promise, Description, Sample.	http://www.law.cornell.edu/ucc/2/2-313.html
Uniform Commercial Code §2-314 LII provides UCC §2-314, Implied Warranty: Merchantability; Usage of Trade..	http://www.law.cornell.edu/ucc/2/2-314.html
Uniform Commercial Code §2-315 LII provides UCC §2-315, Implied Warranty: Fitness for Particular Purpose.	http://www.law.cornell.edu/ucc/2/2-315.html
Uniform Commercial Code §2-316 LII provides UCC §2-316, Exclusion or Modification of Warranties.	http://www.law.cornell.edu/ucc/2/2-316.html
Uniform Commercial Code §2-318 LII provides UCC §2-318, Third Party Beneficiaries of Warranties Express or Implied.	http://www.law.cornell.edu/ucc/2/2-318.html
15 USC §2301-2312 (Magnuson-Moss Warranty Act) LII provides 15 USC §2301-2312, popularly known as the Magnuson-Moss Warranty Act.	http://www.law.cornell.edu/uscode/15/ch50.html
Facts for Consumers-- Warranties Fast Facts The FTC *Warranties Fast Facts* provides guidelines to consumers on different types of warranties, as well as information for resolving disputes over warranties.	http://www.ftc.gov/bcp/conline/pubs/products/warrant.htm
American Law Institute (ALI) The American Law Institute publishes the Restatements (Second) on Torts. ALI does not maintain the Restatements online, but does provide additional information.	http://www.ali.org/
Uniform Commercial Code Article 2A, Leases LII provides UCC's Article 2A, Leases. LII also provides links to Article 2A as enacted by a particular state and to any proposed revisions.	http://www.law.cornell.edu/ucc/2A/overview.html

Chapter 19, Remedies	
Uniform Commercial Code (UCC) §2-703 The Legal Information Institute (LII), maintained by the Cornell Law School, provides a hypertext and searchable version of UCC §2-703, Seller's Remedies in General	http://www.law.cornell.edu/ucc/2/2-703.html
Uniform Commercial Code §2-711 LII provides a hypertext and searchable version of UCC §2-711, Buyer's Remedies in General; Buyer's Security Interest in Rejected Goods.	http://www.law.cornell.edu/ucc/2/2-711.html
Uniform Commercial Code §2-713 LII provides a hypertext and searchable version of UCC §2-713, Buyer's Damages for Non-Delivery or Repudiation.	http://www.law.cornell.edu/ucc/2/2-713.html
Uniform Commercial Code §2-716 LII provides a hypertext and searchable version of UCC §2-716, Buyer's Right to Specific Performance or Replevin.	http://www.law.cornell.edu/ucc/2/2-716.html
Uniform Commercial Code Article 2A, Leases LII provides a hypertext and searchable version of the UCC's Article 2A, Leases. LII also provides links to Article 2A as enacted by a particular state and to proposed revisions.	http://www.law.cornell.edu/ucc/2A/overview.html

Chapter 20, International Sales of Goods: CISG

Pace University School of Law Institute of International Commercial Law (IICL) Pace University School of Law's *IICL* provides the full text of the United Nations Convention on Contracts for the International Sale of Goods (CISG), as well as legislative history, cases, commentaries, and a bibliography.	http://www.cisg.law.pace.edu/
United Nations Commission on International Trade Law (UNCITRAL) UNCITRAL, drafter of the CISG, provides background information, texts and recent documents, case law, and the current status of conventions and model laws.	http://www.un.or.at/uncitral/index.html
International Trade Law (ITL)--Sale of Goods *ITL*, hosted by the University of Tromso, Norway, provides a hypertext version of the CISG (as well as a link to a printable version), the status and contracting parties to the CISG, and a hypertext version of the Uniform Law on International Sale of Goods 1964 (ULIS).	http://ananse.irv.uit.no/trade_law/nav/sales.html
The CISG Website Project The CISG Website Project, maintained by the University of Freiburg, Germany, provides texts, articles, and German case law on the CISG.	http://www.jura.uni-freiburg.de/ipr1/cisg/
ISO Online ISO, drafter of international standards guidelines, such as the ISO 9000 and ISO 14000, provides more on the structure of the organization, as well as a catalog of publications.	http://www.iso.ch/
ISO Integrated Solutions (IIS) IIS, a partnership between the American National Standards Institute and the Global Environment & Technology Foundation, provides news, standards resources, and updates developments and events.	http://www.iso14000.org/
International Chamber of Commerce (ICC) World Business Organization The ICC, developer of the International Rules for the Interpretation of Trade Terms, or incoterms, provides current news, publications, and information on the ICC International Court of Arbitration.	http://www.iccwbo.org/
International Trade Law--International Rules for the Interpretation of Trade Terms (Incoterms) IT provides a listing, description, and explanation of incoterms in a hypertext format.	http://ananse.irv.uit.no/trade_law/documents/sales/incoterms/nav/incoterms.html
International Centre for Commercial Law The International Centre for Commercial Law offers current updates on commercial law, as well as listings for commercial law firms in over forty European countries.	http://www.link.org/

Chapter 21, Introduction to Negotiables: UCC Articles 3 and 7	
Uniform Commercial Code (UCC) Article 3, Negotiable Instruments The Legal Information Institute (LII), maintained by the Cornell Law School, provides a hypertext and searchable version of UCC Article 3, Negotiable Instruments. LII also maintains links to Article 3 as adopted by particular states and to proposed revisions.	http://www.law.cornell.edu/ucc/3/overview.html
Uniform Commercial Code §3-102 LII provides a hypertext and searchable version of UCC §3-102, Subject Matter.	http://www.law.cornell.edu/ucc/3/3-102.html
Uniform Commercial Code §3-104 LII provides a hypertext and searchable version of UCC §3-104, Negotiable Instrument.	http://www.law.cornell.edu/ucc/3/3-104.html
Uniform Commercial Code Article 7, Warehouse Receipts, Bills Of Lading and other Documents of Title LII provides a hypertext and searchable version of UCC Article 7, Warehouse Receipts, Bills Of Lading and other Documents of Title.	http://www.law.cornell.edu/ucc/7/overview.html
Legal Information Institute--Negotiable Instrument Law Materials LII provides an overview of negotiable instruments law, federal and state statutes and regulations, and federal and state court decisions.	http://www.law.cornell.edu/topics/negotiable.html
The National Conference of Commissioners on Uniform State Laws The National Conference of Commissioners on Uniform State Laws (NCCUSL), the drafters of the UCC, provides drafts and revisions of its uniform and model acts.	http://www.law.upenn.edu/library/ulc/ulc.htm

Chapter 22, Negotiability	
Uniform Commercial Code (UCC) §3-103 The Legal Information Institute (LII), maintained by the Cornell Law School, provides a hypertext and searchable version of UCC §3-103, Definitions.	http://www.law.cornell.edu/ucc/3/3-103.html
Uniform Commercial Code §3-104 LII provides a hypertext and searchable version of UCC §3-104, Negotiable Instrument.	http://www.law.cornell.edu/ucc/3/3-104.html
Uniform Commercial Code §3-106 LII provides a hypertext and searchable version of UCC § 3-106, Unconditional Promise or Order.	http://www.law.cornell.edu/ucc/3/3-106.html
Uniform Commercial Code §3-107 LII provides a hypertext and searchable version of UCC §3-107, Instrument Payable in Foreign Money.	http://www.law.cornell.edu/ucc/3/3-107.html
Uniform Commercial Code §3-108 LII provides a hypertext and searchable version of UCC §3-108, Payable on Demand or at Definite Time.	http://www.law.cornell.edu/ucc/3/3-108.html
Uniform Commercial Code §3-111 LII provides a hypertext and searchable version of UCC §3-111, Place of Payment.	http://www.law.cornell.edu/ucc/3/3-111.html
Uniform Commercial Code §3-112 LII provides a hypertext and searchable version of UCC §3-112, Interest.	http://www.law.cornell.edu/ucc/3/3-112.html
Uniform Commercial Code §3-114 LII provides a hypertext and searchable version of UCC §3-114, Contradictory Terms of Instrument.	http://www.law.cornell.edu/ucc/3/3-114.html
Uniform Commercial Code Article 7, Warehouse Receipts, Bills Of Lading and other Documents of Title LII provides a hypertext and searchable version of UCC Article 7, Warehouse Receipts, Bills Of Lading and other Documents of Title.	http://www.law.cornell.edu/ucc/7/overview.html

Chapter 23. Negotiation and Holders in Due Course/ Holders by Due Negotiation	
Uniform Commercial Code (UCC) §3-105 The Legal Information Institute (LII), maintained by the Cornell Law School, provides a hypertext and searchable version of §3-105, Issue of Instrument.	http://www.law.cornell.edu/ucc/3/3-105.html
Uniform Commercial Code §3-201 LII provides UCC §3-201, Negotiation.	http://www.law.cornell.edu/ucc/3/3-201.html
Uniform Commercial Code §3-204 LII provides UCC §3-204, Indorsement.	http://www.law.cornell.edu/ucc/3/3-204.html
Uniform Commercial Code §3-205 LII provides UCC §3-205, Special Indorsement; Blank Indorsement; Anomalous Indorsement.	http://www.law.cornell.edu/ucc/3/3-205.html
Uniform Commercial Code §3-206 LII provides UCC §3-206, Restrictive Endorsement.	http://www.law.cornell.edu/ucc/3/3-206.html
Uniform Commercial Code §3-302 LII provides UCC §3-302, Holder in Due Course.	http://www.law.cornell.edu/ucc/3/3-302.html
Uniform Commercial Code §3-303 LII provides UCC §3-303, Value and Consideration.	http://www.law.cornell.edu/ucc/3/3-303.html
Uniform Commercial Code §3-304 LII provides UCC §3-304, Overdue Instrument.	http://www.law.cornell.edu/ucc/3/3-304.html
Uniform Commercial Code §3-305 LII provides UCC §3-305, Defenses and Claims in Recoupment.	http://www.law.cornell.edu/ucc/3/3-305.html
Uniform Commercial Code §3-402 LII provides UCC §3-402, Signature by Representative	http://www.law.cornell.edu/ucc/3/3-402.html
Uniform Commercial Code §3-403 LII provides UCC §3-403, Unauthorized Signature.	http://www.law.cornell.edu/ucc/3/3-403.html
Uniform Commercial Code §3-406 LII provides UCC §3-406, Negligence Contributing to Forged Signature or Alteration of Instrument.	http://www.law.cornell.edu/ucc/3/3-414.html
Uniform Commercial Code §3-407 LII provides UCC §3-407, Alteration.	http://www.law.cornell.edu/ucc/3/3-414.html
Uniform Commercial Code §3-414 LII provides UCC §3-414, Obligation of Drawer.	http://www.law.cornell.edu/ucc/3/3-414.html
Uniform Commercial Code §3-415 LII provides UCC §3-415, Obligation of Indorser.	http://www.law.cornell.edu/ucc/3/3-415.html

Chapter 24, Liability and Discharge	
Uniform Commercial Code (UCC) §1-207 The Legal Information Institute (LII), maintained by the Cornell Law School, provides a hypertext and searchable version of §1-207, Performance or Acceptance Under Reservation of Rights.	http://www.law.cornell.edu/ucc/3/1-207.html
Uniform Commercial Code §3-311 LII provides a hypertext and searchable version of §3-311, Accord and Satisfaction by Use of Instrument.	http://www.law.cornell.edu/ucc/3/3-311.html
Uniform Commercial Code §3-401 LII provides a hypertext and searchable version of §3-401, Signature.	http://www.law.cornell.edu/ucc/3/3-401.html
Uniform Commercial Code §3-403 LII provides a hypertext and searchable version of §3-403, Unauthorized Signature.	http://www.law.cornell.edu/ucc/3/3-403.html
Uniform Commercial Code §3-404 LII provides a hypertext and searchable version of §3-404, Impostors; Fictitious Payees.	http://www.law.cornell.edu/ucc/3/3-404.html
Uniform Commercial Code §3-416 LII provides a hypertext and searchable version of §3-416, Transfer Warranties.	http://www.law.cornell.edu/ucc/3/3-416.html
Uniform Commercial Code §3-417 LII provides a hypertext and searchable version of §3-417, Presentment Warranties.	http://www.law.cornell.edu/ucc/3/3-417.html
Uniform Commercial Code §3-501 LII provides a hypertext and searchable version of §3-501, Presentment.	http://www.law.cornell.edu/ucc/3/3-501.html
Uniform Commercial Code §3-503 LII provides a hypertext and searchable version of §3-503, Dishonor.	http://www.law.cornell.edu/ucc/3/3-503.html
Uniform Commercial Code §3-504 LII provides a hypertext and searchable version of §3-504, Excused Presentment and Notice of Dishonor	http://www.law.cornell.edu/ucc/3/3-504.html

Chapter 25, Bank-Customer Relations and Electronic Funds Transfer	
Uniform Commercial Code (UCC)--Article 4, Bank Deposits And Collections The Legal Information Institute (LII), maintained by the Cornell Law School, provides a hypertext and searchable version of UCC Article 4, Bank Deposits and Collections. LII also maintains links to Article 4 as adopted by particular states and to proposed revisions.	http://www.law.cornell.edu/ucc/4/ overview.html
Uniform Commercial Code §4-402 LII provides a hypertext and searchable version of §4-402 Bank's Liability to Customer for Wrongful Dishonor; Time of Determining Insufficiency of Account.	http://www.law.cornell.edu/ucc/4/4-402.html
Uniform Commercial Code §4-405 LII provides a hypertext and searchable version of §4-405, Death or Incompetence of Customer.	http://www.law.cornell.edu/ucc/4/4-405.html
Uniform Commercial Code §4-406 LII provides a hypertext and searchable version of §4-406, Customer's Duty to Discover and Report Unauthorized Signature or Alteration.	http://www.law.cornell.edu/ucc/4/4-406.html
Electronic Funds Transfer Act--15 USC §1693 LII provides a hypertext and searchable version of 15 USC §1693, popularly known as the Electronic Funds Transfer Act.	http://www.law.cornell.edu/uscode/15/ 78dd-2.html
Uniform Commercial Code Article 4A, Funds Transfer LII provides a hypertext and searchable version of Article 4A, Funds Transfer.	http://www.law.cornell.edu/ucc/4A/ overview.html

Chapter 26, Secured Transactions: Security Interests and Perfection	
Uniform Commercial Code (UCC) Article 9, Secured Transactions; Sales of Accounts and Chattel Paper The Legal Information Institute (LII), maintained by the Cornell Law School, provides a hypertext and searchable version of UCC Article 9, Secured Transactions; Sales of Accounts and Chattel Paper.	http://www.law.cornell.edu/ucc/9/overview.html
Uniform Commercial Code §9-102 LII provides UCC §9-102, Policy and Subject Matter of Article.	http://www.law.cornell.edu/ucc/9/9-102.html
Uniform Commercial Code §9-103 LII provides UCC §9-103, Perfection of Security Interest in Multiple State Transactions..	http://www.law.cornell.edu/ucc/9/9-103.html
Uniform Commercial Code §9-104 LII provides UCC §9-104, Transactions Excluded from Article.	http://www.law.cornell.edu/ucc/9/9-104.html
Uniform Commercial Code §9-105 LII provides UCC §9-105, Definitions.	http://www.law.cornell.edu/ucc/9/9-105.html
Uniform Commercial Code §9-109 LII provides UCC §9-109, Classification of Goods	http://www.law.cornell.edu/ucc/9/9-109.html
Uniform Commercial Code §9-201 LII provides UCC §9-201, General Validity of Security Agreement.	http://www.law.cornell.edu/ucc/9/9-201.html
Uniform Commercial Code §9-203 LII provides UCC §9-203, Attachment and Enforceability of Security Interest; Proceeds; Formal Requisites.	http://www.law.cornell.edu/ucc/9/9-203.html
Uniform Commercial Code §9-302 LII provides UCC §9-302, When Filing Is Required to Perfect Security Interest; Security Interests to Which Filing Provisions of This Article Do Not Apply.	http://www.law.cornell.edu/ucc/9/9-302.html
Uniform Commercial Code §9-305 LII provides UCC §9-305, When Possession by Secured Party Perfects Security Interest Without Filing.	http://www.law.cornell.edu/ucc/9/9-305.html
Uniform Commercial Code §9-401 LII provides UCC §9-401, Place of Filing; Erroneous Filing; Removal of Collateral.	http://www.law.cornell.edu/ucc/9/9-401.html
Uniform Commercial Code §9-402 LII provides UCC §9-402, Formal Requisites of Financing Statement; Amendments; Mortgage as Financing Statement.	http://www.law.cornell.edu/ucc/9/9-402.html
Uniform Commercial Code §9-403 LII provides UCC §9-403, What Constitutes Filing; Duration of Filing; Effect of Lapsed Filing; Duties of Filing Officer.	http://www.law.cornell.edu/ucc/9/9-403.html

Chapter 27, Secured Transactions: Priorities	
Uniform Commercial Code (UCC) Article 9, Secured Transactions; Sales of Accounts and Chattel Paper The Legal Information Institute (LII), maintained by the Cornell Law School, provides a hypertext and searchable version of UCC Article 9, Secured Transactions; Sales of Accounts and Chattel Paper. LII also maintains links to Article 9 as adopted by particular states and to proposed revisions.	http://www.law.cornell.edu/ucc/9/ overview.html
Uniform Commercial Code §9-107 LII provides a hypertext and searchable version of UCC §9-107, Definitions: "Purchase Money Security Interest".	http://www.law.cornell.edu/ucc/9/9-107.html
Uniform Commercial Code §9-109 LII provides a hypertext and searchable version of UCC §9-109, Classification of Goods: "Consumer Goods"; "Equipment"; "Farm Products"; "Inventory".	http://www.law.cornell.edu/ucc/9/9-109.html
Uniform Commercial Code §9-307 LII provides a hypertext and searchable version of UCC §9-307, Protection of Buyers of Goods.	http://www.law.cornell.edu/ucc/9/9-307.html
Uniform Commercial Code §9-312 LII provides a hypertext and searchable version of UCC §9-312, Priorities among Conflicting Security Interests in the Same Collateral.	http://www.law.cornell.edu/ucc/9/9-312.html
Uniform Commercial Code §9-313 LII provides a hypertext and searchable version of UCC §9-313, Priority of Security Interests in Fixtures.	http://www.law.cornell.edu/ucc/9/9-313.html
The National Conference of Commissioners on Uniform State Laws The National Conference of Commissioners on Uniform State Laws (NCCUSL), the drafters of the UCC, provides drafts and revisions of its uniform and model acts.	http://www.law.upenn.edu/library/ulc/ ulc.htm

Chapter 28, Secured Transactions: Default	
Uniform Commercial Code (UCC) Article 9, Secured Transactions; Sales of Accounts and Chattel Paper The Legal Information Institute (LII), maintained by the Cornell Law School, provides a hypertext and searchable version of UCC Article 9, Secured Transactions; Sales of Accounts and Chattel Paper. LII also maintains links to Article 9 as adopted by particular states and to proposed revisions.	http://www.law.cornell.edu/ucc/9/overview.html
Uniform Commercial Code §9-207 LII provides UCC §9-207, Rights and Duties when Collateral Is in Secured Party's Possession.	http://www.law.cornell.edu/ucc/9/9-207.html
Uniform Commercial Code §9-501 LII provides UCC §9-501, Default; Procedure when Security Agreement Covers Both Real and Personal Property.	http://www.law.cornell.edu/ucc/9/9-501.html
Uniform Commercial Code §9-502 LII provides UCC §9-502, Collection Rights of Secured Party.	http://www.law.cornell.edu/ucc/9/9-502.html
Uniform Commercial Code §9-503 LII provides UCC §9-503, Secured Party's Right to Take Possession After Default.	http://www.law.cornell.edu/ucc/9/9-503.html
Uniform Commercial Code §9-504 LII provides UCC §9-504, Secured Party's Right to Dispose of Collateral After Default; Effect of Disposition.	http://www.law.cornell.edu/ucc/9/9-504.html
Uniform Commercial Code §9-505 LII provides UCC §9-505, Compulsory Disposition of Collateral; Acceptance of the Collateral as Discharge of Obligation.	http://www.law.cornell.edu/ucc/9/9-505.html
Uniform Commercial Code §9-507 LII provides UCC §9-507, Secured Party's Liability for Failure to Comply With This Part.	http://www.law.cornell.edu/ucc/9/9-507.html
The National Conference of Commissioners on Uniform State Laws The National Conference of Commissioners on Uniform State Laws (NCCUSL), the drafters of the UCC, provides drafts and revisions of its uniform and model acts.	http://www.law.upenn.edu/library/ulc/ulc.htm

Chapter 29, Straight Bankruptcy	
Legal Information Institute (LII)--Bankruptcy Law Materials The Legal Information Institute (LII), maintained by the Cornell Law School, provides an overview of bankruptcy law, including the Federal Bankruptcy Code; rules in the Code of Federal Regulations (C.F.R.); state and federal court decisions; and state civil codes.	http://www.law.cornell.edu/topics/ bankruptcy.html
11 USC Chapter 7--Liquidation LII provides Chapter 7, Liquidation, of the U.S. Code.	http://www.law.cornell.edu/uscode/11/ ch7.html
11 USC Chapter 11--Reorganization LII provides Chapter 11, Reorganization, of the U.S. Code.	http://www.law.cornell.edu/uscode/11/ ch11.html
11 USC Chapter 12-- Adjustment of Debts of a Family Farmer with Regular Annual Income LII provides Chapter 12, Adjustment of Debts of a Family Farmer with Regular Annual Income	http://www.law.cornell.edu/uscode/11/ ch12.html
11 USC Chapter 13-- Adjustment of Debts of an Individual with Regular Income LII provides Chapter 13, Adjustment of Debts of an Individual with Regular Income	http://www.law.cornell.edu/uscode/11/ ch13.html
Bankruptcy Reform Act of 1994 The U.S. Congress provides the Bankruptcy Reform Act of 1994.	http://thomas.loc.gov/cgi-bin/query/ z?c103: H.R.5116:
ABI World (American Bankruptcy Institute) ABI World provides daily bankruptcy headlines, legislative news, and materials from the National Bankruptcy Review Commission (NBRC).	http://www.abiworld.org/
InterNet Bankruptcy Library InterNet Bankruptcy Library, maintained by Bankruptcy Creditors' Service, Inc., provides bankruptcy data, news, and information.	http://bankrupt.com/
National Association of Consumer Bankruptcy Attorneys, Inc. (NACBA) NACBA, a national organization of over 600 attorneys, provides consumer bankruptcy information.	http://nacba.com/

Chapter 30, Alternatives to Straight Bankruptcy	
11 U.S.C. Chapter 11--Reorganization The Legal Information Institute (LII), maintained by the Cornell Law School, provides a hypertext and searchable version of Chapter 7, Liquidation, of the U.S. Code.	http://www.law.cornell.edu/uscode/11/ch11.html
11 U.S.C. Chapter 12-- Adjustment of Debts of a Family Farmer with Regular Annual Income LII provides a hypertext and searchable version of Chapter 12, Adjustment of Debts of a Family Farmer with Regular Annual Income	http://www.law.cornell.edu/uscode/11/ch12.html
11 U.S.C. Chapter 13-- Adjustment of Debts of an Individual with Regular Income LII provides a hypertext and searchable version of Chapter 13, Adjustment of Debts of an Individual with Regular Income	http://www.law.cornell.edu/uscode/11/ch13.html
Bankruptcy Alternatives Bankruptcy Alternatives, maintained by Mory Brenner, Attorney at Law, provides questions and answers about alternatives to bankruptcy.	http://www.debtworkout.com/

Chapter 31. The Creation and Termination of an Agency	
The American Law Institute The American Law Institute, publisher of Restatements of the Law, Model Codes, and other proposals for law reform, provides press releases, its newsletter, and other publications.	http://www.ali.org
The Independent Contractor Report The Independent Contractor Report, a monthly newsletter, has materials on employment tax cases, rulings, and issues for users of independent contractors.	http://www.webcom.com/ic_rep/
The Independent Contractor Law Site The Independent Contractor Law Site, maintained by Attorney Stephen Fishman, provides articles, updates, and legislation for independent contractors and employers.	http://www.nolo.com/ic/
Is That Worker an Independent Contractor or Your Employee? "Is That Worker an Independent Contractor or Your Employee?," by Attorney John C. Fox, helps provide a general understanding of the current law relating to independent contractor issues.	http://www.fenwick.com/pub/indepen.html
The Outsourcing Institute The Outsourcing Institute provides general information on outsourcing, including the hiring of independent contractors.	http://www.outsourcing.com/
The Ultimate Employee Handbook--A Workshop Court TV sponsored an on-line seminar, recorded here, in which lawyers from around the world offered advice on the "ultimate" employee handbooks.	http://www.courttv.com/seminars/handbook/
Avoiding Booby Traps in Drafting Employee Manuals "Avoiding Booby Traps in Drafting Employee Manuals," by Attorney James R. Macy, provides basic advice for drafting employment manuals.	http://www.abanet.org/genpractice/compleat/w96man.html
DB Basics, Inc., Company Policy Manual DB Basics Inc., a software development company, maintains its employee handbook online.	http://www.dbbasics.com/Web_Employment_ Manual.htm
U.S. Department of Labor The U.S. Department of Labor provides information and statistics, at the federal level, for workplace and agency issues.	http://www.dol.gov/

Chapter 32, Agency: Liability of Contracts

Getting Around Barriers to Non-Compete Pacts "Getting Around Barriers to Non-Compete Pacts," by James A. DiBoise and David J. Berger and originally published in *The National Law Journal*, discusses whether courts will consider trade secret confidentiality as covenants not to compete.	http://wsgrgate.wsgr.com/Resources/IntProp/Pubs/Articles/barriers.htm
Non-Compete Agreements "Non-Compete Agreements," by Mindy G. Farber and published in *Women Today*, discusses the merits of having an attorney review any covenant not to compete before signing.	http://www.womenconnect.com/bu93051.htm
AHI's Employment Law Resource Center The Alexander Hamilton Institute, Inc., provides newsletters, booklets, and loose-leaf manuals, and discussion groups aimed to help managers.	http://www. ahipubs.com/
The Patent Examiner The Patent Examiner, maintained by the firm of Arent, Fox, Kintner, Plotkin, and Kahn, discusses the basic issues surrounding patent protection and its relevance to the formation of employment contracts.	http://www.patentexaminer.com/patent/corpsurviv.html

Chapter 33, Agency: Liability for Torts and Crimes

EFF "Legal Issues and Policy: Cyberspace and the Law" Archive The Electronic Frontier Foundation, a non-profit civil liberties organization, provides articles and links to information regarding the use of technology and workplace privacy.	http://www.eff.org/pub/Legal/
Legal Information Institute (LII)--Workers Compensation Law Materials LII, maintained by the Cornell Law School, provides an overview of workers compensation law.	http://www.law.cornell.edu/topics/workers_compensation.html

Chapter 34, Business Organization

Smart Business Supersite (SBS)--Company Structure SBS, a distributor of "how-to" business information, provides publications on sole proprietorships, partnerships, corporations, limited liability companies, agreements, forms, and similar topics.	http://www.smartbiz.com/sbs/cats/struct. htm
U.S. Business Advisor The U.S. Business Advisor, a federal government program, provides businesses with access to government information and services.	http://www.business.gov/
U.S. Small Business Administration (SBA) The SBA provides information and materials, such as forms, software, and publications, to help start, finance, and expand a business.	http://www.sba.gov/
Legal Information Institute (LII)—Enterprise Law Materials LII, maintained by the Cornell Law School, provides an overview of corporation and partnership law, including links to state statutes and recent relevant Supreme Court decisions.	http://www.law.cornell.edu/topics/topic2 . html# enterprise law
Internal Revenue Service The Internal Revenue Service and its publication, the "Digital Daily," provide tax advice and information on a variety of issues, including business formation issues	http://www.irs.ustreas.gov/
U.S. Internal Revenue Code—26 USC LII maintains the U.S. Internal Revenue Code, 26 USC, in a hypertext and searchable format.	http://www.law.cornell.edu/uscode/26/
The National Conference of Commissioners on Uniform State Laws The National Conference of Commissioners on Uniform State Laws (NCCUSL), the drafters of the UCC, provides drafts and revisions of its uniform and model acts.	http://www.law.upenn.edu/library/ulc/ ulc.htm
State of Indiana's Uniform Partnership Act The State of Indiana maintains its adopted version of the Uniform Partnership Act.	http://www.law.indiana.edu/codes/in/23/ ch-23-4-1.html
Code of Hammurabi The Yale Law School maintains a hypertext version of the legal Code of Hammurabi.	http://www.yale.edu/lawweb/avalon/ hamframe.htm
State of Arizona's Corporation Laws The State of Arizona maintains its Corporation laws.	http://www.azleg.state.az.us/ars/10/ title10.htm
State of New York's Corporation Laws The State of New York maintains its Corporation laws.	http://www.law.cornell.edu/ny/statutes/ buscorp.htm
General Business Forms The 'Lectric Law Library's™ business forms include a variety of sample partnership and corporation documents.	http://www.lectlaw.com/formb.htm

Chapter 35, Operation of a Business Organization	
Netmarquee: Family Business Netcenter Netmarquee, a legal resource for family-owned businesses, provides news, events, and services.	http://nmq.com/FamBizNC/default.htm
American Success Institute American Success Institute promises a "free business education on the web," provides tips on operating small businesses.	http://www.success.org/
Educom, Inc., Articles of Incorporation Educom (Interuniversity Communications Council, Inc.), a not-for-profit corporation specializing in information about the education process, maintains its articles of incorporation, by-laws, trustees' terms of office, and trustees' names & address, online.	http://educom.edu/web/admin.html
Limited-Liability Companies Attorney Steven E. Davidson provides basic information on limited liability companies, including a state-by-state comparison chart.	http://www.hia.com/llcweb/ll-home.html
Invest in Belgium Invest in Belgium provides information on starting and investing in Belgian corporations.	http://www.ib.be/invest-belgium/mainmenu.html
State of Indiana's Uniform Partnership Act The State of Indiana maintains its adopted version of the Uniform Partnership Act.	http://www.law.indiana.edu/codes/in/23/ch-23-4-1.html
General Business Forms The 'Lectric Law Library's™ business forms include a variety of sample partnership and corporation documents.	http://www.lectlaw.com/formb.htm

Chapter 36, Business Termination and other Extraordinary Events	
General Business Forms The 'Lectric Law Library's™ business forms include a variety of sample partnership and corporation documents.	http://www.lectlaw.com/formb.htm
Limited Liability Companies--USA Limited Liability Companies—USA, sponsored by "The Limited Liability Company Reporter," provides articles, documents, and links relevant to limited liability companies.	http://www.llc-usa.com/
U.S. Chamber of Commerce U.S. Chamber of Commerce provides news, information, services, and products to assist small business owners.	http://www.uschamber.org/
Law Journal EXTRA! (LJX!)—Corporate Law LJX!, sponsored by the New York Law Publishing Company, provides daily corporate law news, case law, and legal analysis.	http://www.ljx.com/practice/corporate/index.html
CNNfn: The Financial Network CNNfn, Turner Broadcasting's financial news complement to CNN, provides reports on mergers and takeovers. CNNfn is interactive, allowing visitors to "ask the experts" or respond to the day's programs.	http://www.cnnfn.com/

Chapter 37, Franchising	
Franchising Online American Bar Association's (ABA's) Forum on Franchising, a Forum Committee of the ABA, provides publiations and information on laws affecting franchising.	http://www.abanet.org/forums/franchising.html
FranInfo FranInfo provides tips and materials on buying a franchise or making a business into a franchise. FranInfo also provides a detailed directory of franchises.	http://www.frannet.com/
Franchising Times Franchising Times provides information on the magazine of the same name.	http://www.franchisingtimes.com/
McDonald's Restaurant Franchise Information McDonald's restaurants, perhaps the most recognized franchise in the world, provides information about how to own a franchise.	http://www.mcdonalds.com/a_system/franchise
Federal Trade Commission Act, 15 U.S.C. §41-58 LII provides a hypertext and searchable version of 15 U.S.C. §41-58, popularly known as the Federal Trade Commission Act.	http://www.law.cornell.edu/uscode/15/41.html
U.S. Federal Trade Commission (FTC) The FTC provides information on proposed franchising rules, as well as news and press releases, speeches and articles, and facts for consumers and businesses.	http://www.ftc.gov/

Chapter 38, Securities Regulation	
Securities and Exchange Commission (SEC) The Securities and Exchange Commission provides information about federal securities laws and investor protection in the securities market.	http://www.sec.gov/
EDGAR EDGAR (Electronic Data Gathering) is a searchable database of corporate information, maintained by the SEC.	http://www.sec.gov/edgarhp.htm
Securities Act of 1933 The University of Cincinnati's Center for Corporate Law maintains the Securities Act of 1933.	http://www.law.uc.edu/CCL/33Act/
Securities Exchange Act of 1934 The University of Cincinnati's Center for Corporate Law maintains the Securities Act of 1934.	http://www.law.uc.edu/CCL/34Act/
Securities Law Home Page The Securities Law Home Page, created by Mark J. Astarita, a New York securities attorney, contains information regarding arbitration, brokers, investors, corporate finance, and securities law and compliance.	http://www.seclaw.com/
Blue Sky Laws: Securities Regulation and Research University of Maryland School of Law maintains a research forum for "blue sky" laws, including publications.	http://www.law.ab.umd.edu/marshall/bluesky/
Indiana Code 23-2 Chapter 1: Securities Regulation The State of Indiana maintains its securities law, also called "blue sky" laws online.	http://www.law.indiana.edu/codes/in/23/ch-23-2-1.html
The Nasdaq Financial Executive Journal The Nasdaq Financial Executive Journal is a short-lived journal on corporate law. Issues from 1993-94 are available.	http://www.law.cornell.edu/nasdaq/nasdtoc.html
Center for Corporate Law at the University of Cincinnati Center for Corporate Law at the University of Cincinnati College of Law maintains rules and forms associated with the 1933 and 1934 Acts, and various SEC regulations.	http://www.law.uc.edu/CCL/
Securities Class Action Clearinghouse Stanford Law School's Securities Class Action Clearinghouse provides full text of complaints, motions, judicial opinions, and other securities class action filings.	http://securities.stanford.edu/
International Organization of Securities Commissions (IOSCO) The International Organization of Securities Commissions (IOSCO) provides reports, guidelines, and links.	http://www.iosco.org/
Foreign Corrupt Practices Act--15 USC §78dd-2 LII provides 15 USC §78dd-2, popularly known as the Foreign Corrupt Practices Act.	http://www.law.cornell.edu/uscode/15/78dd-2.html

Chapter 39, Constitutional Regulation of Business	
U.S. Constitution Emory Law School maintains a hypertext and searchable version of the U.S. Constitution.	http://www.law.emory.edu/FEDERAL/ usconst.html
USSC+--U.S. Supreme Court Database USSC+, maintained by InfoSynthesis, Inc., provides a database of over 5,000 recent Supreme Court opinions, including cases within days of their decision, and news and background on the Court.	http://www.usscplus.com/
The Legal Information Institute (LII)--Decisions of the U.S. Supreme Court LII, maintained by the Cornell Law School, provides recent Supreme Court decisions (1990-present), as well as various historical decisions and background material on the Court.	http://www.law.cornell.edu/supct/supct. table.html
FedWorld/ FLITE Supreme Court Decisions FedWorld, a service of the U.S. Department of Commerce, provides online the U.S. Air Force's database of historic Supreme Court decisions, known as FLITE (Federal Legal Information Through Electronics). The database consists of over 7000 Supreme Court opinions dating from 1937 through 1975.	http://www.fedworld.gov/supcourt/index. htm
Oyez Oyez Oyez: A Supreme Court Resource Oyez Oyez Oyez (pronounced "oh-yay"), maintained by Jerry Goldman and Northwestern University, provides digital recordings (via RealAudio technology) of various Court cases ranging from 1955 to present.	http://oyez.at.nwu.edu/oyez.html
Constitution Society The Constitution Society, a private non-profit organization, provides constitutional research, information, and even pictures.	http://www.constitution.org/
The Free Speech Policy Group The Free Speech Policy Group, a non-profit think tank advocating the protection of First Amendment rights, provides legislation, essays, and links.	http://www.policygroup.com/
International Association of Constitutional Law International Association of Constitutional Law provides information and constitutions for countries around the world.	http://www.eur.nl/iacl/const.html

388

Chapter 40, Antitrust Law	
Sherman Antitrust Act--15 U.S.C. §1-7 LII provides a hypertext and searchable version of 15 U.S.C. §1-7, popularly known as the Sherman Antitrust Act.	http://www.law.cornell.edu/uscode/15/1.html
Clayton Act--15 U.S.C. §12-27 LII provides a hypertext and searchable version of 15 U.S.C. §12-25, popularly known as the Clayton Antitrust Act.	http://www.law.cornell.edu/uscode/15/12.html
Robinson-Patman Act--15 U.S.C. §13 LII provides a hypertext and searchable version of 15 U.S.C. §13, popularly known as the Robinson-Patman Act.	http://www.law.cornell.edu/uscode/15/13.html
Federal Trade Commission Act, 15 U.S.C. §41-58 LII provides a hypertext and searchable version of 15 U.S.C. §41-58, popularly known as the Federal Trade Commission Act.	http://www.law.cornell.edu/uscode/15/41.html
U.S. Department of Justice, Antitrust Division The Antitrust Division of the U.S. Department of Justice provides press releases, speeches and Congressional testimony, antitrust guidelines, court cases since 1994, international agreements and documents, and Division status reports.	http://www.usdoj.gov/atr/atr.htm
U.S. Federal Trade Commission (FTC) The FTC provides news and press releases, speeches and articles, and facts for consumers and businesses.	http://www.ftc. gov/
U.S. Patent and Trademark Office (PTO) The PTO provides general information about patents and trademarks, a search mechanism for patents, and legal information.	http://www.uspto.gov/
Antitrust Policy Antitrust Policy, maintained by Vanderbilt University, provides antitrust case documents (complaints, opinions, and expert testimony), enforcement guidelines and speeches, economic bibliographies, and current antitrust issues in the news.	http://www. antitrust.org/
ABA Section of Antitrust Law The Antitrust Section of the American Bar Association (ABA) provides news and updates, events, and publications.	http://www.abanet.org/antitrust/home.html

Chapter 41, Consumer Protection	
Consumer Credit Protection Act—15 USC § 1601 Legal Information Institute (LII), maintained by the Cornell Law School, provides 15 USC § 1601, the Consumer Credit Protection Act, better known as the Truth in Lending Act.	http://www.law.cornell.edu/uscode/15/1601.html
Federal Reserve Board Regulations The Federal Reserve Board provides summaries of its regulations, including Regulations B and Z.	http://www.bog.frb.fed.us/frregs.htm
U.S. Federal Trade Commission (FTC) The FTC provides news and press releases, speeches and articles, and facts for consumers and businesses.	http://www.ftc.gov/
Fair Credit Reporting Act--15 USC § 1681 LII provides 15 USC § 1681, the Fair Credit Reporting Act.	http://www.law.cornell.edu/uscode/15/1681.html
The Fair Debt Collection Practices Act--15 USC § 1692 LII provides 15 USC § 1692, the Fair Debt Collection Practices Act.	http://www.law.cornell.edu/uscode/15/1692.html
Equal Credit Opportunity Act—15 USC § 1691 LII provides 15 USC § 1691, the Equal Credit Opportunity Act.	http://www.law.cornell.edu/uscode/15/1691.html
Uniform Consumer Credit Code The State of Indiana maintains the Uniform Consumer Credit Code as adopted by the state legislature.	http://www.law.indiana.edu/codes/in/24/art-24-4.5.html
Consumer Product Safety Act—15 USC § 2051 LII provides 15 USC § 2051, the Consumer Product Safety Act	http://www.law.cornell.edu/uscode/15/2051.html
U.S. Consumer Product Safety Commission U.S. Consumer Product Safety Commission provides consumer news and information, as well as notices on recalls and business contracts.	http://www.cpsc.gov/
The Consumer Law Page The Consumer Law Page, maintained by The Alexander Law Firm, provides articles, brochures, and reference materials, including a detailed step-by-step guide to resolving disputes with merchants and manufacturers.	http://consumerlawpage.com/
National Consumer Law Center National Consumer Law Center, a nonprofit corporation founded at Boston College School of Law, provides state manuals, reports, briefs, and legal advice for disadvantaged consumers.	http://www.consumerlaw.org/
The U.S. House of Representatives Internet Law Library-- Consumer Law The U.S. House of Representatives Internet Law Library for consumer law provides links to cases, essays, statutes, and organizations concerned with consumer law.	http://law.house.gov/92.htm

Chapter 42, Environmental Protection	
U.S. Environmental Protection Agency The EPA provides educational materials; regulations, publications, and news; and text for the National Environmental Policy Act of 1969.	http://www.epa.gov/
Council on Environmental Quality (CEQ) The CEQ provides, among other services, NEPANet (National Environmental Policy Act), which includes Environmental Impact Statements (EISs) and a library of environmental resources.	http://www.whitehouse.gov/CEQ/
Clean Air Act—42 USC § 7401 Legal Information Institute (LII), maintained by the Cornell Law School, provides the Clean Air Act, 42 USC § 7401.	http://www.law.cornell.edu/uscode/42/7401.html
Clean Water Act—33 USC § 1251 LII provides the Clean Water Act, 33 USC § 1251.	http://www.law.cornell.edu/uscode/33/1251.html
Noise Control Act—42 USC § 4901 LII provides the Noise Control Act, 42 USC § 4901.	http://www.law.cornell.edu/uscode/42/4901.html
Toxic Substances Control Act—15 USC § 2601 LII provides the Toxic Substances Control Act, 15 USC § 2601.	http://www.law.cornell.edu/uscode/15/2601.html
Insecticide, Fungicide, and Rodenticide Act—7 USC § 121. LII provides the Federal Insecticide, Fungicide, and Rodenticide Act, 7 USC § 121.	http://www.law.cornell.edu/uscode/7/121.html
Resource Conservation and Recovery Act—42 USC § 6901 LII provides the Resource Conservation and Recovery Act, 42 USC § 6901.	http://www.law.cornell.edu/uscode/42/6901.html
Comprehensive Environmental Response, Compensation, and Liability Act (CERCLA)--42 USC § 9601 LII provides the Comprehensive Environmental Response, Compensation, and Liability Act, 42 USC § 9601.	http://www.law.cornell.edu/uscode/42/9601.html
Endangered Species Act--16 USC § 1531 LII provides the Endangered Species Act, 16 USC § 1531.	http://www.law.cornell.edu/uscode/16/1531.html
The U.S. House of Representatives *Internet Law Library--* *Environmental Law* The U.S. House of Representatives Internet Law Library for environmental law provides links to cases, essays, statutes, and organizations.	http://law.house.gov/101.htm

Chapter 43, Labor and Fair employment Practices	
Norris-LaGuardia Act—29 USC § 101 Legal Information Institute (LII), maintained by the Cornell Law School, provides 29 USC § 101, the Norris-LaGuardia Act.	http://www.law.cornell.edu/uscode/29/101.html
Wagner Act—29 USC § 151 LII provides 29 USC § 151, the Wagner Act.	http://www.law.cornell.edu/uscode/29/151.shtml
Taft-Hartely Act—29 USC § 171 LII provides 29 USC § 171, the Taft-Hartley Act.	http://www.law.cornell.edu/uscode/29/171.shtml
Landrum-Griffin Act--29 USC § 185 LII provides 29 USC § 185, the Landrum-Griffin Act.	http://www.law.cornell.edu/uscode/29/185.shtml
National Labor Relations Board The National Labor Relations Board provides speeches, publications, Board decisions, and other materials.	http://cher.eda.doc.gov/nlrb/homepg.html
Civil Rights Act of 1964 LII provides 42 USC § 2000e, the Civil Rights Act of 1964.	http://www.law.cornell.edu/uscode/42/2000e.html
Equal Pay Act of 1963 LII provides 29 USC § 206, the Equal Pay Act of 1963.	http://www.law.cornell.edu/uscode/29/206. shtml
Age Discrimination in Employment Act of 1967 LII provides 29 USC § 621, the Age Discrimination in Employment Act of 1967.	http://www.law.cornell.edu/uscode/29/621.shtml
Rehabilitation Act of 1973 LII provides 29 USC § 701, the Rehabilitation Act of 1973.	http://www.law.cornell.edu/uscode/29/701.shtml
Occupational Safety and Health Act of 1970 LII provides 29 USC § 651, the Occupational Safety and Health Act.	http://www.law.cornell.edu/uscode/29/651.shtml
Americans with Disabilities Act (ADA) Document Center The ADA Document Center, maintained by Attorney Duncan C. Kinder, provides the full ADA and relevant regulations and guidelines.	http://janweb.icdi.wvu.edu/kinder/
Family and Medical Leave Act (FMLA) of 1993 The Department of Labor (DOL), Employment Standards Administration provides the full text of the FMLA, fact sheets, compliance guides, and DOL regulations.	http://www.dol.gov/dol/esa/
Equal Employment Opportunity Commission (EEOC) The EEOC provides publications and media releases, fact sheets, and information on the laws enforced by the EEOC.	http://www.eeoc.gov/
Occupational Safety and Health Administration (OSHA) OSHA provides publications and media releases, program information, software, data, among other services.	http://www.osha.gov/index.html
Social Security Administration (SSA) The SSA maintains publications, information, and forms.	http://www.ssa.gov/
The Labor Letter The Labor Letter, maintained by The Labor Letters, Inc., provides information on state and federal developments.	http://www.laborletter.com/

Chapter 44, Real Property and Joint Ownership	
U.S. Department of Housing and Urban Development (HUD) HUD provides information on real property and planning issues for both consumers and businesses. HUD also provides information on the Fair Housing Act and the Civil Rights Acts.	http://www.hud.gov/
HUD USER HUD USER, PD&R's information source for housing and community development researchers and policy makers, provides Federal Government reports and information on housing policy and programs, building technology, economic development, urban planning, and other housing-related topics.	http://www.huduser.org/
Legal Information Institute (LII)-- Land-Use Law Materials LII provides an overview of land-use law, links to statutes, federal and state judicial court decisions, and other materials.	http://www.law.cornell.edu/topics/ land_use.html
American Bar Association's (ABA) Section of Real Property, Probate and Trust Law. The ABA's Section of Real Property, Probate, and Trust Law provides news, information, and links property.	http://www.abanet.org/rppt/home.html
The U.S. House of Representatives Internet Law Library-- Real Property The U.S. House of Representatives Internet Law Library provides state, federal, and international legal materials concerning real property.	http://law. house.gov/106. htm
Americans with Disabilities Act (ADA) Document Center The ADA Document Center, maintained by Attorney Duncan C. Kinder, provides the full ADA and relevant regulations, guidelines, federally reviewed tech sheets, and other assistance documents.	http://janweb.icdi.wvu.edu/kinder/
"Takings" Resources Page The "Takings" Resource Page, part of the Planning Commissioners Journal's Planning Web, provides articles, news, and analysis concerning eminent domain issues.	http://www.webcom.com/~pcj/takings. html
Legal Information Institute (LII)--Landlord-Tenant Law Materials LII provides an overview of landlord-tenant law, links to statutes, federal and state judicial court decisions, and other materials.	http://www.law.cornell.edu/topics/ landlord_tenant.html
TenantNet TenantNet, an informal network of tenants and tenant leaders in New York, provides news, information, and resources on landlord-tenant law.	http://tenant.net/

Chapter 45, Personal Property and Bailments	
Internal Revenue Service The Internal Revenue Service, and its publication, the Digital Daily, provide tax advice and information on a variety of issues, including personal property issues.	http://www.irs.ustreas.gov/
U.S. Internal Revenue Code—26 USC LII, maintained by the Cornell Law School, provides the U.S. Internal Revenue Code, 26 USC, in a hypertext and searchable format.	http://www.law.cornell.edu/uscode/26/
Legal Information Institute (LII)-- Estate and Gift Tax Law Materials LII provides an overview of estate and gift tax law, including relevant sections from the U.S. Code and Code of Federal Regulation, court cases, and links.	http://www.law.cornell.edu/topics/ estate_gift_tax.html

Chapter 46, Wills, Estates, and Trusts	
Legal Information Institute (LII)-- Estates and Trusts Law Materials LII, maintained by the Cornell Law School, provides an overview of estates and trust law, including relevant sections from the U.S. Code and Code of Federal Regulation, court cases, the Uniform Probate Code, and links.	http://www.law.cornell.edu/topics/ estates_trusts.html
The U.S. House of Representatives Internet Law Library-- Trusts and Estates The U.S. House of Representatives Internet Law Library for trusts and estates provides links to cases, essays, statutes, and organizations concerned with estates and trust law.	http://law.house.gov/112.htm
Crash Course in Wills and Trusts Crash Course in Wills and Trusts, created by attorney and CFP Michael T. Palermo, is a practical guide to what everyone should know about the law of Wills and Trusts before an estate plan is designed.	http://www.mtpalermo.com/
Layne T. Rushforth's Estate Planning & Business Planning Layne T. Rushforth's Estate Planning & Business Planning Page has basic and advanced articles on estate planning, links, and newsgroups.	http://coyote.accessnv.com/rushfort/ planning.html
American Bar Association's Section of Real Property, Probate and Trust Law The Real Property, Probate and Trust Law Section, with over 30,000 members, publishes the scholarly journal, *Real Property, Probate and Trust Law Journal*, and the practical bimonthly magazine, *Probate & Property*.	http://www.abanet.org/rppt/home.html
The American College of Trust and Estate Counsel The American College of Trust and Estate Counsel, a nonprofit association of lawyers and law professors, provides pamphlets on wills and estates.	http://www.actec.org/
Definitions of Estate Planning Legalese Advice & Counsel Incorporated, a California law corporation, provides explanations of estate planning, wills, and trusts "legalese".	http://seamless.com/adviceco/legalese. html
Trusts and Trustees Trusts and Trustees, a journal specializing in international trusts, provides full articles and other resources.	http://www.trusts-and-trustees.com/

Chapter 47, Intellectual Property, Computers, and the Law

Patent and Trademark Office Patent and Trademark Office (PTO) allows for patent searches; as well, it provides forms, legal materials, and the PTO museum.	http://www.uspto.gov/
Intellectual Property Center Intellectual Property Center, sponsored by the New York Law Publishing Company, provides daily news and articles, case law, and analysis.	http://www.ipcenter.com/
Intellectual Property Intellectual Property, part of the American Lawyer Media group, provides articles on laws governing technology and information, links, access to law firms' analysis of legal issues, and intellectual property news.	http://www.ipmag.com/
World Intellectual Property Organization (WIPO) The World Intellectual Property Organization (WIPO) maintains the Berne Convention, Paris Convention WIPO Copyright Treaty, and WIPO Performances and Phonograms Treaty, among other resources.	http://www.wipo.org/eng/general/copyrght/bern.htm
Universal Copyright Convention The United Nation's Universal Copyright Convention is available through Wiretap as a text document.	gopher://wiretap.spies.com:70/00/Gov/Copyright/US.Universal.Copyright.Conv.txt
Copyright Office, Library of Congress The Copyright Office provides publications and extensive information on copyright topics, including the basics of copyright law.	http://lcweb.loc.gov/copyright/
Lanham Act Legal Information Institute, maintained by the Cornell Law School, provides a hypertext and searchable version of the Lanham Act (Trademark Act of 1946).	http://www.law.cornell.edu/lanham/lanham.table.html
The Multilaterals Project The Multilaterals Project, maintained by Tufts University, provides texts of multilateral treaties, including GATT and NAFTA.	http://www.tufts.edu/fletcher/multilaterals.html
U.S. Federal Trade Commission (FTC) The FTC provides news and press releases, speeches and articles, and facts for consumers and businesses.	http://www.ftc.gov/